AWS System Administration

Best Practices for Sysadmins
in the Amazon Cloud

Mike Ryan and Federico Lucifredi

Beijing · Boston · Farnham · Sebastopol · Tokyo

AWS System Administration

by Mike Ryan and Federico Lucifredi

Published by O'Reilly Media, Inc., 1005 Gravenstein Highway North, Sebastopol, CA 95472.

O'Reilly books may be purchased for educational, business, or sales promotional use. Online editions are also available for most titles (*http://oreilly.com/safari*). For more information, contact our corporate/institutional sales department: 800-998-9938 or *corporate@oreilly.com*.

Acquisitions Editor: Rachel Roumeliotis	**Indexer:** WordCo Indexing Services, Inc.
Editor: Andy Oram	**Interior Designer:** David Futato
Production Editor: Melanie Yarbrough	**Cover Designer:** Karen Montgomery
Copyeditor: Kim Cofer	**Illustrator:** Rebecca Demarest
Proofreader: Jasmine Kwityn	

August 2018:   First Edition

Revision History for the First Edition
2018-08-06:   First Release

See *http://oreilly.com/catalog/errata.csp?isbn=9781449342579* for release details.

978-1-449-34257-9

[LSI]

Table of Contents

Foreword

When Amazon created its first cloud, well before anyone had coined the term "DevOps," few if any could conceive of how expansive it would become. From its humble roots in Amazon Elastic Compute Cloud (EC2) in 2002 and Amazon Simple Storage Service (S3) in 2006, AWS has expanded to a collection of over 100 services in over 15 regions around the world. This growing platform of capabilities can be intimidating at first glance and many wonder where to even begin. While there have been scores of blog posts and wikis devoted to passing on the tribal wisdom learned through sometimes painful experiences, it has been difficult to find an entry point that meets the needs of the budding cloud practitioner.

But who exactly is a "cloud practitioner"? We're entering a period where a working knowledge of cloud configuration and administration fundamentals are considered a requirement for a wide series of industries. We're currently in an environment that goes well beyond a concept of self-service IT. We now assume that users will no longer be just consumers of information technology resources, but cocreators. A research scientist developing code to analyze genomic data now not only helps create the data schema but also configures the compute and storage resources necessary to support their analysis. An industrial engineer executing high-performance fluid dynamics calculations has to know how many virtual CPUs and memory to request to best optimize the performance of her application.

We are living in a time of changing infrastructure architectures, serverless applications, and containerization. It takes a complete change in mindset to move from asking how to best configure a rack with an exact number of servers, disks, and network switches to pondering what to do with a potentially unlimited number of configurations of CPUs/GPUs/FPGAs, memory, object, block, and file storage connected through high-speed network connections. The choices can sometimes be overwhelming. The broad expanses of vast computing resources enable us to do things few thought even possible less than a decade ago, and yet the lack of physical constraints can almost induce vertigo at times—like a pilot without a horizon, enveloped in an actual physical cloud, not a virtual computing one.

Boundaries help us to make sense of our surroundings; looking over the edge of the cliff lets us know where to stop; staying between the lines on the road helps us to drive safely. We learn how to best operate within our constraints even though we may occasionally try to push our limitations. We optimize our behavior based upon our limitations. But what do we do when those limitations, which have helped define us for so long, are now removed? How do we begin to think about operating in an era of cloud computing?

Mike and Federico have written a book that is approachable, yet not basic; plain spoken, but not simple; technical, but not overly complex. It addresses the needs of anyone looking to learn how to engage with AWS for the first time. It removes some of the intimidation from the alphabet soup of acronyms and new terminology that will be thrown at the new AWS user: EC2, S3, EBS, AMI, instance, IAM, ELB, RDS, Route 53, CloudWatch, CloudFormation, Glacier, and more. It is a welcome starting point for all who wish to learn more about the essentials of getting started using AWS and beginning their journey into the cloud.

—*Ian Colle, General Manager for AWS Batch and HPC at Amazon Web Services, has a background in economics and philosophy as well as software engineering.*

Preface

System administration is a complicated topic that requires practitioners to be familiar with an ever-expanding range of applications and services. In some ways, Amazon Web Services (AWS) is just another tool to add to your toolkit, yet it can also be considered a discipline in and of itself. Successfully building and deploying infrastructure on AWS involves a thorough understanding of the underlying operating system concerns, software architecture, and delivery practices, as well as the myriad components that make up Amazon Web Services.

Mike runs a DevOps consultancy, helping startups and small businesses reap the benefits of tools and processes that were previously available only to organizations with large teams of system administrators. Many of these businesses do not have a dedicated system administrator, and the development team is responsible for deploying and maintaining the architecture.

In working with these clients, Mike noticed patterns in how people were working with AWS. Those who came from a pure development background, without any sysadmin experience, would often build an infrastructure that left out many of the things sysadmins would take for granted, such as monitoring and logging. The lack of monitoring and logging would then make it difficult to track down issues, leading to more downtime than necessary.

At the other end of the spectrum were clients with a lot of sysadmin experience, but less or no development experience. This group was more likely to treat AWS as nothing more than a virtual machine hosting provider, simply using EC2 to run a fleet of static instances without taking advantage of any high-availability features such as Auto Scaling Groups and Elastic Load Balancing. This is akin to buying a Ferrari and then using it only to buy groceries once per week: fun, but not very cost-effective.

Using AWS requires a fundamentally different mindset than when deploying groups of static servers. You do not simply set up some servers and then periodically perform maintenance. Instead, you use the full AWS toolset (automatic instance replacement, scaling up and down in response to demand, etc.) to build a system. In this sense, it is more like programming than traditional system administration.

Federico's work as the lead Product Manager for Ubuntu Server at Canonical placed him on the front lines from the vendor perspective. Looking at how users and public cloud vendors were integrating Ubuntu into their infrastructure informed the team's decisions as to what user problems to solve first, and led to the creation of Canonical's Certified Public Cloud program, which solves integration problems for public cloud vendors and directly manages the relationship between Ubuntu and the Amazon AWS technical team.

The Ubuntu Server team's cloud-first focus led to the creation of technologies like Cloud-init, and produced the early, smooth integration of Ubuntu with public cloud that resulted in its popularity there today. Federico's aim has been to complement Mike's knowledge as a power user of public cloud with his behind-the-scenes insight into where things can go wrong for users.

The aim of this book is to help you reach a balance between development and operational focus, and help you make the right choice for your application's specific hosting requirements. If you are a developer, this book will give you enough system administration knowledge to ensure that you are using AWS effectively, and help you build a robust and resilient application infrastructure. For system administrators, it will show you how you can keep your favorite tools and processes while working with AWS, and hopefully save you from reinventing some wheels along the way.

AWS is a collection of cloud computing services that can be combined to build scalable and reliable applications and services. It comprises a number of components, each with their own names and configuration options, which are offered under the AWS umbrella. Some of these—such as EC2 and S3—are extremely popular and well-known. Others, such as Kinesis and CloudFormation, are less well-known. Because covering each of these services in detail would result in a multivolume tome of formidable size, this book focuses on the more commonly used services and provides jumping-off points for learning about the others.

If you are familiar with AWS, feel free to hop between chapters to find the information that is most interesting or relevant to your current project. Beginners to AWS should work through the book sequentially, as each chapter builds on information presented in the previous chapters.

Chapter 1 helps you get set up with the tools you will need to interact with AWS and build the example infrastructure.

Chapter 2 introduces what is perhaps the most well-known of all AWS services, EC2. This chapter also introduces our favorite AWS service, CloudFormation.

In Chapter 3, we look at the most important security features provided by AWS, and how they combine with service functionality to enable secure operation.

Chapter 4 introduces configuration management tools, a common requirement when automating a cloud infrastructure. Using these tools, Chapters 5 and 6 demonstrate the process of deploying an example application to AWS.

Chapter 7 looks at some of the methods of deploying application and infrastructure updates to your environment. Chapter 8 builds on this and discusses the creation of reusable components to save time.

Log management, a more traditional sysadmin task that has some interesting implications in the cloud, is the topic of Chapter 9.

Chapter 10 covers another traditional sysadmin task: DNS with Amazon's Route 53 service.

Monitoring with Amazon's CloudWatch service and other monitoring tools is discussed in Chapter 11.

Finally, Chapter 12 looks at some of the ways of backing up your data both in and outside the Amazon cloud.

Audience

This book is written for system administrators and developers. We assume you are comfortable with the basic tools used to administer the operating system and common services such as DNS. If you plan to use Puppet or Chef for automation, you need to learn basic information about those tools elsewhere. You should have a working knowledge of Git or another source code management system. We do not expect you to have prior knowledge of AWS or other virtualization and cloud products.

Where an operating system choice was required, we tested our examples on Ubuntu 16.04 "Xenial" and Ubuntu 14.04 "Trusty." For users on Amazon AWS today, Ubuntu is the most popular option, so we used it as both client environment and for our EC2 instances; examples will nonetheless run on most Linux distributions with minimal or no change. Whenever we used an RPM-based distribution, we checked our work against Amazon Linux, which remains the second most popular choice of distribution as we write.

Conventions Used in This Book

The following typographical conventions are used in this book:

Italic
    Indicates new terms, URLs, email addresses, filenames, and file extensions.

`Constant width`

> Used for program listings, as well as within paragraphs to refer to program elements such as variable or function names, data types, and environment variables.

`Constant width bold`

> Shows commands or other text that should be typed literally by the user.

`Constant width italic`

> Shows text that should be replaced with user-supplied values or by values determined by context.

 This icon signifies a general note.

 This icon signifies a tip or suggestion.

 This icon indicates a warning or caution.

Using Code Examples

This book is here to help you get your job done. Major examples can be downloaded from our GitHub repository (*https://github.com/0xf2/aws-system-administration*). Many other small examples are scattered through the book; we have not bothered to include them in the repository because they are fairly easy to type in.

In general, you may use the code in your programs and documentation. You do not need to contact us for permission unless you're reproducing a significant portion of the code. For example, writing a program that uses several chunks of code from this book does not require permission. Selling or distributing a CD-ROM of examples from O'Reilly books does require permission. Answering a question by citing this book and quoting example code does not require permission. Incorporating a significant amount of example code from this book into your product's documentation does require permission.

We appreciate, but do not require, attribution. An attribution usually includes the title, author, publisher, and ISBN. For example: "*AWS System Administration* by Mike Ryan and Federico Lucifredi (O'Reilly). Copyright 2018 by Mike Ryan and Federico Lucifredi 978-1-449-34257-9."

If you feel your use of code examples falls outside fair use or the permission given above, feel free to contact us at *permissions@oreilly.com*.

O'Reilly Safari

 Safari (formerly Safari Books Online) is a membership-based training and reference platform for enterprise, government, educators, and individuals.

Members have access to thousands of books, training videos, Learning Paths, interactive tutorials, and curated playlists from over 250 publishers, including O'Reilly Media, Harvard Business Review, Prentice Hall Professional, Addison-Wesley Professional, Microsoft Press, Sams, Que, Peachpit Press, Adobe, Focal Press, Cisco Press, John Wiley & Sons, Syngress, Morgan Kaufmann, IBM Redbooks, Packt, Adobe Press, FT Press, Apress, Manning, New Riders, McGraw-Hill, Jones & Bartlett, and Course Technology, among others.

For more information, please visit *http://oreilly.com/safari*.

How to Contact Us

Please address comments and questions concerning this book to the publisher:

O'Reilly Media, Inc.
1005 Gravenstein Highway North
Sebastopol, CA 95472
800-998-9938 (in the United States or Canada)
707-829-0515 (international or local)
707-829-0104 (fax)

We have a web page for this book, where we list errata, examples, and any additional information. You can access this page at *http://bit.ly/aws-system-administration*.

To comment or ask technical questions about this book, send email to *bookquestions@oreilly.com*.

For more information about our books, courses, conferences, and news, see our website at *http://www.oreilly.com*.

Find us on Facebook: *http://facebook.com/oreilly*

Follow us on Twitter: *http://twitter.com/oreillymedia*

Watch us on YouTube: *http://www.youtube.com/oreillymedia*

Acknowledgments

This book would not exist were it not for the many amazing people who helped us along the way. Mike would like to thank his family for their love and support, which allowed him to become the geek he is today. He would also like to thank Cynthia Stolk for supplying endless cups of coffee to fuel this book, and Rachel Kersten and Rebecca Lay for making sure it actually got finished. Federico thanks his wife Irena for being his loving inspiration and Mark Shuttleworth for convincing him "this cloud thing" was really the top priority in a sea of top priorities.

Thanks are due to friends and colleagues who gave feedback and suggestions: Bartek Swedrowski, Dave Letorey, Guyon Morée, Jurg van Vliet, Keith Perhac, Peter van Kampen, Rick van Hattem, Ross Gynn, Sofie Pelmelay, and Thierry Schellenbach. Martin Guenthner, Jess Males, Ilan Rabinovitch, Douglas Knight, Kapil Thangavelu, Ben Howard, Peter Bowen, Kyle Bader, Stephen Walli, and William Ricker patiently reviewed many drafts, told us what the book lacked, and kept us honest. Either directly or indirectly, you helped shape this book.

Finally, we would like to thank the excellent team at O'Reilly for making this happen. Particular thanks are due to our editor, Andy Oram, for persevering on the long road. Nikki McDonald's help was instrumental to getting this first edition past the finish line. And, of course, this book would be empty if not for the amazing team behind Amazon Web Services.

## CHAPTER 1

Setting Up AWS Tools

The role of the system administrator is changing. Just a few years ago, most sysadmins dealt with server farms of physical hardware and performed detailed capacity planning. Scaling up your application meant ordering new hardware and perhaps spending time racking it up in the datacenter. Now there is a huge section of the industry that has never touched physical hardware. We scale up by issuing an API call or clicking a button in a web page to bring new capacity online.

Although the term has been co-opted by marketers, the cloud is an amazing thing. In this context, we are using *cloud* to refer to the idea of scalable, on-demand computing and application services, rather than *cloud-based* services like Google Mail.

As more competition enters the cloud market space, its appeal for sysadmins and business owners alike is increasing on an almost daily basis. Amazon Web Services continues to drive the cloud computing market forward by frequently introducing new tools and services (in fact, they are introduced with such regularity that writing a book about them is a never-ending pursuit).

Economies of scale are constantly pushing down the price of cloud services. Although environments like AWS or Google Compute Engine are not yet suitable for every application, it is becoming increasingly clear that cloud skills are becoming a required part of a well-rounded sysadmin's toolkit.

For businesses, the cloud opens up new avenues of flexibility. Tech teams can do things that would have been prohibitively expensive just a few years ago. The games and applications that are lucky enough to become runaway hits often require a high amount of backend computing capacity. Bringing this capacity online in hours rather than weeks enables these companies to quickly respond to success, without requiring multiyear lease commitments or upfront capital expenditure.

In the age of the Lean Startup, developers and managers know how important it is to quickly iterate and improve their application code. Services like AWS allow you to treat your infrastructure the same way, letting a relatively small team manage massively scalable application infrastructures.

Getting Started

The first step to get your own AWS infrastructure started is to head to *aws.amazon.com* and create a new account, if you do not already have one, as shown in Figure 1-1.

Figure 1-1. Sign up and create your AWS account

AWS accounts do not incur charges until computing, storage, or network resources are allocated for actual use, but you will need to provide a valid credit card number as part of the signup process. The account will be linked to either an email address or a mobile phone number identity that Amazon will require you to verify during the initial setup (see Figure 1-2). While entering payment information and accepting the terms of service you will want to take notice of the current Free Tier (*https://aws.amazon.com/free/*) offering. At the time of this writing Amazon welcomes new account holders with 750 hours of EC2 compute time *per month* and 5 GB of free storage for their first year. Currently this includes free access to 42 different services.

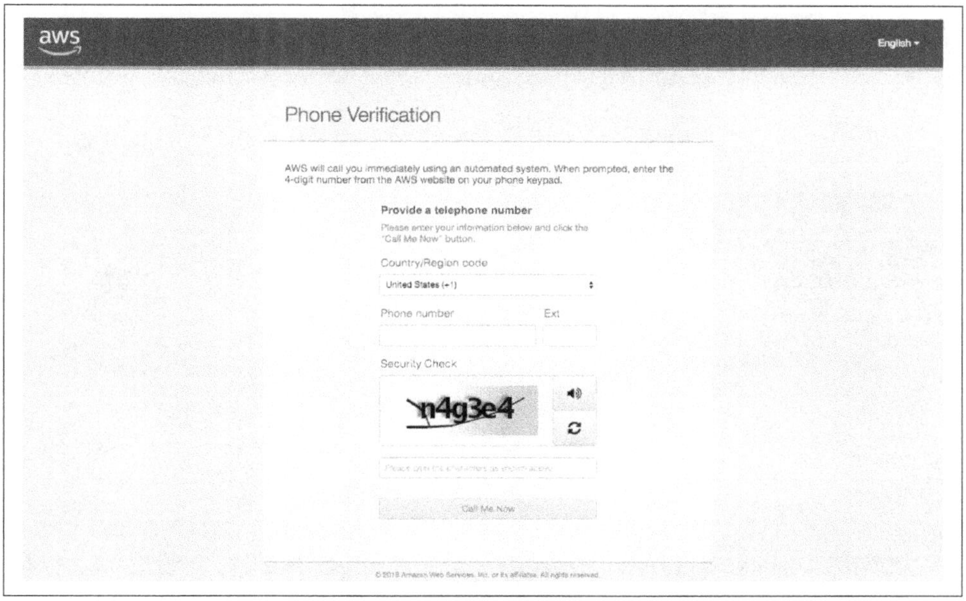

Figure 1-2. Identity validation of new accounts requires a telephone number

The final step of account creation consists in selecting a support plan. You are not required to initiate a support subscription at this time, and we recommend you select the basic, free plan to start. You will be able to revisit this decision at a later time, and selecting the free plan avoids the recurring monthly support charges you would otherwise immediately incur. Amazon has refined its support offerings over the years, and you may find the developer subscription a valuable resource if you want a more predictable turnaround on your technical questions than free community resources like ServerFault (*http://serverfault.com/questions/tagged/amazon-ec2+or+amazon-web-services*) or AskUbuntu (*http://askubuntu.com/questions/tagged/amazon-ec2+or+aws*) may provide.

Account activation will require a few minutes and may take up to several hours. As Amazon completes your account's activation, you will receive an email notice.

Preparing Your Tools

There are various ways to manage your AWS infrastructure components. The AWS Management Console is the first interface most users see (see Figure 1-3). Although great for exploring and learning about the services, it does not lend itself to automation.

Figure 1-3. The EC2 Dashboard section of the AWS Management Console

The AWS APIs are a collection of API endpoints that can be used to manage AWS services from your own application. There are implementations in many popular programming languages and platforms, which can be downloaded from the AWS site (*http://aws.amazon.com*).

The AWS Command Line Interface (AWS CLI) (*http://aws.amazon.com/cli/*) is a command-line tool released by Amazon that directly consumes the AWS API. It can be used to control any AWS component from the command line, making it suitable to use in automated build systems and continuous integration scripts. Before AWS CLI was released, Amazon provided a separate management tool for each service. That is, EC2 was managed by one program and SQS by another. The legacy tools did not all use a consistent naming convention for parameters, making them much less convenient to use.

Amazon's API interface uses access keys composed of an ID and a secret access key. The pair authenticates and authorizes every programmatic request sent to Amazon AWS. AWS provides very sophisticated, advanced access control through the Identity and Access Management service (IAM), but for the sake of simplicity we will start by using the account's root access keys. As a security best practice, AWS recommends avoiding any use of the root access keys and using IAM instead.

Head to the Security Credentials (*https://console.aws.amazon.com/iam/ home#security_credential*) section of the IAM service dashboard. You may see warnings comparable to those you heard about using the *root* user in any UNIX system,

---

and with good reason: the account credentials provide unlimited access to your AWS resources. Click the Create New Access Key button (see Figure 1-4), and you will receive immediate confirmation your new account's access keys have been created. You need to download and save the *rootkey.csv* credentials file once offered, as AWS will not retain the secret component of the key and retrieval at a later time is therefore not possible. Keep the credentials file confidential, never email it, and never share it outside of your organization: it is your virtual datacenter's root password (see "Throwing Away the Root Password" on page 84 for the most forward-thinking best practice in the matter).

Figure 1-4. Creating the master access key

 Make sure you do not accidentally commit these security keys to a public code repository such as GitHub. There have been reports of hackers scanning for accidentally published AWS keys and using them to gain unauthorized access to AWS accounts.

Installing the AWS Command Line Interface

The AWS CLI is written in Python and requires Python in either version 2.6.5, 2.7, 3.3, 3.4, 3.5, or 3.6 as its only prerequisite; this information will change and is kept updated on the project's GitHub site (*https://github.com/aws/aws-cli*). Because AWS CLI is a Python package, it can be installed with *pip*, the Python package management tool. This is included on many systems by default, but you might need to install it manually. On Ubuntu systems, this can be done with the following:

```
sudo apt install python-pip
```

On OS X, the same task can be accomplished thusly:

```
sudo easy_install pip
```

Once you have pip on your system, the AWS CLI installation is incredibly simple:

```
sudo pip install awscli
```

Once you have installed the AWS CLI, you can see general usage information and a list of the services that can be managed with aws help. For help on a specific service, you can use aws ec2 help. Finally, help on a specific command can be displayed with aws ec2 run-instances help. For example:

Command	Action
aws ec2 run-instances	Launch one or more EC2 instances
aws s3 sync	Sync a local directory with an S3 bucket
aws cloudformation create-stack	Create a CloudFormation stack

 We have installed AWS CLI from a source other than the Linux distribution's own repositories, therefore we cannot count on the operating system's security team to alert us to any security issue that may arise with this package. A production environment should monitor the AWS Security Bulletins (*https://aws.amazon.com/security/security-bulletins*) site, which can also be tracked via its RSS feed.

You can verify at any time which version of AWS CLI is installed with the command

```
aws --version
```

to determine if any advisories apply to your present setup.

Command completion is a convenient facility configured by default on all Amazon Linux instances, which come with AWS CLI preinstalled. On Ubuntu, you can add this facility to the default Bash shell with the command:

```
complete -C '/usr/local/bin/aws_completer' aws
```

On other Linux distributions, or if you used a Python virtual environment in your installation, you will want to validate the path location. An active command completion helper will promptly expand partial commands when the Tab key is pressed, or present you with alternatives when more than one completion is applicable:

```
$ aws ec2 ter<TAB>
$ aws ec2 terminate-instances
```

This will assist your recall of less-used commands, not to mention speed up your typing.

You will need to run `aws configure` to initialize the tool with your AWS access key ID and secret access key we retrieved earlier:

```
$ more rootkey.csv
AWSAccessKeyId=AKIAIKVKZ6IGBVXNRSDA
AWSSecretKey=hCJ/Fn3nE378Hb7WjGpHSYa9TRCsia/U4cAd+MG7
$ aws configure
AWS Access Key ID [None]: AKIAIKVKZ6IGBVXNRSDA
AWS Secret Access Key [None]: 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
Default region name [None]: us-east-1
Default output format [None]: json
$
```

Once this step is completed, you have all the resources of Amazon AWS's global infrastructure at your fingertips. For example, let's verify this account is currently not running any cloud instance:

```
$ aws ec2 describe-instances
{
    "Reservations": []
}
$
```

The output format can be controlled with the `--output` option of the command. While JSON output is ideal for parsing in our scripts, it is hardly readable to a human operator as it quickly becomes verbose. The `text` and `table` formats come to our rescue when using `aws` in interactive mode:

```
$ aws ec2 describe-instances --output table
-------------------------------------------------------------------------
|                            DescribeInstances                          |
+-----------------------------------------------------------------------+
||                             Reservations                            ||
|+-----------------------------------+---------------------------------+|
||  OwnerId                          |   740376006796                  ||
||  ReservationId                    |   r-e047ce48                    ||
|+-----------------------------------+---------------------------------+|
|||                              Instances                            |||
||+-----------------------------------+-------------------------------+||
|||  AmiLaunchIndex                   |  0                            |||
|||  Architecture                     |  x86_64                       |||
|||  ClientToken                      |                               |||
|||  EbsOptimized                     |  False                        |||
|||  Hypervisor                       |  xen                          |||
|||  ImageId                          |  ami-d05e75b8                 |||
|||  InstanceId                       |  i-6dd1e1ec                   |||
```

```
|||   InstanceType        |  t2.micro                                   |||
|||   LaunchTime           |  2016-01-17T05:45:01.000Z                   |||
|||   PrivateDnsName       |  ip-172-31-55-216.ec2.internal              |||
|||   PrivateIpAddress     |  172.31.55.216                              |||
|||   PublicDnsName        |  ec2-54-86-1-51.compute-1.amazonaws.com     |||
|||   PublicIpAddress      |  54.86.1.51                                 |||
...
$
```

 Relying on the system-wide Python installation may be undesirable in a production environment, as it creates an update dependency between the AWS tools and any other Python program in the system. You can separate the two by using Virtualenv (*http://virtua lenv.readthedocs.org*), a tool designed to create isolated Python environments. Install it with:

```
sudo pip install virtualenv
virtualenv ~/.python
```

This creates a separate Python environment, including executables, in the *.python* directory. Switching environments is easy with the built-in `activate` script:

```
$ echo $PATH
  /usr/local/sbin:/usr/local/bin:/usr/sbin:/usr/bin:/
sbin:/bin
$ source ~/.python/bin/activate
(.python) $ echo $PATH
  /root/.python/bin:/usr/local/sbin:/usr/local/bin:/usr/
sbin
:/usr/bin:/sbin:/bin
(.python) $
```

This adds the virtualenv's bin directory as the first argument of your $PATH variable, and modifies the prompt to remind you of what environment is currently active. As the separate environment includes its own copy of `pip`, installing `awscli` into it requires no special procedure:

```
pip install awscli
```

If `awscli` will be regularly used from the user's shell, we recommend adding the `activate` script to your *.profile* to ensure the correct environment is always loaded at login. Should you need to exit the virtualenv, this can be done with `deactivate`.

The account's root credentials provide unlimited access to your AWS resources, and you should revisit their use as you learn more about AWS IAM in Chapter 3. You will also be prompted to optionally configure a default region and output format.

The AWS team maintains an extensive command-line interface User Guide (*http:// aws.amazon.com/documentation/cli/*) that details additional native-executable install formats for Microsoft Windows, Linux, and macOS, as well as steps to uninstall and upgrade. A reference to all command options is also available online (*http://docs.aws.amazon.com/cli/latest/*).

Parsing JSON Output with jq

The aws command will often print out JavaScript Object Notation, commonly known as JSON (*http://json.org/*), as part of its results. For example, if you retrieve information about your DNS zones with the aws route53 list-hosted-zones command, you will see something similar to the following:

```
{ "HostedZones": [ {
    "ResourceRecordSetCount": 9, "CallerReference":
    "A036EFFA-E0CA-2AA4-813B-46565D601BAB", "Config": {}, "Id":
    "/hostedzone/Z1Q7O2Q6MTR3M8", "Name": "epitech.nl." }, {
    "ResourceRecordSetCount": 4, "CallerReference":
    "7456C4D0-DC03-28FE-8C4D-F85FA9E28A91", "Config": {}, "Id":
    "/hostedzone/ZAY3AQSDINMTR", "Name": "awssystemadministration.com." } ]
    }
```

In this example, it is trivial to find any information you might be looking for. But what if the results span multiple pages and you are interested in only a subset of the returned information? Enter jq. This handy tool is like *sed* for JSON data. It can be used to parse, filter, and generate JSON data, and is an excellent partner to the aws command.

jq is not installed by default in Amazon Linux or Ubuntu. On the latter, this can be resolved as follows:

```
sudo apt install jq
```

Continuing the DNS zones example, imagine we want to filter the previous list to include only the domain name:

```
$ aws route53 list-hosted-zones | jq '.HostedZones[].Name'
  "epitech.nl."
  "awssystemadministration.com."
```

The output of the aws command is piped to jq in this example. .Hosted Zones[].Name is a jq filter, which acts in a similar way to CSS selectors. It parses the JSON object and returns only the Name element of each of the HostedZones.

jq play (*https://jqplay.org*) provides a convenient online environment that enables you to test jq filters with consistent arbitrary input right in your web browser, potentially accelerating your development cycle when complex queries need to be crafted.

jq can also be used to filter the results. Let's say we want to find the `ResourceRecord SetCount` for the `epitech.nl` domain:

```
aws route53 list-hosted-zones | jq \
'.HostedZones[] | select(.Name=="epitech.nl.").ResourceRecordSetCount' 9
```

This example uses two filters. The first returns all of the `HostedZones`. This list is passed to the next filter, which uses the `select()` function to perform a string comparison. Finally, we request the `ResourceRecordSetCount` element for the item that matched the string comparison.

For installation instructions, extensive documentation, and more usage examples, see the jq homepage (*http://stedolan.github.io/jq/*).

 Before resorting to *grep*, jq, or bringing your Perl skills to the party, make sure you have exhausted the capabilities of the `aws` command's own `--query` option. You can limit the default page of JSON output that launching a new instance produces to the bare essential `InstanceId` with:

```
aws ec2 run-instances --region us-east-1 \
--instance-type t2.micro --image-id ami-43a15f3e \
--output text --query 'Instances[*].InstanceId'
```

This is particularly useful in shell scripts, where the expressive `--query` command option can keep your code shorter and easily readable. The following script terminates all instances in the default EC2 account, a handy way to end an experiment:

```
#! /bin/bash
KILL_LIST=$(aws ec2 describe-instances --output text \
--query 'Reservations[*].Instances[*].InstanceId')
aws ec2 terminate-instances --instance-ids $KILL_LIST
```

The `--query` option uses the JMESPath (*http://jmespath.org*) library to implement a JSON query language. The project site hosts the language's formal specification and a helpful tutorial.

Legacy AWS Command-Line Tools

Prior to AWS CLI, Amazon provided separate tools for each service rather than a unified command-line tool. Mostly obsolete, these tools are still useful in some situations. One such case is evaluating an older script's functionality without refactoring it first. The legacy tools coexist effortlessly with the AWS CLI without side effects (and sometimes even share configuration), so feel free to experiment. We think you should be aware of the existence of these older tools, but advise against using them as part of any new infrastructure design.

Each service had its own collection of tools, which must be download
Because the installation procedure does not vary much between packag
uses the EC2 tools as an example. The process is essentially the same
the tools.

Unfortunately, the legacy tools cannot be found in consistent locations.
tency means it is more difficult than necessary to write a script that automates the
installation of these tools, especially as the URLs for some tools change with each
release.

 Alestic (*http://alestic.com/2012/09/aws-command-line-tools*), a great
blog full of useful AWS tips, has a handy guide containing links to
all of the AWS command-line tools, along with shell snippets (suitable for copying and pasting) to download, extract, and install each
of the packages.

By convention, it is common to store the tools in a subdirectory specific to that tool,
so EC2 tools go in */usr/local/aws/ec2*, and Auto Scaling tools go in */usr/local/aws/as*.
The following commands create this directory, download the EC2 tools, and move
the extracted files into the destination directory:

```
mkdir -p /usr/local/aws/ec2
wget http://s3.amazonaws.com/ec2-downloads/ec2-api-tools.zip
unzip ec2-api-tools.zip
mv ec2-api-tools-*/* /usr/local/aws/ec2
```

Another difference between the legacy tools is in how they handle authentication.
Some require a set of access keys, whereas others use X.509 certificates or SSH keys.
The EC2 tools use access keys, which can be specified in two ways: by setting environment variables containing the access key and secret, or by using the --aws-access-
key and --aws-secret-key arguments on the command line. Using environment
variables is more convenient and can be more secure—because specifying the credentials as command-line options means they will be visible in your shell history and the
list of running processes—so I recommend using this approach where possible.

All of the AWS command-line tools require some environment variables to be set
before they can be used. Set the environment variables as follows, updating the paths
where necessary:

```
export JAVA_HOME=/usr
export EC2_HOME=/usr/local/aws/ec2
export AWS_ACCESS_KEY=your_access_key_ID
export AWS_SECRET_KEY=your_secret_access_key
export PATH=$PATH:/usr/local/aws/ec2/bin
```

JAVA_HOME should point to the directory used as the base when Java was installed. For example, if the output of `which java` is */usr/bin/java*, JAVA_HOME should be set to */usr*.

After setting these variables, you can start using the legacy command-line tools. For example:

Command	Action
`ec2-describe-instance`	Shows information about your running instances
`ec2-describe-regions`	Shows the list of AWS regions

 By default, all AWS command-line tools will operate in the US East region (`us-east-1`). Because US East is one of the cheapest EC2 regions, this is a sensible default. You can override this behavior by setting the `EC2_REGION` environment variable, or otherwise by passing the `--region` option on the command line.

Of course, setting these environment variables every time you wish to run the EC2 tools will quickly become tiresome, so it is convenient to set them automatically upon login. The method for achieving this will vary depending on which shell you use. If you are using Bash, for example, you will need to add the variables to your *$HOME/.bashrc* file. The Alestic blog post mentioned earlier includes an example *.bashrc* that sets the environment variables required for most of the tools, as well as adding each of the tool-specific directories to your PATH. Once you have installed all of the tools, your *.bashrc* might look something like this:

```
export JAVA_HOME=/usr
export EC2_HOME=/usr/local/aws/ec2
export AWS_IAM_HOME=/usr/local/aws/iam
export AWS_RDS_HOME=/usr/local/aws/rds
export AWS_ELB_HOME=/usr/local/aws/elb
export AWS_CLOUDFORMATION_HOME=/usr/local/aws/cfn
export AWS_AUTO_SCALING_HOME=/usr/local/aws/as
export CS_HOME=/usr/local/aws/cloudsearch
export AWS_CLOUDWATCH_HOME=/usr/local/aws/cloudwatch
export AWS_ELASTICACHE_HOME=/usr/local/aws/elasticache
export AWS_SNS_HOME=/usr/local/aws/sns
export AWS_ROUTE53_HOME=/usr/local/aws/route53
export AWS_CLOUDFRONT_HOME=/usr/local/aws/cloudfront
for i in $(find /usr/local/aws -type d -name bin)
  do
    PATH=$i/bin:$PATH
  done
PATH=/usr/local/aws/elasticbeanstalk/eb/linux/python2.7:$PATH
PATH=/usr/local/aws/elasticmapreduce:$PATH
```

```
export EC2_PRIVATE_KEY=$(echo $HOME/.aws-default/pk-*.pem)
export EC2_CERT=$(echo $HOME/.aws-default/cert-*.pem)
export AWS_CREDENTIAL_FILE=$HOME/.aws-default/aws-credential-file.txt
export ELASTIC_MAPREDUCE_CREDENTIALS=$HOME/.aws-default/aws-credentials.json
#Some tools use AWS_ACCESS_KEY, others use AWS_ACCESS_KEY_ID
export AWS_ACCESS_KEY=< your access key ID >
export AWS_SECRET_KEY=< your secret access key >
export AWS_ACCESS_KEY_ID=< your access key ID >
export AWS_SECRET_SECRET_KEY=< your secret access key >
# Change the default region if desired
# export EC2_REGION=us-east-1
```

For more tools and utilities, including all of the AWS command-line tools, visit the AWS developer tools site (*http://aws.amazon.com/developertools*).

Managing Your Costs

AWS service charges are structured in a very granular fashion that attempts to fairly charge customers in proportion to their use of each service. Any and all pricing models inherently have trade-offs, and the potential volatility of your monthly AWS expenditures is the most dramatic one in this case. Not having to face the huge upfront capital outlay that was once required to build a traditional datacenter, CIOs have now begun finding fault with the variability of their operational costs month-to-month.

Managing costs in AWS is a subject worthy of a book in its own right. We certainly do not aspire to settle the eternal game between vendors and CIOs here, but in a more limited scope we wish to offer a few tips to new users that may feel some degree of anxiety at being charged per API call, per resource, or per command executed. In most cases these charges amount to merely a few cents, but the multiple pricing models applicable to different AWS services and their potential interaction can make it rather difficult to forecast more accurately than the order of magnitude of the charges incurred. CIO-level executives could aspire to see the infrastructure reach a kind of steady-state where charges become more roughly predictable, yet one of Amazon AWS's greatest strengths is in its ability to dynamically respond to changes in user demand by scaling according to the volume of service requests—a very desirable property, but also a fact running counter to that very same desire for a predictable budget.

At the individual scale, you can prevent sticker shock in a variety of ways as you learn your way to Amazon AWS mastery. In Chapter 2 we will show you how to set up custom alerts that trigger as you exhaust your free service credit or incur charges crossing a certain predefined threshold. You may also monitor your charges in a more interactive fashion through the billing and cost management dashboard (*https://console.aws.amazon.com/billing/home*) (Figure 1-5), which not only displays current charges but also helpfully tries to forecast what the monthly total cost will be based on your current resource usage. The cost management dashboard lets you drill down into every line item to determine from which service (and in what region) the charge originated. You can then track down and discontinue your perhaps inadvertent use of a service that is padding the bottom line of your bill.

Figure 1-5. The billing and cost management dashboard

 Julio Faerman's amusingly named AWS Daleks tool (*https:// github.com/jfaerman/aws-daleks/tree/master/awsdaleks*) delivers a scripted interface to itemizing and optionally removing every resource associated with an AWS account. Exterminating your AWS account is a rather drastic approach to cost management, but the very existence of this option should make new users more confident in their ability to manage costs during their learning.

Another potentially interesting use of Julio's tool is to easily reset an account to its pristine original state, without needing to create a new account to this end. This can be quite handy where AWS is used as a demo or training environment.

## CHAPTER 2

First Steps with EC2 and CloudFormation

Launched in 2006, *Elastic Compute Cloud* (or *EC2*, as it is universally known) is a core part of AWS, and probably one of the better-known components of the service. It allows customers to rent computing resources by the hour in the form of virtual machines (known as *instances*) that run a wide range of operating systems. These instances can be customized by users to run any software applications supported by their operating system of choice.

The idea of renting computing resources by the hour goes back to the 1960s, when it was simply not financially feasible for a company or university department to own a dedicated computer (the idea of an individual owning a computer seeming, at this point, to be the stuff of science fiction). This changed as computers became cheaper and more popular, and dedicated computing resources became the norm.

The explosive growth of the consumer internet, and thus of the services and applications that make up the motivation for its ever-increasing use, has helped the pendulum swing back the other way, to the point where being able to elastically increase or decrease your computing resources (and therefore costs) has become a key financial advantage.

In the pre-cloud days, capacity planning required a large amount of time and forward thinking. Bringing new servers online was a multistep process with the potential for delays at every step: ordering hardware from the supplier, waiting for its arrival, visiting the datacenter to unpack and rack the server, and installing and configuring the operating system and software. Renting a virtual private server, while usually quicker than provisioning physical hardware, also had its own set of challenges and potential delays. With the launch of EC2, all of this was replaced by a single API call.

Particularly in the consumer-driven web application market, it is possible for new companies to experience month after month of exponential growth. This can lead to service interruption as system administrators struggle valiantly to ensure that the demands of their users do not surpass their supply of computing power. This process is often one of the key factors in the success of young companies and also presents one of their most acute challenges—if you do not have enough computing capacity, your users will quickly tire of seeing error pages and move on to a competitor. But oversupply can be equally terminal, as you will be paying for unused computing capacity. This contributed to the failure of many companies in the 2000 dot-com bubble: they spent a huge amount of money in capital expenses building datacenter capacity to support users who never materialized.

EC2 provides a particularly interesting approach to solving this problem. As instances can be launched and terminated automatically based on your current traffic levels, it is possible to dynamically design your infrastructure to operate at (for example) 80% utilization. Large upfront hardware purchases are then replaced by a much smaller, ongoing operational expense exactly matching your capacity needs.

Flexibility is at the heart of the AWS product offering, and this flexibility also extends to the way one interacts with AWS. For most people, the first steps with EC2 are taken via the Management Console, which is the public face of EC2. This web application lets you control most aspects of your infrastructure, although some features (such as Auto Scaling groups, discussed later in the book) require the use of API calls or command-line tools. Historically, Amazon has usually provided command-line tools and API access to new features before they appear in the Management Console.

At the lowest level, AWS is "simply" an HTTP-based API. You can submit a request asking for 10 t2.micro instances, the API request is processed, and 10 instances are launched. The Management Console is merely another way of interacting with this API.

This book uses all the available methods provided by AWS. In nearly all cases, the methods are interchangeable. If a feature specifically requires you to use the command-line tools, we will indicate this. So, if you are familiar with AWS, you should feel free to ignore our recommendations and use whichever method you feel most comfortable with.

What Is an Instance?

At the simplest level, an *instance* can be thought of as a virtual server, the same as you might rent on a monthly basis from a virtual private server (VPS) provider. Indeed, some people are using EC2 in exactly the same way as they would a VPS. While perfectly serviceable in this respect, to use it in this way ignores several interesting features and technologies that can make your job a lot more convenient.

Amazon Machine Images (AMIs) are the main building blocks of EC2. They allow you to configure an instance once (say, installing Apache or Nginx) and then create an image of that instance. The image can be used to launch more instances, all of which are functionally identical to the original. Of course, some attributes—such as the IP address or instance ID—must be unique, so there will be some differences.

AWS Regions and Availability Zones

AWS services operate in multiple geographic regions around the world. At the time of this writing, there are seventeen public AWS *regions*, each of which is further divided into multiple availability zones. This geographic disparity has two main benefits: you can place your application resources close to your end users for performance reasons, and you can design your application so that it is resilient to loss of service in one particular region or availability zone. AWS provides the tools to build automatic damage control into your infrastructure, so if an availability zone fails, more resources can be provisioned in the other availability zones to handle the additional load.

Each availability zone (AZ) is located in a physically separate datacenter within its region. There are three datacenters in or around Dublin, Ireland, that make up the three availability zones in the EU West 1 region—each with separate power and network connections. In theory, this means that an outage in one AZ will not have any effect on the other AZs in the region. In practice, however, an outage in one AZ can trigger a domino effect on its neighboring AZs, and not necessarily due to any failing on Amazon's part.

Consider a well-architected application that, in the event of an AZ failure, will distribute traffic to the remaining AZs. This will result in new instances being launched in the AZs that are still available. Now consider what happens when hundreds of well-architected applications all failover at the same time—the rush for new instances could outstrip the capability of AWS to provide them, leaving some applications with too few instances.

This is an unlikely event—although AWS has service outages like any other cloud provider, deploying your application to multiple AZs will usually be sufficient for most use cases. To sustain the loss of a significant number of AZs within a region, applications must be deployed to multiple regions. This is considerably more challenging than running an application in multiple AZs.

Chapter 6 demonstrates an example application that can survive the loss of one or more AZs, while reserved and spot instances (see "Processing Power" on page 18) provide a way around capacity shortages in a failover.

A final reminder that AWS services are not uniformly available across all regions—validate deployment plans involving regions you are not already familiar with against the newest version of the official Region Table (*https://amzn.to/2LUREdL*).

Instance Types

EC2 instances come in a range of sizes, referred to as *instance types*, to suit various use cases. The instance types differ wildly in the amount of resources allocated to them. The m3.medium instance type has 3.75 GB of memory and 1 virtual CPU core, whereas its significantly bigger brother c3.8xlarge has 60 GB of memory and 32 virtual CPU cores. Each virtual CPU is a hyperthread of an Intel Xeon core in the m3 and c3 instance classes.

For most of the examples in the book, we will use a t2.micro instance, among the smaller and one of the cheapest instance types suitable for any operating system choice, which makes it ideal for our tests.

In production, picking the right instance type for each component in your stack is important to minimize costs and maximize performance, and benchmarking can be the key when making this decision.

Processing Power

EC2, along with the rest of AWS, is built using commodity hardware running Amazon's software to provide the services and APIs. Because Amazon adds this hardware incrementally, several hardware generations are in service at any one time.

When it comes to discussing the underlying hardware that makes up the EC2 cloud, Amazon used to play the cards close to its chest and reveal relatively little information about the exact hardware specifications. This led to the creation of a dedicated compute unit:

> One EC2 Compute Unit provides the equivalent CPU capacity of a 1.0-1.2 GHz 2007 Opteron or 2007 Xeon processor.

It is easy to encounter this metric in older AWS benchmarks. Amazon now openly identifies what hardware underlies the EC2 compute layer, and these abstract units are obsolete and no longer in use.

Amazon provides a rather vast selection of instance types, the current *generation* of which is described at the EC2 Instance Types page (*http://aws.amazon.com/ec2/instance-types/*). The previously mentioned t2.micro instance type therefore refers to a *second generation* general-purpose burstable performance instance. An immediate update of already running applications is generally not required as older generations (*http://aws.amazon.com/ec2/previous-generation/*) remain available for provisioning, with their original functionality intact. It remains advisable to adopt the latest instance type generation when designing a new (or revised) application, so as to benefit from the capabilities of the newer hosting hardware.

No EC2 instance type has ever been discontinued in almost 10 years. This record is made possible by market forces: as newer instance types become available, their significantly better price/performance ratio induces a user migration away from the previous generation. A reduced demand base in turn allows Amazon to continue to supply those deprecated instance types without having to add capacity with old hardware that may be unavailable.

Older instance types are, however, not available in the newer AWS regions they predate—for example, the first generation to be deprecated, `cc1`, is not found in the newest region `ap-northeast-2` hosted in Seoul, Korea. If our spirited advice and the cost savings produced by migrating to newer instance generations are not sufficient to entice you to regularly update your instance selection, perhaps your global expansion plans will.

AWS machine images may make use of either of the two virtualization types supported by the Xen hypervisor: paravirtualized or hardware virtual machine (HVM). It is not necessary to be conversant in the finer differences of the two technologies to make effective use of AWS, but the two approaches present boot-time differences to the guest OS environment. A given Linux machine image will only support booting one virtualization type as a result, a requirement easily met by filtering any image search with the appropriate virtualization type.

Amazon recommends using HVM virtualization on current-generation AMIs. Where that approach is not suitable, it becomes necessary to determine what virtualization type is supported by the older generation of a specific instance type. This is quickly accomplished by launching a test HVM instance from the AWS CLI and watching for a helpful error message. The AWS documentation also provides insight into what virtualization type (*https://amzn.to/2LVmKCa*) is supported by what older instance type.

Different combinations of CPU, memory, network bandwidth, and even custom hardware differentiate AWS instance types. There are nine instance type classes in the current generation at the time of writing, including general purpose (M4, M3), burstable performance (T2), compute optimized (C4, C3), memory intensive (R3), storage optimized (I2 for performance, or D2 for cost), and GPU enabled (G2). These in turn include multiple types with resource allotments of increasing size, bringing the total number of choices we select from above forty.

Jeff Barr of Amazon has published an interesting timeline (*https://aws.amazon.com/blogs/aws/ec2-instance-history/*) of EC2's instance generations.

Taking a scientific approach to benchmarking is the only way to really be sure you are using the right instance type. AWS makes it really simple to run the very same workload configuration with a succession of different instance types, considerably simplifying this task. The most common approach in the AWS user community is to start with an instance type considered high-CPU for the workload under consideration. While running top, drive the CPU to 100% using your application's load generator of choice. Now examine memory use: if you observe the instance running out of memory before the CPU is at full throttle, switch to a higher-memory instance type. Continue this process until you achieve a reasonable balance.

Alongside fixed-performance instances, including the C4, C3, and R3 types, EC2 offers *burstable performance* instances like the T2 type. Burstable performance instances generally operate at a CPU performance baseline but can "burst" above this limit for a time. Bursting is governed by *CPU credits* that are accumulated when the instance runs without its full allotment of CPU. A CPU credit represents use of a full CPU core for one minute.

A practical example will illustrate the accounting mechanism EC2 employs: a t2.micro instance type allocates one virtual CPU to your cloud instance, with six CPU credits earned each hour, representing a 10% share of a real CPU core. Let's assume our workload is a web server, often idling while waiting for requests. If the CPU load falls below 10%, CPU credits are added to that instance's credit for up to 24 hours. Burstable performance is particularly useful for workloads that do not consistently use their full share of the CPU, but benefit from having access to additional, fast CPUs when the occasion arises—applications include small databases, web servers, and development systems.

Stolen CPU Time

Alongside the traditional CPU shares of us (user), sy (system), id (idle), and wa (IO wait), the EC2 hypervisor exposes the additional metric st, meaning *stolen*:

```
%Cpu(s):  0.1 us,  0.1 sy,  0.1 ni, 98.2 id,  1.0 wa,  0.0 hi,  0.0 si,
0.5 st
```

Stolen CPU time represents the share of time the instance's virtual CPU has been waiting for a real CPU while the hypervisor is using it to service another virtual processor. Stolen CPU has gained prominence as a metric that Netflix, possibly the most prominent AWS tenant, tracks closely. Despite its present fame, Stolen CPU is not as significant for workloads that are not sensitive to network jitter or real-time in nature.

The *Noisy Neighbor* is a related compute *cause célèbre*: in any virtual environment, the noisy neighbor effect occurs when an instance starves other instances for a shared resource, causing performance issues to others on the same infrastructure. You will not observe memory or CPU contention as EC2 instances are generally not overpro-

---

visioned; any potential noisy neighbor problems will be limited to network or disk I/O.

One simple approach countering this issue is to automatically allocate a new instance, replacing the one where the performance problem was encountered. Larger instance types are less likely to present this problem on account of sharing a host with fewer neighbors. SR-IOV support (Enhanced Networking) increases storage and network I/O bandwidth, helping to minimize any noise. The ultimate solution is to use Dedicated Hosts (*https://aws.amazon.com/ec2/dedicated-hosts/*), a facility providing complete control of your instance placement for an additional fee.

Specific instance types may provide the latest advanced features found in Intel hardware, including on-chip support for AES encryption and the Advanced Vector Extensions instruction set. The G2 instance type is currently the most prominent example of enhanced compute support, featuring more than 1,500 NVIDIA GPU cores. Advanced compute options are rapidly evolving; their most recent iteration is documented in the instance types page (*http://aws.amazon.com/ec2/instance-types/*), which we recommend you review often.

EC2 instances can be purchased in three ways. Allocated by the hour and requiring no upfront commitment, *on-demand* instances are the default and are used exclusively throughout this book. *Reserved* instances represent a prepaid commitment on the part of a customer, which is usually rewarded by AWS with very steep discounts, up to 75% of on-demand pricing. *Spot* instance pricing requires no upfront commitment, and their pricing fluctuates according to the supply and demand of compute capacity. The customer may define a maximum hourly price not to be exceeded, and EC2 will automatically shut those instances down if their spot pricing tops the set threshold.

Storage

There are two options when it comes to virtual disk storage for your instances: instance storage (also known as *ephemeral storage*) and Elastic Block Store (or EBS). Both are simply block storage devices that can be attached to instances. Once attached, they can be formatted with your operating system's tools and will act like a standard disk. AWS storage comes in two flavors: magnetic disks and solid-state drives (SSDs). SSDs provide higher read and write performance when compared to magnetic disks, but the cost is slightly higher.

There are some key differences between instance storage and EBS. Instance storage is directly attached to the physical host that runs your instance, whereas EBS is attached over the network. This has implications in terms of disk latency and throughput, so we recommend performing another series of benchmarks to see which is best if your application is sensitive to latency or I/O jitter.

I/O speeds are not the only difference—EBS has features that make it preferable to instance storage in nearly all usage scenarios. One of the most useful is the ability to create a snapshot from an EBS. A snapshot is a copy of an EBS volume at a particular point in time. Once you have created a snapshot, you can then create additional EBS volumes that will be identical copies of the source snapshot. You could, for example, create a snapshot containing your database backups. Every time a new instance is launched, it will have a copy of the data ready for use. EBS snapshots form the backbone of many AWS backup strategies.

When an instance is terminated, any data stored on instance storage volumes is lost permanently. EBS volumes can persist after the instance has been terminated. Given all of the additional features, using EBS volumes is clearly preferable except in a few cases, such as when you need fast temporary storage for data that can be safely discarded.

Multiple volumes (of either type) can be attached to an instance, leading to pretty flexible storage configurations. The Block Device Mapping facility (*https://amzn.to/2LXyxzY*) allows multiple volumes to be associated with an instance at boot time. It is even possible to attach multiple volumes to an instance and build a software RAID array on them—an advantage of volumes appearing as block storage devices to the operating system.

 The `disk_setup` and `mounts` modules of Cloud-init (*http://cloudinit.readthedocs.io*) allow customization of all disks associated with an instance upon boot, including partitioning and formatting disks as well as configuring mount points in */etc/fstab*. The official documentation also sheds light on the details of how many public clouds can initialize their instance storage using Cloud-init (*http://bit.ly/2LXJiSS*).

In June 2012, AWS began offering SSDs as a higher-performance alternative to magnetic storage, and over time introduced multiple options with different performance levels and cost. Some instance types now include an SSD-backed instance store to deliver very-high random I/O performance, with types I2 and R3 being the first to support TRIM extensions. Instance types themselves have evolved to include high-I/O instances (type I2), aimed at delivering high IOPS from up to 8 local SSD drives, while dense storage instances (type D2) offer the lowest price per-disk throughput in EC2 and balance cost and performance, using 24 local magnetic drives.

EBS Magnetic and SSD volumes are currently limited to 16 TB in size, limits easily exceeded by dense storage (d2) instances, which can boot with 48 TB of local disk storage. Whereas EBS volumes can be provisioned at any time and in arbitrary configurations, the number and size of available instance store volumes varies with instance type, and can only be attached to an instance at boot time. In addition, EBS volumes can be dynamically resized, which is also used to redefine their performance at runtime.

EBS SSD options include a number of performance flavors. General-purpose SSD volumes are provisioned with 3 IOPS per GB, with burst performance reaching 3,000 IOPS for extended periods. Provisioned IOPS SSD volumes allow the user to define the desired level of performance, up to 20,000 IOPS and 320 MB/s of throughput. A less costly option is offered by the EBS-optimized (*https://amzn.to/2LVmP8W*) M4 type instances, which include dedicated EBS bandwidth between 450 and 4,000 Mbps depending on the specific instance type. EBS-optimized instances use an optimized configuration stack requiring corresponding support on the machine image's part for optimal performance (see "Finding Ubuntu Images" on page 36 for details on locating optimized images).

Long-term storage options are best supported by the S3 service, but a block storage option is available through Cold HDD EBS volumes. Backed by magnetic drives, Cold HDD volumes offer the lowest cost per GB of all EBS volume types, and still provide enough performance to support a full-volume scan at burst speeds. EBS also supports native at-rest encryption (*https://amzn.to/2LV4Q2m*) that is transparently available to EC2 instances and requires very little effort on the administrator's part to deploy and maintain. EBS encryption has no IOPS performance impact and shows very limited impact on latency, making it a general-purpose architectural option even when high security is not strictly required.

Networking

At its simplest, networking in AWS is straightforward—launching an instance with the default networking configuration will give you an instance with a public IP address. Many applications will require nothing more complicated than enabling SSH or HTTP access. At the other end of the scale, Amazon offers more-advanced solutions that can, for example, give you a secure VPN connection from your datacenter to a Virtual Private Cloud (VPC) within EC2.

At a minimum, an AWS instance has one network device attached. The maximum number of network devices that can be attached depends on the instance type. Running `ip addr show` on your instance will show that it has a private IP address in the default `172.31.0.0/16` range. Every instance has a private IP and may have a public IP; this can be configured at launch time or later, with the association of an Elastic-IP address.

 AWS accounts created after December 2013 no longer have access to the legacy *EC2-classic* networking model. This book covers the current *EC2-VPC* networking model exclusively.

Amazon Virtual Private Cloud enables you to provision EC2 instances in a virtual network of your own design. A VPC is a network dedicated to your account, isolated from other networks in AWS, and completely under your control. You can create subnets and gateways, configure routing, select IP address ranges, and define its security perimeter—a series of complex tasks that are bypassed by the existence of the *default VPC*. The default VPC (*https://amzn.to/2ncTvvM*) includes a default subnet in each availability zone, along with routing rules, a DHCP setup, and an internet gateway. The default VPC enables new accounts to immediately start launching instances without having to first master advanced VPC configuration, but its security configuration will not allow instances to accept connections from the internet until we expressly give our permission, by assigning our own *security group* settings.

The default security group allows all outbound traffic from instances to reach the internet, and also permits instances in the same security group to receive inbound traffic from one another, but not from the outside world. Instances launched in the default VPC receive both a public and a private IP address. Behind the scenes, AWS will also create two DNS entries for convenience.

For example, if an instance has a private IP of `172.31.16.166` and a public IP of `54.152.163.171`, their respective DNS entries will be `ip-172-31-16-166.ec2.inter nal` and `ec2-54-152-163-171.compute-1.amazonaws.com`. These DNS entries are known as the private hostname and public hostname.

It is interesting to note that Amazon operates a split-view DNS system, which means it is able to provide different responses depending on the source of the request. If you query the public DNS name from outside EC2 (not from an EC2 instance), you will receive the public IP in response. However, if you query the public DNS name from an EC2 instance in the same region, the response will contain the private IP:

```
# From an EC2 instance
$ dig ec2-54-152-163-171.compute-1.amazonaws.com +short
172.31.16.166
# From Digital Ocean
$ dig ec2-54-152-163-171.compute-1.amazonaws.com +short
54.152.163.171
```

The purpose of this is to ensure that traffic does not leave the internal EC2 network needlessly. This is important as AWS has a highly granular pricing structure when it comes to networking, and Amazon makes a distinction between traffic destined for the public internet and traffic that will remain on the internal EC2 network. The full breakdown of costs is available on the EC2 Pricing page (*https://aws.amazon.com/ec2/ pricing/#Data_Transfer*).

If two instances in the same availability zone communicate using their private IPs, the data transfer is free of charge. However, using their public IPs will incur *internet transfer* charges on both sides of the connection. Although both instances are in EC2, using the public IPs means the traffic will need to leave the internal EC2 network, which will result in higher data transfer costs.

By using the private IP of your instances when possible, you can reduce your data transfer costs. AWS makes this easy with their split-horizon DNS system: as long as you always reference the public hostname of the instance (rather than the public IP), AWS will pick the cheapest option.

Most of the early examples in the book use a single interface, and we will look at more exotic topologies in later chapters.

Launching Instances

The most useful thing one can do with an instance is launch it, which is a good place for us to start. As an automation-loving sysadmin, you will no doubt quickly automate this process and rarely spend much time manually launching instances. Like any task, though, it is worth stepping slowly through it the first time to familiarize yourself with the process.

Launching from the Management Console

Most people take their first steps with EC2 via the Management Console, which is the public face of EC2. Our first journey through the Launch Instance Wizard will introduce a number of new concepts, so we will go through each page in the wizard and take a moment to look at each of these in turn. Although there are faster methods of launching an instance, the wizard is certainly the best way to familiarize yourself with related concepts.

Launching a new instance of an AMI

To launch a new instance, first log in to Amazon's web console (*http://aws.amazon.com*), open the EC2 section, and click Launch Instance. This shows the first in a series of pages that will let us configure the instance options. The first of these pages is shown in Figure 2-1.

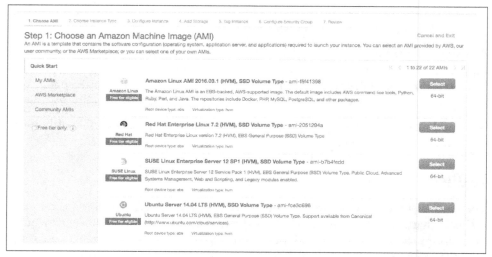

Figure 2-1. AMI selection

As described earlier, Amazon Machine Images (AMIs) are used to launch instances that already have the required software packages installed, configured, and ready to run. Amazon provides AMIs for a variety of operating systems, and the Community and Marketplace AMIs provide additional choices. For example, Canonical provides officially supported AMIs for various versions of its Ubuntu operating system. Other open source and commercial operating systems are also available, both with and without support. The AWS Marketplace lets you use *virtual appliances* created by Amazon or third-party developers. These are Amazon Machine Images already configured to run a particular set of software; for example, many variations of AMIs running the popular WordPress blogging software exist. While some of these appliances are free to use (i.e., you only pay for the underlying AWS resources you use), others require you to pay an additional fee on top of the basic cost of the Amazon resources.

If this is your first time launching an instance, the My AMIs tab will be empty. Later in this chapter, we will create our own custom AMIs, which will subsequently be available via this tab. The Quick Start tab lists several popular AMIs that are available for public use.

Click the Select button next to the Amazon Linux AMI. This gives you instance types to choose from (Figure 2-2).

Figure 2-2. Selecting the instance type

EC2 instances come in a range of shapes and sizes to suit many use cases. In addition to offering increasing amounts of memory and CPU power, instance types also offer differing ratios of memory to CPU. Different components in your infrastructure will vary in their resource requirements, so it can pay to benchmark each part of your application to see which instance type is best for your particular needs. You can also find useful community-developed resources to quickly compare instance types at EC2instances.info (*http://www.ec2instances.info/*).

The Micro instance class is part of Amazon's free usage tier. New customers can use 750 instance-hours free of charge each month with the Linux and Windows *micro* instance types. After exceeding these limits, normal on-demand prices apply.

Select the checkbox next to t2.micro and click Review and Launch. Now you are presented with the review screen, which gives you a chance to confirm your options before launching the instance.

EC2 Instance Details and User Data

So far, we have been using only the most common options when launching our instance. As you will see on the review screen, there are a number of options that we have not changed from the defaults. Some of these will be covered in great detail later in the book, whereas others will rarely be used in the most common use cases. It is worth looking through the advanced options pages to familiarize yourself with the possibilities.

User data is an incredibly powerful feature of EC2, and one that will be used a lot later in the book to demonstrate some of the more interesting things you can do with EC2 instances. Any data entered in this box will be available to the instance once it has launched, which is a useful thing to have in your sysadmin toolbox. Among other things, user data lets you create a single AMI that can fulfill multiple roles depending on the user data it receives, which can be a huge time-saver when it comes to maintaining and updating AMIs. Ubuntu and Amazon Linux support using shell scripts as user data, so you can provide a custom script that will be executed when the instance is launched.

Furthermore, user data is accessible to configuration management tools such as Puppet or Chef, allowing dynamic configuration of the instance based on user data supplied at launch time. This is covered in further detail in Chapter 4.

The Kernel ID and RAM Disk ID options will rarely need to be changed if you are using AMIs provided by Amazon or other developers.

Termination protection provides a small level of protection against operator error in the Management Console. When running a large number of instances, it can be easy to accidentally select the wrong instance for termination. If termination protection is enabled for a particular instance, you will not be able to terminate it via the Management Console or API calls. This protection can be toggled on or off while the instance is running, so there is no need to worry that you will be stuck with an immortal instance. Mike can personally attest to its usefulness—it once stopped him from erroneously terminating a production instance running a master database.

IAM roles are covered in Chapter 3. Briefly, they allow you to assign a security role to the instance. Access keys are made available to the instance so it can access other AWS APIs with a restricted set of permissions specific to its role.

Most of the time your instances will be terminated through the Management Console or API calls. Shutdown Behavior controls what happens when the instance itself initiates the shutdown, for example, after running shutdown -h now on a Linux machine. The available options are to stop the machine so it can be restarted later, or to terminate it, in which case it is gone forever.

Tags are a great way to keep track of your instances and other EC2 resources via the Management Console.

Tags perform a similar role to user data, with an important distinction: user data is for the instance's internal use, whereas tags are primarily for external use. An instance does not have any built-in way to access tags, whereas user data, along with other metadata describing the instance, can be accessed by reading a URL from the instance. It is, of course, possible for the instance to access its own tags by querying the EC2 API, but that would require API access privileges to be granted to the instance itself in the form of a key, something less than desirable in a healthy security posture.

Using the API, you can perform queries to find instances that are tagged with a particular key/value combination. For example, two tags we always use in our EC2 infrastructures are *environment* (which can take values such as *production* or *staging*) and *role* (which, for instance, could be *webserver* or *database*). When scripting common tasks—deployments or software upgrades—it becomes a trivial task to perform a set of actions on all web servers in the staging environment. This makes tags an integral part of any well-managed AWS infrastructure.

If the Cost Allocation Reports feature (on the billing options page of your account settings page) is enabled, your CSV-formatted bill will contain additional fields, allowing you to link line-item costs with resource tags. This information is invaluable when it comes to identifying areas for cost savings, and for larger companies where it is necessary to separate costs on a departmental basis for charge-back purposes. Even for small companies, it can be useful to know where your sources of cost are.

After reviewing the options, click Launch to move to the final screen. At the time of this writing, the wizard's *Quick Start* process will automatically create a convenient `launch-wizard-1` security group granting the instance SSH access from the internet at large. This is not the default security group previously discussed, and this helpfulness is not present when using the AWS CLI or API interfaces to create instances (Figure 2-3).

Figure 2-3. The Review screen (the prominent security warning is alerting you that SSH access has been opened with a default security group)

Key pairs

The next screen presents the available key pairs options (Figure 2-4).

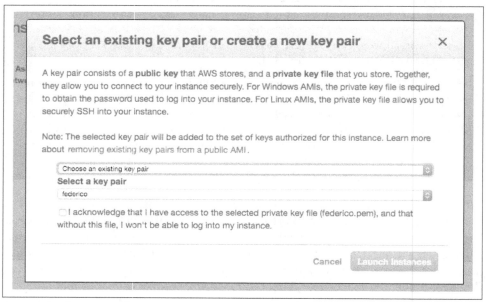

Figure 2-4. Key pair selection

Key pairs provide secure access to your instances. To understand the benefits of key pairs, consider how we could securely give someone access to an AMI that anyone in the world can launch an instance of. Using default passwords would be a security risk, as it is almost certain some people would forget to change the default password at some point. Amazon has implemented SSH key pairs to help avoid this eventuality. Of course, it is possible to create an AMI that uses standard usernames and passwords, but this is not the default for AWS-supplied AMIs.

All AMIs have a *default user*: when an instance is booted, the public part of your chosen key pair is copied to that user's SSH authorized keys file. This ensures that you can securely log in to the instance without a password. In fact, the only thing you need to know about the instance is the default username and its IP address or hostname.

This also means that only people with access to the private part of the key pair will be able to log in to the instance. Sharing your private keys is against security best practices, so to allow others access to the instance, you will need to create additional system accounts and configure them with passwords or SSH authorized keys.

The name of the default user varies between AMIs. For example, Amazon's own AMIs use ec2-user, whereas Ubuntu's official AMIs use ubuntu.

If you are unsure of the username, one trick you can use is to try to connect to the instance as root. The most friendly AMIs present an error message informing you that root login is disabled, and letting you know which username you should use to connect instead.

Changing the default user of an existing AMI is not recommended, but can be easily done. The details of how to accomplish this have been documented by Eric Hammond of Alestic (*https://alestic.com/2014/01/ec2-change-username/*). The following table enumerates default usernames for most popular Linux distributions:

Distribution	Default Username
Amazon Linux	ec2-user
Ubuntu	ubuntu
Debian	admin
RHEL	ec2-user (since 6.4), root (before 6.4)
CentOS	root
Fedora	ec2-user
SUSE	root
FreeBSD	ec2-user
BitNami	bitnami

You can create a new SSH key pair through the EC2 Key Pairs page (*https://console.aws.amazon.com/ec2/v2/home?region=us-east-1#KeyPairs:sort=keyName*) in the AWS Management Console—note that key pairs are region-specific, and this URL refers to the US East 1 region. Keys you create in one EC2 region cannot be immediately used in another region, although you can, of course, upload the same key to each region instead of maintaining a specific key pair for each region. After creating a key, a *.pem* file will be automatically downloaded.

Alternatively, you can upload the public part of an existing SSH key pair to AWS. This can be of great help practically because it may eliminate the need to add the -i / path/to/keypair.pem option to each SSH command where multiple keys are in use (refer to ssh-agent's man page if you need to manage multiple keys). It also means that the private part of the key pair remains entirely private—you never need to upload this to AWS, it is never transmitted over the internet, and Amazon does not need to generate it on your behalf, all of which have security implications.

Alestic offers a handy Bash script (*http://alestic.com/2010/10/ec2-ssh-keys*) to import an existing public SSH key into each region.

If you are a Windows user connecting with PuTTY, you will need to convert this to a PPK file using PuTTYgen before you can use it. To do this, launch PuTTYgen, select Conversions → Import Key, and follow the on-screen instructions to save a new key in the correct format. Once the key has been converted, it can be used with PuTTY and PuTTY Agent.

From the Key Pairs screen in the launch wizard, you can select which key pair will be used to access the instance, or to launch the instance without any key pair. You can select from your existing key pairs or choose to create a new key pair. It is not possible to import a new key pair at this point—if you would like to use an existing SSH key that you have not yet uploaded to AWS, you will need to upload it first, just follow the instructions on the EC2 Key Pairs page (*https:// console.aws.amazon.com/ec2/v2/home?region=us-east-1#KeyPairs:sort=keyName*).

Once you have created a new key pair or imported an existing one, click "Choose from your existing Key Pairs," select your key pair from the drop-down menu, and continue to the next screen. You have now completed the last step of the wizard—click Launch Instances to create the instance.

Waiting for the instance

Phew, we made it. Launching an instance can take a few seconds, depending on the instance type, current traffic levels on AWS, and other factors. The Instances page of the Management Console will show you the status of your new instance. Initially, this will be pending, while the instance is being created on the underlying physical hardware. Once the instance has been created and has begun the boot process, the page will show the running state. This does not mean your instance is servicing requests or ready for you to log in to, merely that the instance has been created.

Selecting an instance in the Management Console will show you its public DNS name, as well as more detail about the settings and status of the instance. At this point, you can try to SSH to the public hostname. If the connection fails, it means SSH is not yet ready to accept connections, so wait a moment and try again. Once you manage to log in to the instance, you will see a welcome screen specific to the AMI you launched.

Querying information about the instance

Now that you have an instance, what can you do with it? The answer is—anything you can do with an equivalent Linux server running on physical hardware. Later chapters demonstrate some of the more useful things you can do with EC2 instances. For now, let's take a look at the *ec2metadata* tool, which is included on most well-designed AMIs.

In the infancy of AWS, EC2 had no real style guide; the question of how to name something was up to the developer. A few different but equivalent tools parsing instance metadata appeared: *ec2metadata* in the case of Ubuntu's, and *ec2-metadata* in the case of Amazon Linux's variant.

The `ec2metadata` tool is useful for quickly accessing the metadata attributes of your instance: for example, the instance ID, or the ID of the AMI from which this instance was created. Running `ec2metadata` without arguments will display all available metadata.

If you are interested in specific metadata attributes, you can read the values one at a time by passing the name of the attribute as a command-line option. For example:

```
$ ec2metadata --instance-id
i-ba932720
$ ec2metadata --ami-id
ami-f5f41398
```

This is useful if you are writing shell scripts that need to access this information. Rather than getting all the metadata and parsing it yourself, you can do this:

```
INSTANCE_ID=$(ec2metadata --instance-id)
AMI_ID=$(ec2metadata --ami-id)
echo "The instance $INSTANCE_ID was created from AMI $AMI_ID"
```

Every instance downloads its metadata from the following URL:

http://169.254.169.254/latest/meta-data/<attribute_name>

So to get the instance ID, you could request the URL *http://169.254.169.254/latest/meta-data/instance-id*.

This URL is accessible only from within the instance, while the IP address maps to the hostname *http://instance-data*, which is easier for users to remember. See AWS's Documentation for full details on instance metadata (*http://docs.aws.amazon.com/AWSEC2/latest/UserGuide/AccessingInstancesLinux.html*).

If you want to query the metadata from outside the instance, you will need to use the `ec2-describe-instances` command.

Terminating the instance

Once you have finished testing and exploring the instance, you can terminate it. In the Management Console, right-click the instance and select Terminate Instance.

Next, we will look at some of the other available methods of launching instances.

In early 2013, Amazon introduced a mobile app (*http://
aws.amazon.com/console/mobile/*) interface to the AWS Management Console with versions supporting both iOS and Android
devices. After multiple updates and enhancements, the app has
become an excellent tool for administrators who need a quick look
at the state of their AWS deployment while on the move.

The app's functionality is not as comprehensive as the web console's, but it showcases remarkable usability in its streamlined
workflow (see Figure 2-5 for an example), and most users enjoy the
quick access to select functionality it provides: some users now
even pull up their mobile phone to execute certain tasks rather
than resorting to their trusted terminal!

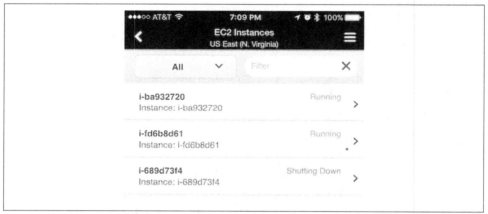

Figure 2-5. The AWS console mobile app

Launching with Command-Line Tools

If you followed the steps in the previous section, you probably noticed a few drawbacks to launching instances with the Management Console. The number of steps
involved and the variety of available options engender complex documentation that
takes a while to absorb. This is not meant as criticism of the Management Console—
EC2 is a complex beast, thus any interface to it requires a certain level of complexity.

Because AWS is a self-service system, it must support the use cases of many users,
each with differing requirements and levels of familiarity with AWS itself. By necessity, the Management Console is equivalent to an enormous multipurpose device that
can print, scan, fax, photocopy, shred, and collate.

This flexibility is great when it comes to discovering and learning the AWS ecosystem, but is less useful when you have a specific task on your to-do list that must be

performed as quickly as possible. Interfaces for managing production systems should be streamlined for the task at hand, and not be conducive to making mistakes.

Documentation should also be easy to use, particularly in a crisis, and the Management Console does not lend itself well to this idea. Picture yourself in the midst of a downtime situation, where you need to quickly launch some instances, each with different AMIs and user data. Would you rather have to consult a 10-page document describing which options to choose in the Launch Instance Wizard, or copy and paste some commands into the terminal?

Fortunately, Amazon gives us precisely the tools required to do the latter. The EC2 command-line tools can be used to perform any action available from the Management Console, in a fashion that is much easier to document and much more amenable to automation.

 As you start exploring dynamic infrastructure provisioning with AWS CLI, we recommend you set up a billing alarm (*https://amzn.to/2vIhVkK*). Leveraging the CloudWatch and Simple Notification services, billing alerts will notify you if you exceed preset spending thresholds.

While not ruinously expensive, forgetting to shut down a few of your test instances and letting them run for the rest of the month (until you notice as you are billed) will easily exceed your personal phone bill. It is a snap to inadvertently make this mistake; we have slipped up ourselves and advise you let the system help keep track with these friendly notifications.

If you have not already done so, you will need to set up the EC2 command-line tools according to the instructions in "Preparing Your Tools" on page 3 before continuing. Make sure you have set the AWS_ACCESS_KEY and AWS_SECRET_KEY environment variables or the equivalent values in the *.aws/credentials* file in your home directory.

Access Key IDs and Secrets

When you log in to the AWS Management Console, you will use your email address and password to authenticate yourself. Things work a little bit differently when it comes to the command-line tools. Instead of a username and password, you use an access key ID and secret access key. Together, these are often referred to as your *access credentials*.

Although access credentials consist of a pair of keys, they are not the same as an SSH key pair. The former is used to access AWS's APIs, while the latter is used to SSH into an instance to perform work on the shell.

When you created your AWS account, you also generated a set of access credentials for your root account identity. These keys have full access to your AWS account—keep them safe! You are responsible for the cost of any resources created using these keys, so if a malicious person were to use these keys to launch some EC2 instances, you would be left with the bill.

"IAM Users and Groups" on page 84 discusses how you can set up additional accounts and limit which actions they can perform, as defined by current security best practices. For the following examples, we will just use the access keys you have already created during CLI setup.

AWS lets you inspect all active access credentials for your account through the Security Credentials page (*https://portal.aws.amazon.com/gp/aws/securityCredentials*) of the Management Console, but for increased security you will be unable to retrieve their secret access keys after creation. This stops any unauthorized access to your account from resulting in a compromise of your API credentials, but has the annoying side effect of requiring you to replace your access keys if they ever were lost.

To launch an instance from the command line, you need to provide values that correspond to the options you can choose from when using the Management Console. Because all of this information must be entered in a single command, rather than gathered through a series of web pages, it is necessary to perform some preliminary steps so you know which values to choose. The Management Console can present you with a nice drop-down box containing all the valid AMIs for your chosen region, but to use the command line, you need to know the ID of the AMI before you can launch it.

The easiest way to get a list of available images is in the Instances tab (*https://console.aws.amazon.com/ec2/home?#s=Images*) of the Management Console, which lets you search through all available AMIs. Keep in mind that AMIs exist independently in EC2 regions—the Amazon Linux AMI in the US East region is not the same image as the Amazon Linux AMI in Europe, although they are functionally identical. Amazon, Canonical, and other providers make copies of their AMIs available in each region as a convenience to their users, but the same AMI will show a different ID in different regions.

Finding Ubuntu Images

Searching for Ubuntu images yields 27,175 results in the `us-east-1` region alone at the time of this writing. Filtering for official images released by Canonical (owner 099720109477) reduces the crop to *only* 6,074 images. These high numbers are due to Ubuntu's high popularity in public cloud environments, and to Canonical's commitment to refreshing AMIs with the newest packages as security updates or bug fixes are published. Older AMIs remain available as new ones are issued by the vendor, the timing of when to switch to newer images being entirely under the admin's control, not AWS's. All these factors conspire to make finding the correct Ubuntu image a rather nontrivial task.

Ubuntu AMIs can be most easily found using Canonical's AMI Locator (*http://cloud-images.ubuntu.com/locator/ec2/*) (see Figure 2-6), which shows only the most recent release by default and which updates results as you search by substring or select from prepopulated pull-down menus. This is an essential resource for navigating the sea of Ubuntu images found on AWS. At the time of this writing, the Locator narrows down our options to twelve images varying in storage and system bit width.

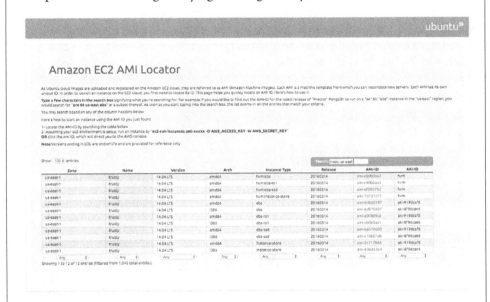

Figure 2-6. Ubuntu EC2 AMI Locator (clicking the selected AMI ID launches it from the Management Console)

Equally interesting to power users is the collection of official Ubuntu cloud images found on Ubuntu.com (*http://cloud-images.ubuntu.com*). This site includes both daily builds and official releases. Finding the latter is accomplished by navigating to the *release/* subdirectory of any Ubuntu version, which is *http://cloud-images.ubuntu.com/releases/16.04/release/* for Xenial.

If you need to find an AMI using the command-line tools, you can do so with the aws ec2 describe-instances command. A few examples follow:

```
# Describe all of your own images in the US East region
aws ec2 describe-images --owners self --region us-east-1
```

```
# Find Amazon-owned images for Windows Server 2012, 64-bit version
aws ec2 describe-images --owners amazon --filters Name=architecture,Val-
ues=x86_64 | grep Server-2012

# List the AMIs that have a specific set of key/value tags
aws ec2 describe-images --owners self --filters Name=tag:role,Values=webserver
Name=tag:environment,Values=production
```

The first query should of course yield no results, unless you have already created some AMIs of your own. Later examples showcase combining the tool's own filtering and grep to find the image you are really looking for. In our second example we are searching for a Windows Server image created by another party. Note that we explicitly searched for Amazon-owned images, as any AWS customer can decide to make her AMIs accessible to all other customers. Image names are freely chosen by their creator just like their contents, thus not only complicating our search with a very large number of results, but potentially posing a security problem if one carelessly selects an unknown party's bits.

At the time of writing, the most popular Ubuntu long-term support (LTS) version on AWS is 16.04, going by the nickname of Xenial Xerus. In the Eastern US EC2 region, the latest version of Canonical's official AMI is ami-43a15f3e (64b, HVM, EBS storage), which is used in many of the examples. Make sure to update this with your chosen AMI. If you are not sure which to use, or have no real preference, the authors recommend using the latest LTS version of Ubuntu for 64-bit systems.

The command used to launch an instance is aws ec2 run-instances. The most basic invocation is simply aws ec2 run-instances --image-id ami-6d060707, which will launch an older m1.small instance in the default us-east-1 region. If you are paying attention, you noticed we used a different AMI ID with paravirtualization support as the older m1.small instance type does not support the newer HVM virtualization style. However, if you run this command and attempt to log in to the instance, you will soon notice a rather large problem: because no key pair name was specified, there is no way to log in to the instance. Instead, try running the command with the -key option to specify one of the SSH key pairs you created earlier. In the following example, we have also changed the instance type to t2.micro, the smallest instance type all AWS operating systems are currently comfortable with:

```
$ aws ec2 run-instances --image-id ami-43a15f3e --region us-east-1 \
--key federico --instance-type t2.micro  --output text
740376006796     r-bbcfff10
INSTANCES         0         x86_64             False    xen      ami-43a15f3e
i-64a8a6fe        t2.micro          federico          2016-04-03T07:40:48.000Z
ip-172-31-52-118.ec2.internal    172.31.52.118              /dev/sda1      ebs
True              subnet-2a45b400 hvm      vpc-934935f7
[ output truncated ]
```

Once EC2 receives the request to launch an instance, it prints some information about the pending instance. The value we need for the next command is the instance ID, in this case, `i-64a8a6fe`.

Although this command returns almost immediately, you will still need to wait a short while before your instance is ready to accept SSH connections. You can check on the status of the instance while it is booting with the `aws ec2 describe-instance-status` command. While the instance is still booting, its status will be listed as `pending`. This will change to `running` once the instance is ready. Remember that `ready` in this context means that the virtual instance has been created, and the operating system's boot process has started. It does not necessarily mean that the instance is ready to receive an SSH connection, which is important when writing scripts that automate these commands.

 Granting access to an already running image can involve multiple manual steps adding the new user's SSH credentials to the authorized keys file. Juggling files can be avoided working with Ubuntu images thanks to the `ssh-import-id` command. Just invoking the following:

```
ssh-import-id lp:f2
```

will retrieve Federico's SSH identity from *Launchpad.net* and grant him access, since he's the user the command was run under. You can accomplish the same for Mike by using his GitHub user ID:

```
ssh-import-id gh:mikery
```

All that is required is the user ID from either site. This is roughly equivalent to running the following (which could be used to derive alternative import strategies for other sites):

```
wget https://launchpad.net/~f2/+sshkeys -0 - >> ~/.ssh/authorized_keys && echo >> ~/.ssh/authorized_keys
```

Once your instance is running, the output should look similar to this:

```
$ aws ec2 describe-instance-status --instance-ids i-64a8a6fe --region us-east-1
--output text
INSTANCESTATUSES        us-east-1a      i-64a8a6fe
INSTANCESTATE   16      running
INSTANCESTATUS  ok
DETAILS reachability     passed
SYSTEMSTATUS    ok
DETAILS reachability     passed
```

Another way to display information about your instance is with `aws ec2 describe-instances`, which will show much more detail. In particular, it will show the public DNS name (for example, `ec2-54-247-40-225.eu-west-1.compute.amazonaws.com`), which you can use to SSH into your instance:

```
$ aws ec2 describe-instances --instance-ids i-64a8a6fe --region us-east-1 --
output text
RESERVATIONS      740376006796    r-bbcfff10
INSTANCES       0      x86_64          False    xen    ami-43a15f3e
i-64a8a6fe      t2.micro       federico       2016-04-03T07:40:48.000Z
ip-172-31-52-118.ec2.internal    172.31.52.118
ec2-52-90-56-122.compute-1.amazonaws.com         52.90.56.122    /dev/sda1
ebs     True            subnet-2a45b400 hvm    vpc-934935f7
BLOCKDEVICEMAPPINGS     /dev/sda1
[ output truncated ]
EBS     2016-04-03T07:40:48.000Z        True    attached       vol-e9c0c637
MONITORING      disabled
NETWORKINTERFACES               12:5a:33:b3:b5:97       eni-ce4084ea
740376006796    ip-172-31-52-118.ec2.internal    172.31.52.118    True    in-use
subnet-2a45b400 vpc-934935f7
ASSOCIATION     amazon  ec2-52-90-56-122.compute-1.amazonaws.com
52.90.56.122
ATTACHMENT      2016-04-03T07:40:48.000Z        eni-attach-2545d3d4    True
0       attached
GROUPS  sg-384f3a41     default
PRIVATEIPADDRESSES      True    ip-172-31-52-118.ec2.internal    172.31.52.118
ASSOCIATION     amazon  52.90.56.122
PLACEMENT       us-east-1a              default
SECURITYGROUPS  sg-384f3a41     default
STATE   16      running
```

To terminate the running instance, issue `aws ec2 terminate-instance`. To verify that this instance has indeed been terminated, you can use the `aws ec2 describe-instances` command again:

```
$ aws ec2 terminate-instances --instance-ids i-64a8a6fe --region us-east-1
INSTANCE        i-64a8a6fe      running shutting-down
$ aws ec2 describe-instances --instance-ids i-64a8a6fe --region us-east-1
RESERVATION     r-991230d1      612857642705    default
INSTANCE        i-64a8a6fe      ami-43a15f3e                    terminated
mike    0       t1.micro        2012-11-25T15:51:45+0000
[ output truncated ]
```

As you find yourself using the command-line tools more frequently, and for more complex tasks, you will probably begin to identify procedures that are good candidates for automation. Besides saving you both time and typing, automating the more complex tasks has the additional benefits of reducing the risk of human error and simply removing some thinking time from the process.

The command-line tools are especially useful when it comes to documenting these procedures. Processes become more repeatable. Tasks can be more easily delegated and shared among the other members of the team.

Trying to connect multiple times as an instance boots is inelegant. Fortunately, we can one-line script our way out of this. The BSD version of ping, notably on macOS, includes a convenient "one ping only" option (-o) that we like to think honors Sean Connery's famous quote in *Hunt for Red October*. The option terminates ping once the first reply is received. Like Captain Marko Ramius, we can use this to ask for "one ping only, please":

```
$ ping -o 52.90.56.122; sleep 2; ssh ubuntu@52.90.56.122
PING 52.90.56.122 (52.90.56.122): 56 data bytes
Request timeout for icmp_seq 0
Request timeout for icmp_seq 1
Request timeout for icmp_seq 2
64 bytes from 52.90.56.122: icmp_seq=3 ttl=48
time=40.492 ms
[ output truncated ]

Welcome to Ubuntu 16.04.4 LTS (GNU/Linux 4.4.0-1052-aws
x86_64)
```

Perhaps less steeped in movie lore, but nonetheless equally effective is this GNU-compatible version that waits in a loop for the SSH service to start up:

```
$ until ssh ubuntu@52.90.56.122; do sleep 1; done
ssh: connect to host 52.90.56.122 port 22: Connection
refused
ssh: connect to host 52.90.56.122 port 22: Connection
refused
[ output truncated ]

Welcome to Ubuntu 16.04.4 LTS (GNU/Linux 4.4.0-1052-aws
x86_64)
```

Launching from Your Own Programs and Scripts

The command-line tools are useful from an automation perspective, as it is trivial to call them from Bash or any other scripting language. While the output for some of the services can be rather complex, it is relatively straightforward to parse this output and perform dynamic actions based on the current state of your infrastructure. At a certain level of complexity, though, calling all of these external commands and parsing their output becomes time-consuming and error prone. At this point, it can be useful to move to a programming language with a client library to help you work with AWS directly.

Officially supported client libraries are available for many programming languages and platforms, including:

- Java

- PHP
- Python
- Ruby
- .NET
- iOS
- Android

The full set of AWS programming resources can be found at the AWS Sample Code site (*http://aws.amazon.com/code*).

Most of the examples in this book use the popular Python-based Boto library (*http://boto.cloudhackers.com/en/latest/index.html*) although other, equally capable libraries exist. Even if you are not a Python developer, the examples should be easy to transfer to your language of choice, because each library is calling the same underlying AWS API.

Regardless of your language choice, the high-level concepts for launching an instance remain the same: first, decide which attributes you will use for the instance, such as which AMI it will be created from, and then issue a call to the RunInstances method of the EC2 API.

When exploring a new API from Python, it can often be helpful to use the interactive interpreter. This lets you type in lines of Python code one at a time, instead of executing them all at once in a script. The benefit here is that you have a chance to explore the API and quickly get to grips with the various functions and objects that are available. We will use this method in the upcoming examples. If you prefer, you can also copy the example code to a file and run it all in one go with python *filename.py*.

If you do not already have the Boto library installed, you will need to install it with pip (pip install boto) before continuing with the examples. Once this is done, open the Python interactive interpreter by running python without any arguments:

```
$ python
Python 2.7.6 (default, Jun 22 2015, 17:58:13)
[GCC 4.8.2] on linux2
Type "help", "copyright", "credits" or "license" for more information.
>>>
```

When you connect to an AWS service with Boto, Boto needs to know which credentials it should use to authenticate. You can explicitly pass the aws_access_key_id and aws_secret_access_key keyword arguments when calling connect_to_region, as shown here:

```
>>> AWS_ACCESS_KEY_ID = "your-access-key"
>>> AWS_SECRET_ACCESS_KEY = "your-secret-key"
>>> from boto.ec2 import connect_to_region
```

```
>>> ec2_conn = connect_to_region('us-east-1',
... aws_access_key_id=AWS_ACCESS_KEY_ID,
... aws_secret_access_key=AWS_SECRET_ACCESS_KEY)
```

Alternatively, if the AWS_ACCESS_KEY_ID and AWS_SECRET_ACCESS_KEY environment variables are set, Boto will use these automatically:

```
$ export AWS_SECRET_ACCESS_KEY='your access key'
$ export AWS_ACCESS_KEY_ID='your secret key'
$ python
Python 2.7.6 (default, Jun 22 2015, 17:58:13)
[GCC 4.8.2] on linux2
Type "help", "copyright", "credits" or "license" for more information.
>>> from boto.ec2 import connect_to_region
>>> ec2_conn = connect_to_region('us-east-1')
```

Boto will also automatically attempt to retrieve your credentials from the file ~/.aws/credentials if one is present, in which case exporting them to environment variables is not necessary.

Once you have connected to the EC2 API, you can issue a call to run_instances to launch a new instance. You will need two pieces of information before you can do this —the ID of the AMI you would like to launch, and the name of the SSH key pair you will use when connecting to the instance:

```
>>> ssh = ec2_conn.create_security_group('ssh', 'SSH access group')
>>> ssh
SecurityGroup:ssh
>>> ssh.authorize('tcp', 22, 22, '0.0.0.0/0')
True
>>> reservation = ec2_conn.run_instances('ami-43a15f3e',
... instance_type='t2.micro', key_name='your-key-pair-name',
... security_group_ids=['ssh'])
>>> instance = reservation.instances[0]
```

The call to run_instances does not, as might initially be suspected, return an object representing an instance. Because you can request more than one instance when calling the run_instances function, it returns a *reservation*, which is an object representing one or more instances. The reservation object lets you iterate over the instances. Here, we requested only one instance, so we simply took the first element of the list of instances in the reservation (in Python, that is done with reservation.instances[0]) to get our instance.

Now the instance is launching, and we have an instance (in the programming sense) of the instance (in the EC2 sense), so we can begin to query its attributes. Some of these are available immediately, whereas others do not get set until later in the launch process. For example, the DNS name is not available until the instance is nearly running. The instance will be in the pending state initially. We can check on the current state by calling the update() function:

```
>>> instance.state
u'pending'
>>> instance.update()
u'pending'
# After some time…
>>> instance.update()
u'running'
```

Once the instance reaches the running state, we should be able to connect to it via SSH. But first we need to know its hostname or IP address, which are available as attributes on the instance object:

```
>>> instance.public_dns_name
u'ec2-54-152-96-69.compute-1.amazonaws.com'
>>> instance.private_ip_address
u'172.31.51.214'
>>> instance.id
u'i-53f2e7c9'
```

Terminating a running instance is just a matter of calling the terminate() function. Before we do that, let's take a moment to look at how Boto can work with EC2 tags to help make administration easier. A tag is a key/value pair that you can assign to any number of instances to track arbitrary properties. The *metadata* stored in tags can be used as a simple but effective administration database for your EC2 resources. Setting a tag is simple:

```
>>> ec2_conn.create_tags([instance.id], {'environment': 'staging'})
True
```

Once an instance has been tagged, we can use the get_all_instances() method to find it again. get_all_instances() returns a list of reservations, each of which, in turn, contains a list of instances. These lists can be iterated over to perform an action on all instances that match a specific tag query. As an example, we will terminate any instances that have been tagged as being part of our staging environment:

```
>>> tagged_reservations = ec2_conn.get_all_instances(filters={'tag:environ
ment': 'staging'})
>>> tagged_reservations
[Reservation:r-6a4a76c1]
>>> tagged_reservations[0]
Reservation:r-6a4a76c1
>>> tagged_reservations[0].instances[0]
Instance:i-53f2e7c9
>>> for res in tagged_reservations:
...     for inst in res.instances:
...         inst.terminate()
>>>
```

Given that nearly all resource types support tagging, and that Amazon provides this feature free of charge, it would be a shame not to take advantage of the many ways this can help you automate and control your infrastructure. Think of it as an incredibly simple query language for your infrastructure. Conceptually, our previous example was similar to `SELECT * FROM instances WHERE tag_environment='staging'`.

The previous example iterated over all the matching instances (only one, in this case) and terminated them. We can now check on the status of our instance and see that it is heading toward the `terminated` state:

```
>>> instance.update()
u'shutting-down'
# After a moment or two...
>>> instance.update()
u'terminated'
```

This example only scratches the surface of what Boto and other client libraries are capable of. The Boto documentation (*http://boto.cloudhackers.com/en/latest/ref/*) provides a more thorough introduction to other AWS services. Having the ability to dynamically control your infrastructure is one of the best features of AWS from a system administration perspective, and it gives you plenty of opportunities to automate recurring processes.

Managing AWS with Python is the subject of Mitch Garnaat's *Python and AWS Cookbook* (O'Reilly). Written by the very author of Boto, this cookbook gets you started with more than two dozen complete recipes.

Introducing CloudFormation

There is another method of launching instances that deserves its own section. Among the many Amazon Web Services features, a favorite is CloudFormation. It fundamentally changes how AWS infrastructure is managed, and is something whose absence is strongly felt when working in non-AWS environments. In a nutshell, CloudFormation is a resource-provisioning tool that accepts a JSON file describing the resources you require and then creates them for you. Such a simple idea, yet so powerful.

Consider this example checklist for launching an instance. Using the three methods of launching instances we have already looked at, how could you most efficiently perform these tasks? More importantly, how would you document the process so it is repeatable?

1. Launch a `t2.micro` instance of `ami-43a15f3e` in the `us-east-1` region. The instance should have a 10 GB EBS volume attached to the `sdf` device and belong to the security group named `webservers`. It should be given the string `webserver` as user data and have a `role` tag with the value of `webserver`.

2. Create a CNAME for *www.example.com* that points to the public hostname of the instance.

If the task is a one-off procedure, it might make sense to perform it using the Management Console, but the documentation would be time-consuming to write and tedious to follow. Automating the task through programming (either by calling the EC2 command-line tools, or using one of the client libraries) means the documentation could be reduced to a single command: "run this script." While benefiting the person following the documentation, this comes at a cost to whomever must write and maintain the script.

Using CloudFormation, the burden of maintaining the tool itself is shifted to Amazon, with the user retaining responsibility solely for maintaining the configuration itself. You simply create a JSON-formatted file (a *stack template*) describing the attributes of the instance, and then let AWS do the rest. The documentation is reduced to one step: "Create a stack named webservers, using the stack template *webserver.json*." A *stack* can be thought of as a collection of resources, along with a list of events associated with changes to those resources and the stack itself.

Successfully submitting a stack template to CloudFormation will result in the creation of a stack, which will, in turn, create one or more AWS resources (such as EC2 instances or Elastic Load Balancers).There are no additional scripts to write or maintain, although writing and maintaining stack templates can become rather complicated as well once your infrastructure starts growing. The CloudFormation stack template language has its own learning curve.

Being plain-text files, stack templates can be stored in your version control system alongside your application code and server configurations. The same processes used to review changes to your code can be applied to changes in your infrastructure. By browsing the history of commits to your stack templates, you can quickly audit changes to your infrastructure, as long as you have a consistent policy in place to run stacks only after they have been committed to version control.

An additional benefit of stack templates is that they can be reused: it is possible to create multiple stacks from the same template. This can be used to give each developer a self-contained copy of their development stack. When new members join the team, they simply need to launch a new copy of the stack, and they can start familiarizing themselves with the application and infrastructure almost immediately.

The same stack template can also be used to create multiple copies of the stack in the different AWS regions. Operating an application across multiple AWS regions requires a lot of careful planning at both the application and infrastructure layers, but CloudFormation makes one aspect of the task very easy: by deploying a stack template to multiple regions, you can be sure that your infrastructure is identical in each region, without needing to manually configure a series of resources in each one.

Aside from the cost of the underlying resources, CloudFormation is free of charge. Although it adds a small bump in the AWS learning curve, it is well worth taking the time to deploy your infrastructure with CloudFormation, especially if you find yourself managing complicated or frequently changing infrastructures. Routing all changes to your infrastructure through a single process (i.e., updating the CloudFormation stack) is imperative when working with a team, as it gives you an easy way to answer those questions of "who changed what, and when."

For more examples of what can be achieved with CloudFormation, have a look at the example templates provided by Amazon (*http://aws.amazon.com/cloudformation/aws-cloudformation-templates/*).

 Are there limits on just how many servers you can dynamically request from AWS? New accounts are usually limited to 20 on-demand instances, an additional 20 reserved instances, and up to 20 (*https://amzn.to/2niY7k6*) spot instances in each region. Additional restrictions (*https://amzn.to/2nidRnA*) are enforced on certain instance types, and filing a support request (*https://amzn.to/2n42peT*) is all that is necessary to increase your account limits (*https://console.aws.amazon.com/ec2/v2/home?region=us-east-1#Limits:*).

Working with CloudFormation Stacks

CloudFormation stacks are themselves a type of AWS resource, and can thus be managed in similar ways. They can be created, updated, and deleted via the same methods we use for interacting with other AWS services—the Management Console, command-line tools, or client libraries. They can also be tagged for ease of administration.

Creating the Stack

In this section, we will start with a basic stack template that simply launches an EC2 instance. Example 2-1 shows one of the simplest CloudFormation stacks.

Example 2-1. Basic CloudFormation stack in JSON

```
{
  "AWSTemplateFormatVersion" : "2010-09-09",
  "Description" : "A simple stack that launches an instance.",
  "Resources" : {
    "Ec2Instance" : {
      "Type" : "AWS::EC2::Instance",
      "Properties" : {
        "InstanceType": "t2.micro",
        "ImageId" : "ami-43a15f3e"
      }
    }
  }
}
```

 CloudFormation requires stack templates to be strictly valid JSON, so keep an eye out for trailing commas when copying or modifying templates.

Templates can be validated and checked for errors with the AWS command-line tool. For example:

```
aws cloudformation validate-template \
--template-body file://MyStack.json
```

Some editors, including Eclipse and Vim, can be extended with plug-ins to help produce and validate JSON files.

The Resources section is an object that can contain multiple children, although this example includes only one (EC2Instance). The EC2Instance object has attributes that correspond to the values you can choose when launching an instance through the Management Console or command-line tools.

CloudFormation stacks can be managed through the Management Console, with the command-line tools, or with scripts leveraging client-side libraries such as Boto.

One advantage of using the Management Console is that a list of events is displayed in the bottom pane of the interface. With liberal use of the refresh button, this will let you know what is happening when your stack is in the *creating* or *updating* stages. Any problems encountered while creating or updating resources will also be displayed here, which makes it a good place to start when debugging CloudFormation problems. These events can also be read by using the command-line tools, but the Management Console output is a much more friendly human interface.

It is not possible to simply paste the stack template file contents into the Management Console. Rather, you must create a local text file and upload it to the Management Console when creating the stack. Alternatively, you can make the stack accessible on a website and provide the URL instead. The same applies when using the command-line tools and API.

To see the example stack in action, copy the JSON shown in Example 2-1 into a text file. You may need to substitute the AMI (`ami-43a15f3e`) with the ID of an AMI in your chosen EC2 region (our preset value comes from the ever-popular default us-east-1). Use the command-line tools or Management Console to create the stack. Assuming you have stored your stack template in a file named *example-stack.json*, you can create the stack with this command:

```
aws cloudformation create-stack --template-body file://example-stack.json \
--stack-name example-stack
```

If your JSON file is not correctly formed, you will see a helpful message letting you know the position of the invalid portion of the file. If CloudFormation accepted the request, it is now in the process of launching an EC2 instance of your chosen AMI. You can verify this with the `aws cloudformation describe-stack-resources` and `aws cloudformation describe-stack-events` commands:

```
$ aws cloudformation describe-stack-events--stack-name example-stack \
--output text
STACKEVENTS      9b5ea230-fcc7-11e5-89de-500c217b26c6      example-stack
arn:aws:cloudformation:us-east-1:740376006796:stack/example-stack/7b1d5700-
fcc7-11e5-a700-50d5cd2758d2             CREATE_COMPLETE             AWS::CloudForma-
tion::Stack      arn:aws:cloudformation:us-east-1:740376006796:stack/example-
stack/7b1d5700-fcc7-11e5-a700-50d5cd2758d2         example-stack
2016-04-07T13:49:53.884Z
STACKEVENTS      Ec2Instance-CREATE_COMPLETE-2016-04-07T13:49:52.222Z
Ec2Instance      i-ebe00376
{"ImageId":"ami-43a15f3e","InstanceType":"t2.micro"}
        CREATE_COMPLETE         AWS::EC2::Instance
arn:aws:cloudformation:us-east-1:740376006796:stack/example-stack/7b1d5700-
fcc7-11e5-a700-50d5cd2758dexample-stack 2016-04-07T13:49:52.222Z
STACKEVENTS      Ec2Instance-CREATE_IN_PROGRESS-2016-04-07T13:49:05.313Z
Ec2Instance      i-ebe00376
{"ImageId":"ami-43a15f3e","InstanceType":"t2.micro"}
        CREATE_IN_PROGRESS        Resource creation Initiated
AWS::EC2::Instance       arn:aws:cloudformation:us-east-1:740376006796:stack/
example-stack/7b1d5700-fcc7-11e5-a700-50d5cd2758d2      example-stack
2016-04-07T13:49:05.313Z
STACKEVENTS      Ec2Instance-CREATE_IN_PROGRESS-2016-04-07T13:49:04.113Z
Ec2Instance              {"ImageId":"ami-43a15f3e","InstanceType":"t2.micro"}
        CREATE_IN_PROGRESS        AWS::EC2::Instance
arn:aws:cloudformation:us-east-1:740376006796:stack/example-stack/7b1d5700-
fcc7-11e5-a700-50d5cd2758d2      example-stack   2016-04-07T13:49:04.113Z
STACKEVENTS      7b1fc800-fcc7-11e5-a700-50d5cd2758d2      example-stack
arn:aws:cloudformation:us-east-1:740376006796:stack/example-stack/7b1d5700-
fcc7-11e5-a700-50d5cd2758d2             CREATE_IN_PROGRESS      User Initiated
AWS::CloudFormation::Stack       arn:aws:cloudformation:us-
east-1:740376006796:stack/example-stack/7b1d5700-fcc7-11e5-a700-50d5cd2758d2
example-stack   2016-04-07T13:48:59.905Z
```

```
$ aws cloudformation describe-stack-resources --stack-name example-stack \
--output text
STACKRESOURCES   Ec2Instance      i-ebe00376      CREATE_COMPLETE
AWS::EC2::Instance      arn:aws:cloudformation:us-east-1:740376006796:stack/
example-stack/7b1d5700-fcc7-11e5-a700-50d5cd2758d2      example-stack
2016-04-07T13:49:52.222Z
```

aws cloudformation describe-stack-events prints a list of events associated with the stack, in reverse chronological order. Following the chain of events, we can see that AWS first created the stack, and then spent around 60 seconds creating the instance, before declaring the stack creation complete. The second command shows us the ID of the newly launched instance: i-5689cc1d.

Updating the Stack

Updating a running stack is an equally straightforward task. But before doing this, a brief digression into the way AWS handles resource updates is called for.

Some attributes of AWS resources cannot be modified once the instance has been created. Say, for example, you launch an EC2 instance with some user data. You then realize that the user data was incorrect, so you would like to change it. Although the Management Console provides the option to View/Change User Data, the instance must be in the stopped state before the user data can be modified. This means you must stop the instance, wait for it to enter the stopped state, modify the user data, and then start the instance again.

This has an interesting implication for CloudFormation. Using the previous example, imagine you have a CloudFormation stack containing an EC2 instance that has some user data. You want to modify the user data, so you update the stack template file and run the aws cloudformation update-stack command. Because CloudFormation is unable to modify the user data on a running instance, it must instead either reload or replace the instance, depending on whether this is an EBS-backed or instance store –backed instance.

If this instance was your production web server, you would have had some unhappy users during this period. Therefore, making changes to your production stacks requires some planning to ensure that you won't accidentally take down your application. We won't list all of the safe and unsafe types of updates here, simply because there are so many permutations to consider that it would take an additional book to include them all. The simplest thing is to try the operation you want to automate by using the Management Console or command-line tools to find out whether they require stopping the server.

We already know that user data cannot be changed without causing the instance to be stopped, because any attempt to change the user data of a running instance in the

Management Console will fail. Conversely, we know that instance tags can be modified on a running instance via the Management Console; therefore, updating instance tags with CloudFormation does not require instance replacement.

Changing some other attributes, such as the AMI used for an instance, will also require the instance to be replaced. CloudFormation will launch a new instance using the update AMI ID and then terminate the old instance. Obviously, this is not something you want to do on production resources without taking care to ensure that service is not disrupted while resources are being replaced. Mitigating these effects is discussed later, when we look at Auto Scaling and launch configurations.

If in doubt, test with an example stack first. CloudFormation lets you provision your infrastructure incredibly efficiently—but it also lets you make big mistakes with equal efficiency. With great power (which automation offers) comes great responsibility.

> Be careful when updating stacks that provide production resources. Once you submit the request to modify the stack, there is no going back. Furthermore, you cannot request any additional changes until the update is complete, so if you accidentally terminate all of your production resources, you will have no option but to sit back and watch it happen, after which you can begin re-creating the stack as quickly as possible.
>
> To remove any doubt, review the CloudFormation documentation for the resource type you are modifying. The documentation will let you know if this resource can be updated in place, or if a replacement resource is required in order to apply changes.

To see this in action, we will first update the instance to include some tags. Update the *example-stack.json* file so that it includes the following line in bold—note the addition of the comma to the end of the first line:

```
...
    "InstanceType": "t2.micro",
    "Tags": [ {"Key": "foo", "Value": "bar"}]
  }
...
```

Now we can update the running stack with `aws cloudformation update-stack` and watch the results of the update process with `aws cloudformation describe-stack-events`:

```
$ aws cloudformation update-stack --template-body file://example-stack.json \
--stack-name example-stack --output text
arn:aws:cloudformation:us-east-1:740376006796:stack/example-stack/7b1d5700-
fcc7-11e5-a700-50d5cd2758d2

$ aws cloudformation describe-stack-events --stack-name example-stack \
```

```
--output text
STACKEVENTS    beaeaca0-fcca-11e5-a119-500c2866f062    example-stack
arn:aws:cloudformation:us-east-1:740376006796:stack/example-stack/7b1d5700-
fcc7-11e5-a700-50d5cd2758d2             UPDATE_COMPLETE          AWS::CloudForma-
tion::Stack    arn:aws:cloudformation:us-east-1:740376006796:stack/example-
stack/7b1d5700-fcc7-11e5-a700-50d5cd2758d2    example-stack
2016-04-07T14:12:21.550Z
STACKEVENTS    bda21ea0-fcca-11e5-b6dd-50d5ca6e60ae    example-stack
arn:aws:cloudformation:us-east-1:740376006796:stack/example-stack/7b1d5700-
fcc7-11e5-a700-50d5cd2758d2             UPDATE_COMPLETE_CLEANUP_IN_PROGRESS
AWS::CloudFormation::Stack       arn:aws:cloudformation:us-
east-1:740376006796:stack/example-stack/7b1d5700-fcc7-11e5-a700-50d5cd2758d2
example-stack    2016-04-07T14:12:19.911Z
STACKEVENTS    Ec2Instance-UPDATE_COMPLETE-2016-04-07T14:12:18.229Z
Ec2Instance    i-ebe00376    {"ImageId":"ami-43a15f3e","Tags":
[{"Value":"bar","Key":"foo"}],"InstanceType":"t2.micro"}
         UPDATE_COMPLETE         AWS::EC2::Instance
arn:aws:cloudformation:us-east-1:740376006796:stack/example-stack/7b1d5700-
fcc7-11e5-a700-50d5cd2758dexample-stack 2016-04-07T14:12:18.229Z
STACKEVENTS    Ec2Instance-UPDATE_IN_PROGRESS-2016-04-07T14:12:02.354Z
Ec2Instance    i-ebe00376    {"ImageId":"ami-43a15f3e","Tags":
[{"Value":"bar","Key":"foo"}],"InstanceType":"t2.micro"}
         UPDATE_IN_PROGRESS         AWS::EC2::Instance
arn:aws:cloudformation:us-east-1:740376006796:stack/example-stack/7b1d5700-
fcc7-11e5-a700-50d5cd2758d2    example-stack    2016-04-07T14:12:02.354Z
STACKEVENTS    b0537140-fcca-11e5-bc1e-500c286f3262    example-stack
arn:aws:cloudformation:us-east-1:740376006796:stack/example-stack/7b1d5700-
fcc7-11e5-a700-50d5cd2758d2             UPDATE_IN_PROGRESS       User Initiated
AWS::CloudFormation::Stack       arn:aws:cloudformation:us-
east-1:740376006796:stack/example-stack/7b1d5700-fcc7-11e5-a700-50d5cd2758d2
example-stack    2016-04-07T14:11:57.557Z

$ aws cloudformationdescribe-stack-resources --stack-name example-stack \
--output text
STACKRESOURCES Ec2Instance    i-ebe00376       UPDATE_COMPLETE
AWS::EC2::Instance       arn:aws:cloudformation:us-east-1:740376006796:stack/
example-stack/7b1d5700-fcc7-11e5-a700-50d5cd2758d2    example-stack
2016-04-07T14:12:18.229Z
```

Finally, the `aws ec2 describe-tags` command will show that the instance is now
tagged with `foo=bar`:

```
$ aws ec2 describe-tags --filters Name=resource-type,Values=instance \
Name=resource-id,Values=i-ebe00376 --output text
TAGS    aws:cloudformation:logical-id    i-ebe00376       instance
Ec2Instance
TAGS    aws:cloudformation:stack-id    i-ebe00376       instance
arn:aws:cloudformation:us-east-1:740376006796:stack/example-stack/7b1d5700-
fcc7-11e5-a700-50d5cd2758d2
TAGS    aws:cloudformation:stack-name    i-ebe00376       instance    example-
stack
TAGS    foo    i-ebe00376       instance       bar
```

Notice the additional tags in the `aws:cloudformation` namespace. When provisioning resources that support tagging, CloudFormation will automatically apply tags to the resource. These tags let you keep track of that stack, which "owns" each resource, and make it easy to find CloudFormation-managed resources in the Management Console.

Looking Before You Leap

When you have more than one person working on a stack template, it can be easy to find yourself in a situation where your local copy of the stack template does not match the template used by the running stack.

Imagine that two people are both making changes to a stack template stored in a Git repository. If one person makes a change and updates the stack without committing that change to Git, the next person to make an update will be working with an out-of-date stack template. The next update will then revert the previous changes, which, as previously discussed, could have negative consequences. This is a typical synchronization problem whenever you have two independent activities that could be happening concurrently: in this case, updating Git and updating the actual AWS stack.

Happily, Amazon has provided a tool that, in combination with a couple of Linux tools, will let you make certain that your local copy of the stack does indeed match the running version. Use the `aws cloudformation get-template` command to get a JSON file describing the running template, clean the output with `sed` and `head`, and finally use `diff` to compare the local and remote versions. If we did this before updating the example stack to include tags, we would have obtained the following results:

```
$ aws cloudformation get-template --stack-name example-stack \
| grep -v "TemplateBody" | head -n -1 > example-stack.running
$ diff <(jq '.' example-stack.running) <(jq '.' example-stack.json)
9c9,10
4a5,10
<         "Tags": [
<           {
<             "Value": "bar",
<             "Key": "foo"
<           }
<         ],
```

 We use `jq` to pretty-print the JSON in a consistent format that saves `diff` from getting caught up in formatting or whitespace differences. Element ordering is still a factor; however, one easily addressed by making your initial `git commit` of a new stack with the format exported by `aws cloudformation get-template`.

These commands could be wrapped in a simple script to save typing. Changes to production CloudFormation stacks should always be preceded by a check like this, especially if working in a team. This check should be incorporated into the script used for updating the stack: if it happens automatically, there is no chance of forgetting it.

Deleting the Stack

Deleting a running stack will, by default, result in the termination of its associated resources. This is quite frequently the desired behavior, so it makes for a sensible default, but at times, you would like the resources to live on after the stack itself has been terminated. This is done by setting the `DeletionPolicy` attribute on the resource. This attribute has a default value of `Delete`.

All resource types also support the `Retain` value. Using this means that the resource will not be automatically deleted when the stack is deleted. For production resources, this can be an added safety net to ensure that you don't accidentally terminate the wrong instance. The downside is that, once you have deleted the stack, you will need to manually hunt down the retained resources if you want to delete them at a later date.

The final option for the `DeletionPolicy` attribute is `Snapshot`, which is applicable only to the subset of resources that support snapshots. Currently, these include the Relational Database Service (RDS) database instances, Amazon Redshift data warehouse clusters, and EBS volumes. With this value, a snapshot of the database or volume will be taken when the stack is terminated.

Remember that some resources will be automatically tagged with the name of the CloudFormation stack to which they belong. This can save some time when searching for instances that were created with the `Retain` deletion policy.

Deleting a stack is done with the `aws cloudformation delete-stack` command. Again, you can view the changes made to the stack with `aws cloudformation describe-stack-events`:

```
$ aws cloudformation delete-stack \
--stack-name example-stack

$ aws cloudformation describe-stack-events --stack-name example-stack --output
text
STACKEVENTS      Ec2Instance-DELETE_IN_PROGRESS-2016-04-08T07:22:22.919Z
Ec2Instance      i-05fe1098
{"ImageId":"ami-43a15f3e","InstanceType":"t2.micro"}
        DELETE_IN_PROGRESS              AWS::EC2::Instance
arn:aws:cloudformation:us-east-1:740376006796:stack/example-stack/76b64990-
fd5a-11e5-9750-500c286f3262      example-stack    2016-04-08T07:22:22.919Z
[ output truncated ]
```

Events are available only until the stack has been deleted. You will be able to see the stack while it is in the DELETE_IN_PROGRESS state, but once it has been fully deleted, aws cloudformation describe-stack-events will fail.

Which Method Should I Use?

As we have already seen, AWS provides a lot of choices. When deciding which method is best for your use case, there are several things to consider. One of the most important is the return on investment of any effort spent automating your system administration tasks.

The main factors to consider are as follows:

- How frequently is the action performed?
- How difficult is it?
- How many people will have to perform it?

If you are part of a small team that does not make frequent changes to your infrastructure, the Management Console might be all you need. Personal preference will also play a part: some people are more at home in a web interface than they are on the command line. Once you have a complicated infrastructure or a larger team, it becomes more important that processes are documented and automated, which is not a strong point of the Management Console.

For production services, we cannot recommend using CloudFormation strongly enough. Given the benefits outlined in the previous section—an audit trail, stack templates stored in source control—how could any sysadmin not immediately fall in love with this technology? Unless you have a compelling reason not to, you should be using CloudFormation for any AWS resources that are important to your infrastructure.

Mike's golden rule for any infrastructure he is responsible for is "If it's in production, it's in Git." Meaning that if a resource—application code, service configuration files, and so on—is required for that infrastructure to operate, it must be under version control. CloudFormation ties into this philosophy perfectly.

No matter how useful CloudFormation is, at times you will need to perform tasks that fall outside its capabilities. For these occasions, some combination of the command-line tools and client libraries are the next best thing in terms of ease of documentation and automation.

Combining the AWS client libraries with existing system management software can be a powerful tool. Packages such as Fabric (*http://fabfile.org*) (Python) and Capistrano (*https://github.com/capistrano/capistrano/wiki*) (Ruby) make it easy to efficiently administer large numbers of systems. By combining these with the respective language's client library, you can use them to administer a fleet of EC2 instances.

Automating too early can waste as much time as automating too late, as demonstrated in Figure 2-7. Especially at the beginning of a project, processes can change frequently, and updating your automation scripts each time can be a drain on resources. For this reason, I recommend using the Management Console when first learning a new AWS service—once you have performed the same task a few times, you will have a clear idea of which tasks will provide the most "automation ROI."

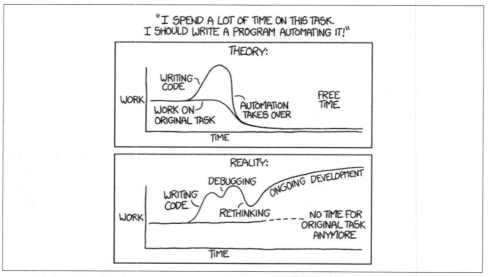

Figure 2-7. XKCD's take on automation (https://xkcd.com/1319/), courtesy of Randall Munroe

 If you are interested in strategies to help decide which tasks warrant automation, the authors would like to recommend *Time Management for System Administrators* by Thomas A. Limoncelli (O'Reilly).

Regardless of which method you choose, it is important to have a documented process describing how to perform updates. Errors will inevitably occur if there is no policy in place to organize everyone in a coherent fashion.

Amazon Machine Images

Some AMIs are virtual appliances—preconfigured server images running a variety of operating systems and software stacks. Amazon provides a number of its own images, running open source and commercial software, and allows any third party to distribute their images through the AWS Marketplace. You can also create your own images, configured exactly to meet your requirements, and share them with a few selected accounts or choose to make them public altogether.

Building your own AMIs has a number of benefits. You get to customize the software selection and configure which services will start when the instance is launched. Any services that are not required can be disabled to cut down on wasted resources. Later chapters show how to launch instances automatically in response to external conditions such as traffic levels (when instances are launched in response to growing demand, it is important they are ready for service as soon as possible).

Once an instance has been configured and an image created from it, that configuration is baked into the AMI. As we look at configuration management tools in Chapter 4, we will see how tools like Puppet can be used to dynamically configure an instance. This raises the question of how much of the configuration should be baked into the AMI, and how much should be dynamically configured.

At one end of the spectrum, you can deploy an entirely vanilla Ubuntu image, automatically install a configuration management tool such as Puppet, and then apply your desired configuration to start up the correct services (such as Nginx for a web server). At the other end of the spectrum, you could create a custom AMI for each specific role within the application: one for the database server, one for the web server, and so on. In the latter case, all configuration options are baked into the AMI, and no dynamic configuration is performed when the instance is launched.

In our experience, the best option is somewhere in the middle: some roles have their own AMI, whereas other AMIs perform multiple roles. The most efficient place will depend on various factors, including the type of software you deploy and how frequently you modify the server configuration. If it is important for newly launched instances to start serving requests as quickly as possible (which includes practically all uses of Auto Scaling), you'll want to reduce the amount of automatic configuration that takes place on boot.

At its core, an AMI is essentially a disk image and a metadata file describing how that disk image can be used to launch a virtual server. The metadata file keeps track of some internal information that is required when launching instances from this AMI, such as which Linux kernel to use.

In the early days of EC2, the only available AMI type was what is now known as an *instance store–backed AMI*. As the Elastic Block Store service was introduced and evolved, an additional type of AMI was created: the EBS-backed AMI. The key architectural difference between the two is in where the disk image that contains the root volume is stored.

EBS-backed AMIs, this is simply an EBS snapshot. When launching a new instance from such an image, a volume is created using this snapshot, and this new volume is used as the root device on the instance.

Instance store–backed AMIs are created from template disk images stored in S3, which means the disk image must be copied from S3 each time an instance is launched, introducing a startup delay over EBS-backed instances. Because the image must be downloaded from S3 each time, the root volume size is also limited to 10 GB, whereas EBS-backed instances have their root volumes limited to a more generous 16 TB.

In practice, an EBS-backed AMI is nearly always the best option. This type of AMI can be temporarily stopped and restarted without losing any data, whereas instance store–backed AMIs can only be terminated, at which point all data stored on the volume is lost.

Upgrading a Running Instance's Hardware

AWS's capability to change the hardware underlying your instance with just a few API calls is a great perk: you can upgrade your systems (or scale back your expense) with unprecedented ease. This complements AWS's ability to *scale out* by adding more instances with the ability to *scale up* by moving existing instances to more powerful virtual hardware.

To take advantage of this capability your instances must be EBS-backed, as they will need to be restarted in order to change instance type. You will want to use an elastic IP address to be able to maintain the same network endpoint for your existing service. Lastly you should standardize on 64-bit AMIs across your EC2 deployment, as changing bit width requires replacing the AMI itself. For this very same reason the instance's existing virtualization technology and root volume support choices cannot be altered.

Let's play it all out in practice:

```
$ aws ec2 run-instances --image-id ami-43a15f3e --region us-east-1 \
--instance-type t2.micro  --output text
740376006796    r-40546f92
INSTANCES       0       x86_64          False   xen     ami-43a15f3e
i-995fa01e      t2.micro        2016-04-10T14:52:12.000Z
ip-172-31-5-195.ec2.internal    172.31.5.195            /dev/sda1       ebs
True            subnet-d14ae8a7 hvm     vpc-934935f7
[ output truncated ]

$ aws ec2 describe-instances --instance-ids i-995fa01e | grep Type
                "InstanceType": "t2.micro",
                "RootDeviceType": "ebs",
                "VirtualizationType": "hvm",
```

```
$ aws ec2 stop-instances --instance-ids i-995fa01e --output text
STOPPINGINSTANCES          i-995fa01e
CURRENTSTATE    64         stopping
PREVIOUSSTATE   16         running

$ aws ec2 modify-instance-attribute --instance-type m4.xlarge --instance-id
i-995fa01e

$ aws ec2 start-instances --instance-ids i-995fa01e --output text
STARTINGINSTANCES          i-995fa01e
CURRENTSTATE    0          pending
PREVIOUSSTATE   80         stopped

$ aws ec2 describe-instances --instance-ids i-995fa01e | grep Type
                "InstanceType": "m4.xlarge",
                "RootDeviceType": "ebs",
                "VirtualizationType": "hvm",
```

After you re-associate the elastic IP address, your server will have just received an on-the-fly upgrade from a flimsy single core with only one gigabyte of RAM to a considerably beefier 16 GBs powered by four cores—not bad for a few seconds' work.

Building Your Own AMI

AMI builds should be automated as soon as possible, if you do it with any kind of regularity. It is tedious work and involves a lot of waiting around. Automating the process means you'll probably update AMIs more frequently, reducing a barrier to pushing out new features and software upgrades. Imagine you learn of a critical security flaw in your web server software that must be updated immediately. Having a procedure in place to create new AMIs and push them into production will help you respond to such scenarios rapidly and without wasting lots of time.

To demonstrate the procedures for creating an AMI and some of the useful features that AMIs provide, let's create an AMI using the command-line tools. This AMI will run an Nginx web server that displays a simple welcome page. We will look at a method of automating this procedure later in the book, in "Building AMIs with Packer" on page 166.

Begin by selecting an AMI to use as a base. We will be using our usual Ubuntu 16.04 image with the ID ami-43a15f3e. Launch an instance of this AMI with aws ec2 run-instances, remembering to specify a valid key pair name and security group granting access to SSH, then use aws ec2 describe-instances to find out the public DNS name for the instance:

```
$ # if you have not created a security group for SSH access yet,
$ # you need to do that first:

$ aws ec2 create-security-group --group-name ssh --description "SSH Access"
```

```
{
    "GroupId": "sg-4ebd8b36"
}

$ aws ec2 authorize-security-group-ingress --group-name ssh --protocol tcp \
--port 22 --cidr 0.0.0.0/0

$ aws ec2 describe-security-groups --group-names ssh --output text
SECURITYGROUPS  SSH Access      sg-4ebd8b36     ssh     740376006796
vpc-934935f7
IPPERMISSIONS   22      tcp     22
IPRANGES        0.0.0.0/0
IPPERMISSIONSEGRESS     -1
IPRANGES        0.0.0.0/0

$ aws ec2 run-instances --image-id ami-43a15f3e --region us-east-1 \
--key your-key-pair-name  --security-groups ssh --instance-type t2.micro
740376006796    r-315a9492
INSTANCES       0       x86_64          False   xen     ami-43a15f3e    i-
d9c83544        t2.micro        federico        2016-04-10T22:40:26.000Z
ip-172-31-55-4.ec2.internal     172.31.55.4             /dev/sda1       ebs
True            subnet-2a45b400 hvm     vpc-934935f7
[ output truncated ]

$ aws ec2 describe-instances --instance-ids i-d9c83544 --region us-east-1 \
--output text
RESERVATIONS    740376006796    r-315a9492
INSTANCES       0       x86_64          False   xen     ami-43a15f3e    i-
d9c83544        t2.micro        federico        2016-04-10T22:40:26.000Z
ip-172-31-55-4.ec2.internal     172.31.55.4
ec2-54-84-237-158.compute-1.amazonaws.com       54.84.237.158   /dev/sda1
ebs     True            subnet-2a45b400 hvm     vpc-934935f7
[ output truncated ]
```

Once the instance has launched, we need to log in via SSH to install Nginx. If you are not using Ubuntu, the installation instructions will differ slightly. On Ubuntu, update the package repositories and install Nginx as follows:

```
$ ssh ubuntu@ec2-54-84-237-158.compute-1.amazonaws.com
The authenticity of host 'ec2-54-84-237-158.compute-1.amazonaws.com
(54.84.237.158)' can't be established.
ECDSA key fingerprint is a0:d1:5a:ef:02:32:bd:72:28:41:fd:f1:b1:c6:75:4e.
Are you sure you want to continue connecting (yes/no)? yes

$ sudo apt update
[ output truncated ]

$ sudo apt install nginx-full --assume-yes
[ output truncated ]
```

By default, Nginx is installed with a welcome page stored at *usr/share/nginx/www/ index.html*. If you like, you can modify this file to contain some custom content.

Once the instance is configured, we need to create a matching AMI using `aws ec2 create-image`. This command will automatically create an AMI from a running instance. Doing so requires that the instance be stopped and restarted, so your SSH session will be terminated when you run this command. In the background, a snapshot of the EBS volumes used for your instance will be made. This snapshot will be used when launching new instances through a newfangled AMI ID. Because it can take some time before snapshots are ready to use, your new AMI will remain in the `pending` state for a while after `aws ec2 create-image` completes. The image cannot be used until it enters the `available` state. You can check on the status in the Management Console or with the `aws ec2 describe-images` command:

```
$ aws ec2 create-image --instance-id i-d9c83544 --region us-east-1 \
--name test-image --output text
ami-4dc5d527

$ aws ec2 describe-images --region us-east-1 --image-ids ami-4dc5d527\
--output text
IMAGES  x86_64  2016-04-10T22:51:06.000Z        xen     ami-4dc5d527
740376006796/test-image machine test-image      740376006796    False   /dev/
sda1    ebs     simple  pending hvm
BLOCKDEVICEMAPPINGS      /dev/sda1
EBS     True    False   snap-f407b282   8       standard
BLOCKDEVICEMAPPINGS      /dev/sdb        ephemeral0
BLOCKDEVICEMAPPINGS      /dev/sdc        ephemeral1
```

When your new image is ready, it can be launched by any of the means described previously. Launch a new instance based on this image and get the public DNS name with `aws ec2 describe-instances`. Connect via SSH, then confirm that Nginx has started automatically:

```
$ service nginx status
 * nginx is running
```

Although we have configured Nginx and have a running web server, you can't access the Nginx welcome page just yet. If you try to visit the instance's public DNS name in your web browser, the request will eventually time out. This is because EC2 instances are, by default, protected by a firewall that allows only connections from instances in the same security group—incoming HTTP connections have to be explicitly enabled with the same processes we used to allow inbound SSH connections. These firewalls, known as *security groups*, are discussed in the next chapter.

SUSE studio

We have focused on automation where AMIs are concerned, but an interactive approach to build AMIs reminiscent of the Management Console also exists. SUSE Studio (*https://susestudio.com*) (Figure 2-8) provides a web-based interface to building various types of images based on the eponymous Linux distribution. A creation of Nat Friedman's fertile imagination during his time as SUSE's CTO, SUSE Studio possibly offers the best interactive path to AMI building, the trade-off being the use of a distribution decidedly off the mainstream of public cloud adoption.

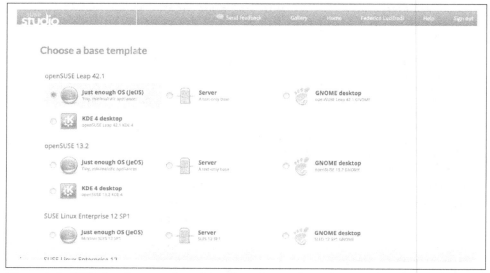

Figure 2-8. SUSE Studio provides a friendly web interface to AMI creation

Remember that both this instance and the original instance from which we created the image are still running. You might want to terminate those before moving on to the next section. The two-line script in "Parsing JSON Output with jq" on page 9 can be used to terminate all running EC2 instances in your account to clean the slate after running a few experiments.

Tagging your images is a good way to keep track of them. This can be done with the `aws ec2 create-tags` command. By using backticks to capture the output of shell commands, you can quickly add useful information, such as who created the AMI, as well as static information like the role:

```
$ aws ec2 create-tags --resources ami-4dc5d527 --tags Key=role,Value=webserver\
Key=created-by,Value=`whoami` Key=stage,Value=production

$ aws ec2 describe-tags --output text
```

```
TAGS    created-by      ami-4dc5d527    image   federico
TAGS    role    ami-4dc5d527    image   webserver
TAGS    stage   ami-4dc5d527    image   production
```

Tagging Strategy

Your AMI tagging strategy should let you keep track of the purpose of the image, when it was created, and its current state. Consider the lifecycle of an image: first it will be created and tested, then used in production for a while, and then finally retired when a new instance is created to replace it. The `state` tag can be used to keep track of this process, with values such as `dev`, `production`, or `retired`. A companion `state-changed` tag can track when changes were made.

Automate the process of moving images through the lifecycle so that you never forget to add or remove the relevant tags.

Deregistering AMIs

Once an AMI is no longer required, it should be *deregistered*, which means it will no longer be available to use for launching new instances. Although they are not particularly expensive, it is important to regularly remove old AMIs because they clutter up the interface and contribute to a gradual increase of your AWS costs.

 A good way to identify snapshots in your account ripe for deletion is to retrieve the complete listing of snapshots associated with your OwnerID and applying additional filtering. The OwnerID for your account can be found in the *Account Identifiers* section of the Security Credentials (*https://console.aws.amazon.com/iam/home?#security_credential*) page, but the handy alias `self` is always available. To list all your snapshots, enter:

```
aws ec2 describe-snapshots --owner-ids self --output
text
```

You must also delete the snapshot used to create the root volume. This will not happen automatically.

AWS allows you to delete the snapshot before deregistering the AMI. Doing so means you will have an AMI that looks as though it is available and ready for use, but will, in fact, fail when you try to launch an instance. If the deregistered AMI is referenced in Auto Scaling groups, it might be some time before you notice the problem. The only option in that case is to quickly create a new AMI and update the Auto Scaling group.

You can check to see whether a particular AMI is in use by running instances with the `aws ec2 describe-instances` command. For example:

```
$ aws ec2 describe-instances --filters Name=image-id,Values=ami-4dc5d527 \
--output text
RESERVATIONS    740376006796    r-726ca2d1
INSTANCES       0       x86_64          False   xen     ami-4dc5d527
i-8d30cd10      t2.micro        federico        2016-04-10T23:05:25.000Z
ip-172-31-55-118.ec2.internal   172.31.55.118
ec2-52-91-46-86.compute-1.amazonaws.com 52.91.46.86     /dev/sda1       ebs
True            subnet-2a45b400 hvm     vpc-934935f7
[ output truncated ]
TAGS    aws:cloudformation:logical-id   Ec2Instance
TAGS    aws:cloudformation:stack-id     arn:aws:cloudformation:us-
east-1:740376006796:stack/example-stack/ffad2160-069c-11e6-b07a-50d5caf92cd2
TAGS    aws:cloudformation:stack-name   example-stack
```

This works for individual instances. For instances that were launched as part of an Auto Scaling group, we can use the `aws autoscaling describe-launch-configurations` command. Unfortunately, this command does not accept a filter argument, so it cannot be used in quite the same way. As a workaround, you can `grep` the output of `aws autoscaling describe-launch-configs` for the AMI ID.

Performing these checks before deleting AMIs en masse can save you from a rather irritating cleanup exercise.

Once you are sure the AMI is safe to deregister, you can do so with `aws ec2 deregister-image`:

```
$ aws ec2 deregister-image --image-id ami-4dc5d527 --region us-east-1
```

Remember to delete the snapshot that was used as the root volume of the AMI. You can find it through the `aws ec2 describe-snapshots` command. When AWS creates a new snapshot, it uses the description field to store the ID of the AMI it was created for, as well as the instance and volume IDs referencing the resources it was created from. Therefore, we can use the AMI ID as a filter in our search, returning the ID of the snapshot we want to delete:

```
$ aws ec2 describe-snapshots --region us-east-1 \
--filters Name=description,Values="Created by CreateImage*for ami-4dc5d527*" \
--output text

SNAPSHOTS       Created by CreateImage(i-d9c83544) for ami-4dc5d527 from
vol-7df10dac    False   740376006796    100%    snap-f407b282
2016-04-10T22:51:18.000Z                completed       vol-7df10dac    8
```

```
$ aws ec2 delete-snapshot --region us-east-1 --snapshot-id snap-f407b282
```

Automatic snapshot management has long made everyone's list of Amazon AWS missing features. Any Google search can produce a long list of (mostly out of date) scripts using the EC2 API meant by different users to manage this deficiency. The AWS CLI has improved over the years to the point where finding snapshots is much easier; it just requires a little skill with the --query filter. For example, one can find all the snapshots taken before a certain date with the following:

```
$ aws ec2 describe-snapshots --owner-ids self --output text \
--query 'Snapshots[?StartTime<=`2016-05-31`]'

False    740376006796    100%    snap-bde3fbcf    2016-04-20T04:52:43.000completed
vol-00b633d1    8
False    740376006796    100%    snap-ca0c4487    2016-04-20T04:53:10.000completed
vol-00b633d1    8
```

Similarly, we can tabulate all snapshots belonging to our account with only selected attributes included in our query's results:

```
$ aws ec2 describe-snapshots --owner-ids self \
--query 'Snapshots[*].{ID:SnapshotId,Time:StartTime}'

[
    {
        "ID": "snap-bde3fbcf",
        "Time": "2016-04-20T04:52:43.000Z"
    },
    {
        "ID": "snap-ca0c4487",
        "Time": "2016-04-20T04:53:10.000Z"
    },
    {
        "ID": "snap-514c5be2",
        "Time": "2016-09-25T23:22:52.000Z"
    },
    {
        "ID": "snap-6d9afde5",
        "Time": "2016-10-16T07:39:19.000Z"
    },
    {
        "ID": "snap-428f90da",
        "Time": "2016-09-03T20:49:26.000Z"
    }
]
```

Combining and extending these commands, we can automate our annual snapshot cleanup with just a little bit of help from the Linux shell to manipulate dates:

```
#! /bin/bash
REGION=us-east-1

echo "Clearing all EC2 snapshots older than one year from $REGION"

AGE_FILTER=\`\`date +%Y-%m-%d --date '1 year ago'\`\`\`
SNAPSHOTS=$(aws ec2 describe-snapshots --owner-ids self \
--query "Snapshots[?StartTime<=$AGE_FILTER].{ID:SnapshotId}" --output text)
for i in $SNAPSHOTS
do
```

```
      echo "deleting $i"
      aws ec2 delete-snapshot --region $REGION --snapshot-id $i
done
```

The application of `--filters` enables searching for items tagged with a certain value. The following searches for any images tagged as retired from our production environment:

```
$ aws ec2 describe-images --filters Name=tag-key,Values="environment" \
Name=tag-value,Values="retired" --output text
IMAGES    x86_64   2017-05-29T04:16:43.000Z           xen      ami-838ac495
740376006796/test-image machine test-image            740376006796    False    /dev/
sda1     ebs       simple    available       hvm
BLOCKDEVICEMAPPINGS          /dev/sda1
EBS       True     False     snap-1b793584   8        standard
BLOCKDEVICEMAPPINGS          /dev/sdb        ephemeral0
BLOCKDEVICEMAPPINGS          /dev/sdc        ephemeral1
TAGS      environment        retired
```

The cleanup we performed manually can be automated with a single consolidated Boto script, shown in Example 2-2. This script will delete all images with a staging environment tag set to a value of `retired`.

Example 2-2. Deleting images with a Python script

```
#!/usr/bin/env python

from boto.ec2 import connect_to_region

ec2_conn = connect_to_region('us-east-1')

print 'Deleting retired AMI images.\n'

for image in ec2_conn.get_all_images(owners='self', filters={'tag:environment':
'retired'}):
    print ' Deleting image %s and associated snapshot' % (image.id)
    image.deregister(delete_snapshot=True)
```

This script relies on your AWS_ACCESS_KEY_ID and AWS_SECRET_ACCESS_KEY environment variables being set—Boto will attempt to read these automatically. It will delete all images (and the associated snapshots) that have been placed in the `retired` staging environment. To use this script, make sure your instances follow the tagging strategy described in "Tagging Strategy" on page 63. Save this file as *delete-retired-amis.py* and use `chmod` to make it executable.

The call to `get_all_images` specifies some filter conditions: we are interested in images that have an `environment` tag with a value of `retired`.

Deleting an image does not automatically delete the snapshot it uses for its root volume so we must do this by setting the `delete_snapshot` parameter of `deregister` to `True`.

 A snapshot can be shared with other organizations by modifying its permissions to include another account's ID in the AWS console. Make sure you avoid making public any snapshots containing private data, even for short intervals. Hackers can use the AWS API to trivially discover and instantly clone any such snapshots in their quest for valuable data and credentials.

Security researchers have demonstrated exfiltration (*https://www.nvteh.com/news/problems-with-public-ebs-snapshots*) of SSH login keys, AWS credentials, API access keys, confidential genome sequences, and even the full payroll of a Fortune 100 company from snapshots that were lazily configured with public access permissions.

Pets versus Cattle

Microsoft's Bill Baker is credited with originating the metaphor popularized by OpenStack's Randy Bias (*http://www.slideshare.net/randybias/pets-vs-cattle-the-elastic-cloud-story*) that so vividly illustrates two radically opposite approaches to managing servers. In this tale, pets are lovingly cared for, taken to the vet when they get sick, and tenderly nursed back to health—cattle, on the other hand, are replaced without a second thought, even slaughtered. This distinction is humorously used to illustrate the more formal distinction delineated by Gartner in IT operations: traditional *Mode 1* IT (*http://blogs.gartner.com/it-glossary/files/2015/01/bimodaltable.png*) servers are highly managed assets that *scale up* to bigger, more costly hardware and are carefully restored to health should anything go amiss. *Mode 2* IT, on the other hand, espouses a radically different operational philosophy: servers are highly disposable entities that are instantiated through automation, eliminated at the drop of a hat when no longer needed, and "scale out" in herds. Replacing a server with an expensive many-socket system and more complex memory architecture is decidedly Mode 1, while adding as many equally sized web servers behind a load balancer as required by today's service load is the Mode 2 way.

Mode 1 IT is the mainstay of traditional datacenter operations, whereas Mode 2 has emerged as the prim and proper way to design and operate applications in a public cloud environment. AWS gives you plenty of choices in how you achieve your goals, and we have been introducing all the technical details you need in order to scale services either up or out, but as we proceed to design a realistic application in the coming chapters, we will decidedly lean the way a cloud architect would, and adopt a Mode 2 mindset in our design exclusively. You should do the same; pets do not belong in your cloud architecture.

## CHAPTER 3

Access Management and Security Groups

In all of the previous examples, we have been using access keys that have root-level access to our AWS accounts. This means they can perform any action—including actions that potentially cost thousands of dollars in resource fees—through a few simple API calls. The thought of your AWS keys leaking should be a scary one indeed, so now is a good time to look at some of the tools Amazon provides to securely deploy and manage your applications.[1]

The AWS Security Model

AWS infrastructure services rely on a shared responsibility model (*http://media.amazonwebservices.com/AWS_Security_Best_Practices.pdf*) for security. Unlike in the traditional datacenter, where the full responsibility for the environment's security falls squarely on the IT team, EC2 customers share this burden with the AWS team in significant ways (Figure 3-1).

In this shared responsibility model, the user owns the operating system's login credentials but AWS bootstraps initial access to that same operating system. The end user may or may not have administrative control of the provisioning process and a separate administrator may be in charge of configuring and operating the identity management system that provides access to the user layer of the virtualization stack. The separation between AWS's sphere of security oversight and the customer's is clearly defined, but it is entirely up to the customer to delineate the level of access end users and administrators are granted, and whether there is any distinction between the two.

---

[1] A sad cautionary tale about AWS security is that of Code Spaces (*http://bit.ly/2v5hlNr*).

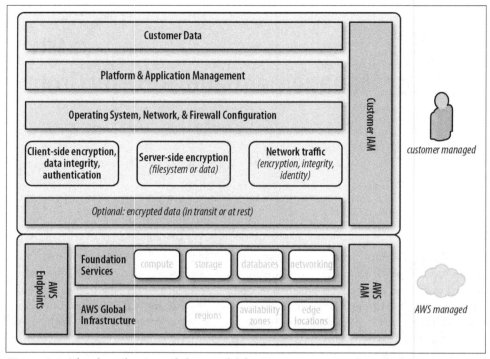

Figure 3-1. The shared responsibility model for IAAS services as described in AWS Security Best Practices (http://media.amazonwebservices.com/AWS_Security_Best_Practices.pdf)

Amazon manages the security of facilities and is obviously responsible for the physical security of all hardware assets and network infrastructure. Beyond its global infrastructure, AWS is responsible for the software foundation underlying its services. In EC2's case, this includes virtual provisioning infrastructure as well as the issuing of any credentials required to access it. The customer's security area of responsibility includes the following:

- Amazon Machine Images (AMIs)
- Operating system(s)
- Applications
- Data in transit
- Data at rest
- Data stores
- Credentials

- Policies and configuration

The attack surface exposed varies conspicuously: leaving an operating system image unpatched may expose a number of instances to attack, while an error handling access credentials could lead to the loss of all infrastructure hosted by the account—or the total loss of data confidentiality.

Securing EC2 images is no different than securing a machine in a traditional datacenter: OS images and running instances need to be patched, applications need to be updated, and AWS provides technology to protect data at rest and in transit. What changes, in implementation if not in spirit, is the way to define processes and levels of access for different classes of users. IAM is the mechanism AWS uses to provide access control and privilege separation, and we will examine it in detail in the next section—right after we tighten the security of your AWS account.

Account Security Checklist

Let's enumerate some generally accepted security best practices to operate safely in public cloud environments:

Do not use root credentials.
> Production use of root credentials breaks auditing in the shared responsibility model: were anything untoward to happen, you may not be able to reliably track down the real user responsible. You should secure the account with MFA and read "Throwing Away the Root Password" on page 84 for the most aggressive approach to securing the root account.

Do use IAM users, user groups, and roles.
> This chapter will teach you how to minimize the attack surface of compromised credentials by assigning separate keys to users and compute tasks. Credentials can further be limited in what actions they allow on which resources. Roles are used to eliminate the need to bake credentials into AMIs, eliminating a major leak vector for credentials.

Leverage password policy.
> You can set a password policy to define complexity requirements for user passwords. More importantly, you should use this feature to define password expiration windows while also implementing a matching key rotation policy.

Enable AWS CloudTrail.
> CloudTrail logs each AWS API call executed by the entire account, including what credentials were used to authenticate it. These records permit monitoring user behavior, and enable auditing after a security incident has occurred.

Multi-Factor Authentication

Multi-factor authentication (MFA) adds a layer of security to your AWS account. When signing in to AWS, you will need to enter an authentication code in addition to your username and password. This authentication code can be generated by a physical device or by an application running on your computer or smartphone.

Adding a second factor to the authentication process (your password being the first one) gives you a lot of protection against unauthorized account access. It is no magic bullet, but it certainly prevents a lot of common attacks that rely on a single password giving access to your account.

To the cheers of sysadmins everywhere, Amazon decided to base its multi-factor implementation (known as *AWS MFA*) on an open standard. The Time-Based One-Time Password Algorithm (TOTP—RFC 6238) is a method of generating passwords based on a shared secret. These passwords are valid for only a short period of time, and are typically regenerated every 30 seconds or so.

Google has made multi-factor authentication an option for logging in to its services, and as a result, published Google Authenticator. This is a smartphone application—available for Android, iOS, and BlackBerry—that acts as a virtual multi-factor authentication device. Because it is also based on the TOTP algorithm, it works perfectly with AWS MFA, giving you a quick way to increase your AWS account security without any monetary cost.

There is, of course, a small-time cost, as you will need to look up your access code whenever your AWS session expires. From a security perspective, it seems like a cost worth paying.

 If you have purchased a hardware multi-factor authentication device or downloaded a virtual device for your smartphone, see the AWS Multi-Factor Authentication page (*http://aws.amazon.com/ mfa*) to tie it into AWS.

Identity and Access Management

Identity and Access Management (IAM) is the name given to the suite of features that lets you manage who and what can access AWS APIs using your account. This permissions-based system can be somewhat overwhelming at first, but resist the temptation to give in and grant all permissions to all users. Having a well-planned policy based on IAM is an important part of AWS security, and fits in well with the *defense in depth* strategy.

IAM makes a distinction between *authentication* ("who is this person?") and *authorization* ("are they allowed to perform this action?"). Authentication is handled by users and groups, whereas authorization is handled by IAM policies.

 Amazon's CloudTrail service (*http://aws.amazon.com/cloudtrail/*) keeps track of the API calls made by users in your account. You can use this to review the full history of AWS API calls that have been made by your account, whether they came from the Management Console, CLI tools, or services like CloudFormation. This service is the preferred method to audit user actions, and is invaluable when it comes to diagnosing permissions problems.

Amazon Resource Names

You may already know that S3 bucket names must be unique across the whole of S3. Have you ever wondered how that can be the case, considering there are surely many IAM users named `mike` or `admin`?

The answer lies with ARNs and how they are formatted.

To identify IAM users and other resource types, AWS uses an *Amazon Resource Name (ARN)*. An ARN is a globally unique identifier that references AWS objects. Most AWS resource types have ARNs, including S3 buckets and IAM users. ARNs take the following format:

```
arn:aws:serviceregionaccount_IDrelative_ID
```

For example, here is the ARN for Mike's IAM account (with the 12-digit account ID replaced by Xs):

```
arn:aws:iam::XXXXXXXXXXXX:user/mike
```

Notice that the region is not specified in the user's ARN. This means that this ARN is a global resource, not tied to any specific region.

Some resources, such as S3 buckets, also omit the account ID in the ARN. S3 buckets use this ARN format:

```
arn:aws:s3:::bucket_name
```

For example:

```
arn:aws:s3:::mike-image-resize
```

Notice that the only variable is the bucket name. Because S3 ARNs do not include the account number, creating two S3 buckets with the same name would result in a duplicate ARN, so this is not allowed.

IAM Policies

The idea behind IAM is to separate users and groups from the actions they need to perform. You do this by creating an *IAM policy*, which is a JSON-formatted document describing which actions a user can perform. This policy is then applied to users or groups, giving them access only to the services you specifically allowed.

The best way to show the flexibility of IAM policies is with an example. Let's say you use a tagging strategy described in the previous chapter, and have given all of your images a `state` tag that represents its current status, such as `production` or `retired`. As a good sysadmin who dislikes repetitive tasks, you have decided to automate the process of deleting retired images—AMIs that have been replaced by newer versions and are no longer required.

Example 2-2 shows a simple Boto script that deletes any AMIs that are in the `retired` state (according to our "Tagging Strategy" on page 63).

This script calls a number of Boto functions, which, in turn, call AWS APIs to perform the requested actions. If you were to run this script, it would connect to the API using the access key and secret that are stored in your `AWS_ACCESS_KEY_ID` and `AWS_SECRET_ACCESS_KEY` environment variables. While convenient, those access keys have far more permissions than are strictly required to run this script. Using them to authorize this script is overkill, and comes with a potential security risk: the more places in which your keys are stored, the more likely they are to be accidentally exposed to someone who does not need them.

There is another downside of reusing the same keys for multiple roles: it becomes very difficult to change them. Good security practices dictate that security credentials should be regularly rotated. If your AWS access credentials are reused in multiple scripts, keeping track of where each access key is being used becomes problematic. Replacing a key involves making the old one inactive so it can no longer be used to access APIs. If you accidentally deactivate the credentials that are used for making your database backups, you have a rather serious problem. If you do not segregate your IAM roles, you will end up being scared to deactivate old access keys because some vital component of your infrastructure will stop working.

A better solution would be to create a set of access credentials that are authorized to perform only the specific actions required by the script. Then you have a set of access credentials specific to each identifiable role—for example, `AMI-cleaner`, `database-backups`, and so on.

Let's create an AMI policy with enough permissions to run the script that cleans old images and snapshots. Looking at the code, we see four Boto function calls. In most cases, Boto's functions map quite well to AWS action types. Here are the four function calls and the action invoked by each one:

Function call	Action invoked
connect_to_region	ec2:DescribeRegions
get_all_images	ec2:DescribeImages
delete_snapshot	ec2:DeleteSnapshot
delete_image	ec2:DeregisterImage

A permission is a combination of two items: an action and one or more resources. AWS will check to see whether the authenticated user is allowed to perform the requested action on a specific resource—for example, is the user allowed to create a file (the action) in an S3 bucket (the resource)?

Actions are namespaced strings that take the form *service_name:Permission*. All EC2-related permissions are prefixed with ec2:, such as ec2:DeleteSnapshot.

Because policies can reference highly granular, dynamic permissions across all AWS services, they can be time-consuming to write. When you create a policy, Amazon's web interface gives you a list of permissions from which you can pick to save some time, but unfortunately no tool can magically remove the time it takes to plan out exactly which permissions each of your users or groups will require.

Using the Management Console is a great way of becoming familiar with the available permissions. Even if you are a hardcore command-line user, we suggest taking a few clicks around the interface to discover which actions are available. Because we already know which permissions to use for this script, we can use the command-line tools to create a user and attach a new policy to it, using the aws iam create-user and iam create-access-key commands.

First, we create a new user for this role, named ami-cleaner:

```
$ aws iam create-user --user-name ami-cleaner
{
    "User": {
        "UserName": "ami-cleaner",
        "Path": "/",
        "CreateDate": "2016-06-01T03:18:35.032Z",
        "UserId": "AIDAILRZI2G4XH3QC6J4W",
        "Arn": "arn:aws:iam::740376006796:user/ami-cleaner"
    }
}
$ aws iam create-access-key --user-name ami-cleaner
{
    "AccessKey": {
        "UserName": "ami-cleaner",
        "Status": "Active",
        "CreateDate": "2016-06-01T03:19:02.919Z",
        "SecretAccessKey": "wSelXh56SYP0f5ZxPkpSNL+kThTqU0nc3JeBNsC2",
        "AccessKeyId": "AKIAJBYS5AQKKUN7MZJQ"
```

```
        }
    }
```

The `iam create-access-key` command generates an access key ID and secret access key for our new user. Store these somewhere safe, as we will need them later.

Next, we create an AMI policy and embed it directly in the user:

```
$ aws iam put-user-policy --user-name ami-cleaner --policy-name ami-cleaner \
--policy-document '{"Version":"2008-10-17","Statement":[{"Effect":"Allow", \
"Action":["ec2:DescribeImages","ec2:DeleteSnapshot", \
"ec2:DeregisterImage"],"Resource":["*"]}]}'
```

 If you succeed in creating a malformed policy despite IAM's validation safeguards, it will be waiting for your corrections in the claws of the policy validator (*http://docs.aws.amazon.com/IAM/latest/ UserGuide/access_policies_policy-validator.html*), in the IAM section of the console.

In this case, the user and policy names are both `ami-cleaner`. We chose to inline the policy directly in our user for simplicity, but a standalone policy object is more practical for production use as it can be associated with multiple users or even multiple groups of users. Using inlined JSON syntax, we are creating an `Allow` policy that applies to all resources. We specified a short list of actions that will be allowed, but you can specify as many permissions as you need.

Now we have an IAM user with a policy matching its role, so we can update the script to use the new keys. There are a few ways to do this, depending on your approach to managing your access keys. If no credentials are specified when opening a new connection to an AWS API, Boto will check whether the `AWS_ACCESS_KEY_ID` and `AWS_SECRET_ACCESS_KEY` environment variables are set, before falling back to the contents of the ~/.aws/credentials file. Run the script by executing the following commands in a terminal:

```
export AWS_ACCESS_KEY_ID='AKIAJBYS5AQKKUN7MZJQ'
export AWS_SECRET_ACCESS_KEY='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'

python delete-retired-amis.py
```

The script is now being run with the most restrictive set of permissions that will still allow it to function.

By running `aws iam put-user-policy`, we created a new IAM policy and added it to the user. But what does this policy actually look like? Through the IAM section in the Management Console, you can view the JSON-formatted version of our new AMI. First, find the `image-cleaner` user and then look in the Permissions tab (Figure 3-2).

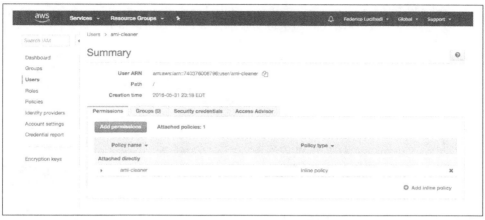

Figure 3-2. The newly created policy is found in the user's permissions

You can also view the body of this embedded policy with the `aws iam get-user-policy` command:

```
$ aws iam get-user-policy --user-name ami-cleaner --policy-name ami-cleaner
{
    "UserName": "ami-cleaner",
    "PolicyName": "ami-cleaner",
    "PolicyDocument": {
        "Version": "2008-10-17",
        "Statement": [
            {
                "Action": [
                    "ec2:DescribeImages",
                    "ec2:DeleteSnapshot",
                    "ec2:DeregisterImage"
                ],
                "Resource": [
                    "*"
                ],
                "Effect": "Allow"
            }
        ]
    }
}
```

Readers familiar with JSON formatting will recognize that the `Statement` attribute is actually a list. Although our example includes only one statement, a single policy can contain multiple statements. Notice that a statement can have only a single `Effect`. So to create a policy that allows some actions but denies others, we must combine multiple statements with different `Effect` attributes.

Determining what set of actions to allow a given policy is not simple, and even more complex is the task of mapping the interactions of multiple sets of permissions on a single user. Amazon provides the IAM Policy Simulator (*https://policysim.aws.amazon.com*) to help you evaluate how multiple policies interact to allow (or deny) a given action. The policy we just created is shown in the simulator undergoing testing in Figure 3-3.

Figure 3-3. Evaluating our first policy in the simulator

Referencing resources in IAM policies

The `Resource` attribute of an IAM policy lets you control exactly which resources an action can be performed on. In the previous example, the policy granted the user permissions to delete any EBS snapshot owned by this account. What if you want a more granular policy that applies only to a subset of resources?

As discussed previously, ARNs are used to globally identify AWS resources. Used in IAM policies, they let you control exactly which resources are included when granting or denying permissions.

Suppose you use S3 buckets across your organization. Although most buckets contain data that could be easily replaced if lost (such as resized versions of images), you have one bucket that contains your database backups—something you certainly don't want to lose. Your users are creating and deleting buckets via the Management Console, and you would like to make sure nobody accidentally deletes your backup bucket.

The cleanest solution to this problem is to create an IAM policy that allows users to perform any action on S3 buckets, with the exception of the one containing your backups. We do this by creating a policy containing two statements. The first grants the user all S3-related permissions, allowing them to be performed on any resource. The second statement denies all S3-related permissions, but only on the protected bucket.

When conflicting permissions are encountered, Deny takes precedence over Allow. So, users will be able to do anything they want on any bucket, except the one containing your backups.

The policy document describing these permissions looks like this:

```
{
  "Statement": [
    { "Action": [
        "s3:*"
      ],
      "Effect": "Allow",
      "Resource": [
        "*"
      ]
    },
    { "Action": [
        "s3:*"
      ],
      "Effect": "Deny",
      "Resource": [
        "arn:aws:s3:::db-backups"
      ]
    }
  ]
}
```

These examples use the s3:* action to grant all S3-related permissions. In practice, this is nearly always a bad idea.

When creating an IAM policy to suit a particular role, grant the role as few permissions as possible. It might take a while (and a bit of trial and error!) to find the fewest permissions you need to fulfill a particular task, but it's worth spending the time to do so.

Resist the temptation to assign *:* permissions!

To implement this policy, first find the ARN of your critical bucket. Assuming that your bucket is named db-backups, the ARN will be as follows:

```
arn:aws:s3:::db-backups
```

When creating a policy, remember to replace the ARNs used in our examples.

Next, create the policy using the command-line tools or Management Console.

If using the Management Console, you can create the policy as follows:

1. Navigate to the IAM service.
2. Select the Policies tab.
3. Click Create Policy.
4. Select Create Your Own Policy.
5. Paste the text into the Policy Document box.

Using `aws iam put-user-policy` to attach a policy defined with inline JSON is not the most satisfying of user experiences. If you want to create a policy from the command line, you will have a much easier time writing it to a temporary file and uploading it. Assuming you have saved the policy to a file named *s3-policy.json*, you can create the policy with this command:

```
aws iam put-user-policy --user-name mike --policy-name s3_policy \
--policy-document file://./s3-policy.json
```

Because denying rights to a particular activity is quite a common requirement, Amazon has provided an additional element in its resource policy language to handle this use case. Using `NotResource` as a shorthand, the preceding policy could be rewritten as follows:

```
{
  "Statement": [
    { "Action": [
        "s3:*"
      ],
      "Effect": "Allow",
      "NotResource": [
        "arn:aws:s3:::db-backups"
      ]
    }
  ]
}
```

This is almost (but not entirely—see "How Permissions Are Evaluated" on page 81) the same as the longer policy we defined previously. `NotResource` refers to all objects other than the `db-backups` bucket, so this policy is effectively saying "grant all S3 permissions on all buckets except `db-backups`."

The `Action` element of a policy document also has a negated counterpart, `NotAction`. Thus, to allow a user to perform all S3 actions except `DeleteBucket`, you could include this in your policy document:

```
"NotAction": "s3:DeleteBucket"
```

How Permissions Are Evaluated

Whenever you make a request to AWS, Amazon must evaluate the request and decide whether it should be allowed. The logic behind this process means there is a subtle but important difference between the two IAM policies in the previous section.

A request typically includes three bits of information: the user making the request, the action that is to be performed, and the target of the action. For example, Alice wants to terminate an EC2 instance. When receiving the request, AWS will use this information to decide whether it should be allowed by performing the following steps:

1. All policies pertaining to the user making the request are combined, including those applied by way of group membership.

2. If a permission is denied by one of the policies (an *explicit deny*), the request can be immediately denied.

3. If a permission is explicitly granted by one of the policies (an *allow*), the request is allowed.

4. Finally, if the permission was not explicitly granted, it is denied (a *default deny*).

Given this logic, consider the differences between the policies that used `Resource` and `NotResource` as two ways to deny access to a bucket.

The first example includes an *explicit deny* that ensures no users have permissions to modify the `db-backups` S3 bucket. The second example, however, merely grants permissions to all S3 buckets except `db-backups`. There is no explicit deny on the `db-backups` bucket in the latter case; it is handled by the *default deny*.

Consequently, if the user were assigned a further policy that granted permissions to all S3 buckets, that user would have permissions to delete the `db-backups` bucket and all of its contents.

Creating IAM policies is another area where being explicit is definitely better than being implicit.

For more details on how AWS evaluates permissions, see the AWS Identity and Access Management page (*http://docs.amazonwebservices.com/IAM/latest/UserGuide/Access PolicyLanguage_EvaluationLogic.html*) describing its evaluation logic.

Dynamic policies

Conditions can be used to create dynamic IAM policies that behave differently, depending on one or more factors. The attributes of the request (such as the ARN of the requesting user or the source IP address) can be used in Boolean expressions to control whether a request should be allowed or denied.

Some of the available attributes on which you can base your conditions are as follows:

- Time of day
- Source IP address
- Whether the request is being made using HTTP or HTTPS

Of particular use is the SecureTransport attribute, which lets us check whether Secure Sockets Layer (SSL) is being used to make the request. Many of the AWS APIs can be accessed in both secure (HTTPS) and insecure (HTTP) modes. IAM policies provide the only way to force your users to use the secure versions of these APIs.

Let's say you have an S3 bucket that is used for storing backups of confidential customer information. For regulatory reasons (or perhaps merely because of a healthy level of sysadmin paranoia), you must maintain a remote backup of this data, and the files must be transferred over an SSL connection.

This policy document would ensure that users could not perform any actions against the db-backups bucket if they are connected via plain old HTTP:

```
{
    "Statement":[{
        "Effect":"Allow",
        "Action":"s3:*",
        "Resource":"arn:aws:s3:::db-backups",
        "Condition":{
            "Bool":{
                "aws:SecureTransport":"true"
            }
        }
    }
    ]
}
```

Using conditions, you could further enhance this policy to indicate the following:

- All connections must be secured by SSL.
- Files can be written to the bucket by only the database server (say, IP address 192.168.10.10).
- Files can be read by only the off-site backup server (say, IP address 192.168.20.20).

Of course, you could simply remember to enable the "use SSL" option of the client you use for transferring files from S3, but unless security features are enforced at a technical policy level, they will eventually be accidentally forgotten.

For a more thorough look at the elements of an IAM policy, have a look at Amazon's Access Policy Language (*http://docs.amazonweb services.com/IAM/latest/UserGuide/AccessPolicyLanguage.html*) documentation.

Limitations of IAM policies

Although powerful, IAM policies do have some drawbacks that can take some effort to work around. Chief among these is that some AWS services do not yet provide support for ARNs in all actions, and can therefore not be fully managed by IAM policies drawing a distinction between different resource instances.

EC2 instances are a good example. Resource-level permissions have been introduced in EC2 since July 2013, but not all `ec2:` actions support their use yet. Actions without resource-level permissions have no way to reference a specific EC2 instance from an IAM policy. Whenever you allow such an EC2 action in a policy, the resource will be `*`, which means it will apply to every instance owned by your AWS account. AWS maintains a continuously updated list of Supported resource-level permissions for Amazon EC2 API actions (*http://docs.aws.amazon.com/AWSEC2/latest/UserGuide/ec2-supported-iam-actions-resources.html*). A number of other things are simply not yet possible with IAM.

To work around this limitation, some people have taken to operating multiple AWS accounts—one for each department. IAM roles, covered later in this chapter, give you a way to securely share resources between accounts, making this a viable option in the remaining cases where resource-level permissions are not yet available.

Operating with multiple accounts is a valid advanced security strategy in its own right. Table 3-1 lists a few sensible strategies for your consideration. To be clear, we are not taking the position that multiple accounts are a recommended default strategy for every user; we believe a supporting rationale needs to be identified to justify the cost in time and effort of the additional complexity. Whether it is hosted in a single AWS account or multiple ones, we recommend you consider the impact of your security structure on the team's velocity. The insight found in Conway's Law (*https://en.wikipedia.org/wiki/Conway%27s_law*) is critical to designing effective security boundaries for any team: "any organization [..] will inevitably produce a [product] design whose structure is a copy of the organization's communication structure."

Table 3-1. Security strategies

Account strategy	Consequences
Single AWS account	Centralized management with minimum overhead. Secure with tailored users limited in access to actions and resources.
Separate production, development, and testing AWS accounts	Supplement single account capabilities with separation between multiple AWS accounts. Additional effort required for staging resources between accounts.

Account strategy	Consequences
Multiple AWS accounts, one per department	Access to actions and resources can follow radically different procedures for each organization. Cooperation on private shared resources marginally more complex.
Multiple AWS accounts, one per function	Functionally centralized management with different accounts for DNS, DBMS, CDN, CMS, or any other services.

IAM Users and Groups

Because users and groups need to deal only with authentication, they are relatively simple compared to other AWS facilities. If you are familiar with how Unix or Windows handles user and group permissions, you already know the core principles behind IAM users and groups.

A *user* can be a human who logs in to the Management Console with a username and password, or a program that uses a set of access credentials to interact with AWS APIs. The user can be assigned one or more IAM policies, which specify the actions the user is allowed to perform.

To ease administration, users can be placed in *groups*. When an IAM policy is assigned to a group, all members of that group inherit the permissions designated by the IAM policy. It is not possible to nest groups; a group cannot contain other groups.

IAM is a *global* AWS service, meaning it is not tied to any particular region. An IAM user will be able to access APIs in any region, if allowed by its assigned IAM policies.

You should create a separate user for each person who will access your account, rather than sharing the master password for your AWS account. As people leave and join the organization, it will be a lot easier to revoke old security keys and assign permissions to new accounts.

Assigning permissions to specific users has its purposes, but it is often a sign that tasks and knowledge are not being shared across the team. If Alice is the only person with CreateSnapshot permissions, how is Bob going to handle backups while she is on vacation?

Aim to map AWS groups to specific roles within your organization, and apply the policy to the group instead. Managing updates to permissions is also a lot easier, as they will need to be made in only one place.

Throwing Away the Root Password

Throwing away the root password for your AWS account is an increasingly popular security best practice: you cannot lose control of credentials you do not know and have no access to. If for any reason you ever needed it, you could always regain access to your root account identity as long as you have access to the email address the

---

account is bound to. Eric Hammond (*https://alestic.com/2014/09/aws-root-password/*) of Alestic shared this security best practice:

1. Create an IAM user with full administrative privileges, including access to account billing information. This grants the user ability to update payment methods and most account information.
2. Change the AWS root account password to a long, locally generated random string which you will retain no copies of. On Ubuntu, you can use `pwgen -s 24 1` to generate such a password.

Although an intruder who manages to gain rogue access to the AIM user with full administrative privileges could still do a lot of damage—running up costs, destroying resources and data, etc.—at least they could not lock you out and change the associated email address to prevent your team from recovering access. When you detect the intrusion, you can re-create the root password and lock out the intruder.

Eric has identified the following seven exceptions as the only AWS functionality you may ever need your root account for:

- Changing the email and password of the AWS root account
- Transferring a Route 53 Domain registration
- Canceling AWS services, like support
- Closing the account
- Submitting a penetration testing inquiry form
- Setting up consolidated billing
- Activating (or deactivating) IAM user access to billing information

Organizing users and groups with paths

If you are coming from a Lightweight Directory Access Protocol (LDAP) or Active Directory background, you might be used to a little more flexibility in user and group layout. In particular, the inability to nest groups within groups can feel like a big limitation when moving from one of these systems to IAM.

Paths are an optional feature of IAM users that can be used to implement more complicated user and group scenarios. In combination with IAM policies, they can be used to create a hierarchical structure for your users and groups.

Suppose you have several departments in your organization, and you would like each department to manage its own users. No one likes resetting passwords or setting up new accounts, so delegating this to a group of trusted users within that department will save time and headaches on all sides.

Start by creating two new groups: one to hold the users of the group and one for the group admins. Let's use a development team as an example and create groups named dev_admins and dev_users:

```
$ aws iam create-group --group-name dev_admins --path "/dev/"
{
    "Group": {
        "Path": "/dev/",
        "CreateDate": "2016-06-05T14:03:57.681Z",
        "GroupId": "AGPAIHLR2VSAFC2VNVXCQ",
        "Arn": "arn:aws:iam::740376006796:group/dev/dev_admins",
        "GroupName": "dev_admins"
    }
}
$ aws iam create-group --group-name dev_users --path "/dev/"
{
    "Group": {
        "Path": "/dev/",
        "CreateDate": "2016-06-05T14:05:45.019Z",
        "GroupId": "AGPAI7PNSRYTT573CEYH6",
        "Arn": "arn:aws:iam::740376006796:group/dev/dev_users",
        "GroupName": "dev_users"
    }
}
```

Next, create two users. Alice is the most responsible member of the dev team, so she will be in the dev_admins and dev_users groups. Bob, being slightly less responsible (or at least feigning irresponsibility to avoid being assigned additional tasks), is only in the dev_users group:

```
$ aws iam create-user --user-name alice --path "/dev/"
{
    "User": {
        "UserName": "alice",
        "Path": "/dev/",
        "CreateDate": "2016-06-05T22:48:26.833Z",
        "UserId": "AIDAJKWL3DGB6E4OHBTYK",
        "Arn": "arn:aws:iam::740376006796:user/dev/alice"
    }
}
$ aws iam add-user-to-group --user-name alice --group-name dev_admins
$ aws iam add-user-to-group --user-name alice --group-name dev_users
$ aws iam create-user --user-name bob --path "/dev/"
{
    "User": {
        "UserName": "bob",
        "Path": "/dev/",
        "CreateDate": "2016-06-05T23:27:59.704Z",
        "UserId": "AIDAIVVPCRZA4V26N4J52",
        "Arn": "arn:aws:iam::740376006796:user/dev/bob"
    }
```

```
    }
    $ aws iam add-user-to-group --user-name bob --group-name dev_users
```

We can verify that the users and groups have been created with the correct paths by issuing the aws iam list-users and aws iam list-groups commands:

```
$ aws iam list-users --output text
USERS    arn:aws:iam::740376006796:user/dev/alice
2016-06-05T22:48:26Z    /dev/    AIDAJKWL3DGB6E4OHBTYK    alice
USERS    arn:aws:iam::740376006796:user/dev/bob    2016-06-05T23:27:59Z    /dev/
AIDAIVVPCRZA4V26N4J52    bob
[...]
$ aws iam list-groups --output text
GROUPS   arn:aws:iam::740376006796:group/dev/dev_admins    2016-06-05T14:03:57Z
AGPAIHLR2VSAFC2VNVXCQ    dev_admins    /dev/
GROUPS   arn:aws:iam::740376006796:group/dev/dev_users     2016-06-05T14:05:45Z
AGPAI7PNSRYTT573CEYH6    dev_users    /dev/
```

Now that the users and groups are set up, we need to create an IAM policy next.

Notice that the ARNs for our new users and groups include /dev as part of the identifier. This is the magic that makes it all work. Because we can use wildcards when specifying resources in IAM policies, we can simply grant the user permission to execute IAM actions on resources that exist under the /dev hierarchy. As before, the asterisk indicates "all resources":

```
{
    "Statement": {
        "Effect": "Allow",
        "Action": "iam:*",
        "Resource": [
            "arn:aws:iam::740376006796:group/dev/*",
            "arn:aws:iam::740376006796:user/dev/*"
        ]
    }
}
```

Save the preceding policy document in a text file and apply it to Alice's group with the aws iam put-group-policy command, taking care to replace the ARN with your own account's:

```
$ aws iam put-group-policy --group-name dev_admins --policy-name dev_admin \
--policy-document file://./dev_admin.json
```

Once this policy is applied, Alice will be able to reset Bob's password or create a new user in the /dev hierarchy, but she will not be able to create a new user in the /support hierarchy.

Auditing and rotating access keys

Security best practices include the removal of keys no longer in use, as well as regularly changing keys, a practice known as *key rotation*. IAM assists the administrator in this tedious task by providing ready access to all the information that is needed to promptly identify accounts or keys no longer in use. The IAM console reports when access keys were last used, in what region, and for what AWS service. Details concerning a user's password last use complement this data to form a complete picture of when an account was last active.

The Credential Report is found in the IAM console (Figure 3-4) and can be generated from the CLI as follows:

```
$ aws iam generate-credential-report
{
    "State": "STARTED",
    "Description": "No report exists. Starting a new report generation task"
}
$ aws iam get-credential-report | jq -r '.Content' | base64 -d > report.csv
$ more report.csv
user,arn,user_creation_time,password_enabled,password_last_used [...]
alice,arn:aws:iam::740376006796:user/dev/alice,2016-06-05T22:48:26+00:00 [...]
[output truncated]
```

Figure 3-4. The credential report is only one click away in the IAM console

The report is returned in base64 encoding wrapped in a JSON envelope, requiring the use of jq and base64 to save the comma-separated CSV file's contents.

Once your audit has identified any idle accounts to be deactivated, the task turns to rotating the old keys of the remaining accounts to newly generated ones. This is a well-defined process requiring a number of well-planned steps. Let's say our audit identified that Bob's key is due for rotation: our first step would be adding a second access key to the account (up to two active access keys are allowed for each user):

```
$ aws iam list-access-keys --user-name Bob
{
    "AccessKeyMetadata": [
```

```
        {
            "UserName": "bob",
            "Status": "Active",
            "CreateDate": "2015-06-05T00:41:52Z",
            "AccessKeyId": "AKIAI33YRI5D4IIJOANA"
        }
    ]
}
$ aws iam create-access-key --user-name Bob
{
    "AccessKey": {
        "UserName": "bob",
        "Status": "Active",
        "CreateDate": "2016-06-21T04:27:41.291Z",
        "SecretAccessKey": "CFgIptAtrqUKhfe/p3v1OBHciK5sY/n8EBX8JyO/",
        "AccessKeyId": "AKIAIL5TWIUC2M76F3PQ"
    }
}
$ aws iam list-access-keys --user-name Bob
{
    "AccessKeyMetadata": [
        {
            "UserName": "bob",
            "Status": "Active",
            "CreateDate": "2016-06-21T04:27:41Z",
            "AccessKeyId": "AKIAIL5TWIUC2M76F3PQ"
        },
        {
            "UserName": "bob",
            "Status": "Active",
            "CreateDate": "2015-06-05T00:41:52Z",
            "AccessKeyId": "AKIAI33YRI5D4IIJOANA"
        }
    ]
}
```

The new secret access key needs to be forwarded to Bob securely, preferably in some automated fashion. Key IDs (AKIDs) will help you track a key through its lifecycle; once you are satisfied the new key has replaced the old one in all uses and everything is still functioning as expected, you can retire the old key as inactive:

```
$ aws iam update-access-key --access-key-id AKIAI33YRI5D4IIJOANA \
--status Inactive --user-name Bob
$ aws iam list-access-keys --user-name Bob
{
    "AccessKeyMetadata": [
        {
            "UserName": "bob",
            "Status": "Active",
            "CreateDate": "2016-06-21T04:27:41Z",
            "AccessKeyId": "AKIAIL5TWIUC2M76F3PQ"
        },
```

```
{
    "UserName": "bob",
    "Status": "Inactive",
    "CreateDate": "2015-06-05T00:41:52Z",
    "AccessKeyId": "AKIAI33YRI5D4IIJOANA"
}
]
}
```

Functionally equivalent to being deleted, an inactive key has the salient property of being ready to return to service immediately upon a single command being issued. This makes turning a key inactive the safest way to retire it from production, with the comfort of an immediate "undo" option should anything go wrong. The final step of actually deleting the key is performed by passing the AKID and username to `aws iam delete-access-key`. There is no urgency to taking this action, but it will be required before the next key rotation is performed as AWS limits users to two access keys.

Password policy

A *password policy* enables you to define length and complexity requirements for user passwords account-wide. Equally important and perhaps more interesting, it permits setting an expiration window for user passwords matching your key rotation policy. For example:

```
$ aws iam update-account-password-policy --allow-users-to-change-password \
--max-password-age 90 --minimum-password-length 14
```

This will require that users change their passwords every 90 days, while simultaneously granting them permission to actually change their passwords. Federico typically requires 14-character minimum length passwords (AWS defaults to 6), without forcing their character composition. The intent is to nudge users toward the use of safe and more easily recalled passphrases—see XKCD's common-sense summary of password security in Figure 3-5. You will need to weigh the inconvenience to your users against your organization's threat profile as you alter these settings. Note that the `aws iam update-account-password-policy` command does not support partial updates: no parameters are required, but those not supplied will silently return to their default values—this can be both convenient when resetting defaults, and confusing if you are not aware of this command's behavior.

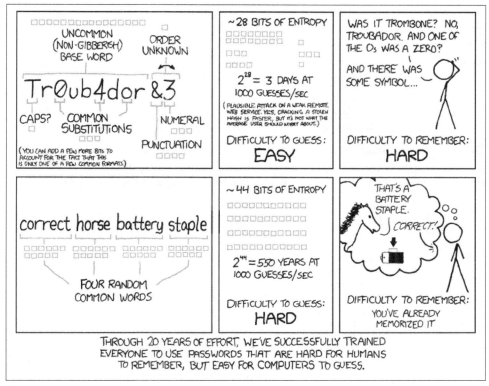

Figure 3-5. XKCD's uniquely elegant explanation of password strength (https://xkcd.com/936/), courtesy of Randall Munroe

CloudTrail

CloudTrail can log all activity occurring in the account by creating a record of every API call in a specified region or globally, irrespective of the tool originating the call—CLI, console, and even other AWS services. These records greatly enhance your ability to determine what user performed what action at a given time, and is essential to reconstruct what has really happened in the event of a security incident.

 CloudTrail will include in its logs all API calls generated by any AWS service on the user's behalf. You will be startled when you notice this for the first time, and may wonder if another, possibly rogue, user is carrying out some kind of unauthorized activity. To determine if an API call was generated automatically by another service, examine the *invokedBy* field of the CloudTrail record in question.

CloudTrail generates log files recording all activity occurring in the account (or in a specific AWS region), storing them in an S3 bucket. Trails can be created using the `aws cloudtrail create-trail` command. This command requires a preexisting S3 bucket to store logs to—remember that as the namespace of the s3 service is flat, you will need to find a unique name for your trail's bucket:

```
$ aws s3 mb s3://global-trail
make_bucket: s3://global-trail/
$ aws s3api put-bucket-policy --bucket global-trail --policy file://cbp.json
```

The second command sets a bucket policy that grants CloudTrail all the permissions it requires to perform its logging. The file defines the same policy the AWS console would set automatically if you choose to initialize your trail in the UI instead:

```
{
  "Version": "2012-10-17",
  "Statement": [
            {
          "Sid": "AWSCloudTrailAclCheck20150319",
            "Effect": "Allow",
            "Principal": {
                        "Service": "cloudtrail.amazonaws.com"
                },
            "Action": "s3:GetBucketAcl",
            "Resource": "arn:aws:s3:::global-trail"
        },
        {
          "Sid": "AWSCloudTrailWrite20150319",
          "Effect": "Allow",
          "Principal": {
                        "Service": "cloudtrail.amazonaws.com"
                },
          "Action": "s3:PutObject",
          "Resource": "arn:aws:s3:::global-trail/AWSLogs/740376006796/*",
          "Condition": {
          "StringEquals": {
                        "s3:x-amz-acl": "bucket-owner-full-control"
                }
            }
        }
    ]
}
```

Next, we create a trail logging the account's activity in all AWS regions:

```
$ aws cloudtrail create-trail --name global-trail --s3-bucket-name global-trail\
--is-multi-region-trail
{
    "IncludeGlobalServiceEvents": true,
    "Name": "global-trail",
    "TrailARN": "arn:aws:cloudtrail:us-east-1:740376006796:trail/global-trail",
    "LogFileValidationEnabled": false,
```

```
    "IsMultiRegionTrail": true,
    "S3BucketName": "global-trail"
}
$ aws cloudtrail start-logging --name global-trail
```

Examining a trail's contents requires sifting through the S3 bucket configured earlier, and retrieving the log file for the region and day of interest (see Figure 3-6). This is most easily accomplished in the AWS console, in particular if your browser is equipped with an extension like Chrome's JSONview (*https://chrome.google.com/webstore/detail/jsonview/chklaanhfefbnpoihckbnefhakgolnmc?hl=en*), which makes cursory examination of JSON files that much more efficient (Figure 3-7).

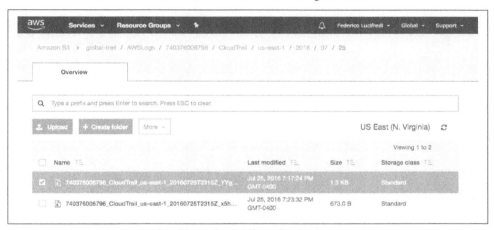

Figure 3-6. Navigating to a log file in the trail's S3 bucket

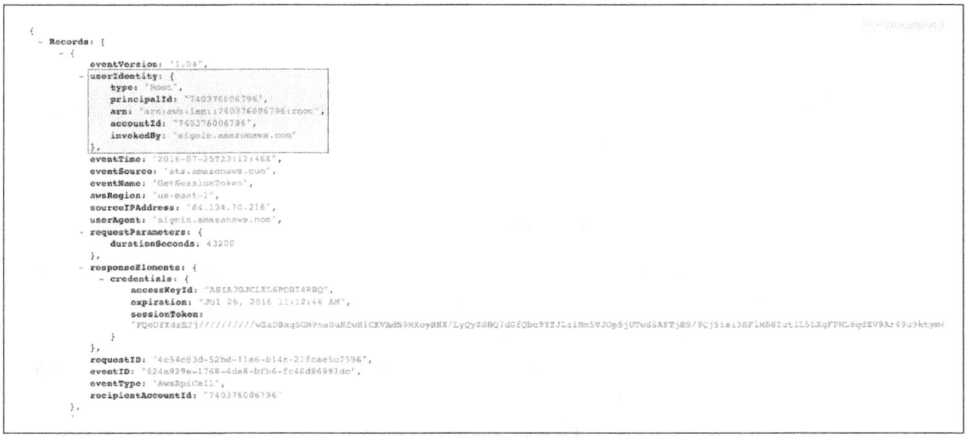

Figure 3-7. A CloudTrail login record examined inline in Chrome with JSONview—someone logged in as root, contrary to our policy!

Navigating to CloudTrail S3 bucket in the AWS console (Figure 3-6) also provides download access to the trail's files for offline analysis in your tool of choice. The granularity of single files may hinder your analysis when examining sequences of events spanning longer than a single day or more than one AWS region, which is the reason why the AWS console provides the API Activity view (*https://console.aws.amazon.com/cloudtrail/home?region=us-east-1#/events*). Consolidating events for the last seven days, this interface selectively visualizes *create*, *delete*, and *modify* events. The interface provides convenient direct access to the API call metadata as well as limited search functionality (Figure 3-8).

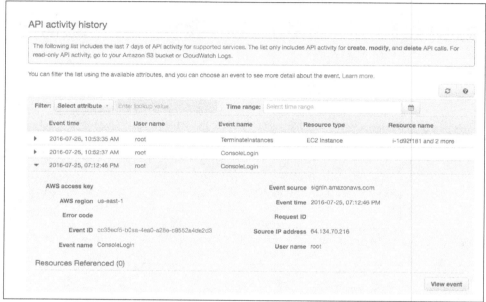

Figure 3-8. The API Activity History interface to CloudTrail, visualizing the same login record we reviewed earlier

Resource Limits

Denial of service is one of the most common security attack vectors: what if a user logged in to AWS and launched the public cloud equivalent of a *fork bomb*? Launching thousands upon thousands of instances would quickly exhaust the region's capacity and disrupt provisioning for other users. For this reason, AWS accounts have default service limits (*https://console.aws.amazon.com/ec2/v2/home?region=us-east-1#Limits:*) enforced on a regional basis (Figure 3-9). You can request these resource ceilings be raised at any time by opening a support request on the very same page—some of Federico's teams have access to accounts with spot limits exceeding thousands of instances for large-scale benchmarking, AWS can be very accommodating to customers' needs if you make a good case, so don't be shy about your goals.

EC2 Service Limits

Amazon EC2 provides different resources that you can use, such as instances and volumes. When you create your AWS account, AWS sets limits for these resources on a per-region basis. This page lists your EC2 service limits in US East (N. Virginia).

Instance Limits

Name	Current Limit	Action
Running On-Demand EC2 Instances	20	Request limit increase
Running On-Demand c1.medium instances	20	Request limit increase
Running On-Demand c1.xlarge instances	20	Request limit increase
Running On-Demand c3.2xlarge instances	20	Request limit increase
Running On-Demand c3.4xlarge instances	20	Request limit increase
Running On-Demand c3.8xlarge instances	20	Request limit increase
Running On-Demand c3.large instances	20	Request limit increase
Running On-Demand c3.xlarge instances	20	Request limit increase
Running On-Demand c4.2xlarge instances	20	Request limit increase
Running On-Demand c4.4xlarge instances	20	Request limit increase
Running On-Demand c4.8xlarge instances	20	Request limit increase
Running On-Demand c4.large instances	20	Request limit increase
Running On-Demand c4.xlarge instances	20	Request limit increase
Running On-Demand cc1.4xlarge instances	20	Request limit increase

Figure 3-9. Some of the default account limits listed in the AWS console of a new account

Trusted Advisor

True to its name, the AWS Trusted Advisor is a part of AWS's support package offering automated advice in the areas of cost reduction, performance, security, and fault tolerance. Full access to Trusted Advisor is only available with an enterprise support package, but some functionality is generally available to all users. The freebies include very useful basic security advice as well as analysis of usage thresholds meant to prevent outages caused by exceeding account resource limits.

The Trusted Advisor dashboard (Figure 3-10) provides access to useful information even to those not subscribing to AWS's support services, making it a useful resource to monitor the health of your account with minimum effort. In particular, the security scan includes a summary of open ports that is hard to beat for convenience—Figure 3-11 illustrates the point with a section of the spreadsheet produced by auditing an account running this chapter's examples. The AWS team regularly adds new checks to Trusted Advisor, which are usually announced by Jeff Barr in AWS's official blog (*https://aws.amazon.com/blogs/aws/*).

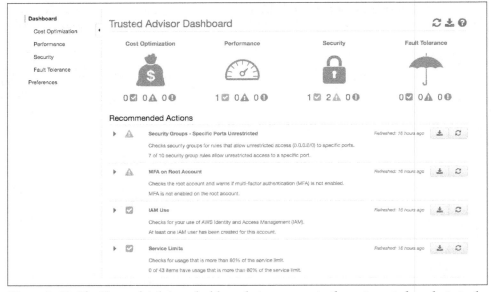

Figure 3-10. The Trusted Advisor dashboard gives access to the automated analysis tooling as well as a summary of their most recent findings

Naturally, Trusted Advisor reports can be retrieved programmatically and integrated in your automation—a security dashboard could retrieve the open port numbers on your account, for example. A premium support subscription is required for API access, and the lowest-cost option (developer support) is excluded as of this writing. We start by retrieving the identifier of the Trusted Advisor check in question, then forcing a refresh for this particular report:

```
$ aws support describe-trusted-advisor-checks --language en | jq \
'.checks[] | select(contains({name:"Ports Unrestricted"})).id'
"HCP4007jGY"
$ aws support refresh-trusted-advisor-check --check-id HCP4007jGY
{
    "status": {
        "checkId": "HCP4007jGY",
        "status": "enqueued",
        "millisUntilNextRefreshable": 3599988
    }
}
$ aws support refresh-trusted-advisor-check --check-id HCP4007jGY
{
    "status": {
        "checkId": "HCP4007jGY",
        "status": "success",
        "millisUntilNextRefreshable": 270266
    }
}
```

We can now retrieve the results and parse them for local use to our heart's content (or our CIO's):

```
$ aws support describe-trusted-advisor-check-result --check-id HCP4007jGY
{
  "result": {
      "checkId": "HCP4007jGY",
      "status": "warning",
      "flaggedResources": [
          {
              "status": "warning",
              "resourceId": "4lPCS_Zw5DRIqfc6yKAu4Vc2r2F96s_YmiVOpKmqoRA",
              "region": "us-east-1",
              "isSuppressed": false,
              "metadata": [
                "us-east-1",
                "image-resizing-ImageResizingSecurityGroup-SYAMMMJ89PVX",
                "sg-c38beab8 (vpc-934935f7)",
                "tcp",
                "Yellow",
                "22"
[ output truncated ]
```

Status: warning
Summary

Total number of resources processed: 10
Number of resources flagged: 7
Number of suppressed resources: 0

Region	Security Group Name	Security Group ID	Protocol	Status	Ports
us-east-1	image-resizing-ImageResizingSecurityGroup-SYAMMMJ89PVX	sg-c38beab8 (vpc-934935f7)	tcp	Yellow	22
us-east-1	launch-wizard-1	sg-b9f35fc2 (vpc-934935f7)	tcp	Yellow	22
us-east-1	launch-wizard-2	sg-a53672de (vpc-934935f7)	tcp	Yellow	22
us-east-1	openvpn-server-OpenVPNSecurityGroup-14J41Q46XR9WW	sg-feccae85 (vpc-934935f7)	udp	Yellow	1194
us-east-1	openvpn-server-OpenVPNSecurityGroup-14J41Q46XR9WW	sg-feccae85 (vpc-934935f7)	tcp	Yellow	22
us-east-1	openvpn-server-OpenVPNSecurityGroup-14J41Q46XR9WW	sg-feccae85 (vpc-934935f7)	tcp	Yellow	943
us-east-1	ssh	sg-4ebd8b36 (vpc-934935f7)	tcp	Yellow	22

Figure 3-11. Trusted Advisor's audit: open ports found in the authors' security groups

Users who do not have access to a support subscription will not be able to leverage Trusted Advisor's most advanced features, but a handy third-party alternative is also available: Security Monkey (*https://github.com/Netflix/security_monkey*). Hailing from one of the earliest teams to adopt public cloud as the computing platform of choice in a large enterprise, Security Monkey populates a database tracking configuration changes in your accounts' critical infrastructure and then runs rule-based checks every time a change occurs. Some noteworthy differences arise due to the different nature of the two tools—one a SaaS solution, the other an Open Source software package: Security Monkey empowers end users with the capability to define custom security checks, which Trusted Advisor does not.

IAM Roles

Consider the following scenario: you regularly need to resize images stored in an S3 bucket. Knowing a bit about Boto, you write a script that will look in the *incoming* directory of your S3 bucket for new images, perform the resize operations, and save the resulting images in the *processed* directory.

You want to launch an EC2 instance that will run this script after it has finished booting. For the script to work, it needs to use a set of AWS credentials with permissions to read the source files and write the output files to the S3 bucket.

In the previous section, we have already created the IAM user, applied the appropriate policy to it, and downloaded the access key and secret. But how will you provide these keys to the instance so they can be used by the log-processing script?

Until June 2012, the process of distributing AWS keys to your EC2 instances was somewhat painful. There were essentially two main options: bake the keys into the AMI so they were available when an instance booted, or provide them to the instance at runtime, perhaps with user data.

Both had their own downsides. If keys were baked into the AMI, replacing keys meant building a new AMI. If you went for the user data option, your unencrypted AWS keys were easily visible in the Management Console and other places. The Amazon team recognized that both options lacked security and simplicity, so they introduced IAM roles in response.

IAM roles almost entirely remove the problems surrounding this issue. Like users and groups, IAM roles can have one or more policies applied to them. When you launch an instance, you assign it a role that you have previously created. AWS will automatically generate access credentials and make them available to the instance. These credentials can then be used to access AWS services, with the permissions specified by the role's policies.

Best of all, Amazon will regularly rotate the keys during the lifetime of the instance, without requiring any action on your part. This can be a big relief if you are working with long-running instances, as it seriously reduces the time in which compromised keys are usable.

Given these advantages, we can't recommend using IAM roles highly enough. If all of your AWS scripts use roles, you will never need to worry about rotating these access credentials, even when people leave your organization. Furthermore, you will no longer run the risk of accidentally revoking keys that are still in use in some little-visited corner of your infrastructure (although you could still delete an IAM policy that you need).

If not properly configured, IAM roles can be used for privilege escalation. Imagine a nefarious user who has permissions to launch instances with IAM roles, but does not have permissions to delete Route 53 DNS records. By launching an instance with a role that does have these permissions, the user could easily SSH into the instance and retrieve the credentials.

IAM policies can be used to control which roles can be assigned by a user when they launch an instance, by explicitly referencing the ARN of the role when granting the user the `iam:PassRole` permission.

To see IAM roles in action, let's implement the example just given. To start, we will need an S3 bucket containing an example image. Although we will use `aws s3` in the following example, you could, of course, create the S3 bucket and upload an example file via the Management Console.

s3cmd (*http://s3tools.org/s3cmd*) is a popular command-line tool for interacting with S3, which Mike has found very useful when creating S3-based backup systems and Federico's team uses to test compatibility with the S3 interface. It is readily available in the default package repositories of many Linux systems.

If you are using Ubuntu, you can install this alternative command-line tool with `sudo apt install s3cmd`. Before using `s3cmd`, you will need to run `s3cmd --configure`. This will write a file in your home directory containing your AWS credentials, along with some other settings.

First, create a new S3 bucket. Because S3 bucket names must be unique, you will need to choose your own name for it:

```
$ aws s3 mb s3://mike-image-resize
make_bucket: s3://mike-image-resize/
```

Download an example image file and copy it to the S3 bucket. We will use the O'Reilly logo for this example:

```
$ wget -q http://cdn.oreillystatic.com/images/sitewide-headers/ml-header-home-
blinking.gif
$ aws s3 cp ml-header-home-blinking.gif s3://mike-image-resize/incoming/
upload: ./ml-header-home-blinking.gif to s3://mike-image-resize/incoming/ml-
header-home-blinking.gif
$ aws s3 ls --recursive s3://mike-image-resize
2016-06-05 23:21:43       9067 incoming/ml-header-home-blinking.gif
$
```

Now that we have a bucket, we can create a policy that will allow the script to create and delete the contents of the bucket. As with most tasks involving IAM, the first step is to think about which permissions the script will require. Thankfully, our example script is quite simple—the tasks it performs map to the following actions:

1. List the contents of the bucket: `s3:ListBucket`.

2. Get the original file: `s3:GetObject`.

3. Store the resized images in the bucket: `s3:PutObject`.

4. Delete the processed files: `s3:DeleteObject`.

To make our application as secure as possible, this role will have access only to the bucket we created earlier, so malicious users who managed to access these credentials would not be able to affect other parts of your application. To do this, we need to know the ARN of the bucket.

As we saw near the beginning of this chapter, the ARN for an S3 bucket takes the format `arn:aws:s3:::`*name-of-bucket*. The consecutive colons are not merely decoration: other resource types use these fields to store additional attributes that are not used by S3 ARNs.

Because permissions can apply to either the contents of the bucket or the bucket itself, we actually need to specify two ARNs:

- `arn:aws:s3:::`*name-of-bucket*
- `arn:aws:s3:::`*name-of-bucket*/*

 You might consider saving some typing and simply specifying the ARN as `arn:aws:s3:::`*my-bucket**. But if you have a bucket named, say, `my-bucket-secure`, you will be granting this role permissions on this bucket too. To quote the Zen of Python, "explicit is better than implicit"—even if it does sometimes involve more typing.

The first ARN references the bucket itself, and the second references any keys stored within that bucket. If we wanted to, we could assign an even more stringent set of permissions that allows the application to read and delete files in the *incoming* directory, but only write to the *processed* directory.

We now have all the information we need to create a role and assign a policy to it. We do this with the `aws iam create-role` command, creating a role named `image-resizing`:

```
$ aws iam create-role --role-name image-resizing --assume-role-policy-document \
file://./ec2-assume-role.json
{
    "Role": {
        "AssumeRolePolicyDocument": {
            "Version": "2012-10-17",
            "Statement": {
                "Action": "sts:AssumeRole",
                "Effect": "Allow",
                "Principal": {
                    "Service": "ec2.amazonaws.com"
                }
            }
        },
        "RoleId": "AROAIJSFDM5WJNR2M5ZVI",
        "CreateDate": "2016-06-07T05:22:34.145Z",
        "RoleName": "image-resizing",
        "Path": "/",
        "Arn": "arn:aws:iam::740376006796:role/image-resizing"
    }
}
```

The last line of the output is the ARN of the newly created role; we will use this later. The trust policy document controls which services may assume this role—at the time of writing, EC2, AWS Data Pipeline, Amazon Elastic Transcoder, or AWS OpsWorks are the only services that can assume roles.

We used the following trust policy document to create the `image-resizing` role:

```
{
  "Version": "2012-10-17",
  "Statement": {
    "Effect": "Allow",
    "Principal": {"Service": "ec2.amazonaws.com"},
    "Action": "sts:AssumeRole"
  }
}
```

Once the role has been created, we can create a policy and embed it into the role:

```
{
    "Version": "2012-10-17",
    "Statement": [
```

```
        {
            "Sid": "Stmt1465279863000",
            "Effect": "Allow",
            "Action": [
                "s3:DeleteObject",
                "s3:GetObject",
                "s3:ListBucket",
                "s3:PutObject"
            ],
            "Resource": [
                "arn:aws:s3:::mike-image-resize/*",
                "arn:aws:s3:::mike-image-resize"
            ]
        }
    ]
}
$ aws iam put-role-policy --role-name image-resizing \
--policy-name image-resizing --policy-document file://image-resizing.json
```

The role and policy are both named image-resizing. If you wish to distinguish between them (or you just like Hungarian notation), you might want to call the latter policy-image-resizing, but making consistent naming choices will help you maintain your sanity as you navigate AWS. If this command completed without any errors, the policy has been created and applied to the role.

Finally, we need to create an IAM instance profile, which will let us launch an EC2 instance using the role:

```
$ aws iam create-instance-profile --instance-profile-name image-resizing \
--output text
INSTANCEPROFILE arn:aws:iam::740376006796:instance-profile/image-resizing
2016-06-07T06:33:09.622Z        AIPAIAUTOO3GIHBKVG67G   image-resizing  /
$ aws iam add-role-to-instance-profile --instance-profile-name image-resizing \
--role-name image-resizing
```

 As an automation-loving sysadmin, your attachment to the command-line interface should not deter you from exploring the IAM facilities found in the console. A good example of this is the *policy generator* wizard found in the permissions section of the users, groups, or roles tab in the IAM console (Figure 3-12).

The JSON policies we are using in this book were seldom hand-written, and even in such cases IAM wizards conveniently assisted with validation. We invite you to follow our example.

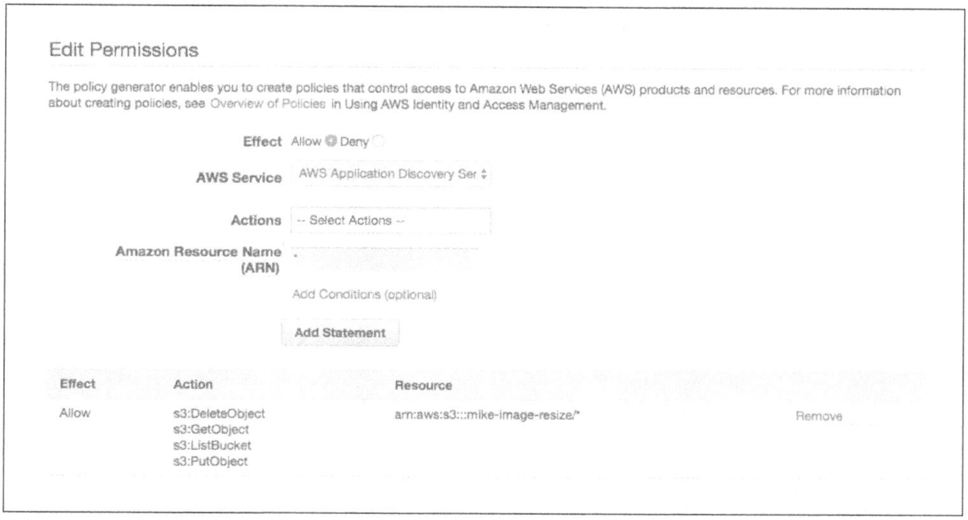

Edit Permissions

The policy generator enables you to create policies that control access to Amazon Web Services (AWS) products and resources. For more information about creating policies, see Overview of Policies in Using AWS Identity and Access Management.

Effect Allow ⊙ Deny ○

AWS Service AWS Application Discovery Ser ⬦

Actions -- Select Actions --

Amazon Resource Name (ARN)

Add Conditions (optional)

Add Statement

Effect	Action	Resource	
Allow	s3:DeleteObject s3:GetObject s3:ListBucket s3:PutObject	arn:aws:s3:::mike-image-resize/*	Remove

Figure 3-12. Defining a JSON policy using the IAM wizard

To see it in action, we can now launch a new EC2 instance that assumes this role. We do this by passing the name of the profile when running ec2-run-instances (or by selecting from the list of IAM roles in the Launch Instance Wizard). Note that IAM roles can only be assigned to new instances and that it is not possible to assign a different role to a running instance.

To launch an instance using this role, execute the following command—remembering to update the security group and the name of your SSH key pair. Note the last argument, which specifies the name of the instance profile we just created:

```
$ aws ec2 run-instances --image-id ami-43a15f3e --region us-east-1 --key mike \
--security-groups ssh --instance-type t2.micro \
--iam-instance-profile Name="image-resizing"

{
    "OwnerId": "740376006796",
    "ReservationId": "r-6e6b93cc",
    "Groups": [],
    "Instances": [
    [...]
            "IamInstanceProfile": {
                "Id": "AIPAIAUTOO3GIHBKVG67G",
                "Arn": "arn:aws:iam::740376006796:instance-profile/image-
resizing"
            },
    [...]
```

Once the instance has booted, open an SSH session to it. In the previous section, we used the ec2metadata tool to display the instance's metadata. At the time of writing, `ec2metadata` does not have support for IAM roles, so we must use the common Unix `curl` command to display the credentials. The limited-access URL to access the credentials with `curl` is always *http://169.254.169.254/latest/meta-data/iam/security-credentials/<instance-profile-name>*:

```
$ curl http://169.254.169.254/latest/meta-data/iam/security-credentials/image-
resizing
{
  "Code" : "Success",
  "LastUpdated" : "2016-06-11T03:44:36Z",
  "Type" : "AWS-HMAC",
  "AccessKeyId" : "ASIAJ5HOGZLCDMXIMARA",
  "SecretAccessKey" : "hPaw27itOOxc2Sq2fZxKKgzM9pbctYg5GjnAsUbI",
  "Token" : "FQoDYXdzECUaDAPhEgucj01B4VLx6SKZA/WqJVcs9JDkV83vL62J9dypgAq-
LIMu2zGajKfJg/xCc57yOh+yBgWx85XLzpQoQNc5oof5Kd1mxW4mkIGeW9uktKrVI
+oD1FdgEg4ve9U2irMurcYZxlFA9wiZcb2ohrUWDnRMOvIHJEOV3cK1fGOWLVTsetkFAASmOw8jobQ-
Viy2eocMnFd3bksriq+oy/khsHpm+7SoAcd2cDfpZmhH+ibIl8+fHWD2iLr5pfvqQ2bYsHKW2o6ROY0H
+18vRXcDaBU9qnHSKTWlw7P7Vv0zE3Vde1y7AH0XPwYp7sbfeQJiKFWBUhNCUTIsHaYoXp-
JARjJPRLo1Z+gaWipkLc4NSTNgu3m9mSLtS4JjCEJvfLbJ5sF1XxqYJe-
peGDspTu4YX4DWvpPQuDkvCDswjgASNDR1cdR+jebYuCPiIIQCiUBZeD
+EKtp3SxKa13mX5EcrH5OSkcOoOq8m9nKNa9HfljVox8TNcwYIvFLNUvWRUWABPt0MyN2YXvGpAA/
JqFMHzni25+av7noGL2+UJxAgBC8h3BicZyrN4ouZLuugU=",
  "Expiration" : "2016-06-11T09:55:33Z"
}
```

Fortunately, the authors of the AWS SDKs have decided to make things easy for us when using the client libraries. Boto, for example, has built-in support for IAM roles. If you connect to an AWS service without specifying any credentials, Boto will check to see whether it is running on an EC2 instance and whether this instance has an IAM role. If so, Boto will use the credentials supplied by IAM to authorize your API requests.

Example 3-1 shows a simple Boto script that looks in the S3 bucket's *incoming* directory and resizes all the files it finds. Processed files will be stored in the bucket's *processed* directory.

Example 3-1. Script accessing S3 buckets

```
#!/usr/bin/python

import tempfile
from PIL import Image
import shutil
import sys
from boto.s3.connection import S3Connection
from boto.s3.key import Key

IMAGE_SIZES = [
    (250, 250),
    (125, 125)
```

```
]
bucket_name = sys.argv[1]
# Create a temporary directory to store local files
tmpdir = tempfile.mkdtemp()
conn = S3Connection()
bucket = conn.get_bucket(bucket_name)
for key in bucket.list(prefix='incoming/'):
    filename = key.key.strip('incoming/')
    print 'Resizing %s' % filename
    # Copy the file to a local temp file
    tmpfile = '%s/%s' % (tmpdir, filename)
    key.get_contents_to_filename(tmpfile)
    # Resize the image with PIL
    orig_image = Image.open(tmpfile)
    # Find the file extension and remove it from filename
    file_ext = filename.split('.')[-1]
    for resolution in IMAGE_SIZES:
        resized_name = '%s%sx%s.%s' % (filename.rstrip(file_ext), resolution[0], res
olution[1], file_ext)
        print 'Creating %s' % resized_name
        resized_tmpfile = '%s/%s' % (tmpdir, resized_name)
        resized_image = orig_image.resize(resolution)
        resized_image.save(resized_tmpfile)
        # Copy the resized image to the S3 bucket
        resized_key = Key(bucket)
        resized_key.key = 'processed/%s' % resized_name
        resized_key.set_contents_from_filename(resized_tmpfile)
    # Delete the original file from the bucket
    key.delete()

# Delete the temp dir
shutil.rmtree(tmpdir)
```

This script has a few dependencies, which can be installed on Ubuntu systems as follows:

```
sudo apt install gcc python-dev python-pip
sudo pip install --upgrade boto
sudo apt install libtiff5-dev libjpeg8-dev zlib1g-dev libfreetype6-dev \
liblcms2-dev libwebp-dev tcl8.6-dev tk8.6-dev python-tk
sudo pip install pillow
```

 Make sure you are using a recent version of Boto that has support for IAM roles.

Notice that the script contains no mention of access credentials. Boto will fall back to using those provided by the IAM metadata.

Save the program to a file on the instance and execute it, passing the name of your S3 bucket as a command-line argument. If everything goes according to plan, you should see something similar to the following:

```
$ python image-resizing.py your-bucket-name
Resizing 1-header-home-blinking.gif
Creating 1-header-home-blinking.250x250.gif
Creating 1-header-home-blinking.125x125.gif
$
```

On your computer (not the instance we just launched), you can now use s3cmd to show the contents of the bucket and verify that the resized images were indeed created:

```
$ aws s3 ls --recursive s3://your-bucket-name
2016-06-11 22:32:01     8001 processed/1-header-home-blinking.125x125.gif
2016-06-11 22:32:01    26902 processed/1-header-home-blinking.250x250.gif
$
```

Once you have finished with the example script and your own experiments, remember to terminate the instance.

There are a number of problems with the previous example that would prevent you from using it in a high-traffic application, primarily because it would be impossible to *scale out* by launching multiple instances to process the files. Because multiple instances would be processing the bucket simultaneously, race conditions could emerge when two instances try to process the same image.

If you are building something like this for production use, Simple Queue Service (SQS) would be a better bet.

By using IAM roles, we removed the need to manually distribute and manage AWS credentials. Although there was a human behind the keyboard executing the image-resizing script, it is easy to see how IAM roles can save a lot of administration overhead, particularly when building applications based on Auto Scaling or CloudFormation.

Using IAM Roles from Other AWS Accounts

In "Limitations of IAM policies" on page 83, we mentioned that it is not always possible to define an IAM policy that—for example—allows users from the Development department to perform an action on certain instances, while preventing them from performing the same action on instances launched by the Marketing team. For most situations, this limitation is not a huge problem; an instance might be accidentally clobbered on occasion, but that is not the end of the world.

However, in some situations you might want to have a strict border between your AWS resources. You might need to guarantee for regulatory purposes that only members of the Support team are allowed to perform *any* action at all on production instances. The solution in those cases where resource permissions currently fall short is to create separate AWS accounts.

A side effect of maintaining separate AWS accounts is that you will receive a separate bill for each one, separating costs automatically—with a single account, the same can be accomplished through a careful tagging strategy. AWS Consolidated Billing lets you combine the bills from multiple AWS accounts, while still seeing exactly which account is responsible for each line item. This can save a lot of time in budget meetings, as arguments over who launched those m4.10xlarge instances for testing and forgot to terminate them become a thing of the past.

In November 2012, Amazon released a feature called cross-account API access to help customers who have gone down this route. As the name suggests, cross-account API access provides a framework for securely sharing resources between AWS accounts. Today, *roles* are the mechanism used to grant cross-account access. This feature is described more fully in IAM's common scenarios documentation (*https:// amzn.to/2ni8Efq*).

Using IAM in CloudFormation Stacks

IAM policies are a powerful tool on their own, but they become even more useful when combined with CloudFormation. Creating IAM policies and users from CloudFormation templates means that your CloudFormation stack contains everything required to run your application. The more self-contained your application is, the easier it will be to deploy and manage.

Building on the previous steps that introduced IAM roles, we will now create a CloudFormation stack that runs the image-resizing application. Everything—the S3 bucket, the IAM policy and role, and the EC2 instance that does the work—is contained within the stack template.

As always, a little planning is required before we start writing the CloudFormation stack template. First, consider the resources we need to create:

- IAM role
- IAM policy
- S3 bucket
- EC2 instance

These resources need to reference each other—for example, the stack will create a new S3 bucket and an IAM policy that references the bucket. When CloudFormation creates resources, they are given automatically generated names, which are not human-friendly and cannot be predicted in advance. Because of this, we must use the Ref function whenever we want to reference another resource in the stack.

Ref is an intrinsic function of CloudFormation templates. Passing it the logical name of a CloudFormation resource (the name you specify for the resource in the stack template) will return a value that can be used to reference that resource in other parts of the same template. It can be thought of as similar to variables in programming terms: the logical name of the resource will be replaced with the actual value at run-time.

The CloudFormation template language supports built-in functions that can add a bit of flexibility to your stack templates. You can find the full list of available functions on the AWS Intrinsic Functions page (*https://amzn.to/2LXDAAj*).

This example uses the Join and Ref functions to refer to other resources in the stack. Although not quite as flexible as the domain-specific language included in tools like Chef or Puppet, this small set of functions can be combined to add some interesting features to your stack templates.

With that in mind, let's begin creating the stack template. Create a file named *image-resizing.json* and add the preliminary boilerplate common to all templates:

```
{
    "AWSTemplateFormatVersion" : "2010-09-09",
    "Description" : "Image resizing stack",
    "Resources" : {
```

The first resource we will define is the S3 bucket, which is the simplest:

```
    "ImageResizingBucket": {
        "Type": "AWS::S3::Bucket"
    },
```

This creates a simple S3 bucket with a logical name of ImageResizingBucket.

Next, we create the IAM role, profile, and policy:

```
    "ImageResizingRole" : {
        "Type": "AWS::IAM::Role",
        "Properties": {
            "AssumeRolePolicyDocument": {
                "Statement": [ {
                    "Effect": "Allow",
                    "Principal": {
                        "Service": [ "ec2.amazonaws.com"]
                    },
                    "Action": ["sts:AssumeRole"]
```

```
                } ]
            },
            "Path": "/"
        }
    },
    "ImageResizingPolicies": {
        "Type": "AWS::IAM::Policy",
        "Properties": {
            "PolicyName": "root",
            "PolicyDocument": {
                "Statement": [ {
                    "Effect": "Allow",
                    "Action": [
                        "s3:ListBucket", "s3:GetObject",
                        "s3:PutObject", "s3:DeleteObject"
                    ],
                    "Resource": [
                        {"Fn::Join": [ "", [ "arn:aws:s3:::", {"Ref": "ImageRe-
sizingBucket"} ] ] },
                        {"Fn::Join": [ "", [ "arn:aws:s3:::", {"Ref": "ImageRe-
sizingBucket"}, "/*" ] ] }
                    ]
                } ]
            },
            "Roles": [ {
                "Ref": "ImageResizingRole"
            } ]
        }
    },
    "ImageResizingProfile": {
        "Type": "AWS::IAM::InstanceProfile",
        "Properties": {
            "Path": "/",
            "Roles": [ {
                "Ref": "ImageResizingRole"
            } ]
        }
    },
```

The `ImageResizingRole` is an IAM role that will be assigned to our instance.

`ImageResizingPolicies` contains IAM policies (or, as in this case, a single policy) defining which actions the user is allowed to perform. Note the use of the `Fn::Join` and `Ref` intrinsic functions. `Ref` lets us assign `ImageResizingBucket`, a logical name for the S3 bucket, to an actual bucket name, such as `simage-resizing-imageresizingbucket-86q5y1qzusge`. This is necessary as the actual bucket name will become available only at runtime.

This value is, in turn, passed to the `Fn::Join` function. `Join` combines a list of strings into a single string, separated by the given delimiter character. In this case, we use an empty delimiter ("") and join two strings to create a valid ARN for the new S3 bucket.

The second use of Fn::Join also appends /* to the bucket's ARN, which is used to declare actions that reference the bucket's contents, rather than the bucket itself.

By combining Ref and Fn::Join, we can dynamically create the ARN string used in IAM policies.

The ImageResizingProfile simply acts as a container, allowing us to assign the role to an instance.

The next step is to declare an EC2 instance and a security group that will let us SSH into this instance:

```
"ImageResizingInstance" : {
    "Type" : "AWS::EC2::Instance",
    "Properties" : {
      "InstanceType": "t2.micro",
      "ImageId": "ami-43a15f3e",
      "KeyName": "your-ssh-key-name",
      "SecurityGroups" : [
          {"Ref": "ImageResizingSecurityGroup"}
      ],
      "IamInstanceProfile": {
          "Ref": "ImageResizingProfile"
      },
      "Tags" : [
          {"Key" : "role", "Value": "image-resizing"}
      ],
      "UserData" : {
          "Fn::Base64": {"Ref": "ImageResizingBucket"}
      }
    }
},
"ImageResizingSecurityGroup" : {
    "Type" : "AWS::EC2::SecurityGroup",
    "Properties" : {
      "GroupDescription" : "Allow SSH from anywhere",
      "SecurityGroupIngress" : [ {
        "IpProtocol" : "tcp",
        "FromPort" : "22",
        "ToPort" : "22",
        "CidrIp" : "0.0.0.0/0"
        }
      ]
    }
}
```

This section creates a micro instance and assigns to it the newly created IAM instance profile. It also populates the user data with the name of the S3 bucket.

The `ImageResizingSecurityGroup` is a simple security group that allows SSH access from any IP address—not the most secure of firewalls, but it will serve for this example.

Remember to update the `ImageID` and `KeyName` attributes to refer to a valid AMI and SSH key pair name.

The final step is to add an `Outputs` section:

```
  },
    "Outputs" : {
      "BucketName" : {
        "Description" : "The name of the S3 bucket",
        "Value" : { "Ref" : "ImageResizingBucket" }
      },
      "InstanceIP" : {
        "Description" : "Public IP address of the newly created EC2 instance",
        "Value" : { "Fn::GetAtt" : [ "ImageResizingInstance", "PublicIp" ] }
      }
    }
  }
```

While not strictly required, outputs can be useful, especially when debugging new stacks. Outputs are visible in the Management Console, and can also be accessed from the command line with `aws cloudformation describe-stacks`. We define two outputs so we can easily see the IP address of the instance and the name of the S3 bucket.

Save all of these combined sections to *image-resizing.json* and create the stack:

```
$ aws cloudformation create-stack --stack-name image-resizing \
--template-body file://image-resizing.json  --capabilities CAPABILITY_IAM
{
    "StackId": "arn:aws:cloudformation:us-east-1:740376006796:stack/image-
resizing/4dc95850-3375-11e6-8a60-50d5cd148236"
}
```

You can watch the progress of the stack creation in the Management Console.

 If this command fails, make sure you have set up your command-line tools correctly. Also, check that the IAM credentials you are using have permissions to launch new instances with IAM roles and create all of the resources referenced in the stack template.

Now that the instance is running, you can connect to it and run the image-resizing script. Copy the script in Example 3-1 to a file named *image-resize.py* and install the requirements listed in "IAM Roles" on page 98.

The last time we ran the script, we had to pass the bucket name as an argument. This time, we parse the bucket name from the output of the ec2metadata command. Alternatively, you could update the script to read the value directly from user data instead of a command-line argument.

As before, place an example image in the *incoming/* directory of your S3 bucket and then run the following commands to resize your test image:

```
$ BUCKET=$(ec2metadata --user-data)
$ python image-resizing.py $BUCKET
Resizing l-header-home-blinking.gif
Creating l-header-home-blinking.250x250.gif
Creating l-header-home-blinking.125x125.gif
```

Although we had to log in to the instance to run the script manually, it is clear that combining all of the resources required for a particular business task into a single CloudFormation stack has benefits. Later, we will look at methods of running tasks automatically when an instance boots.

Security Groups

Given the dynamic nature of EC2, which launches and terminates instances in response to changes in demand, it would be difficult to easily manage firewall rules with a traditional firewall, such as iptables or pf. Defining rules when you know neither the hostname nor the IP address in advance could be tricky.

AWS provides *security groups* as an alternative (or sometimes, a supplement) to standard firewall software. Security groups consist of a series of access rules. When launching an instance, one or more security groups are assigned to it. Their combined rulesets define which traffic is allowed to reach the instance.

VPC security groups operate on inbound and outbound network traffic, and don't provide all the features you might be used to. If you want quality of service or deep packet inspection, or if you use your firewall logs for bandwidth reporting, you will need to combine security groups with your own firewall software. Security groups do, however, have some bells and whistles of their own, which we will look at in this chapter.

When you first launch an instance from the AWS console, a security group named `launch-wizard-1` will be created automatically. The wizard will apply this security group to the instance being launched and, amidst prominent warnings, instruct AWS to provide unimpeded two-way `ssh` connectivity to them.

It can be tempting to add your custom rules to this default group and use it for all of your instances. This leads to a maintenance and security nightmare, where the most disparate services rely on the same security group's policy, and making changes to the group itself effectively means running the risk of breaking potentially unknown services in production.

Having a well-planned security group strategy from the beginning of a project can save a lot of headaches later.

The rules that make up a security group combine a source, a destination port, and a protocol. As in a traditional firewall, the source can be a single IP address (`192.168.1.10`) or a network block in Classless Inter-Domain Routing (CIDR) notation (`192.168.0.0/24`). Using this, you can define rules that allow your office IP address access to SSH on your EC2 instances, for example. A default rule allows all outbound traffic, but this can be deleted and replaced with more granular controls.

The source can also be the name of another security group, which is where they really begin to shine. Suppose you have a PostgreSQL server running on port 5432, which should be accessible only to a particular subset of your EC2 instances. Because instances are launched dynamically, you do not know their IP addresses in advance, so you cannot create rules using that method. To solve this problem, you can create security groups and dynamically assign instances to groups as the instances are created.

Also of note is the *stateful* nature of security groups, which permits replies to allowed traffic to flow without impediment in either direction—see the section on *connection tracking* (*https://amzn.to/2nefmCW*) in the official AWS documentation for the complete details.

For this example, first create a security group. We give it a custom name, `db_clients`:

```
aws ec2 create-security-group --group-name db_clients --description "Database
client security group"
```

Next, create a security group named `db_servers`:

```
aws ec2 create-security-group --group-name db_servers --description "Database
server security group"
```

Finally, create a rule in the `db_servers` group that allows members of the `db_clients` group access on TCP port 5432:

```
aws ec2 authorize-security-group-ingress --group-name db_servers --protocol tcp
--port 5432 --source-group db_clients
```

When launching new instances, you will need to assign the newly created security groups as appropriate—for example, PostgreSQL servers in the db_servers group. With this setup, you can easily ensure that all of your database clients can access PostgreSQL, while locking it down to protect it from external access.

 This method also works across AWS accounts—that is, you can reference security groups belonging to other AWS accounts within your own group rules, provided the two VPCs are first peered (*https://amzn.to/2LVzSHB*).

Security groups can also reference themselves—that is, allow members of a security group to access other members of that group. To see this in action, update the db_servers security group to allow itself access on TCP port 5432:

```
aws ec2 authorize-security-group-ingress --group-name db_servers --protocol tcp
--port 5432 --source-group db_servers
```

Now, if you have two instances in the db_servers group, they will each be able to access the other's PostgreSQL instance—perfect for streaming replication.

This design pattern of role-based security group pairs is a good way of controlling access to your instances. It is likely that many types of instances will need to access your database server, such as web servers, monitoring systems, and reporting tools. Placing all of the database-access rules in a single db_servers group gives you only one thing to change if you, for example, change the port your database is running on.

 At the time of this writing, AWS allows users to create 500 security groups per VPC, each spanning up to 50 rules. Up to five security groups can be assigned to each network interface, providing plenty of flexibility for the design of your security posture.

One capability that has received little notice in the transition from EC2 Classic to VPC networking is that the new model allows changing at runtime what security groups are assigned to a running instance. Security group changes are no longer limited to boot time. This has interesting applications, particularly in security incidents. Admins can now quarantine a running instance and remove it from production during forensic analysis without having to connect to it to modify its internal state in any way. This permits immediate recovery of production to proceed with new instances while incident analysis is still being conducted.

Mark Nunnikhoven has demonstrated an automated workflow that responds to security events (e.g., the detection of malware) by changing the security group of the affected instance to isolate it for analysis, then forcing the health check of an Auto Scaling group to fail to automatically replace the compromised instance with a new one. This process cannot resolve the underlying cause of the vulnerability, which requires human intervention, but the automated process frees the operations team to perform the analysis, knowing that automation is taking care of restoring production. Mark's presentation (*https://markn.ca/2014/11/sec313-updating-security-operations-for-the-cloud/*) is Federico's AWS re:Invent all-time favorite, and food for thought when designing the infosec process of your production workloads. While a persistent attacker may continue to breach vulnerable instances until a fix is manually introduced, the prompt removal of the compromised instance poses a formidable obstacle to any attacker trying to expand their foothold deeper in your infrastructure.

 As your operations grow more sophisticated, the sheer number of security groups in your account can become a challenge. While creating different security groups on a per-application basis will limit the number of rules one needs to track in a single task, security oversight becomes increasingly complex.

Anay Nayak has developed aws-security-viz (*https://github.com/anaynayak/aws-security-viz*) as a way to manage this difficulty. Anay's tool visualizes the rules defining a collection of security groups, enabling you to examine an entire account's ruleset (or a select subset), and the relationships existing between your security groups.

aws-security-viz requires Ruby 2.0, and works equally well on macOS and Ubuntu hosts. Setup is quite simple:

```
apt install graphviz
gem install aws_security_viz
```

Once installed aws-security-viz can inspect an account's current security groups directly by invoking the AWS CLI, or import a previously saved JSON dump. Visualize an entire account's setup with the following:

```
aws_security_viz -a AWS access key -s aws secret key -f
viz.svg --color=true
```

Output takes the form of an SVG image (Figure 3-13) or a small website. Consider integrating and automatically refreshing this view in your dashboards.

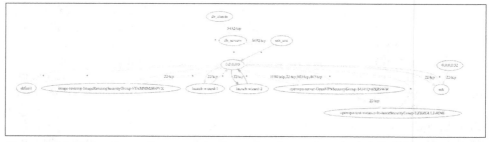

Figure 3-13. View of security groups in the authors' account generated with aws_security_viz

Protecting Instances with SSH Whitelists

Defense in depth is one of the key principles of successful IT security. SSH has an amazing track record when it comes to security, but there is no reason to let the whole world look for insecurities in your SSH setup. Security groups can be used to limit which IP address can access SSH on your instances, creating a whitelist of trusted addresses.

Depending on your organization, this whitelist might not change frequently, and might be small enough for you to recognize each IP address. In larger teams, maintaining the whitelist can become a chore, and it becomes difficult to know which address belongs to whom.

Implementing your SSH whitelist as a CloudFormation-managed security group can alleviate this headache and provide other benefits in the process. First, consider the alternative—manually adding and removing addresses via the Management Console. This is undesirable for a number of reasons, chiefly that there is no audit trail. If someone accidentally deletes a rule, there is no way of tracking down who did this and reverting the change.

Maintain Strong Security Policies When Moving to the Cloud

Securely setting up your infrastructure takes time and effort. It will sometimes be an inconvenience. The trade-off between security and convenience is well understood in the IT industry. You will need to choose the right position on this spectrum for your company's specific situation.

One common mistake is to add a rule to your default security group that allows SSH traffic from anywhere (0.0.0.0/0). This makes it convenient to access your servers remotely, but will also result in your SSH port being probed 24 hours a day. Given how easy it is to manage SSH whitelists with security groups, there is no excuse for not taking the time to set it up.

We have seen people who should know better take some horribly insecure shortcuts on AWS, including the one just mentioned. These are things that they would never consider doing on physical hardware. Just because we are on the cloud does not mean we should forget security best practices.

AWS provides a lot of tools to securely operate your infrastructure, but it does not enforce their use—that's up to your organizational policies.

The text-based nature of CloudFormation templates means we have an easy way of tracking changes to the whitelist—committing them to a version control system such as Git when updating the list. This immediately gives us an audit trail, a change log, and an easy way to revert unwanted changes.

There is, however, one downside to managing whitelists in this way: the CloudFormation template syntax. Here is the section required to allow ingress from a single IP address:

```
"InstanceSecurityGroup" : {
      "Type" : "AWS::EC2::SecurityGroup",
      "Properties" : {
        "GroupDescription" : "A test IP address",
        "SecurityGroupIngress" : [ {
          "IpProtocol" : "tcp",
          "FromPort" : "22",
          "ToPort" : "22",
          "CidrIp" : "192.168.1.10/32"
        } ]
      }
    }
```

Most of this template must be repeated for every IP address you want to whitelist. Typing this stanza over and over again will quickly get repetitive, so some people like to automate this. One common method is to have a CSV file containing IP addresses, which is used to generate the CloudFormation stack template file.

A security group created as part of a CloudFormation stack will have a name like *xxx*-ssh-whitelist. Resources created by CloudFormation have automatically generated names, which can make them a little difficult to reuse in other stacks. You will need to remember this name and reference it in your other CloudFormation stacks to assign instances to this security group. Also, if you replace this stack (i.e., delete it and re-create it), the security group will have a new name. This limitation can be worked around by using a two-stage approach to creating security groups.

Our current stack template performs two actions: creating the security group and populating it with addresses. Breaking this into two stages makes it much easier to manage security group whitelists with CloudFormation.

There are two ways to define which security group an *ingress rule* (as inbound security group rules are known) belongs to. In the previous example, we specified a list of ingress rules as an attribute on the `AWS::EC2::SecurityGroup` resource type. Thus, the rules are *children* of the security group, so CloudFormation implicitly knows that they belong to the parent.

The other method involves creating `AWS::EC2::IngressRule` resources and explicitly listing which security groups they belong to. So we can create the security group outside of CloudFormation (i.e., with the Management Console or command-line tools) and then use CloudFormation to populate the list of IP addresses.

Either way, two-stage definitions give the best of both worlds. We can control which name is assigned to our security group and still store the stack template in Git.

Now, you might be already jumping ahead and planning an even better security group layout. What about having an `ssh_whitelist` group that contains further security groups such as `devs_whitelist`, `support_whitelist`, and so on? Unfortunately, this is not supported: security groups cannot be nested, so this will not work as expected.

Virtual Private Networks and Security Groups

What if a whitelist is not enough? The overhead of adding and removing IP addresses from the list is not particularly grueling, but there is an overhead. If you are frantically trying to SSH into an instance to diagnose a problem that is causing production downtime, the last thing you want is to waste time updating CloudFormation stacks before you can get to work fixing things.

Or perhaps you would like an additional layer of security in front of SSH, such as a VPN server that requires client-side certificates before allowing connections.

In these scenarios, a solution based solely on security groups won't quite cut it; we need a dedicated VPN server running within EC2. The VPN server acts as a bastion host: the secure entry point to your other instances.

This means your public servers do not need to accept SSH connections from the public internet. Instead, their security groups can be configured to allow only those SSH connections that originate from the VPN instance. You no longer need to worry about script kiddies probing your ports, and there is no SSH whitelist to manage.

Because the instances will not need to receive any inbound connections from the public internet, we can use Amazon's Virtual Private Cloud service in this example.

Amazon Virtual Private Cloud

Amazon Virtual Private Cloud (VPC) is the current iteration of EC2's networking feature set, designed to improve the security of your EC2 instances. When EC2 was launched, the default network model (now referred to as "EC2 Classic" and no longer available to new accounts) automatically assigned a public IP address to each instance. Although instances were still protected by a security group, they were routable from the public internet by default.

In 2009, Amazon introduced VPC. The VPC model allows users to create logically isolated sections in their network architectures, rather than having a single section containing all of their EC2 instances.

VPC makes it possible to create a variety of network topologies within AWS. This has benefits for people using AWS as an extension of their own datacenter, or those with specific network security requirements that cannot be satisfied by security groups alone.

VPC introduced components to EC2 that emulate features found when running your own network outside AWS. These include subnets and routing tables, network access control lists (ACLs), and the ability to specify IP address ranges for your EC2 instances and other AWS resources.

In 2013, VPC became the default for new AWS accounts. Upon using an EC2 region for the first time, a default VPC is automatically created, including a default subnet, routing table, and other required components of a VPC. This process is essentially invisible to the user: new EC2 instances will be launched in the default VPC automatically, as we have seen in Chapter 2.

Our example will include a VPC consisting of two subnets. The first subnet will be accessible via the public internet, and will be home to our bastion host. The second subnet will be private: it will not be routable from the internet, and will be accessible only to the bastion host after we implement the required routing and access control rules.

As a demonstration, we will use the free OpenVPN as our VPN server, although the same general procedure will apply to other VPN servers as well. Luckily, the makers of OpenVPN have published an AMI that contains everything you need to run an OpenVPN server. To cut down on the installation time, we will use this ready-to-go AMI instead of installing it from scratch ourselves.

In "Security Groups" on page 112, we looked at some strategies for defining security groups for client/server applications such as PostgreSQL. In this section, we will be creating two security groups:

openvpn
> This will be assigned to OpenVPN instances, and will allow the public internet to access the OpenVPN server.

protected_ssh
> This will be assigned to all other instances, and will allow SSH access only from the OpenVPN instance(s).

These security groups will be created as part of the CloudFormation stacks.

The instance could be launched in any number of ways. We are going to use Cloud-Formation so we can have one stack that contains the VPN instance and security group, and another that contains a *protected* EC2 instance and its own security group.

You can find the ID of the OpenVPN AMI by searching for it in the Launch Instance Wizard in the Management Console. Alternatively, OpenVPN maintains a list of AMIs for each EC2 region in the EC2 Appliance (AMI) Quick Start Guide (*http://bit.ly/2nfBgFZ*).

At the time of writing, the ID for the OpenVPN AMI in us-east-1 is ami-7ab25917. You will need to replace this if you are using a different region, or if a new OpenVPN AMI has since been created.

The OpenVPN AMI has two configuration phases. First, the OpenVPN installation process requires some configuration data such as the instance's hostname and the admin user's password. This takes place when the instance is booting. This configuration data can be provided as user data or entered using the OpenVPN installer on the command line.

The second configuration phase takes place after OpenVPN is installed and running, and is done through the OpenVPN web interface. It is at this point that you can create additional users who will be allowed to access the VPN.

In this example, we will perform the first configuration stage manually using the OpenVPN installer. Although using user data is more convenient, it will leave the OpenVPN administrative account password visible in both the CloudFormation and EC2 web consoles, which is not desirable.

Example 3-2 shows the CloudFormation stack we will use to create the OpenVPN instance and associated resources.

Example 3-2. OpenVPN CloudFormation stack

```
{
  "AWSTemplateFormatVersion" : "2010-09-09",
  "Description" : "OpenVPN EC2 Instance and Security Group",

  "Parameters" : {
    "KeyName": {
      "Description" : "EC2 KeyPair name",
      "Type": "String",
      "MinLength": "1",
      "MaxLength": "255",
      "AllowedPattern" : "[\\x20-\\x7E]*",
      "ConstraintDescription" : "can contain only ASCII characters."
    },
    "AllowedIPRange" : {
      "Description" : "IP Range allowed to access OpenVPN via SSH and HTTP(S)",
      "Type": "String",
      "MinLength": "9",
      "MaxLength": "18",
      "Default": "0.0.0.0/0",
      "AllowedPattern": "(\\d{1,3})\\.(\\d{1,3})\\.(\\d{1,3})\\.(\\d{1,3})/(\
\d{1,2})",
      "ConstraintDescription": "Must be a valid IP CIDR range of the form x.x.x.x/
x."
    },
    "AMI" : {
      "Description" : "OpenVPN AMI ID",
      "Type": "String"
    }
  },

  "Resources" : {
    "OpenVPNInstance" : {
      "Type" : "AWS::EC2::Instance",
      "Properties" : {
        "InstanceType" : "t2.micro",
        "SecurityGroups" : [ { "Ref" : "OpenVPNSecurityGroup" } ],
        "KeyName" : { "Ref" : "KeyName" },
        "ImageId" : { "Ref" : "AMI"},
        "SourceDestCheck" : "false"
      }
    },

    "OpenVPNSecurityGroup" : {
      "Type" : "AWS::EC2::SecurityGroup",
      "Properties" : {
        "GroupDescription" : "Allow SSH, HTTPS and OpenVPN access",
        "SecurityGroupIngress" : [
                {
                  "IpProtocol" : "tcp",
                  "FromPort" : "22",
```

```
          "ToPort" : "22",
          "CidrIp" : { "Ref" : "AllowedIPRange"}
        },
        {
          "IpProtocol" : "tcp",
          "FromPort" : "443",
          "ToPort" : "443",
          "CidrIp" : { "Ref" : "AllowedIPRange"}
        },
        {
          "IpProtocol" : "tcp",
          "FromPort" : "943",
          "ToPort" : "943",
          "CidrIp" : { "Ref" : "AllowedIPRange"}
        },
        {
          "IpProtocol" : "udp",
          "FromPort" : "1194",
          "ToPort" : "1194",
          "CidrIp" : { "Ref" : "AllowedIPRange"}
        }
      ]
    }
  }
},

"Outputs" : {
  "InstanceId" : {
    "Description" : "InstanceId of the OpenVPN EC2 instance",
    "Value" : { "Ref" : "OpenVPNInstance" }
  },
  "OpenVPNSecurityGroup" : {
    "Description" : "ID of the OpenVPN Security Group",
    "Value" : { "Fn::GetAtt" : [ "OpenVPNSecurityGroup", "GroupId" ] }

  },
  "PublicIP" : {
    "Description" : "Public IP address of the newly created EC2 instance",
    "Value" : { "Fn::GetAtt" : [ "OpenVPNInstance", "PublicIp" ] }
  }
}
}
}
```

Save this stack template to a file named *openvpn.json* and create the stack with the
CloudFormation command-line tools:

```
aws cloudformation create-stack --stack-name openvpn-server \
  --template-body file://./openvpn.json --region=us-east-1 \
  --parameters  ParameterKey=KeyName,ParameterValue=your-key-name \
  ParameterKey=AllowedIPRange,ParameterValue=0.0.0.0/0 \
  ParameterKey=AMI,ParameterValue=ami-7ab25917
```

This stack template introduces a new feature of CloudFormation: parameters. *Parameters* can be thought of as variables within your stack template. They can be given a default value that can be overridden when creating the stack. They are not quite as flexible as variables, as they can be set only once (when launching or updating the stack), but they do allow for a certain amount of reusability within your stack templates.

The parameters required by this stack are specified on the command line with the syntax `ParameterKey=`*KeyName*`,ParameterValue=`*value*. You will need to replace the SSH key name and IP range with your own values.

If you are not launching the stack in the `us-east-1` region, you will also need to change the AMI parameter to match the OpenVPN AMI ID for your region. You can find the ID on the OpenVPN AWS AMI Marketplace page (*https://aws.amazon.com/marketplace/pp?sku=a6vjvrelz10rgvvemklxv2dow*).

After the stack has been created, we can find the IP address of the instance by querying its outputs:

```
aws cloudformation describe-stacks --stack-name openvpn-server
```

This will output a full description of the stack, including the outputs and their values. Instead of searching through this information manually, you could use the `jq` tool to filter the JSON and print only the required values. We use the following filter:

```
aws cloudformation describe-stacks --stack-name openvpn-server | \
    jq '.Stacks[0].Outputs[] | select(.OutputKey=="OpenVPNSecurityGroup"
or .OutputKey=="PublicIP").OutputValue'
```

This will parse the JSON and print the `OutputValue` for the `OpenVPNSecurityGroup` and `PublicIP` outputs. For example:

```
"54.164.47.241"
"sg-feccae85"
```

Now that the instance is running, it must be configured. Begin by connecting to the instance via SSH as the `openvpnas` user. After logging in to the connection, an OpenVPN configuration process will be automatically started. The default choices presented by the application are suitable for our uses, so press the Enter key on each line to accept them.

Once this process exits, you will need to set the password for the `openvpn` user, used to configure OpenVPN through its web interface. Generate a password and set it by executing the following:

```
sudo passwd openvpn
```

You can now open the configuration page in your web browser. The address will be displayed after the OpenVPN configuration process completes, and will be something like *https://54.77.153.76:943/admin*.

When you open this address in your web browser, you should see the OpenVPN welcome page. Using the OpenVPN Quick Start Guide (*http://bit.ly/2nfBgFZ*), you can now configure the OpenVPN server according to your requirements.

 It is possible to create DNS records from CloudFormation templates, so we could, in fact, set up a CNAME so we can access this instance by visiting, for example, *vpn.example.com*.

After the VPN server has been configured, you should now be able to connect to the VPN, using the OpenVPN documentation for your platform of choice.

 This OpenVPN server is a single point of failure, which is not desirable when it is the only way you can SSH into your other instances. Before using a solution like this in production, you should explore methods of making this system more robust. For example, you could run an Auto Scaling group with one or more instances of OpenVPN so that failed instances are automatically replaced.

Now that the VPN server is up and running, we can verify that it is working as expected when it comes to protecting our instances. We will do this by launching a new instance and assigning it to the `protected_ssh` security group. Example 3-3 shows a simple CloudFormation stack template that declares a single instance using this security group.

Example 3-3. Launching a protected instance with CloudFormation

```
{
  "AWSTemplateFormatVersion" : "2010-09-09",
  "Description" : "Example EC2 instance behind an OpenVPN server",

  "Parameters" : {
    "KeyName": {
      "Description" : "EC2 KeyPair name",
      "Type": "String",
      "MinLength": "1",
      "MaxLength": "255",
      "AllowedPattern" : "[\\x20-\\x7E]*",
      "ConstraintDescription" : "can contain only ASCII characters."
    },
    "AMI" : {
      "Description" : "AMI ID",
      "Type": "String"
    },
    "OpenVPNSecurityGroup" : {
```

```json
        "Description" : "OpenVPN Security Group ID",
        "Type": "String"
    }
  },

  "Resources" : {
    "Ec2Instance" : {
      "Type" : "AWS::EC2::Instance",
      "Properties" : {
        "InstanceType" : "t2.micro",
        "SecurityGroups" : [ { "Ref" : "InstanceSecurityGroup" } ],
        "KeyName" : { "Ref" : "KeyName" },
        "ImageId" : { "Ref" : "AMI"}
      }
    },

    "InstanceSecurityGroup" : {
      "Type" : "AWS::EC2::SecurityGroup",
      "Properties" : {
        "GroupDescription" : "Allows SSH access from the OpenVPN instance",
        "SecurityGroupIngress" : [
              {
                "IpProtocol" : "tcp",
                "FromPort" : "22",
                "ToPort" : "22",
                "SourceSecurityGroupId" : { "Ref" : "OpenVPNSecurityGroup"}
              }
          ]
        }
      }
    },

  "Outputs" : {
    "PrivateIP" : {
      "Description" : "Private IP address of the EC2 instance",
      "Value" : { "Fn::GetAtt" : [ "Ec2Instance", "PrivateIp" ] }
    },
    "PublicIP" : {
      "Description" : "Public IP address of the  EC2 instance",
      "Value" : { "Fn::GetAtt" : [ "Ec2Instance", "PublicIp" ] }
    }
  }
}
```

Save this file as *protected_instance_cloudformation.json* and execute the following command to create the stack:

```
aws cloudformation create-stack --stack-name openvpn-test-instance \
  --template-body file://protected_instance_cloudformation.json \
  --region=us-east-1 --parameters ParameterKey=KeyName,ParameterValue=federico \
  ParameterKey=AMI,ParameterValue=ami-43a15f3e.
  ParameterKey=OpenVPNSecurityGroup,ParameterValue=sg-feccae85
```

As before, you will need to adjust some of the parameters to match your environment. The value for the `OpenVPNSecurityGroup` should be the value retrieved from the `describe-stacks` command executed earlier.

Find out the public and private IPs of the instance by running the following:

```
aws cloudformation describe-stacks --stack-name openvpn-test-instance |\
jq '.Stacks[0].Outputs[]'
```

Once the stack has been created, make sure your VPN is disconnected and try to SSH to the public IP of the instance. This should time out, because your public IP address is not allowed to access instances in this security group.

Connect to the VPN and then try to SSH to the instance's private IP address. This time you should be presented with the familiar Ubuntu prompt, confirming that your security groups are doing their job and traffic is being routed over the VPN.

Setting up the OpenVPN server and performing ongoing maintenance adds overhead that is not present when working with security groups on their own. However, for some companies, the additional layer of security is a must. Managing this stack with CloudFormation will keep the maintenance to a minimum.

This is just an introduction to running OpenVPN with CloudFormation. TurnKey Linux has published an example CloudFormation template that includes a VPN and separate subnets for the OpenVPN server and protected instances. Available on their GitHub page (*http://bit.ly/2nh7Mrg*), this is a great starting point for building highly available and secure VPNs in Amazon's cloud.

A Security State of Mind

Security is a job that by its very nature is never complete, and subject to some of the strongest trade-offs in IT. Too little security may be as bad as too much security—the former leading to catastrophic incidents, the latter preventing your team from being effective. We have laid a solid foundation for your security thinking in a public cloud environment, and we offer a few key takeaways:

- Most of the security concepts you already know have direct parallels in AWS.
- Manually maintaining security groups and whitelists is time-consuming and error prone—don't do it. Automate these processes using CloudFormation or your own custom scripts.
- It is a lot easier to build a secure infrastructure from the beginning than it is to improve security on a running infrastructure.
- Time spent defining a sensible IAM policy at the beginning of a project will pay off in reduced headaches later in the project.

- The cloud is not a magic place where security rules do not apply. Just as your datacenter managers would not prevent you from deploying a physical server with a misconfigured firewall, AWS will not prevent you from building an insecure infrastructure.

- Public cloud security may be stronger than a private datacenter's when properly architected around a clear understanding of the shared responsibility model, particularly for smaller IT teams that are invariably resource-constrained.

- A VPN-based bastion host can add a security and auditing layer, at the cost of increased maintenance.

- Allowing SSH from `0.0.0.0/0` is nearly always a bad idea.

## CHAPTER 4

Configuration Management

Why Use Configuration Management?

Mike originally became enamored (*obsessed* might be a better word) with the idea of automatically configuring and deploying infrastructures after reading the classic "Bootstrapping an Infrastructure" paper (*http://www.infrastructures.org/papers/boot strap/bootstrap.html*) from the LISA '98 system administration conference.

The paper described the experiences of system administrators and architects responsible for building and maintaining large Unix environments for financial trading floors, and outlined some philosophies they adopted as a result. While somewhat dated in terms of the software used, the underlying principles are still highly relevant to managing today's cloud infrastructures:

> We recognize that there really is no "standard" way to assemble or manage large infrastructures of UNIX machines. While the components that make up a typical infrastructure are generally well-known, professional infrastructure architects tend to use those components in radically different ways to accomplish the same ends. In the process, we usually write a great deal of code to glue those components together, duplicating each others' work in incompatible ways. Because infrastructures are usually ad hoc, setting up a new infrastructure or attempting to harness an existing unruly infrastructure can be bewildering for new sysadmins. The sequence of steps needed to develop a comprehensive infrastructure is relatively straightforward, but the discovery of that sequence can be time-consuming and fraught with error. Moreover, mistakes made in the early stages of setup or migration can be difficult to remove for the lifetime of the infrastructure.

The authors of this paper recognized that automation is the key to effective system administration, and that a huge amount of time was being wasted by duplicating efforts to automate common tasks like installing software packages. By describing some battle-tested experiences, they hoped to reduce the amount of redundant work performed by their peers.

Configuration management software evolved out of a wider need to address this problem. Puppet, Chef, and Ansible are just a few examples of configuration management packages. They provide a framework for describing your application/server configuration in a text-based format. Instead of manually installing Apache on each of your web servers, you can write a configuration file that says, "All web servers must have Apache installed."

As well as reducing manual labor, storing your configurations as text files means you can store them in a version control system with your application code so that changes can be audited and reverted.

Your infrastructure effectively becomes *self-documenting*, as your server and application configurations can be reviewed at any time by browsing your version control system. Of course, the bits only answer *how* something is done, therefore authors must take care to document the *why* in their commit message.

Finally, the entire unit is a self-contained unit and can be deployed with minimal human interaction. Once the first server hosting the configuration management application is running, the rest of the infrastructure can be brought into service without having to manually configure operating systems or applications.

This is especially important when a small team is responsible for a large infrastructure, or in the case of consulting companies, a number of disparate infrastructures. Manually installing software does not scale up very well—if it takes you one hour to configure a server manually, it will take you two hours to configure two servers, to the extent that you are not parallel.

However, if it takes one hour to configure a server with configuration management software, that configuration can be reused for as many servers as you need.

Adopting the configuration management philosophy does involve an initial time investment if you have not used it before, but it will soon pay off by reducing the amount of time you spend configuring servers and deploying changes.

OpsWorks

Amazon recognizes how important configuration management tools are, and is doing its bit to make these tools more effective when working within AWS. In February 2013, it announced the OpsWorks service, bringing joy to the hearts of sysadmins everywhere.

OpsWorks made configuration management a core part of AWS, bringing support for Chef directly into the Management Console. It works by letting the users define the *layers* that make up their application—for example, clusters of web and database servers would be two separate layers. These layers consist of EC2 instances (or other AWS resources) that have been configured using Chef recipes. Once your layers have been defined, AWS will take care of provisioning all the required resources.

Your running application—and all of its layers—are visible in the Management Console, making it easy to see the overall health of your application.

This makes it a lot easier for people who are familiar with Chef to use it to manage their AWS infrastructure. More importantly, it makes configuration management tools a lot more discoverable for companies that do not have dedicated system administrators. A lot of people avoid implementing configuration management because the return on investment is not always clear in advance. OpsWorks will hopefully lead to a lot more people using professional system administration practices when setting up AWS applications.

Another advantage of OpsWorks is that it further commoditizes many parts of designing and deploying an application infrastructure. It is possible to find shared Chef recipes for installing common software packages such as PostgreSQL or HAProxy. Instead of manually designing your own database setup and writing custom Chef recipes, you can just take a working example and tweak it if necessary.

Over time, AWS may build on this platform to offer entire "off-the-shelf" application stacks—for example, a "social media stack" that contains all the elements required to run a typical social media website, such as web servers, a database cluster, and caching servers.

Amazon maintains a choice of multiple overlapping services for template-based application provisioning. OpsWorks is best suited to users who have already adopted Chef as their configuration management tool of choice and therefore do not feel limited by this choice. Outside of this group, OpsWorks is best thought of as a service abstracting the creation of web application stacks to a lesser degree than the easy-to-use AWS Elastic Beanstalk. OpsWorks provides more customization of application instances at the cost of potentially higher complexity, thanks to the integration of Chef. The authors prefer a third application template option for most automation tasks: AWS CloudFormation. CloudFormation is a lower-level foundation service that delivers complete control of the application template to the administrator, allowing us to tailor every detail. The effort caused by the additional complexity is offset by the need to operate only one tool, and our use of it through API automation, which makes this a setup-time cost only.

For more information about OpsWorks, see Amazon's OpsWorks page (*http://aws.amazon.com/opsworks/*).

Choosing a Configuration Management Package

A plethora of tools are available in the configuration management software space. We believe the number of options is a result of the fact that many of their users are system administrators who can code. When a tool does not quite meet users' needs, they begin working on their own version to scratch their individual itch, as eloquently illustrated by the XKCD comic shown in Figure 4-1.

The top-tier tools all have their own approaches and architecture decisions, but share a common fundamental set of features. For example, they all provide the capability to install software packages and ensure services are running, or to create files on client hosts (such as Apache configuration files).

Figure 4-1. XKCD on standards (https://xkcd.com/927/), courtesy of Randall Munroe

There are a few things to keep in mind when choosing a package.

Nearly all of the available configuration management tools have the concept of reusable pieces of code that can be shared to save even more time. Instead of doing all of the work yourself, you can take some prewritten modules and customize them to fit your needs. In Puppet, these are known as modules (*https://docs.puppet.com/puppet/3/reference/modules_fundamentals.html*), Chef calls them recipes (*https://docs.chef.io/recipes.html*), and Ansible calls them playbooks (*http://docs.ansible.com/ansible/playbooks.html*).

Puppet, Inc., operates the Puppet Forge (*https://forge.puppet.com*), a site where users from the community can share Puppet modules written for common tasks.

The availability of external modules should factor into your decision; building on the work of others will usually be easier than building from scratch.

The language used to build the tool might also come into play, if you anticipate needing to extend it in some way (such as creating your own managed resource types). Chef and Puppet are both written in Ruby, whereas Ansible is a Python tool.

Most of the mature tools come from the pre-cloud days, and have evolved to support the needs of a more dynamic infrastructure. Chef and Puppet in particular have very good integration with AWS.

Given the relative similarity of features, choosing the right tool is often merely a case of finding the one that you feel most comfortable using. Amazon's choice of Chef as the backend to OpsWorks will add to Chef's popularity in the future, but that does not necessarily mean it is the right tool for everyone.

Our recommendation, especially if you are new to configuration management, is to try out a few packages and see which suits your team's workflow.

Puppet on AWS

Instead of dedicating half of the book to configuration management tools, we use Puppet to demonstrate the key concepts in the rest of this chapter. It has a good amount of overlap with other tools in terms of the available features, so all of the core principles can be applied with any of the available configuration management packages.

A Quick Introduction to Puppet

Initially launched by Luke Kanies in 2005, Puppet is perhaps the most popular open source configuration management tool. It uses a declarative language to let users describe the configuration and state of Unix or Windows hosts in text files known as Puppet *manifests*. These manifests describe the desired state of the system—*this* package should be installed, and *this* service should be running.

Typically, these manifests are stored on a central server known as the Puppet *master*. Client hosts periodically connect to the master server and describe their current system state. The Puppet master calculates the changes required to move from the current state to the desired state, as described in the manifests for that host, and lets the client know which changes it needs to make. Finally, the Puppet client performs these actions.

Because clients connect to the master server at regular intervals, configuration changes can be made on the master server and they propagate throughout your network as each client connects and picks up the new configuration.

The */etc/puppet/manifests/sites.pp* file is used to map server hostnames to configuration manifests, which are known as *node definitions*. The best way to illustrate this is with an example, which contains two node definitions:

```
# demo sites.pp with two nodes

node "www.example.com" {
    package { "nginx":
```

```
            ensure => installed
        }
    }

    node "db.example.com" {
        package { "postgresql":
            ensure => installed
        }
    }
```

When a client named *www.example.com* connects to the Puppet master, the Nginx package will be installed. When *db.example.com* requests its configuration from the Puppet master, the PostgreSQL package will be installed.

In addition to matching explicit hostnames, regular expressions can be used in node definitions: `www-\d+\.example\.com` would match *www-01.example.com* and *www-999.example.com*.

Puppet supports a module-based system for creating reusable Puppet manifests. Consider the common example of needing to ensure that user accounts are automatically managed by Puppet across all of your servers. Rather than explicitly listing all of your users over and over again, they can be listed once in a `users` module that is reused in multiple node definitions.

Modules are Puppet manifests that exist in a particular directory, usually */etc/puppet/ modules*. A simple `users` module, stored in */etc/puppet/modules/users/manifests/ init.pp*, might look like this:

```
user { 'mike':
  ensure => present
  }

user { 'federico':
  ensure => present
  }
```

This is applied to nodes by including it in their node definition. For example:

```
node 'www.example.com' {
  include users
  package { 'nginx':
  ensure => installed
  }
}
node 'db.example.com' {
  include users
  package { 'postgresql':
  ensure => installed
  }
}
```

This would ensure that users named `mike` and `federico` are created on both *www.example.com* and *db.example.com*.

 Puppet offers multiple ways to test a module locally during development, without having to wait for the server (known as the *master* in Puppet lingo). One of the simplest is to manually apply a manifest matching the current node locally:

```
puppet apply manifest.pp
```

The client's parser can also validate syntax without actually executing any configuration changes:

```
puppet parser validate module.pp
```

Additionally, a very convenient validation tool called `puppet-lint` is available. `puppet-lint` will go beyond reporting errors and will also deliver style warnings and flag potential inconsistencies. Found in Ubuntu's universe repository, it is installed thus:

```
sudo apt install puppet-lint
```

One last option is to cause the client to immediately contact the server and apply any outstanding action. Although this is a more involved and time-consuming strategy, this "all up" test should provide final validation to your manifests:

```
sudo puppet agent --test
```

Another way of achieving this is to use the default node definition, which applies to every client that connects to the Puppet master. This configuration in the default node is applied to clients that do not have a node definition explicitly assigned to them.

To see Puppet in action, we will launch two EC2 instances—one to act as the master, the other as a client. The initial Puppet manifest will simply install the Nginx web server package and make sure it is running—something akin to a "Hello, World" for Puppet.

Example 4-1 shows a CloudFormation stack that will create the two EC2 instances, as well as two security groups. These are required to access both instances with SSH, and to allow the Puppet client to contact the master on TCP port 8140.

Example 4-1. Puppet master and client CloudFormation stack

```
{
    "AWSTemplateFormatVersion": "2010-09-09",
    "Description": "Example Puppet master and client stack (manual install)",

    "Parameters" : {
        "KeyName": {
```

```
            "Description" : "EC2 KeyPair name",
            "Type": "String",
            "MinLength": "1",
            "MaxLength": "255",
            "AllowedPattern" : "[\\x20-\\x7E]*",
            "ConstraintDescription" : "can contain only ASCII characters."
        },
        "AMI" : {
            "Description" : "AMI ID",
            "Type": "String"
        }
    },

    "Resources": {
        "PuppetClientGroup": {
            "Type": "AWS::EC2::SecurityGroup",
            "Properties": {
                "SecurityGroupIngress": [
                    {
                        "ToPort": "22",
                        "IpProtocol": "tcp",
                        "CidrIp": "0.0.0.0/0",
                        "FromPort": "22"
                    }
                ],
                "GroupDescription": "Group for Puppet clients"
            }
        },
        "PuppetMasterGroup": {
            "Type": "AWS::EC2::SecurityGroup",
            "Properties": {
                "SecurityGroupIngress": [
                    {
                        "ToPort": "8140",
                        "IpProtocol": "tcp",
                        "SourceSecurityGroupName" : { "Ref" : "PuppetClientGroup" },
                        "FromPort": "8140"
                    },
                    {
                        "ToPort": "22",
                        "IpProtocol": "tcp",
                        "CidrIp": "0.0.0.0/0",
                        "FromPort": "22"
                    }
                ],
                "GroupDescription": "Group for Puppet master"
            }
        },
        "PuppetMasterInstance": {
            "Type": "AWS::EC2::Instance",
            "Properties": {
                "ImageId" : { "Ref" : "AMI"},
```

```
                    "KeyName" : { "Ref" : "KeyName" },
                    "SecurityGroups": [
                        {
                            "Ref": "PuppetMasterGroup"
                        }
                    ],
                    "InstanceType": "t2.micro"
                }
            },
            "PuppetClientInstance": {
                "Type": "AWS::EC2::Instance",
                "Properties": {
                    "ImageId" : { "Ref" : "AMI"},
                    "KeyName" : { "Ref" : "KeyName" },
                    "SecurityGroups": [
                        {
                            "Ref": "PuppetClientGroup"
                        }
                    ],
                    "InstanceType": "t2.micro",
                    "UserData": {
                        "Fn::Base64": {
                            "Fn::GetAtt": [ "PuppetMasterInstance", "PrivateDnsName" ]
                        }
                    }
                }
            }
        },
        "Outputs" : {
            "PuppetMasterIP" : {
              "Description" : "Public IP of the Puppet master instance",
              "Value" : { "Fn::GetAtt" : [ "PuppetMasterInstance", "PublicIp" ] }
            },
            "PuppetClientIP" : {
              "Description" : "Public IP of the Puppet client instance",
              "Value" : { "Fn::GetAtt" : [ "PuppetClientInstance", "PublicIp" ] }
            },
            "PuppetMasterPrivateDNS" : {
              "Description" : "Private DNS of the Puppet master instance",
              "Value" : { "Fn::GetAtt" : [ "PuppetMasterInstance", "PrivateDnsName" ] }
            },
            "PuppetClientPrivateDNS" : {
              "Description" : "Private DNS of the Puppet client instance",
              "Value" : { "Fn::GetAtt" : [ "PuppetMasterInstance", "PrivateDnsName" ] }
            }
        }
    }
}
```

Save this stack template to a file named *puppet-stack.json*. Next, create the stack with the AWS command-line tools, remembering to replace the KeyName parameter to match your own key's:

```
$ aws cloudformation create-stack --region us-east-1 --stack-name puppet-stack \
    --template-body file://puppet-stack.json \
    --parameters ParameterKey=AMI,ParameterValue=ami-43a15f3e \
    ParameterKey=KeyName,ParameterValue=federico
{
    "StackId": "arn:aws:cloudformation:us-east-1:740376006796:stack/puppet-
stack/fdd3bed0-6838-11e8-aaa5-500c21792a35"
}
```

We used Ubuntu 16.04 "Xenial" in this example, but we will showcase this kind of
stack with different OS choices throughout the chapter. Once the stack has been created, list the stack resources to find out the IP address and DNS names of the two
instances:

```
$ aws cloudformation describe-stacks --stack-name puppet-stack | jq \
'.Stacks[0].Outputs[]'
{
  "OutputValue": "54.166.216.73",
  "OutputKey": "PuppetMasterIP",
  "Description": "Public IP of the Puppet master instance"
}
{
  "OutputValue": "54.175.109.196",
  "OutputKey": "PuppetClientIP",
  "Description": "Public IP of the Puppet client instance"
}
{
  "OutputValue": "ip-172-31-50-245.ec2.internal",
  "OutputKey": "PuppetClientPrivateDNS",
  "Description": "Private DNS of the Puppet client instance"
}
{
  "OutputValue": "ip-172-31-62-113.ec2.internal",
  "OutputKey": "PuppetMasterPrivateDNS",
  "Description": "Private DNS of the Puppet master instance"
}
```

Now we need to install the Puppet master and create the manifests that will install
Nginx on the client and make sure it is running.

Log in to the Puppet master host with SSH and install the Puppet master package—
this will also install the Puppet client package:

```
sudo apt update
sudo apt install --yes puppetmaster
sudo systemctl status puppetmaster
```

With the Puppet master installed, we can begin configuration. The following is a simple example of a *site.pp* file, which should be saved to */etc/puppet/manifests/site.pp*:

```
node default {
  package { 'nginx':
  ensure => installed
```

```
    }
    service { 'nginx':
    ensure => running,
    require=> Package['nginx']
    }
    file { '/tmp/hello_world':
    ensure => present,
    content=> 'Hello, World!'
    }
}
```

This *site.pp* file uses the default node definition, so it will be applied to any client that connects to the server. It will install Nginx and create a text file.

Now we can move on to the client. Connect to the client instance with SSH and install the Puppet client package:

```
sudo apt update
sudo apt install --yes puppet
```

Once installed, Puppet will run every 30 minutes by default. Unfortunately, this will not work immediately—usually your Puppet master will have a more friendly DNS name such as *puppet.example.com*. Because we have not yet set up DNS for the Puppet master, we must use its AWS-supplied DNS name. We further restrict access to the Puppet master by limiting client access exclusively to its private DNS and corresponding IP address. Security concerns dictate this policy, which we implement through dedicated security groups.

Puppet uses a key-based system for security. This provides two levels of protection: it ensures that communications between the master and clients are encrypted, and it also makes sure that only authorized clients can connect to the Puppet master and retrieve the configuration.

When a Puppet client first connects to the master, it will create a *key signing request* on the Puppet master. An administrator must authorize this request by running `puppet sign <hostname>`, which signs the key and confirms that the client is allowed to connect and retrieve its manifests file.

On the client, we configure the Puppet client by editing the file */etc/puppet/ puppet.conf* to point to the master. Append the following line to the [main] section:

```
server = internal DNS name of master
```

Now initialize the client by executing the following command:

```
$ sudo puppet agent --waitforcert 120 --test
Info: Creating a new SSL key for ip-172-31-50-245.ec2.internal
Info: Caching certificate for ca
Info: csr_attributes file loading from /home/ubuntu/.puppet/csr_attributes.yaml
Info: Creating a new SSL certificate request for ip-172-31-50-245.ec2.internal
Info: Certificate Request fingerprint (SHA256): 85:50:1D:FB:94:0F:50:0B:8B:3B:
```

```
5E:20:70:B9:7C:62:87:D9:89:76:85:90:70:79:AA:42:99:A1:CA:E9:19:77
Info: Caching certificate for ca
```

This command tells Puppet that it should wait up to 120 seconds for the key to be signed on the master.

On the master, immediately list the waiting requests with this command:

```
$ sudo puppet cert list
  "ip-172-31-50-245.ec2.internal" (SHA256) 85:50:1D:FB:94:0F:50:0B:8B:3B:5E:
20:70:B9:7C:62:87:D9:89:76:85:90:70:79:AA:42:99:A1:CA:E9:19:77
```

Sign the request, taking care to update the client's hostname to match that listed:

```
$ sudo puppet cert sign ip-172-31-50-245.ec2.internal
Notice: Signed certificate request for ip-172-31-50-245.ec2.internal
Notice: Removing file Puppet::SSL::CertificateRequest
ip-172-31-50-245.ec2.internal at '/var/lib/puppet/ssl/ca/requests/
ip-172-31-50-245.ec2.internal.pem'
```

Once you sign the request on the master, Puppet is nearly ready to do its job. Enable the client and make it spring into action and begin applying the configuration:

```
$ sudo puppet agent --enable
$ sudo puppet agent --test
Info: Caching certificate_revocation_list for ca
Info: Retrieving plugin
Info: Caching catalog for ip-172-31-50-245.ec2.internal
Info: Applying configuration version '1471818168'
Notice: /Stage[main]/Main/Node[default]/Package[nginx]/ensure: ensure changed
'purged' to 'present'
Notice: /Stage[main]/Main/Node[default]/File[/tmp/hello_world]/ensure: created
Info: Creating state file /var/lib/puppet/state/state.yaml
Notice: Finished catalog run in 6.77 seconds
```

Once Puppet finishes, the client instance will have installed and started Nginx, which can be verified by checking that the Nginx service is running:

```
sudo systemctl status nginx
```

The text file will also have been created:

```
cat /tmp/hello_world
```

Auto Scaling and Autosign: Disabling Certificate Security

Puppet's key-signing system is great when clients have a certain level of permanence, but when you are constantly creating and destroying hosts, it can become an impediment. Manually signing key requests is clearly not an option when combined with AWS Auto Scaling, which automatically launches instances in response to changes in required capacity.

Aware that this method of signing keys might not be suitable for all situations, Puppet makes it easy to disable it with a feature known as *autosigning*. This is done by populating the */etc/puppet/autosign.conf* file with a list of hostnames for which autosigning is enabled—when these hosts connect to the Puppet master, key checking will be bypassed. Autosign can be enabled globally by using a wildcard (*) as the hostname.

Disabling security measures always involves a trade-off. It is our view that, as long as your Puppet master is sufficiently protected by security groups or firewalls, enabling autosigning is an acceptable risk. This is the only practical way of using Puppet in conjunction with Auto Scaling, and to a lesser extent EC2 as a whole.

This example uses only two types of Puppet resources: a service and a file. The Puppet Documentation site maintains a list of all available resource types on its Type Reference page (*https://docs.puppet.com/puppet/latest/reference/type.html*).

Puppet is a very broad subject, covered in full detail in the recent *Learning Puppet 4* by Jo Rhett (O'Reilly). Jo's book is the most up-to-date tome covering Puppet, and the first to cover version 4 in depth.

Puppet and CloudFormation

The previous example shows how Puppet can make it easy to manage the configuration of EC2 instances. Previous chapters have shown how CloudFormation provides a similar function for provisioning EC2 resources. What about the combination of the two?

Amazon has built some aspects of configuration directly into CloudFormation. In addition to creating EC2 instances, it can automatically install packages and run services on those instances after they have launched. This means there is quite a lot of overlap between Puppet and CloudFormation, which can sometimes lead to questions over which should be responsible for particular tasks. If CloudFormation can handle many of the tasks usually handled by Puppet, do you even need to use Puppet?

CloudFormation's configuration management system works by embedding configuration data into the stack template, via the AWS::CloudFormation::Init metadata (*https://amzn.to/2nhZmAc*) attribute, which can be specified when declaring EC2 resources in stack templates. For example, this snippet would install the `puppet-server` package, using the Yum package manager:

```
"Resources": {
  "MyInstance": {
    "Type": "AWS::EC2::Instance",
    "Metadata" : {
      "AWS::CloudFormation::Init" : {
        "config" : {
          "packages" : {
```

```
      "yum": {
        "puppet-server": []
      }
    },
  [ truncated ]
```

When the instance is launched, this metadata is parsed, and the required packages are installed. The metadata is parsed by the cfn-init script (*http://docs.aws.amazon.com/ AWSCloudFormation/latest/UserGuide/cfn-init.html*), which also performs the actual package installation. This script, developed by Amazon, is preinstalled on all Amazon Linux AMIs and is also available for installation on other operating systems.

> The `cfn-init` script is preinstalled on Amazon Linux AMIs, but can also be installed manually on most Linux operating systems. Amazon provides RPM packages (for RedHat-based systems, and source code for others).
>
> `cfn-init` is short for *CloudFormation initialization*, which is a hint as to its purpose. It is executed during the instance's boot process, at a similar point in time to when */etc/rc.local-like* scripts are executed, by passing a shell script as user data to the instance.
>
> The script is responsible for performing post-boot configuration of the instance. It queries the EC2 API to find out information about the CloudFormation stack it is part of—for example, it looks at the `Metadata` attribute for the instance, to see which software packages should be installed.
>
> Remember that accessing the EC2 API requires the use of IAM credentials with permissions to query the API interface. Data such as tags and CloudFormation metadata is not directly available to the instance in the same way that user data is.

Because configuration information is contained within CloudFormation stack templates, it must be valid JSON. This means certain characters must be escaped, and strings can consist of only a single line (multiline strings can be created with the `Fn::Join` function).

Stack templates have a maximum size of 450 KB (50 KB when not using S3 to pass the template), which acts as a hard limit to how much configuration can be contained in a single stack. Nested stacks (*https://amzn.to/2M1xUFG*), though often less than convenient, may be a way to work around this limit.

Working around these limitations may make a dedicated configuration management tool like Puppet easier to work with, but that does not mean CloudFormation's tools are redundant.

Amazon maintains and supports its own Linux distribution, Amazon Linux, a derivative of Red Hat Enterprise Linux. Amazon Linux AMIs come preinstalled with a number of AWS tools, such as the latest versions of all command-line tools, and the `cfn-init` package.

More information is available on the Linux AMI page (*http://aws.amazon.com/amazon-linux-ami/*).

Combining CloudFormation and Puppet accomplishes the majority of the aims set out in the "Bootstrapping an Infrastructure" paper. CloudFormation can create the AWS resources that make up your infrastructure, and Puppet can configure the operating system and application.

Because both use text-based template files, everything can be stored in a version control system. By checking out a copy of your repository, you have absolutely everything you need to bootstrap your infrastructure to a running state.

To demonstrate a few of the CloudFormation configuration management features and see how they interact with Puppet, we will create an example stack that automatically installs and configures a Puppet master.

This can provide the base of an entirely bootstrapped infrastructure. Information describing both resources (EC2 instances) and application-level configuration is contained within a single stack template.

In this example we will be using the Amazon Linux AMI, which does not have Puppet *baked in*—that is, Puppet has not previously been installed when the instance launches. Instead, it will be installed by `cfn-init` when the instance has finished booting.

Example 4-2 shows a CloudFormation stack template that declares an EC2 instance resource and uses its metadata to install, configure, and run the Puppet master service. The template also includes some supplementary resources—the security groups required to access the SSH and Puppet services running on the instance.

The `PuppetMasterGroup` is a security group that will contain the Puppet master instance. It allows Puppet clients to access the master, and also allows SSH from anywhere so we can administer the instance.

Example 4-2. Puppet master CloudFormation stack

```
{
    "AWSTemplateFormatVersion": "2010-09-09",
    "Description": "Example Puppet master stack",
    "Parameters" : {
        "KeyName": {
            "Description" : "EC2 KeyPair name",
```

```json
            "Type": "String",
            "MinLength": "1",
            "MaxLength": "255",
            "AllowedPattern" : "[\\x20-\\x7E]*",
            "ConstraintDescription" : "can contain only ASCII characters."
        },
        "AMI" : {
            "Description" : "AMI ID",
            "Type": "String"
        }
    },
    "Resources": {
        "CFNKeys": { ❶
            "Type": "AWS::IAM::AccessKey",
            "Properties": {
                "UserName": {
                    "Ref": "CFNInitUser"
                }
            }
        },
        "CFNInitUser": {
            "Type": "AWS::IAM::User",
            "Properties": {
                "Policies": [
                    {
                      "PolicyName": "AccessForCFNInit",
                      "PolicyDocument": {
                         "Statement": [
                             {
                               "Action": "cloudformation:DescribeStackResource",
                               "Resource": "*",
                               "Effect": "Allow"
                             }
                         ]
                      }
                    }
                ]
            }
        },
        "PuppetClientSecurityGroup": { ❷
            "Type": "AWS::EC2::SecurityGroup",
            "Properties": {
             "SecurityGroupIngress": [
                 {
                   "ToPort": "22",
                   "IpProtocol": "tcp",
                   "CidrIp": "0.0.0.0/0",
                   "FromPort": "22"
                 }
             ],
             "GroupDescription": "Group for SSH access to Puppet clients"
            }
```

```
        },
    "PuppetMasterSecurityGroup": {❸
        "Type": "AWS::EC2::SecurityGroup",
        "Properties": {
         "SecurityGroupIngress": [
           {
            "ToPort": "8140",
            "IpProtocol": "tcp",
            "SourceSecurityGroupName": { "Ref": "PuppetClientSecurityGroup"},
            "FromPort": "8140"
           },
           {
            "ToPort": "22",
            "IpProtocol": "tcp",
            "CidrIp": "0.0.0.0/0",
            "FromPort": "22"
           }
         ],
         "GroupDescription": "Group for Puppet client to master communication"
        }
    },
    "PuppetMasterInstance": {
        "Type": "AWS::EC2::Instance",
        "Properties": {
            "UserData": {❹
                "Fn::Base64": {
                    "Fn::Join": [
                        "",
                        [
"#!/bin/bash\n",
"/opt/aws/bin/cfn-init --region ", { "Ref": "AWS::Region" },  " -s ",
{ "Ref": "AWS::StackName" }, " -r PuppetMasterInstance ",
" --access-key ", { "Ref": "CFNKeys" },
" --secret-key ", { "Fn::GetAtt": [ "CFNKeys", "SecretAccessKey" ] }, "\n"
                        ]
                    ]
                }
            },
            "KeyName": { "Ref" : "KeyName" },
            "SecurityGroups": [
                {
                    "Ref": "PuppetMasterSecurityGroup"
                }
            ],
            "InstanceType": "t2.micro",
            "ImageId": { "Ref" : "AMI" }❺
        },
        "Metadata": {
            "AWS::CloudFormation::Init": {
                "config": {
                    "files": {❻
                        "/etc/puppet/autosign.conf": {
```

```
                    "content": "*.internal\n",
                    "owner": "root",
                    "group": "wheel",
                    "mode": "100644"
                },
                "/etc/puppet/manifests/site.pp": {
                    "content": "import \"nodes\"\n",
                    "owner": "root",
                    "group": "wheel",
                    "mode": "100644"
                },
                "/etc/puppet/manifests/nodes.pp": {
                    "content": {
                        "Fn::Join": [
                            "",
                            [
                                "node basenode {\n",
                                " include cfn\n",
                                " package { 'nginx':\n",
                                " ensure => installed\n",
                                " }\n",
                                " service { 'nginx':\n",
                                " ensure => running,\n",
                                " require=> Package['nginx']\n",
                                " }\n",
                                "}\n",
                                "node /^.*internal$/ inherits basenode {\n",
                                "}\n"
                            ]
                        ]
                    },
                    "owner": "root",
                    "group": "wheel",
                    "mode": "100644"
                },
                "/etc/puppet/modules/cfn/lib/facter/cfn.rb": {
                    "owner": "root",
                    "source": "https://s3.amazonaws.com/cloudformation-
examples/cfn-facter-plugin.rb",
                    "group": "wheel",
                    "mode": "100644"
                },
                "/etc/yum.repos.d/epel.repo": {
                    "owner": "root",
                    "source": "https://s3.amazonaws.com/cloudformation-
examples/enable-epel-on-amazon-linux-ami",
                    "group": "root",
                    "mode": "000644"
                },
                "/etc/puppet/fileserver.conf": {
                    "content": "[modules]\n allow *.internal\n",
                    "owner": "root",
```

```
                    "group": "wheel",
                    "mode": "100644"
            },
            "/etc/puppet/puppet.conf": {
                "content": {❼ ❽
                    "Fn::Join": [
                        "",
                        [
                            "[main]\n",
                            " logdir=/var/log/puppet\n",
                            " rundir=/var/run/puppet\n",
                            " ssldir=$vardir/ssl\n",
                            " pluginsync=true\n",
                            "[agent]\n",
                            " classfile=$vardir/classes.txt\n",
                            " localconfig=$vardir/localconfig\n"
                        ]
                    ]
                },
                "owner": "root",
                "group": "root",
                "mode": "000644"
            },
            "/etc/puppet/modules/cfn/manifests/init.pp": {
                "content": "class cfn {}",
                "owner": "root",
                "group": "wheel",
                "mode": "100644"
            }
        },
        "packages": {❾
            "rubygems": {
                "json": []
            },
            "yum": {
                "gcc": [],
                "rubygems": [],
                "ruby-devel": [],
                "make": [],
                "puppet-server": [],
                "puppet": []
            }
        },
        "services": {❿
            "sysvinit": {
                "puppetmaster": {
                    "ensureRunning": "true",
                    "enabled": "true"
                }
            }
        }
    }
}
```

```
            }
          }
        }
      },
      "Outputs": {⓫
        "PuppetMasterPrivateDNS": {
          "Description": "Private DNS Name of PuppetMaster",
          "Value": {
            "Fn::GetAtt": [ "PuppetMasterInstance", "PrivateDnsName" ]
          }
        },
        "PuppetMasterPublicDNS": {
          "Description": "Public DNS Name of PuppetMaster",
          "Value": {
            "Fn::GetAtt": [ "PuppetMasterInstance", "PublicDnsName" ]
          }
        },
        "PuppetClientSecurityGroup": {
          "Description": "Name of the Puppet client Security Group",
          "Value": { "Ref" : "PuppetClientSecurityGroup" }
        }
      }
    }
}
```

❶ Remember that `cfn-init` requires an IAM user with access to the EC2 API. The `CFNKeys` and `CFNInitUser` resources declare an IAM user with permissions to describe all CloudFormation stack resources, and also an IAM access key and secret. These credentials are passed to the Puppet master instance via user data. The same result could be achieved by using IAM roles.

❷ The `PuppetClientGroup` is a security group that will be populated with Puppet client instances. Any members of this group will be allowed to contact the Puppet master on TCP port 8140 (the default Puppet master port).

❸ The `PuppetMasterGroup` is a security group that will contain the Puppet master instance. It allows Puppet clients to access the master, and also allows SSH from anywhere so we can administer the instance.

❹ The `User Data` attribute for the instance is a Base64-encoded shell script. This script runs the `cfn-init` program, passing it some information about the stack that it is part of. This includes the EC2 region, the stack name, and the IAM access key and secret that will be used to query the EC2 API.

Because JSON does not support multiline strings, the `Fn::Join` function is used to create a multiline shell script.

❺ Find the latest ID for the Amazon Linux AMI (*http://aws.amazon.com/amazon-linux-ami/*)—ami-6869aa05, built with Amazon Linux 2016.03, is a good choice at the time of writing. This value is passed as a parameter when creating the stack.

❻ Here is where the interesting part begins. Remember that the `cfn-init` script will retrieve this metadata after the instance has launched. The file's `Metadata` attribute lists a number of files that will be created on the instance, along with information about the file's user and group permissions.

❼ Files can be retrieved from remote sources such as web servers or S3. They will be downloaded when the instance launches. Basic HTTP authorization is supported.

❽ Alternatively, the content can be explicitly set, using the `Fn::Join` function to create multiline files.

❾ Software packages can be installed from multiple sources—this example shows some Ruby gems being installed, along with some packages from the Yum package manager.

❿ Finally, we specify that the Puppet master service should be enabled (i.e., it should start automatically when the instance boots) and running.

⑪ The `Outputs` section makes it easier to retrieve information about the resources in your stack. Here, we are specifying that we want to access the private DNS name of the Puppet master instance and the name of the Puppet client security group.

 This example is based on Amazon's documentation (*http://bit.ly/2LUKhmB*), which you can access for further information and additional examples of what can be done with Puppet and Cloud-Formation.

Create the stack with the command-line tools:

```
aws cloudformation create-stack --stack-name puppet-master --template-body \
    file://puppet_master_cloudformation.json \
    --region us-east-1 --capabilities CAPABILITY_IAM \
    --parameters ParameterKey=AMI,ParameterValue=ami-6869aa05 \
    ParameterKey=KeyName,ParameterValue=federico
```

Because this stack will create an IAM user, we need to add the `--capabilities CAPABILITY_IAM` option to the command. Without this setting,

CloudFormation would refuse to create the IAM user. Capabilities are used to prevent some forms of privilege escalation, such as a malicious user creating an IAM policy granting access to resources that the user would not otherwise have access to.

Once the stack has been created, we can find out the Puppet master's DNS name and the security group by querying the stack's outputs:

```
aws cloudformation describe-stacks --stack-name puppet-master | jq \
  '.Stacks[0].Outputs[]'
```

To verify that everything is working as expected, log in to the instance with SSH and check whether the puppetmaster service is running.

 cfn-init halts client-side execution upon encountering the first error, but the default behavior of a stack is to rollback a failed initialization, decommissioning all stack resources. In order to more easily troubleshoot a problem, set DisableRollback in your create-stack calls (in the console, this is called *Rollback on failure*). This makes debugging a very linear process, but also a straightforward one. All support binaries are found under */opt/aws/bin/*, and initialization is logged at */var/log/cfn-init.log* and */var/log/cfn-init-cmd.log*.

Now that we know the Puppet master is up and running, we can bring up a client to demonstrate it in action.

Example 4-3 shows a CloudFormation stack that declares a Puppet client instance. This instance, when launched, will connect to our Puppet master and retrieve its configuration—in this case, it will install Nginx on the client.

We will use two parameters—one for the Puppet master's DNS name and one for the Puppet client security group. The parameters to this stack are the output of the previous stack.

Example 4-3. Puppet client CloudFormation stack

```
{
    "AWSTemplateFormatVersion": "2010-09-09",
    "Description": "Example Puppet client stack",
    "Parameters" : {❶
      "KeyName": {
        "Description" : "EC2 KeyPair name",
        "Type": "String",
        "MinLength": "1",
        "MaxLength": "255",
        "AllowedPattern" : "[\\x20-\\x7E]*",
        "ConstraintDescription" : "can contain only ASCII characters."
      },
```

```json
    "AMI" : {
      "Description" : "AMI ID",
      "Type": "String"
    },
    "PuppetMasterDNS" : {
      "Description" : "Private DNS name of the Puppet master instance",
      "Type": "String"
    },
    "PuppetClientSecurityGroup" : {
      "Description" : "Name of the Puppet client Security Group",
      "Type": "String"
    }
  },

  "Resources": {
      "CFNKeys": {
          "Type": "AWS::IAM::AccessKey",
          "Properties": {
              "UserName": {
                  "Ref": "CFNInitUser"
              }
          }
      },
      "CFNInitUser": {
          "Type": "AWS::IAM::User",
          "Properties": {
              "Policies": [
                  {
                  "PolicyName": "AccessForCFNInit",
                  "PolicyDocument": {
                      "Statement": [
                          {
                          "Action": "cloudformation:DescribeStackResource",
                          "Resource": "*",
                          "Effect": "Allow"
                          }
                      ]
                  }
                  }
              ]
          }
      },
      "PuppetClientInstance": {
          "Type": "AWS::EC2::Instance",
          "Properties": {
              "UserData": {❷
                  "Fn::Base64": {
                      "Fn::Join": [
                          "",
                          [
"#!/bin/bash\n",
"/opt/aws/bin/cfn-init --region ", { "Ref": "AWS::Region" },  " -s ",
```

```
                { "Ref": "AWS::StackName" }, " -r PuppetClientInstance ",
        " --access-key ", { "Ref": "CFNKeys" },
        " --secret-key ", { "Fn::GetAtt": [ "CFNKeys", "SecretAccessKey" ] }
                                        ]
                                    ]
                                }
                            },
                    "KeyName": { "Ref" : "KeyName" },
                    "SecurityGroups": [
                        {
                            "Ref": "PuppetClientSecurityGroup"
                        }
                    ],
                    "InstanceType": "t2.micro",
                    "ImageId": { "Ref" : "AMI" }
                },
            "Metadata": {
                "AWS::CloudFormation::Init": {
                    "config": {
                        "files": {
                            "/etc/puppet/puppet.conf": {
                                "content": {
                                    "Fn::Join": [
                                        "",
                                        [
                    "[main]\n",
                    " server=", { "Ref": "PuppetMasterDNS" }, "\n",
                    " logdir=/var/log/puppet\n",
                    " rundir=/var/run/puppet\n",
                    " ssldir=$vardir/ssl\n",
                    " pluginsync=true\n",
                    "[agent]\n",
                    " classfile=$vardir/classes.txt\n",
                    " localconfig=$vardir/localconfig\n"
                                        ]
                                    ]
                                },
                                "owner": "root",
                                "group": "root",
                                "mode": "000644"
                            }
                        },
                        "packages": { ❸
                            "rubygems": {
                                "json": []
                            },
                            "yum": {
                                "gcc": [],
                                "rubygems": [],
                                "ruby-devel": [],
                                "make": [],
                                "puppet": []
```

```
                    }
                },
                "services": { ❹
                    "sysvinit": {
                        "puppet": {
                            "ensureRunning": "true",
                            "enabled": "true"
                        }
                    }
                }
            }
        }
    }
},
"Outputs" : {
    "PuppetClientIP" : {
        "Description" : "Public IP of the Puppet client instance",
        "Value" : { "Fn::GetAtt" : [ "PuppetClientInstance", "PublicIp" ] }
    },
    "PuppetClientPrivateDNS" : {
        "Description" : "Private DNS of the Puppet client instance",
        "Value" : { "Fn::GetAtt" : [ "PuppetMasterInstance", "PrivateDnsName" ] }
    }
}
}
```

❶ The parameters define values that can be specified by the user when the stack is launched. If a value is not specified, the default is used. If no default is set, attempting to create the stack without specifying a value will result in an error message.

❷ The user data for this instance is the same as in the previous example: run `cfn-init`, and let it configure the instance according to the `Metadata` attributes.

❸ We need to install only the Puppet package, as Puppet master is not required on clients.

❹ Finally, we start the Puppet agent, which will periodically connect to the master and retrieve its configuration.

Because this stack uses parameters, creating it requires a slightly different invocation of the command-line tools. We need to pass the output of the previous stack as parameters, like so:

```
aws cloudformation create-stack --stack-name puppet-client --template-body \
    file://puppet_client_cloudformation.json \
    --region us-east-1 --capabilities CAPABILITY_IAM \
    --parameters ParameterKey=AMI,ParameterValue=ami-6869aa05 \
```

```
ParameterKey=KeyName,ParameterValue=federico \
ParameterKey=PuppetMasterDNS,ParameterValue=ip-172-31-48-10.ec2.internal \
ParameterKey=PuppetClientSecurityGroup,ParameterValue=puppet-master-
PuppetClientSecurityGroup-YI5PIW673C1N
```

Once the stack has been created, we can log in to the client instance and check its status. Remember, it takes a few minutes for Puppet to run, so if you log in to the instance immediately after it finishes booting, the Puppet run might still be in progress. Puppet will write its logs to /var/log/puppet/, so check this location first if you need to troubleshoot.

Consider what this example achieves, in the context of the "Bootstrapping an Infrastructure" paper. We have deployed a fully automated Puppet master, which did not require any manual configuration whatsoever. Once that was running, we used it to bootstrap the rest of the environment—again, without any manual configuration.

If your CloudFormation stacks are stored in (for example) GitHub, your disaster recovery plan can be summarized in four steps:

1. Check out your GitHub repository.
2. Install the AWS command-line tools.
3. Launch the Puppet master stack.
4. Launch the Puppet client stack.

This is incredibly easy to document, and the steps can be followed without requiring expertise in Puppet (or indeed, Nginx).

There are a few deficiencies in this workflow that make it somewhat inconvenient to use in production. For example, if your Puppet master's DNS name changes—which will happen if the instance is stopped and restarted, or terminated and replaced with a new instance—you will need to delete and re-create your Puppet client stack to pick up the new changes. This is clearly suboptimal—as we improve on this stack through the rest of the book, we will look at ways to make this easier to use in production. To solve the "changing DNS name" problem, we will use Route 53 to automatically assign DNS names to our instances, so our Puppet master will always be reachable at puppet.example.com.

Another potential improvement is in how files are created on the instance. The Puppet master stack demonstrates two methods: pulling files from HTTP sites and explicitly defining the content in the stack template. There are other options available, such as retrieving files from an S3 bucket.

It is worth noting that there is nothing specific to Puppet in this example. The same concept could be used to bootstrap any configuration management software, such as Chef or Ansible, or indeed any software package that can be installed with Apt, Yum, Ruby gems, pip, or any other package manager supported by CloudFormation.

There is a lot of overlap between CloudFormation and configuration management tools. While it would technically be possible to replace most of Puppet's core features with CloudFormation, it would be a lot less convenient than using a dedicated configuration management tool. If your instance configuration is very simple, CloudFormation might suffice on its own—we find it simpler to put configuration management in place from the beginning.

User Data and Tags

AWS provides two built-in mechanisms to provide data to your EC2 instances: user data and tags. User data is supplied to the instance at launch time and cannot be changed without restarting the instance. Tags are more flexible—these key/value pairs can be changed at any point during the instance's lifecycle.

Both of these methods can be used to provide data to your EC2 instances, which can then be used by your scripts and applications. These building blocks enable several useful features. For example, you can create an AMI that can perform two roles (e.g., running a web server or a database, but not both). When launching an instance from this AMI, you could set a role=web or role=dbms tag. The launch scripts on the AMI would read this tag and know whether it should start Nginx or PostgreSQL.

Before the introduction of tags, it was necessary to build your own inventory storage system if you wanted to keep track of particular details about your instances. With tags, EC2 is itself its own inventory system. While user data is available only within an individual EC2 instance, tags can be queried externally by any party with authorized API access.

Tags and user data—and the differences between them—are described in more detail in "Mapping Instances to Roles" on page 272. For now, it is worth knowing that we can use tags both within EC2 instances and from applications running outside AWS, a kind of inventory management system that stores metadata for each instance.

CloudFormation also uses tags. For example, when an EC2 instance is created as part of a CloudFormation stack, it is automatically tagged with the name and ID of the CloudFormation stack to which it belongs.

In relation to configuration management tools, tags and user data are both extremely useful features. Through the use of Facter plug-ins (which gather additional information about your systems), Puppet is able to access user data and tags and use them as standard variables in its configuration manifests.

CloudFormation is most commonly used as a boot-time configuration tool—something reflected in its general design. However, the availability of the cfn-hup helper daemon (*https://amzn.to/2nfgrKX*) overturns this assumption: cfn-hup monitors resource metadata for changes, and applies any new client-side configuration when necessary. The stack template of a running stack can be updated with the update-stack CLI command (*https://amzn.to/2ni99Gk*).

Typically, Puppet uses the hostname of the instance to decide which configuration should be applied. Because EC2 instances have autogenerated hostnames, this is not immediately useful. One way to work around this problem is to use user data to control which configuration should be applied. We will do this by providing JSON-formatted user data that can be read by Puppet.

To begin, launch a new Ubuntu instance—we will use 14.04 "Trusty" this time, with the following user data:

```
{"role": "web"}
```

This is a JSON-formatted string simply containing a role=web key/value pair:

```
$ aws ec2 run-instances --image-id ami-c80b0aa2 --region us-east-1 \
  --key federico --security-groups ssh --instance-type t2.micro \
  --user-data '{"role": "web"}' --output text
740376006796    r-453484fb
INSTANCES       0       x86_64          False   xen     ami-c80b0aa2
i-4f5f827e      t2.micro        federico        2016-08-29T11:37:54.000Z
ip-172-31-54-180.ec2.internal   172.31.54.180           /dev/sda1       ebs
True            subnet-2a45b400 hvm     vpc-934935f7
[output truncated]
```

Once the instance has launched, you can verify the user data has reached the instance by logging in and running the ec2metadata command:

```
$ ec2metadata
ami-id: ami-c80b0aa2
ami-launch-index: 0
ami-manifest-path: (unknown)
ancestor-ami-ids: unavailable
availability-zone: us-east-1a
block-device-mapping: ami
ephemeral0
ephemeral1
root
instance-action: none
instance-id: i-4f5f827e
instance-type: t2.micro
local-hostname: ip-172-31-54-180.ec2.internal
local-ipv4: 172.31.54.180
kernel-id: unavailable
```

```
mac: unavailable
profile: default-hvm
product-codes: unavailable
public-hostname: ec2-54-208-246-122.compute-1.amazonaws.com
public-ipv4: 54.208.246.122
public-keys: ['ssh-rsa AAAAB3NzaC1yc2EAAAABIwAAAQEA83H2O96JIchWxmFMI-
TAfQ4mgfgP4CgF2mZteBdwHnWVgiMlzwnL/zfAoAUeKCgFZ+H5L2qxv3aERoipnFwUVI1Y0Ym7IjWs
+CgadDMsfJr1MsitFdLhRTu8D8kYg4E32FeKn4ZNJN/QxANj15bNDZ2XYTE1v/0QWSorao0NQv7bK/
anN7IuPtfPjbhXwTLVVbHSG5SErIMSqVbksj0r1pzjnBxAmmeXdHHmQV889oMsHEpvWFroGIRsTo-
pYmVe7H8d2+P6lZgkz3WrDCOdoGwTWvbnfNHonYvE0wSQro/
nEa1b7OB3i23tLzque7Z0PdUPKvg48JaLSEBiL6ydLCyw== federico']
ramdisk-id: unavailable
reserveration-id: unavailable
security-groups: ssh
user-data: {"role": "web"}
```

We install Puppet and its stdlib library from the upstream Puppet repositories, as we need a newer version of Facter than what is included in Ubuntu 14.04 for our code to work correctly. Using Trusty in this run enables us to illustrate how to work with packages not part of the default repositories—these steps are not required if you use Xenial or Bionic instead, which carry newer versions of Facter in their repositories (see Example 4-4).

Example 4-4. Installing Puppet's upstream release

```
wget --quiet http://apt.puppet.com/puppetlabs-release-trusty.deb
sudo dpkg -i puppetlabs-release-trusty.deb
sudo apt update
# Should not be installed, but just in case we caught you using an old instance...
sudo apt remove --yes puppet puppet-common
# Install latest version of puppet from PuppetLabs repo
sudo apt install --yes puppet facter -t trusty
#install the stdlib module
sudo puppet module install puppetlabs-stdlib
rm puppetlabs-release-trusty.deb
```

Now create a new file */etc/puppet/manifests/site.pp* with the contents shown in Example 4-5.

Example 4-5. Puppet and user data

```
require stdlib

node default {

    $userdata = parsejson($ec2_userdata)

    $role = $userdata['role']

    case $role {
```

```
    "web": {
        require my_web_module
    }
    "db": {
        require my_database_module
    }
    default: { fail("Unrecognised role: $role") }
    }

}
```

This file is responsible for changing the behavior of Puppet so that it ignores the hostname of the instance and instead looks at the user data. node default indicates that the following configuration should be applied to all nodes, regardless of their hostname. We then use the parsejson function to read the EC2 user data string into a Puppet variable. Finally, we include a different module depending on the value of the $role variable.

You could proceed with running this example by executing puppet apply /etc/puppet/manifests/site.pp. Because we have not yet created a my_web_module, Puppet will fail. However, it will fail with an error that my_web_module could not be found, demonstrating that our underlying theory is indeed working as planned:

```
$ facter --version
2.4.6
$ puppet apply /etc/puppet/manifests/site.pp
Error: Could not find class my_web_module for ip-172-31-54-180.ec2.internal on
node ip-172-31-54-180.ec2.internal
Error: Could not find class my_web_module for ip-172-31-54-180.ec2.internal on
node ip-172-31-54-180.ec2.internal
```

In the following section, we will use tags to look up instances based on the role they are tagged with and then execute shell scripts on the returned instances.

Executing Tasks with Fabric

The standard way to run Puppet is to allow the clients to contact the master according to a regular schedule, either using Puppet's internal scheduling (when running as a daemon) or a tool such as cron. This lets you make changes on the central Puppet server, knowing that they will eventually propagate out to your instances.

Sometimes, it can be useful to take more control over the process and run Puppet only when you know there are changes you would like to apply. To take a common example, let's say you have a cluster of Nginx web servers behind an Elastic Load Balancer, and you would like to deploy a configuration change that will cause Nginx to restart. Allowing Puppet to run on all instances at the same time would restart all of your Nginx servers at the same time, leaving you with zero functional web servers for a brief period.

In this case, it would be better to run Puppet on a few instances at a time, so that there are always enough running Nginx instances to service incoming requests.

In some cases, it is necessary to do additional work either before or after a Puppet run. Continuing with the example of web servers behind an Elastic Load Balancer—if you just need to restart Nginx, it is sufficient to leave the machine *in service* (active) while Puppet runs, as Nginx will not take a long time to restart. But what if you need to perform an operation that might take a few minutes? In this rolling-update scenario, you will need to remove the instance from the ELB, update it, and then return it to service—not something easily achieved with Puppet alone.

Several tools are dedicated to simplifying the task of running commands on groups of servers. Fabric is particularly flexible when it comes to working with EC2 instances and traditional hardware alike, and we will use it for the following examples.

Fabric is a Python tool used to automate system administration tasks. It provides a basic set of operations (such as executing commands and transferring files) that can be combined with some custom logic to build powerful and flexible deployment systems, or simply make it easier to perform routine tasks on groups of servers or EC2 instances. Because Boto is also Python-based, we can use it to quickly integrate with AWS services.

Tasks are defined by writing Python functions, which are usually stored in a file named *fabfile.py*. These functions use Fabric's Python API to perform actions on remote hosts. Here is a simple example of a Fabric file supplied by *fabfile.org*:

```
from fabric.api import run

def host_type():
    run('uname -s')
```

The `host_type` task can be executed on numerous servers. For example:

```
$ fab -H localhost,linuxbox host_type
[localhost] run: uname -s
[localhost] out: Darwin
[linuxbox] run: uname -s
[linuxbox] out: Linux

Done.
Disconnecting from localhost... done.
Disconnecting from linuxbox... done.
```

Fabric understands the concept of *roles*—collections of servers, grouped by the role they perform (or some other factor). Using roles, we can easily do things like running Task A on all web servers, followed by Task B on all database servers.

Roles are typically defined in your Fabric file as a static collection of roles and the hostnames of their members. However, they can also be created dynamically by executing Python functions, which means roles can be populated by querying the AWS API with Boto. This means we can execute Task A on all EC2 instances tagged with role=webserver, without needing to keep track of a list of instances.

To demonstrate this, we will launch an instance and then use Fabric to execute commands on that host.

Mike has written a small Python package containing a helper function that makes it easy to look up EC2 instances using tags. It is used in the following example and can be downloaded from GitHub (*https://github.com/mikery/fabric-ec2*).

Begin by installing Fabric and the helper library as follows:

```
pip install fabric
sudo apt install git --yes
pip install git+git://github.com/mikery/fabric-ec2.git
```

Using the Management Console or command-line tools, launch a t2.micro EC2 instance and provide it with some EC2 tags. For this example, we will use two tags— *staging:true* and *role:web*:

```
aws ec2 create-tags --resources i-3b20870a --tags Key=role,Value=web \
    Key=staging,Value=true
```

While the instance is launching, create a file named *fabfile.py*, which will store our Fabric tasks and configuration. You could also give it another name, but you will need to pass this as an option when executing Fabric—for example, fab --fabfile=/ some/file.py. The file should contain the following contents:

```
from fabric.api import run, sudo, env
from fabric_ec2 import EC2TagManager

def configure_roles():
    """ Set up the Fabric env.roledefs, using the correct roles for the given
    environment
    """
    tags = EC2TagManager(common_tags={'staging': 'true'})

    roles = {}
    for role in ['web', 'db']:
        roles[role] = tags.get_instances(role=role)

    return roles

env.roledefs = configure_roles()

def hostname():
        run('hostname')
```

Once the instance has launched, the Fabric task can be executed thus:

```
$ fab -u ubuntu hostname --roles web
[ec2-54-161-199-160.compute-1.amazonaws.com] Executing task 'hostname'
[ec2-54-161-199-160.compute-1.amazonaws.com] run: hostname
[ec2-54-161-199-160.compute-1.amazonaws.com] out: ip-172-31-62-71
[ec2-54-161-199-160.compute-1.amazonaws.com] out:


Done.
Disconnecting from ec2-54-161-199-160.compute-1.amazonaws.com... done.
```

Fabric will use the EC2 API to find the hostname of any instances that match the tag query and then perform the requested task on each of them. In our example case, it will have found only our single test instance.

With this in place, you have a simple way of running tasks—including applying Puppet manifests—selectively across your infrastructure. Fabric provides an excellent base for automating your deployment and orchestration processes.

Because tasks are just Python functions, they can be used to do helpful things. Before deploying to a web server instance, Fabric can first remove it from an ELB and wait for live traffic to stop hitting the instance before it is updated.

Masterless Puppet

So far, we have been working with Puppet in the typical master/client topology. This is the most common way to run Puppet, especially when working with physical hardware, outside of a cloud environment.

Puppet has another mode of operation, which does not require a master server: in *local mode*, where the client is responsible for applying its own configuration rather than relying on a master server.

There are two key reasons that make this useful when working with AWS.

The first is availability. When Puppet runs during the instance boot process, it becomes a core part of your infrastructure. If the Puppet master is unavailable, Auto Scaling will not work properly, and your application might become unavailable. Although you can deploy a cluster of Puppet masters to increase resilience to failures and load, it can be simply easier to remove it from the equation.

The second reason relates to Auto Scaling. Given that AWS can launch new instances in response to changing factors such as traffic levels, we cannot predict when new instances will be launched. In environments where large numbers of instances are launched simultaneously, it is possible to overwhelm the Puppet master, leading to delays in auto scaling or even instances that fail to launch properly as Puppet is never able to complete its configuration run.

When operating in local mode, an instance is more self-contained: it does not rely on an operational Puppet master in order to become operational itself. As a result, you have one less single point of failure within your infrastructure.

As always, there is a trade-off to be considered—there's no such thing as a free lunch, after all. A number of useful features rely on a master/client setup, so moving to a masterless topology means these features are no longer available. These include things like Puppet Dashboard (*https://github.com/sodabrew/puppet-dashboard*), which provides an automatically populated inventory based on data supplied by clients, and exported resources (*http://bit.ly/2vyi2PC*).

In practical terms, applying a configuration without a Puppet master is simply a case of executing the following:

```
puppet apply /etc/puppet/manifests/site.pp
```

This will trigger the usual Puppet logic, where the node's hostname is used to control which configuration will be applied. It is also possible to apply a specific manifest:

```
puppet apply /etc/puppet/modules/mymodule/manifests/site.pp
```

This does mean that the Puppet manifests must be stored on every instance, which can be achieved in various ways. They can be baked into the AMI if they do not change frequently, or deployed alongside your application code if they do.

We can use a modified version of Example 4-3 to create a CloudFormation stack with embedded Puppet manifests. Example 4-6 shows the updated stack template.

Example 4-6. Masterless Puppet CloudFormation stack

```
{
    "AWSTemplateFormatVersion" : "2010-09-09",
    "Description": "Example Puppet masterless stack",
    "Parameters" : {
        "KeyName": {
            "Description" : "EC2 KeyPair name",
            "Type": "String",
            "MinLength": "1",
            "MaxLength": "255",
            "AllowedPattern" : "[\\x20-\\x7E]*",
            "ConstraintDescription" : "can contain only ASCII characters."
        },
        "AMI" : {
            "Description" : "AMI ID",
            "Type": "String"
        }
    },
    "Resources" : {
        "CFNKeys": {
            "Type": "AWS::IAM::AccessKey",
```

```json
        "Properties": {
            "UserName": {
                "Ref": "CFNInitUser"
            }
        }
    },
    "CFNInitUser": {
        "Type": "AWS::IAM::User",
        "Properties": {
            "Policies": [
                {
                    "PolicyName": "AccessForCFNInit",
                    "PolicyDocument": {
                        "Statement": [
                          {
                            "Action": "cloudformation:DescribeStackResource",
                            "Resource": "*",
                            "Effect": "Allow"
                          }
                        ]
                    }
                }
            ]
        }
    },
    "NginxInstance" : {
        "Type" : "AWS::EC2::Instance",
        "Metadata" : {
            "AWS::CloudFormation::Init" : {
                "config" : {
                    "packages" : {
                        "yum" : {
                            "puppet" : [],
                            "ruby-devel" : [],
                            "gcc" : [],
                            "make" : [],
                            "rubygems" : []
                        },
                        "rubygems" : {
                            "json" : []
                        }
                    },
                    "files" : {
                        "/etc/yum.repos.d/epel.repo" : {
                        "source" : "https://s3.amazonaws.com/cloudformation-
examples/enable-epel-on-amazon-linux-ami",
                        "mode" : "000644",
                        "owner" : "root",
                        "group" : "root"
                        },
                        "/etc/puppet/autosign.conf" : {
                            "content" : "*.internal\n",
```

```
                    "mode" : "100644",
                    "owner" : "root",
                    "group" : "wheel"
                },
                "/etc/puppet/puppet.conf" : {
                    "content" : { "Fn::Join" : ["", [
                        "[main]\n",
                        " logdir=/var/log/puppet\n",
                        " rundir=/var/run/puppet\n",
                        " ssldir=$vardir/ssl\n",
                        " pluginsync=true\n",
                        "[agent]\n",
                        " classfile=$vardir/classes.txt\n",
                        " localconfig=$vardir/localconfig\n"]] },
                    "mode" : "000644",
                    "owner" : "root",
                    "group" : "root"
                },
                "/etc/puppet/manifests/site.pp" : {
                    "content" : { "Fn::Join" : ["", [
                        "node basenode {\n",
                        "  package { 'nginx':\n",
                        "    ensure => present\n",
                        "  }\n\n",
                        "  service { 'nginx':\n",
                        "    ensure => running,\n",
                        "    require=> Package['nginx']\n",
                        "  }\n",
                        "}\n",
                        "node /^.*internal$/ inherits basenode {\n",
                        "}\n"
                        ]]
                    }
                },
                "mode" : "100644",
                "owner" : "root",
                "group" : "wheel"
            }
        }
    }
},
"Properties" : {
    "InstanceType" : "t2.micro",
    "SecurityGroups" : [ { "Ref" : "NginxGroup" } ],
    "KeyName": { "Ref" : "KeyName" },
    "ImageId": { "Ref" : "AMI" },
    "UserData" : { "Fn::Base64" : { "Fn::Join" : ["", [
"#!/bin/bash\n",
"/opt/aws/bin/cfn-init --region ", { "Ref" : "AWS::Region" },
" -s ", { "Ref" : "AWS::StackName" }, " -r NginxInstance ",
" --access-key ", { "Ref" : "CFNKeys" },
" --secret-key ", { "Fn::GetAtt" : ["CFNKeys", "SecretAccessKey"]}, "\n",
```

```
"/usr/bin/puppet apply /etc/puppet/manifests/site.pp", "\n"]]}}
            }
        },
        "NginxGroup" : {
            "Type" : "AWS::EC2::SecurityGroup",
            "Properties" : {
                "SecurityGroupIngress": [
                    {
                        "ToPort": "22",
                        "IpProtocol": "tcp",
                        "CidrIp": "0.0.0.0/0",
                        "FromPort": "22"
                    }
                ],
                "GroupDescription" : "Security Group for managed Nginx"
            }
        }
    },
    "Outputs" : {
     "NginxDNSName" : {
      "Value" : { "Fn::GetAtt" : [ "NginxInstance", "PublicDnsName" ] },
      "Description" : "DNS Name of Nginx managed instance"
     }
    }
}
```

The CloudFormation metadata on the `NginxInstance` resource ensures that the Puppet client package is installed, but that the Puppet agent service is not running. If it were, it would be regularly trying to connect to a nonexistent Puppet master.

The metadata also declares the Puppet configuration files that will be created on the instance. In this example, */etc/puppet/manifests/sites.pp* contains a basic manifest that installs the Nginx web server package and ensures it is running.

One of the properties, `UserData`, contains a script that runs `puppet apply` when the instance launches, applying the configuration manifest stored in *site.pp*.

Creating this stack will launch an EC2 instance that automatically installs and runs Nginx, without any reliance on a Puppet master. Although the Puppet manifests used in the example were basic, they can be expanded upon to build a more complicated infrastructure.

For more information about running Puppet in standalone mode, and other ways of scaling Puppet, see Puppet's documentation (*https://puppet.com/blog/deploying-puppet-client-server-standalone-and-massively-scaled-environments*).

Building AMIs with Packer

AMI creation is a tedious process that should be automated as soon as possible. Making AMIs manually is slow and error prone, and installing the same packages over and over will soon get tiresome, making some type of configuration management tool a necessity.

This section presents some ways to automate the process of developing and building AMIs.

When starting out with AWS, a lot of people use a simple workflow for creating AMIs: launch an instance, manually install packages and edit configuration files, and then create an AMI (version 1).

To change the AMI, the same process is followed: launch the current version of the AMI, make some configuration changes, and then create a new AMI (version 2).

This is all well and good for getting up and running quickly, but by the time you reach version 10, you have a problem on your hands. Unless you have been meticulously documenting the changes you have made, repeating this process will be difficult. You will have no changelog describing what was changed when, why, and by whom.

This trap should be avoided as soon as possible. You should always use a configuration management tool to help create AMIs so that the process can be easily automated. Automating this process means you can release changes faster, without wasting time manually creating AMIs.

HashiCorp's Packer (*http://packer.io*) is a tool for automating the process of creating machine images. It can use various configuration management tools—including Chef, Puppet, and Salt—to create images for several platforms, including AWS. Where AMIs are concerned, we already discussed SUSE studio as the interactive tool of choice, while Packer is by far the most widely preferred automation option.

Packer automates the following processes:

- Launching a new EC2 instance
- Applying a configuration
- Creating an AMI
- Adding tags to the AMI
- Terminating the instance

Once configured, these processes can be performed with a single command. Integrating Packer with continuous integration tools such as Jenkins means you can completely automate the process of creating new AMIs and perhaps release newly created AMIs into your staging environment automatically.

We will use Packer to build an AMI with Nginx installed. Nginx will be installed by Puppet, demonstrating how to use configuration management tools in combination with Packer.

Begin by installing Packer according to its installation instructions (*http://www.packer.io/docs/installation.html*). Packer 0.10.1 ships as a single compressed binary on its developer's site:

```
wget https://releases.hashicorp.com/packer/0.10.1/packer_0.10.1_linux_amd64.zip
unzip packer_0.10.1_linux_amd64.zip
```

Once Packer has been installed in your path, create a new directory to work in, containing the subdirectories required for the Puppet manifest files:

```
mkdir packer_example
cd packer_example
mkdir -p puppet/{manifests,modules/nginx/manifests}
```

Create a file named *puppet/manifests/site.pp* with the following contents:

```
node default {
    require nginx
}
```

This will instruct Puppet to apply the Nginx class to any node using this configuration. Next, create a file named *puppet/modules/nginx/manifests/init.pp* with the following contents:

```
class nginx {
    package { 'nginx':
        ensure => present
    }

    service { 'nginx':
        ensure => running
    }
}
```

This is a riff on the theme of our previous manifests, accomplishing the same outcome but using Puppet classes for variety. There are no virtual hosts configured, so Nginx will just display the default welcome page as configured on your operating system.

In this example, we will be using Ubuntu 14.04. We already demonstrated the use of newer builds than those available in Trusty's repositories in the Ubuntu Archive to sidestep some bugs in Facter's EC2 user data parsing, and we want to maintain this capability. We will use a shell script to add Puppet Lab's *apt* repository and install the most recent version of Puppet.

Create a file named *install_puppet.sh* in our example's directory, containing the same code used in Example 4-4.

We can now move on to the Packer configuration.

It is important to understand two Packer concepts for this section:

Provisioners

These control which tools will be used to configure the image—for example, Puppet or Chef. Multiple provisioners can be specified in the Packer configuration, and they will each be run sequentially.

Builders

These are the outputs of Packer. In our case, we are building an AMI. You could also build images for VMware, OpenStack, VirtualBox, and other platforms. By using multiple builders with the same provisioner configuration, it is possible to create identical virtual machines across multiple cloud environments.

Example 4-7 shows the configuration file we will use to build our example AMI.

Example 4-7. Packer example

```
{
  "variables": {
    "aws_access_key": "",
    "aws_secret_key": ""
  },
  "provisioners": [
    {
      "type": "shell",
      "script": "install_puppet.sh"
    },
    { "type": "puppet-masterless",
      "manifest_file": "puppet/manifests/site.pp",
      "module_paths": ["puppet/modules"]
    }
  ],
  "builders": [{
    "type": "amazon-ebs",
    "access_key": "",
    "secret_key": "",
    "region": "us-east-1",
    "source_ami": "ami-c80b0aa2",
    "instance_type": "t2.small",
    "ssh_username": "ubuntu",
    "ami_name": "my-packer-example-",
    "associate_public_ip_address": true
  }]
}
```

In the `provisioners` section, we have our two provisioners: first Packer will run the shell script to install Puppet, and then it will use the `puppet-masterless` provisioner to apply the Puppet manifests.

Next, we have the `builders` section, which contains a single builder object. This contains the information Packer needs to launch an EC2 instance and begin configuring it using the provisioners.

Applying the Puppet configuration to a vanilla installation of the operating system ensures that the instance can be re-created from scratch if necessary. It also ensures that everything required to configure the instance is contained within Puppet's configuration, as any manual changes will be removed the next time the image is made.

The `variables` section provides your AWS credentials to Packer. If these are not hardcoded in the configuration file, Packer will attempt to retrieve the credentials from the `AWS_ACCESS_KEY_ID` and `AWS_SECRET_ACCESS_KEY` environment variables or the local *~/.aws/credentials* file.

Save the Packer configuration file to *packer_image.json*, after changing the `region` and `source_ami` parameters if desired.

First, we check and validate the configuration file, as Packer runs are too time consuming to be needlessly used as a debugging tool:

```
$ packer validate packer_image.json
Template validated successfully.
```

To create the AMI, execute Packer:

```
$ packer build packer_image.json
amazon-ebs output will be in this color.

==> amazon-ebs: Prevalidating AMI Name...
==> amazon-ebs: Inspecting the source AMI...
==> amazon-ebs: Creating temporary keypair: packer 57cb368f-1381-3d49-
e634-764b35662582
==> amazon-ebs: Creating temporary security group for this instance...
==> amazon-ebs: Authorizing access to port 22 the temporary security group...
==> amazon-ebs: Launching a source AWS instance...
    amazon-ebs: Instance ID: i-a6844bbe
==> amazon-ebs: Waiting for instance (i-a6844bbe) to become ready...
==> amazon-ebs: Waiting for SSH to become available...
==> amazon-ebs: Connected to SSH!
==> amazon-ebs: Provisioning with shell script: install_puppet.sh
...
[output truncated]
...
    amazon-ebs: Notice: Finished catalog run in 8.91 seconds
==> amazon-ebs: Stopping the source instance...
==> amazon-ebs: Waiting for the instance to stop...
==> amazon-ebs: Creating the AMI: my-packer-example-1472935567
```

```
    amazon-ebs: AMI: ami-6a5d367d
==> amazon-ebs: Waiting for AMI to become ready...
==> amazon-ebs: Terminating the source AWS instance...
==> amazon-ebs: Cleaning up any extra volumes...
==> amazon-ebs: No volumes to clean up, skipping
==> amazon-ebs: Deleting temporary security group...
==> amazon-ebs: Deleting temporary keypair...
Build 'amazon-ebs' finished.

==> Builds finished. The artifacts of successful builds are:
--> amazon-ebs: AMIs were created:

us-east-1: ami-6a5d367d
```

Packer is quite verbose in its output, so you can follow through as it launches the EC2 instance, runs the shell script, runs Puppet, and finally creates the AMI. In a successful run, the ID of the newly minted AMI will be the closing result of Packer's output.

Once Packer has finished, you can use the AWS Management Console to verify the existence of your new AMI. If you launch an instance of this image and connect to its public DNS name in your web browser, you will be greeted with the default Nginx welcome page.

This simple example demonstrates how Packer can be used to build AMIs. Packer can significantly reduce the amount of time you spend involved in the AMI building process, and just like our other automation examples, it enables you to entirely rebuild from scratch another key infrastructure component by using just a few files checked out of your trusted version controlsystem.

Automate All the Things

The Chef team successfully co-opted the "all the things" internet meme to summarize the philosophy of automation we subscribe to. Even if you are not already using configuration management tools, it takes little time to implement an automation strategy that readily pays for itself in saved time and mistakes avoided, to say nothing of cloud-native tasks that are simply ill-suited to manual, step-by-step execution. The AWS console is there to make us comfortable with the cloud environment and help us discover functionality, but it is really not the way AWS was meant to be used.

## CHAPTER 5

An Example Application Stack

Because this book covers how to run a production application in AWS, it is useful to have an example application stack that can demonstrate the various principles and strategies introduced in later chapters. Therefore, this chapter describes how to plan an application deployment and gradually builds up a working application using AWS components. As the chapter progresses, we will create Puppet manifests and a Cloud-Formation stack template that, when combined, can be used to deploy the entire application as a single self-contained stack.

By the end of this chapter, you will have a web-based application running in AWS, provisioned using CloudFormation and Puppet. This application consists of multiple services: a web application, a background task-processing service, a database, and a caching service.

This stack is something Mike has deployed many times, and is similar to those used by popular websites like Pinterest. You can, of course, replace the components we describe with your own application's components. This chapter is concerned with general processes you must go through when planning a new application, rather than the specific technologies used in this stack.

Overview of Application Components

This example deploys a content management system (CMS). A CMS provides a GUI-based interface for bloggers, journalists, and others to create and update web pages without requiring knowledge of HTML or other markup languages.

The infrastructure required to operate a CMS (or indeed, most web-based applications) consists of these components:

Component	Role
Application layer	Handle incoming HTTP requests
Task-processing layer	Perform scheduled and ad hoc application tasks
Database layer	Provide persistent storage
Caching layer	Provide temporary quick-access storage

We'll build the infrastructure in this chapter using a combination of AWS services. The application and task-processing layers will be handled by EC2 instances. The database layer will use AWS RDS (a hosted database service), and the caching layer will use AWS ElastiCache.

The Web Application

We will use the open source Mezzanine CMS (*http://mezzanine.jupo.org*), which is based on Django (*https://www.djangoproject.com*), a Python web development framework. We chose Mezzanine because it provides a good compromise between ease of installation and customization: we get a working CMS out of the box, without having to spend too much time installing it.

The Mezzanine application will be served by the Nginx web server because it offers better performance than Mezzanine's built-in HTTP server.

Database and Caching

This application requires database and caching servers, which usually means installing software such as MySQL or Memcache. Amazon provides services that act as replacements for these software packages. Instead of running your own MySQL database, you can use Amazon's Relational Database Service (RDS).

Memcache can be replaced with ElastiCache, which is a protocol-compatible replacement: that is, any valid Memcache client will work with ElastiCache without any modification.

The point of this chapter is to get an application up and running, not to spend time installing and configuring software. Therefore, the example application stack will use RDS and ElastiCache instead of installing the corresponding standalone software packages.

Background Task Processing

Many applications require some form of background task processing. We want our websites to be as fast as possible from the user's perspective, so waiting around for slow tasks to complete is not an option. Today's web applications rarely live in isolation, and it is common for one website to interact with many others through the use of external API requests.

For example, your website might give users the opportunity to invite their friends from social networks such as Facebook or Twitter. This requires API requests to query these services for a list of the users' friends, and to send out the invitations.

These API requests can take some time to complete, and making the user wait around until they do so does not make a good user experience. The best practice in this case is to move long-running tasks out of the HTTP request/response cycle and into a dedicated background processing application. This way, the tasks can be processed asynchronously. From the user's perspective, the action is completed immediately, but, in fact, all the work happens in another process.

For blogs that accept comments from users, there is another popular use case for asynchronous task processing: anti-spam checks. We want to keep our blog's comments spam-free, which means every new comment must be checked by an anti-spam service.

Our example blog will use background task processing to check posted comments for spam. For this application, we will use Celery (*http://www.celeryproject.org/*), a distributed task queue application written in Python. Celery works extremely well with Django, and is the de facto standard task processing application for many Django and Python developers.

Celery works by sending messages between your application and the processes that are actually executing your task. It requires a message broker to store these messages. One of the most common (and most efficient) Celery message brokers is RabbitMQ, which operates using the Advanced Message Queuing Protocol (AMQP).

Celery can also work with Amazon's Simple Queuing Service (SQS), which is a highly scalable message-queuing service. SQS can act as a replacement to tools like RabbitMQ. By using SQS as our Celery message broker, we do not need to install or maintain a RabbitMQ cluster.

In this architecture, we have to install and maintain only a single EC2 instance, which runs both the web application and the Celery task-processing application. The rest of the services are provided by AWS.

Installing the Web Application

The first step is to launch and configure the EC2 instance that will run the web and task-processing applications. Once it is configured and working properly, create an Amazon Machine Image so it can be used as part of a CloudFormation stack.

First, we will install the software manually, and then "translate" these manual steps into Puppet manifests.

Start by creating a new security group named web. This security group should allow inbound TCP traffic from 0.0.0.0/0 on ports 8000 and 80:

```
$ aws ec2 create-security-group --group-name web --description "global web \
  server access"
{
    "GroupId": "sg-b7d15acd"
}
$ aws ec2 authorize-security-group-ingress--group-name web --protocol tcp \
  --port 80 --cidr 0.0.0.0/0
$ aws ec2 authorize-security-group-ingress --group-name web --protocol tcp \
  --port 8000 --cidr 0.0.0.0/0
$ aws ec2 describe-security-groups --group-names web
SECURITYGROUPS   global webserver access sg-b7d15acd     web       740376006796
vpc-934935f7
IPPERMISSIONS    80      tcp      80
IPRANGES         0.0.0.0/0
IPPERMISSIONS    8000    tcp      8000
IPRANGES         0.0.0.0/0
IPPERMISSIONSEGRESS      -1
IPRANGES         0.0.0.0/0
```

Next, launch an EC2 instance using the Ubuntu 16.04 AMI, making sure that this instance is a member of the web and ssh security groups. Once the instance has launched, log in with SSH:

```
$ aws ec2 run-instances --image-id ami-43a15f3e --region us-east-1 \
--key federico --security-groups ssh web --instance-type t2.micro
[output truncated]
SECURITYGROUPS   sg-4ebd8b36     ssh
SECURITYGROUPS   sg-b7d15acd     web
STATE   0        pending
STATEREASON      pending pending
```

Mezzanine is a Python package available from PyPI (*https://pypi.python.org/pypi*), Python's package management system. Python packages can be installed with the pip command. First, we need to install pip itself in our new instance, along with the Python development libraries:

```
sudo apt install python-pip python-dev
sudo apt install libtiff5-dev libjpeg8-dev zlib1g-dev libfreetype6-dev
```

Once this is done, Mezzanine itself can be installed with pip. This will also install Django, as well as any other package dependencies required to run Mezzanine:

```
sudo pip install Mezzanine==4.2.3
```

We are forcing a specific version of Mezzanine in order to ensure the examples in this chapter are not affected by development changes occurring after its publication: pip defaults to installing the latest version of any package its upstream developers have released to the world. pip does this irrespective of the incompatible changes inevitably taking place between some versions, always providing access to the latest and greatest software. Without the second layer of consistency that the independent versioning of a Linux distribution implicitly provides, some additional management by the operator has to take place. We discuss in "Package Management" on page 263 how to strictly manage pip package versioning.

We need to create a directory to store the files that make up the Mezzanine project. For security purposes, we will create a new user to own this directory:

```
sudo useradd mezzanine
sudo mkdir /srv/mezzanine
sudo chown mezzanine /srv/mezzanine
sudo -u mezzanine mezzanine-project myblog /srv/mezzanine
```

Unless otherwise configured, Mezzanine will use SQLite (*http://www.sqlite.org/*) as its database. SQLite is a self-contained database engine: unlike MySQL or PostgreSQL, it does not require a dedicated database server. Instead, the entire database is contained in a C library file, which can be embedded into a compiled program.

Because database access is not mediated by a server program, concurrent writes are not SQLite's forte. This makes it unsuitable for many production applications, but SQLite remains a great choice for development, as there is no need to spend time setting up a database server when beginning the project. So we will use SQLite to make sure Mezzanine is working, before moving to an RDS-based database.

Mezzanine provides a createdb command that initializes the database and populates it with some example pages. The command will also prompt you to create a superuser account, which is required to access the admin interface of the site and begin making changes. Make sure to have the public DNS name of the instance, then execute the following, binding to the public DNS and port 8000 when prompted:

```
$ cd /srv/mezzanine
$ sudo -u mezzanine python manage.py createdb
[output truncated]
A site record is required.
Please enter the domain and optional port in the format 'domain:port'.
For example 'localhost:8000' or 'www.example.com'.
Hit enter to use the default (127.0.0.1:8000):
ec2-54-172-21-112.compute-1.amazonaws.com:8000

Creating default site record: ec2-54-172-21-112.compute-1.amazonaws.com:8000 ...

Creating default account ...

Username (leave blank to use 'mezzanine'):
Email address: federico@ubuntu.com
Password: ••••••
Password (again): ••••••
Superuser created successfully.
Installed 2 object(s) from 1 fixture(s)
```

```
Would you like to install some initial demo pages?
Eg: About us, Contact form, Gallery. (yes/no): yes

Creating demo pages: About us, Contact form, Gallery ...

Installed 16 object(s) from 3 fixture(s)
```
Once this command is complete, Mezzanine is ready to run.

 If you have to interrupt Mezzanine's createdb command because of an error entering configuration settings, you will need to remove the file */srv/mezzanine/dev.db* first before running the command again. Mezzanine has built-in safeguards designed to prevent accidental database overwrites, something you will come to appreciate in highly automated environments.

To ease development, Django has a built-in HTTP server that can be used to quickly test pages, without having to set up Apache or Nginx. While in the */srv/mezzanine/* directory, the server can be started as follows:

```
sudo -u mezzanine python manage.py runserver 0.0.0.0:8000
```

Open your browser and visit the public IP address of your EC2 instance on port 8000 (for example, *http://ec2-54-172-21-112.compute-1.amazonaws.com:8000/*); do not use SSL, as the built-in server does not support it. You should now see the Mezzanine welcome page, ushering you into the newly created website. You could validate the CMS system's functionality by logging in the administrative interface and publishing a short test blog.

The Django development server is not fast enough for production use, but saves plenty of time in the development phase. In production, a Web Server Gateway Interface (WSGI) server such as Gunicorn is used to serve the Python application, and traffic is proxied by a web server such as Nginx or Apache. These servers are much better at dealing with higher numbers of concurrent users, while still providing fast responses to user requests.

To make this example more closely match a production environment, we will set up Nginx and configure it to serve the Mezzanine blog application instead of using Django's development server. In this configuration, Nginx acts as a proxy to the actual application. The user's request is received by Nginx, which then forwards the request to the application server before returning the result to the client.

Nginx can communicate with the application in a few ways, two of the most popular being HTTP and Unix sockets. Unix sockets can offer improved performance over HTTP, but they require Nginx and the application to run on the same physical server (or virtual server instance, in the case of AWS). Using HTTP to communicate with the proxy involves a little more overhead—network sockets must be created, for example—but allows Nginx and the application to run on separate servers, increasing resilience and scalability.

Install Nginx with the following:

```
sudo apt install nginx
```

 If any apt sofware install ends unsuccessfully, your first check should be for stale metadata. Run the following and try the install command once more:

```
sudo apt update
```

Remove the link to the placeholder configuration file found in */etc/nginx/sites-available/default*—as indicated in its comments, one may keep it as a reference:

```
sudo unlink /etc/nginx/sites-enabled/default
```

Example 5-1 shows a simple Nginx virtual host definition. This configures Nginx to act as a proxy server and relay traffic to an upstream application server, running on port 8000 on the same host.

Example 5-1. Nginx configuration

```
upstream myblog_app {

  server localhost:8000;

}

server {
  listen              *:80 default;

  server_name         blog.example.com;
  access_log          /var/log/nginx/blog.example.com.access.log;
  location / {
    proxy_pass http://myblog_app;
    proxy_read_timeout 90;
    proxy_set_header Host $http_host;
  }
}
```

Save this configuration to */etc/nginx/sites-available/myblog.conf*. Soft-link that file from */etc/nginx/sites-enabled/myblog.conf* and restart Nginx:

```
sudo ln -s /etc/nginx/sites-available/myblog.conf /etc/nginx/sites-enabled/\
myblog.conf
sudo systemctl restart nginx
```

Make sure the Django development server is not already running and then start it:

```
cd /srv/mezzanine
sudo -u mezzanine python manage.py runserver
```

Without parameters, Mezzanine will bind to localhost only, port 8000. Now visit the public hostname of the EC2 instance in your browser again, this time on the default port 80. You should again see the Mezzanine welcome page, but this time it is being served by Nginx instead of Django's development server.

Of course, running the Django development server manually is inconvenient. We don't want to have to start it manually every time the server starts, nor do we want to have to restart it if it crashes. Therefore, stop the server and turn to our next step, which is a superserver that starts and monitors other processes.

Supervisor (*http://supervisord.org/*) is a process-control system that can help solve this problem. It will automatically start processes when the instance is launched, and will restart them if they crash unexpectedly. Supervisor is just one example of many tools that perform a similar function. It can be installed as follows:

```
sudo apt install supervisor
```

Example 5-2 shows the Supervisor configuration file required to start our Django development server. This file provides all the information Supervisor needs to run the server. The process will be started automatically when the instance boots, and it will be automatically restarted if it crashes unexpectedly.

Example 5-2. Supervisor configuration file

```
[program:myblog_app]
command=/usr/bin/python /srv/mezzanine/manage.py runserver
autostart=true
autorestart=unexpected
stopwaitsecs=10
stopasgroup=true
killasgroup=true
user=mezzanine
```

Save this file to */etc/supervisor/conf.d/myblog_web.conf* and issue the `sudo supervisorctl update` command, instructing Supervisor to read and process the new configuration file. Make sure you stop the manually launched development server before doing this. Otherwise, the Supervisor-launched process will not start correctly because it will be unable to bind to port 8000 which is already in use:

```
$ sudo supervisorctl update
myblog_app: added process group
$ sudo supervisorctl status
myblog_app                      STARTING
```

```
$ sudo supervisorctl status
myblog_app                     RUNNING    pid 13012, uptime 0:00:10
```

Confirm that everything is working by reloading the welcome page in your web browser. Once more, the page should be displayed—only this time, the Django development server process is being managed by Supervisor. When the instance starts, the development server will be started. If the server process crashes for some reason, it will be automatically restarted.

Preparing Puppet and CloudFormation

Now that the server is configured correctly, we can retrace our steps and convert this manual process into a Puppet manifest. We will also begin creating the CloudFormation stack that describes all the EC2 resources required to provision the application.

Puppet Files

Let's first recap the steps we have taken:

1. Install some packages from Apt and pip repositories.
2. Create a directory to store the application, and a user to own the application files.
3. Initialize the application and database.
4. Create configuration files for Nginx and Supervisor.

To make this a repeatable process across any number of AWS instances, we will use a Puppet module that performs all of these configuration steps. We will call this module myblog. The Puppet Style Guide recommends that modules consist of multiple classes, each responsible for a subset of the module's functionality. Therefore, the logic to complete the preceding tasks will be spread across multiple classes:

- The myblog::requirements class will handle installing the Apt and pip requirements.
- The logic specific to the web application server will be contained in myblog::web.
- Later, when we add the Celery server to the stack, its Puppet configuration will be handled by the myblog::celery class.

Because both the web and Celery servers have the same basic set of requirements, both of these classes can include the myblog::requirements class instead of duplicating the requirements list.

To save time, we will use modules from the Puppet Forge where possible; this saves us from having to reinvent the wheel. Puppet modules are available for Nginx and

Supervisor, and the rest of the configuration can be handled with Puppet's built-in capabilities.

Begin by creating a new repository in your version control system and setting up the initial directory structure for Puppet's configuration files. We will be using Git for these examples:

```
sudo apt install git
git config --global user.name "Federico Lucifredi"
git config --global user.email federico@ubuntu.com
git init ~/myblog
cd ~/myblog
mkdir -p puppet/{manifests,modules}
mkdir puppet/modules/myblog
```

 The Puppet Forge (*https://forge.puppetlabs.com/*) is a repository of reusable Puppet modules that you can use in your Puppet manifests. Many of these are incredibly high quality, and will give you a lot of control over how the underlying software or service is configured. You will find modules for a huge range of open source and proprietary software, as well as physical devices such as Juniper network switches.

Starting in Puppet version 2.7.14, modules can be installed with the `puppet module` command. For example:

```
puppet module install puppetlabs/stdlib
```

In previous versions, module files were manually placed in the */etc/ puppet/modules/* directory.

Example 5-3 contains the basic *site.pp* file used by Puppet to control which configurations are applied to each node.

Example 5-3. Puppet role assignment with EC2 user data

```
require stdlib

node default {

    $userdata = parsejson($ec2_userdata)

    # Set variables from userdata
    $role = $userdata['role']

    case $role {
        "web": { $role_class = "myblog::web" }
        default: { fail("Unrecognized role: $role") }
    }
```

```
# Main myblog class
class { "myblog":
}
# Role-specific class, e.g. myblog::web
class { $role_class:
}
}
```

This file uses EC2 user data, which you first learned about in "EC2 Instance Details and User Data" on page 27, to determine which configuration should be applied to a node. This method was described in further detail in "User Data and Tags" on page 155. Here, we are setting the $role variable from user data. $role is then used in the case statement to set the $role_data variable to the name of the class that should be used for this node.

Finally, the main myblog class is declared, along with the role-specific class (myblog::web).

Save this file to *puppet/manifests/site.pp* and commit your changes to the repository:

```
git add puppet/site.pp
git commit -m 'Added site.pp'
```

Next, we can add the Nginx (*https://forge.puppet.com/jfryman/nginx/readme*) and Supervisor (*https://github.com/plathrop/puppet-module-supervisor*) Puppet modules to our repository. We will do this using the git subtree command, which pulls the content of these external Git repositories into our own repository. Execute the following commands:

```
git subtree add --prefix puppet/modules/supervisor \
https://github.com/plathrop/puppet-module-supervisor.git master --squash
git subtree add --prefix puppet/modules/nginx \
https://github.com/jfryman/puppet-nginx.git master --squash
```

As we have previously installed Puppet modules using the convenient puppet module install command, questions naturally arise around our changed strategy. puppet module install *name* will deliver the latest version of a module, which can lead to unexpected code changes not acceptable in our automatically provisioned infrastructure. git subtree imports a copy of the module into our version control system instead, ensuring such updates only occur at a time of our choosing.

Provisioning Puppet Runtime and Modules

Deploying a consistent Puppet environment complete with one's choice of modules is a broad topic that cannot be exhausted here. A number of alternatives exist; we introduce here the most popular options and leave a deeper exploration of the trade-offs to our readers.

r10k (*https://github.com/puppetlabs/r10k*) is currently Puppet's default choice for environment and module deployment. It provides no dependency resolution, meaning that modules used within other modules must be declared explicitly. This creates more work, but the net positive result is that all module versions, including the dependencies, can be strictly controlled.

puppet module install (*http://bit.ly/2LTQ0Jv*) is the simplest and fastest approach to installing a set of Puppet modules. It performs automatic dependency resolution, so while the modules installed explicitly can be pinned to specific versions, automatically resolved dependencies will default to the newest version available.

git subtree imports the code of the module into an application's own Git repository, ensuring no version change occurs unless a developer initiates it first. The (very reasonable) trade-off is the need to master the appropriate Git merge strategy (*http://bit.ly/2LTQf7n*).

librarian-puppet (*https://github.com/voxpupuli/librarian-puppet*) provides dependency resolution as well a version pinning through a *puppetfile.lock* file. While some cosider librarian-puppet slow and would see it replaced with r10k, it remains the tool of choice in masterless Puppet environments.

The Nginx module uses Puppet's stdlib (standard library) module, which provides useful functions such as variable validation. This can be installed with the following:

```
git subtree add --prefix puppet/modules/stdlib \
https://github.com/puppetlabs/puppetlabs-stdlib.git master --squash
```

Now we can begin writing our custom module, myblog, which will use the Nginx and Supervisor modules, as well as performing the rest of the configuration required to run the application.

The Puppet Style Guide (*https://docs.puppet.com/guides/style_guide.html*) suggests that, when modules contain multiple Puppet classes, each class should be saved to its own file. This is best illustrated with an example.

Example 5-4 shows the top-level myblog class, which is the class we referenced in *site.pp*.

Example 5-4. Initial MyBlog Puppet manifest

```
class myblog {

    $app_path = "/srv/mezzanine"

    class {"supervisor": }

    require myblog::requirements

}
```

This class references a subclass, `myblog::requirements`. It also sets the `$app_path` variable, which is used in the other classes. If we wanted to change the location of the Mezzanine project files, we would need to update only this variable instead of making changes in multiple files. Save this file to *puppet/modules/myblog/manifests/init.pp*.

Example 5-5 contains the `myblog::requirements` class. This class installs all of the software packages required to run Mezzanine. It also creates the `mezzanine` user, and creates a directory to store the project files.

Example 5-5. MyBlog requirements Puppet manifest

```
class myblog::requirements {

    $packages = ["python-dev", "python-pip", "libtiff5-dev", "libjpeg8-dev",
"zlib1g-dev", "libfreetype6-dev"]

    package { $packages:
        ensure  => installed
    }

    $pip_packages = ["Mezzanine"]

    package { $pip_packages:
        ensure  => installed,
        provider => pip,
        require => Package[$packages]
    }

    user { "mezzanine":
        ensure  => present
    }

    file { "$myblog::app_path":
        ensure  => "directory",
        owner   => "mezzanine",
        group   => "mezzanine"
    }
```

```
}
```

Save this file to *puppet/modules/myblog/manifests/requirements.pp*.

The next subclass actually launches some servers. It is shown in Example 5-6.

Example 5-6. MyBlog initialization Puppet manifests

```
class myblog::create_project {

    # Create the Mezzanine project
    exec { "init-mezzanine-project":
        command => "/usr/local/bin/mezzanine-project myblog $myblog::app_path",
        user => "mezzanine",
        creates => "$myblog::app_path/__init__.py",
        notify  => Exec["init-mezzanine-db"]
    }

    # Create the development SQLite database
    exec { "init-mezzanine-db":
        command => "/usr/bin/python manage.py createdb --noinput",
        user => "mezzanine",
        cwd => "$myblog::app_path",
        refreshonly => true
    }

}
```

This class uses Puppet's Exec resource type to execute two commands. The
mezzanine-project command creates the initial Mezzanine project, which will set up
a simple website with example pages. The createdb command creates the SQLite
database used in development.

> Be careful when creating database resources from tools like Puppet.
> An incorrect configuration could result in a database being unin-
> tentionally dropped and replaced with a freshly created database.
>
> For this reason, it can be desirable to create the database outside
> the configuration management tool.

The Exec resource type accepts parameters that determine when it should be executed. The init-mezzanine-project Exec uses the creates parameter, which
informs Puppet that executing this command will create a particular file and prevents
the Exec from executing if that file already exists.

Thus, this command will execute only if */srv/mezzanine/__init__.py* does not exist. Because we know that `mezzanine-project` will always create this file, it is a reliable method of ensuring we do not overwrite an existing project.

The `init-mezzanine-db` Exec uses another of Puppet's control methods. It sets the `refreshonly` parameter to `true`, which means it will be executed only if explicitly requested by another resource. In this example, the `init-mezzanine-project` Exec notifies `init-mezzanine-db`, causing the latter to execute when `init-mezzanine-project` is executed. Save this file to *puppet/modules/myblog/manifests/create_project.pp*.

Example 5-7 shows the `myblog::nginx` class.

Example 5-7. Nginx Puppet module

```
class myblog::mynginx {

    class { "nginx": }

    nginx::resource::upstream { "myblog_app":
        ensure  => present,
        members => [
            'localhost:8000',
        ]
    }

    nginx::resource::vhost { "blog.example.com":
        ensure  => enable,
        listen_options => "default",
        proxy   => "http://myblog_app"
    }

}
```

Similar to the `myblog::supervisor` class, this class installs the Nginx package and writes the configuration file describing our desired Nginx setup. In this case, a single Nginx virtual host is created. This virtual host will proxy all traffic to the `myblog_app` proxy, which is running on port 8000.

Because we already have a class named `nginx` in the Nginx module, we can't call our class `myblog::nginx`. Instead, we call it `myblog::mynginx` to prevent a naming collision.

Example 5-7 should be saved to *puppet/modules/myblog/manifests/mynginx.pp*.

The final piece of the puzzle is the `myblog::web` class, shown in Example 5-8.

Example 5-8. myblog::web class

```
class myblog::web {
    Class["myblog::web"] -> Class["myblog"]

    require myblog::mynginx

    supervisor::service { "myblog_app":
        ensure  => present,
        enable  => true,
        command => "/usr/bin/python ${myblog::app_path}/manage.py runserver",
        stopasgroup => true,
        killasgroup => true,
        user    => "mezzanine",
        group   => "mezzanine"
    }

}
```

This class contains everything specifically related to running an application server. It imports the `myblog::nginx` class to configure the web server. It also declares a `supervisor::service` resource, which will create a configuration file at */etc/supervisor/myblog_web.ini*, causing Supervisor to start the Mezzanine application when the instance launches.

Save this file to *puppet/modules/myblog/manifests/web.pp*.

Now the first step of the Puppet configuration is complete. The `myblog` module will take a fresh Ubuntu 16.04 instance and turn it into a working Mezzanine blog, served by Nginx.

CloudFormation Files

Now we set up CloudFormation to provision the EC2 instance and security group. Example 5-9 shows the first version of the CloudFormation stack.

Example 5-9. Initial CloudFormation stack

```
{
  "AWSTemplateFormatVersion" : "2010-09-09",
  "Description" : "Mezzanine-powered blog, served with Nginx.",
  "Parameters" : {
    "KeyName" : {
      "Description" : "Name of an existing EC2 KeyPair to enable SSH access to the
instance",
      "Type" : "String"
    }
  },
  "Resources" : {
```

```
    "WebInstance" : {
      "Type" : "AWS::EC2::Instance",
      "Properties" : {
        "SecurityGroups" : [ { "Ref" : "WebSecurityGroup" } ],
        "KeyName" : "federico",
        "ImageId" : "ami-43a15f3e",
        "UserData": {
            "Fn::Base64": {
                "{\"role\" : \"web\"}"
            }
        }
      }
    },
    "WebSecurityGroup" : {
      "Type" : "AWS::EC2::SecurityGroup",
      "Properties" : {
        "GroupDescription" : "Allow SSH and HTTP from anywhere",
        "SecurityGroupIngress" : [
          {
            "IpProtocol" : "tcp",
            "FromPort" : "22",
            "ToPort" : "22",
            "CidrIp" : "0.0.0.0/0"
          },
          {
            "IpProtocol" : "tcp",
            "FromPort" : "80",
            "ToPort" : "80",
            "CidrIp" : "0.0.0.0/0"
          }
        ]
      }
    }
  }
 }
}
```

This stack does not deploy the Puppet manifests to the instance when it launches—
we'll add that later. Save this version of the stack template to *myblog/cloudformation/
myblog.json*.

Another point to note is the use of the `UserData` parameter on the `WebInstance`
resource. This provides the instance with a JSON string describing the role for the
instance, which will be used in Puppet's *manifest/site.pp* file to decide which classes to
apply to the node during configuration. Because the CloudFormation manifest is
itself written in JSON, we must escape quotation marks in the user data with a back-
slash to ensure they are not treated as part of the manifest.

Finally, add the Puppet modules and CloudFormation stack to the Git repository:

```
cd ~/myblog
git add -A
git commit -m 'added Puppet modules and CloudFormation stack'
```

Creating an RDS Database

The Mezzanine `createdb` command used in the previous step created a SQLite database. Now that the application is working, we can replace SQLite with Amazon's Relational Database Service (RDS).

This involves two steps: creating the RDS database, and reconfiguring the Mezzanine application to use the new database instead of SQLite. First, we will perform these steps manually for testing purposes, before updating the Puppet manifests and CloudFormation stacks to reflect the updated application.

Before we can create the RDS database, we need to create a security group. This procedure can protect your database instances just as it protects EC2 instances. The two security groups perform exactly the same function: limiting access to resources, based on the source of the request.

For our purposes, we need a security group that permits access from our web server instances. We will do this with the AWS console for variety, but the task can be equally accomplished from the CLI as we have previously demonstrated.

Create this group by visiting the EC2 Security Groups page (*https://console.aws.amazon.com/ec2/v2/home?region=us-east-1#SecurityGroups*) and clicking Create Security Group. Name the new group db and set the description to "Myblog DB access."

After the group has been created, add an ingress rule that permits access for the web security group by referencing the groupid in a custom rule, as shown in Figure 5-1. This will allow any member of the web security group to access the database.

Figure 5-1. Creating the DB security group

Now we can create a new RDS database through the Management Console or command line. We will continue to use the Management Console here and later create the same database using CloudFormation. On the RDS Console Dashboard page (*https://console.aws.amazon.com/rds/home*), click Launch a DB Instance, which will open a wizard that guides you through the process of creating a database.

The first screen presents you with a list of database engines—such as PostgreSQL, MySQL, Microsoft SQL Server, and Oracle—that can be used with RDS. Select the MySQL icon, and click Next.

Multi-AZ Deployment allows you to deploy a master/slave database pair that spans multiple availability zones. This increases resilience to failure, but also increases cost, and it is not required for this test database. Select the MySQL "Dev/Test" option when prompted, ignoring the Multi-AZ and Amazon Aurora alternatives for now.

Figure 5-2 shows the third screen in the process, where the initial MySQL options are set.

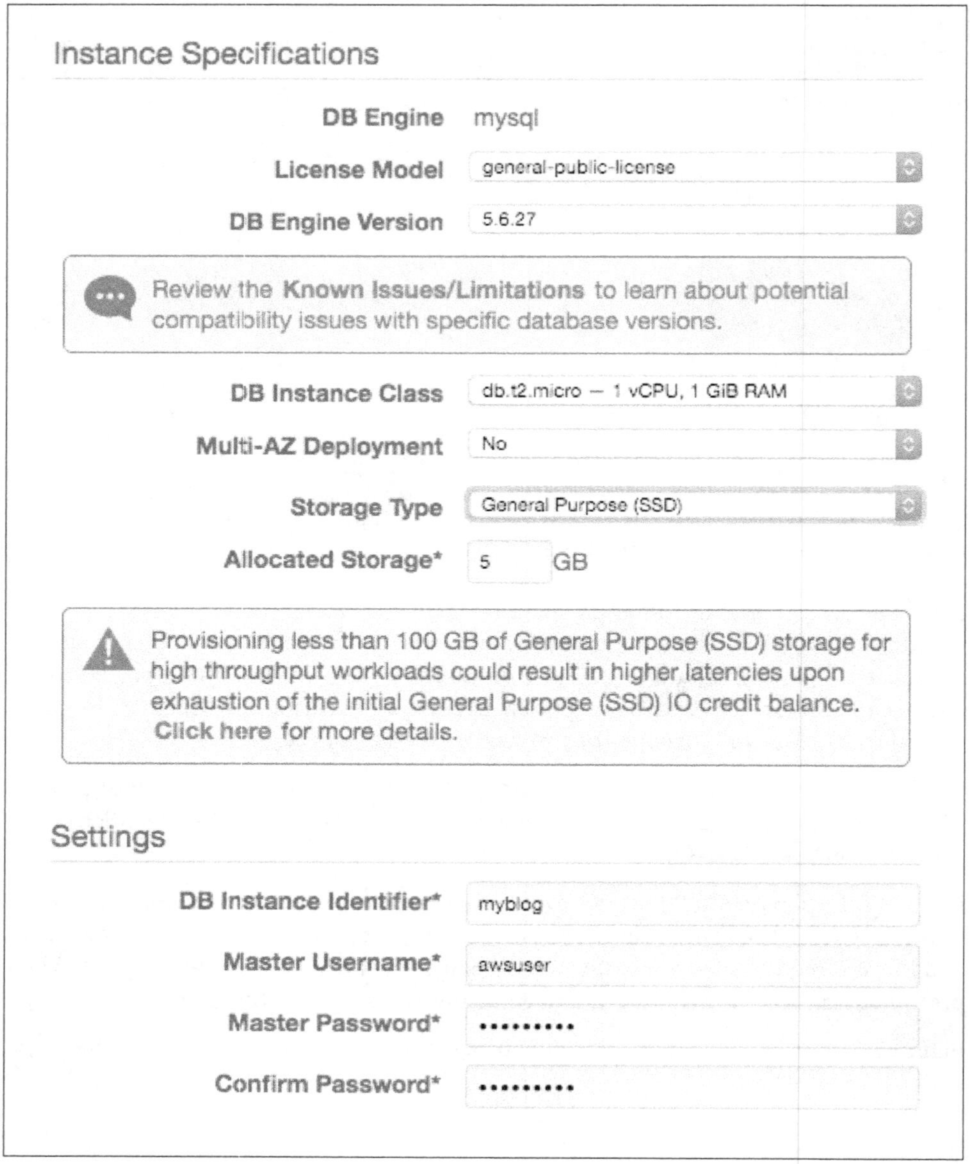

Instance Specifications

DB Engine	mysql
License Model	general-public-license
DB Engine Version	5.6.27

> Review the **Known Issues/Limitations** to learn about potential compatibility issues with specific database versions.

DB Instance Class	db.t2.micro — 1 vCPU, 1 GiB RAM
Multi-AZ Deployment	No
Storage Type	General Purpose (SSD)
Allocated Storage*	5 GB

> ⚠ Provisioning less than 100 GB of General Purpose (SSD) storage for high throughput workloads could result in higher latencies upon exhaustion of the initial General Purpose (SSD) IO credit balance. **Click here** for more details.

Settings

DB Instance Identifier*	myblog
Master Username*	awsuser
Master Password*	··········
Confirm Password*	··········

Figure 5-2. DB instance details

The DB Instance Identifier, Master Username, and Master Password options can be set to any values you want—but keep track of them, as they will be needed in the next step. Then click Next Step to move on to the Configure Advanced Settings screen, shown in Figure 5-3.

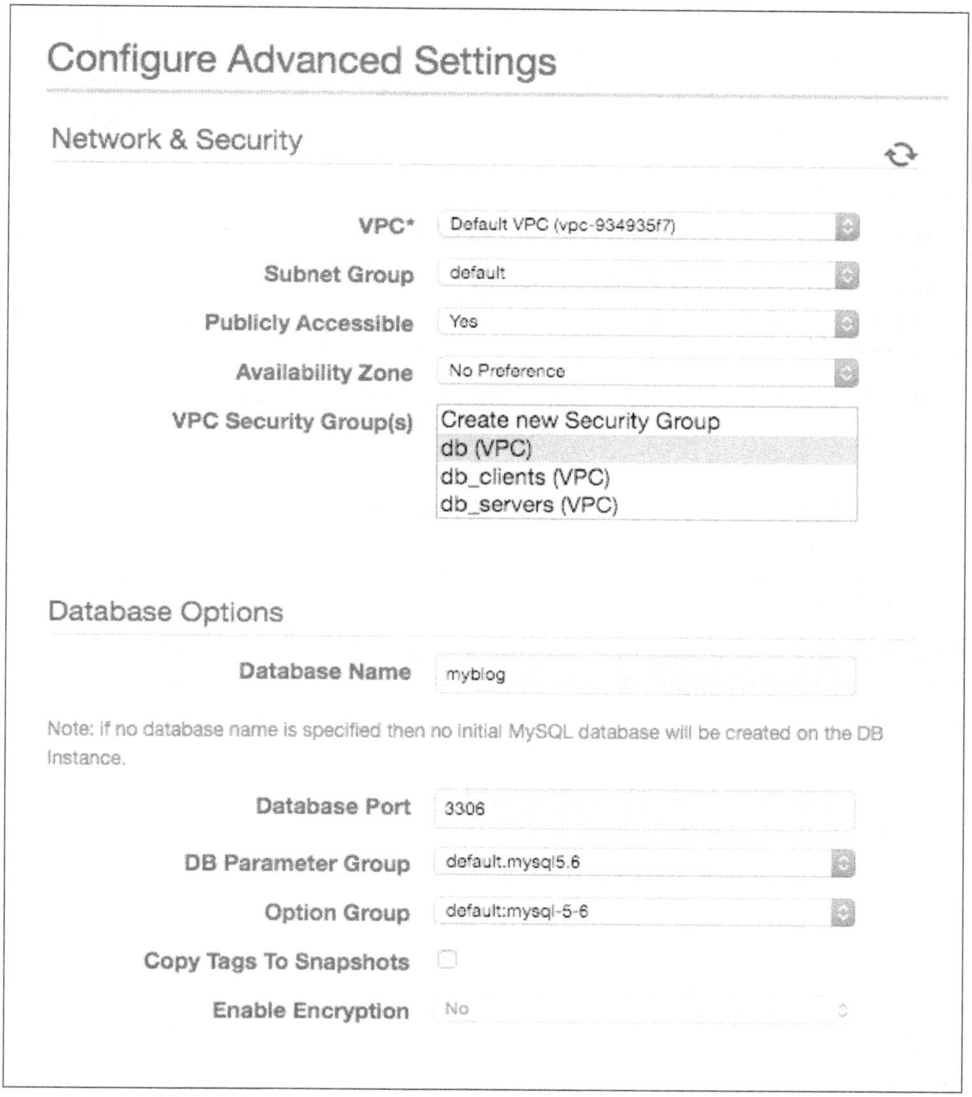

Configure Advanced Settings

Network & Security

VPC*	Default VPC (vpc-934935f7)
Subnet Group	default
Publicly Accessible	Yes
Availability Zone	No Preference
VPC Security Group(s)	Create new Security Group db (VPC) db_clients (VPC) db_servers (VPC)

Database Options

Database Name	myblog

Note: if no database name is specified then no initial MySQL database will be created on the DB Instance.

Database Port	3306
DB Parameter Group	default.mysql5.6
Option Group	default:mysql-5-6
Copy Tags To Snapshots	☐
Enable Encryption	No

Figure 5-3. Additional configuration

Enter a name for your database (e.g., `myblog`). This database will be created automatically when the DB instance launches.

In the DB Security Groups box, select the `db` security group and click Next Step.

This screen lets you also configure the automatic backup settings. For the purposes of this test, we will disable automatic backups by defining a backup retention period of zero days. While we do not wish to incur additional data charges for our development instance, the automatic backup, tagging, minor version upgrade, and monitoring functionality offered by AWS just in this screen make a clear case of why public cloud environments are not just convenient, but also effective: in a classic datacenter, you would be in charge of performing (or automating away) each of those tasks. You should absolutely make use of these facilities in production, particularly the automated backup option.

After reviewing your chosen settings, click Launch DB Instance.

Once the database instance has been created, its record in the console will be updated to include an endpoint. This is the hostname you will use to configure your MySQL clients—for example, *myblog.cvqj2dqsvoab.us-east-1.rds.amazonaws.com.*

Now that you have a database instance running, you can reconfigure Mezzanine to use this database instead of the local SQLite database.

Mezzanine settings are controlled by a Python file located at */srv/mezzanine/myblog/ settings.py.* Because it is quite common for different environments to require different settings (for example, a local database is used during development, and a remote database is used during production), Django and Mezzanine make it easy to override individual settings.

If a file named *local_settings.py* exists, any settings it contains will override those set in the main *settings.py* file. The settings that are consistent across all environments can be stored in *settings.py*, and any custom settings in *local_settings.py*.

 There are many ways to set different configuration options, depending on the environment in which the instance is running. The Twelve-Factor App (*https://12factor.net/config*) describes one such alternative method that uses a system-level environment variable to control which settings file is used.

Example 5-10 shows a *local_settings.py* file that specifies the use of an RDS database. Modify this file to reflect your database endpoint, as well as the username and password settings. The latter two should be set to the values you chose for Master Username and Master Password, respectively.

Example 5-10. Mezzanine database configuration

```
ALLOWED_HOSTS = "*"

DEBUG = True

DATABASES = {
    "default": {
        "ENGINE": "django.db.backends.mysql",
```

```
    "NAME": "myblog",
    "USER": "awsuser",
    "PASSWORD": "foobarbaz",
    "HOST": "myblog.cvqj2dqsvoab.us-east-1.rds.amazonaws.com",
    "PORT": "3306"
  }
}
```

Do not use the master user in your production applications; create for each a separate user with limited access. Doing so will limit the impact of a security breach.

Setting ALLOWED_HOSTS to * will make our example application work regardless of the domain name in use. This is convenient in our example, but for production deployments you will want to limit the IP addresses and domain names that your project is allowed to serve. ALLOWED_HOSTS (*http://bit.ly/2LXEpsT*) is a security feature meant to counteract HTTP host header attacks (*http://bit.ly/2LXEzjZ*).

After making the required changes, save this file to */srv/mezzanine/myblog/local_settings.new* with appropriate user and group ownership, then execute the following to preserve the hash salt variable generated at project creation:

```
sudo su mezzanine
cd /srv/mezzanine/myblog
mv local_settings.py local_settings.old
cat local_settings.old | grep 'SECRET_KEY =\|NEVERCACHE_KEY =' > local_set-
tings.py
cat local_settings.new >> local_settings.py
exit
```

We no longer need the SQLite database file, so proceed to delete it:

```
sudo rm /srv/mezzanine/dev.db
```

Because we will now be using MySQL instead of SQLite, we must ensure that the Python client libraries for MySQL are installed:

```
sudo apt install python-mysqldb mysql-client-5.6 libmysqlclient-dev
```

Before we can use the new database, we must create the initial table structure and example setup by running createdb again:

```
sudo -u mezzanine python /srv/mezzanine/manage.py createdb --noinput
```

As we have just replaced the existing database with a fresh one, do not expect to see any of your test blog entries. Further, you will need to re-initialize access with the following—make sure to use the same password for the default user:

```
cd /srv/mezzanine
sudo -u mezzanine python manage.py createsuperuser
```

The Mezzanine application must be restarted to pick up the changed settings file. This is done with Supervisor's `supervisorctl` command:

```
sudo supervisorctl restart myblog_app
```

Once the process has been restarted, use your web browser to verify once again that the Mezzanine site is still working.

You may notice that the web page feels a bit slower than it did previously. This is because the database is no longer on the same machine as the web application, which introduces some delay. After updating the Puppet and CloudFormation files with the changes we have just made, we will add a caching server to alleviate some of this delay.

RDS: Updating Puppet and CloudFormation

Now that we have completed and tested our changes manually, it is time to update the Puppet manifests to reflect them.

As part of the manual process, we created a database with the Management Console and hardcoded its endpoint into the settings file, along with the username and password. Our end goal is to have a stack that can be deployed without any manual configuration, which means that the RDS database will need to be created by CloudFormation. Hardcoding the connection details will not be an option for a dynamically created database.

How do we solve the problem of dynamically changing configuration files based on other resources in the CloudFormation stack? "User Data and Tags" on page 155 demonstrated one way of solving this problem.

CloudFormation's `Fn::GetAtt` function can access the attributes of resources in the stack template. So we can use this function to send the database's endpoint as user data to the instance. Puppet can then access that user data and use it when writing the configuration files.

Example 5-11 shows an updated version of the *myblog.json* stack template.

Example 5-11. MyBlog CloudFormation stack with RDS database

```
{
  "AWSTemplateFormatVersion" : "2010-09-09",
  "Description" : "Mezzanine-powered blog with RDS, served with Nginx.",
  "Parameters" : {
    "KeyName" : {
      "Description" : "Name of an existing EC2 KeyPair to enable SSH access to the
instance",
```

```
      "Type" : "String"
    },
    "WebAMI": {
      "Type": "String"
    },
    "KeyPair": {
      "Type": "String"
    },
    "DBUser": {
      "Type": "String"
    },
    "DBPassword": {
      "Type": "String",
      "NoEcho": "TRUE"
    }
  },
  "Resources" : {
    "BlogDB" : {  ❶
      "Type" : "AWS::RDS::DBInstance",
      "Properties" : {
        "DBSecurityGroups" : [ {"Ref" : "DBSecurityGroup"} ],
        "DBName" : "myblog",
        "AllocatedStorage" : 5,
        "DBInstanceClass" : "t2.micro",
        "Engine" : "MySQL",
        "EngineVersion" : "5.5",
        "MasterUsername" : { "Ref" : "DBUser" },  ❷
        "MasterUserPassword" : { "Ref" : "DBPassword" }
      },
      "DeletionPolicy" : "Snapshot"  ❸
    },
    "DBSecurityGroup" : {  ❹
      "Type" : "AWS::EC2::SecurityGroup",
      "Properties" : {
        "GroupDescription" : "Allow inbound MySQL access from web instances",
        "SecurityGroupIngress" : [
          {
            "IpProtocol" : "tcp",
            "FromPort" : "3306",
            "ToPort" : "3306",
            "SourceSecurityGroupName" : { "Ref" : "WebSecurityGroup" }
          }
        ]
      }
    },
    "WebInstance" : {
      "Type" : "AWS::EC2::Instance",
      "Properties" : {
        "SecurityGroups" : [ { "Ref" : "WebSecurityGroup" } ],
        "KeyName" : { "Ref" : "KeyPair",
        "ImageId" : { "Ref" : "WebAMI" },
        "UserData" : {  ❺
          "Fn::Base64" : {
```

```
            "Fn::Join" : [ "", [
              "{\"db_endpoint\": \"",
                { "Fn::GetAtt": [ "BlogDB", "Endpoint.Address" ] }, "\",",
              " \"db_user\": \"", { "Ref": "DBUser" }, "\",",
              " \"db_password\": \"", { "Ref": "DBPassword" }, "\" }"
            ] ]
          }
        }
      }
    },
    "WebSecurityGroup" : {
      "Type" : "AWS::EC2::SecurityGroup",
      "Properties" : {
        "GroupDescription" : "Allow SSH and HTTP from anywhere",
        "SecurityGroupIngress" : [
          {
            "IpProtocol" : "tcp",
            "FromPort" : "22",
            "ToPort" : "22",
            "CidrIp" : "0.0.0.0/0"
          },
          {
            "IpProtocol" : "tcp",
            "FromPort" : "80",
            "ToPort" : "80",
            "CidrIp" : "0.0.0.0/0"
          }
        ]
      }
    }
  }
}
```

The key items in the stack are as follows:

❶ The BlogDB resource is the RDS database instance, using the same settings as the database we created using the Management Console.

❷ The MasterUsername database parameter is used in two places. First, it is used when creating the RDS instance, and it is also passed to the WebInstance resource as part of its user data, making it accessible to scripts running on that instance.

❸ The DeletionPolicy database parameter ensures that when the stack is deleted, your data is not lost. Before CloudFormation terminates the database, it will perform a final snapshot.

❹ The DBSecurityGroup allows members of the WebSecurityGroup to access the database instance.

❺ The user data of the `WebInstance` contains the database hostname, username, and password.

Update *~/myblog/cloudformation/myblog.json* to reflect these changes. The `WebSecuri tyGroup` is unchanged, so you won't have to update that part of the file.

Now that the database name will be sent as user data, we need to update the Puppet manifests so that the *local_settings.py* file contains the correct endpoint, username, and password settings.

 The user data is JSON-formatted to make it easy to read in Puppet. Because CloudFormation stacks are themselves JSON-formatted, it means the user data must be escaped in order to be valid JSON. This, admittedly, can lead to rather ugly syntax in stack templates.

Here is an example of the user data produced by this statement:

```
{ "db_endpoint": "myblog.cvqj2dqsvoab.us-
east-1.rds.amazonaws.com",
  "db_user": "awsuser",
  "db_password": "foobarbaz"
}
```

Currently, this is the process for setting up a new Mezzanine project with Puppet:

1. Initialize the project with `mezzanine-project`.
2. Create the database with `createdb`.

We need to insert an additional step in the middle:

- Create a *local_settings.py* file based on the given user data.

This must be done before running `createdb`; otherwise, the default Mezzanine settings will be used, and a SQLite database will be created.

Create the new file by adding a `File` resource in the Puppet manifest and using a template to populate the contents of this file. The template uses variables that are set in the Puppet manifests by querying the user data for the instance.

Although this is a small change, implementing it cleanly requires changing a few of the Puppet manifest files. We could access the user data variable directly from the `myblog::create_project` class, but this goes against Puppet's best practice guidelines.

Instead, we will convert the top-level `myblog` class to a parameterized class, which takes the DB endpoint, username, and password as parameters. Placing variables in a class is the recommended way to introduce variation into Puppet templates, as it helps make modules a lot more reusable by avoiding variable scoping issues.

Example 5-12 shows an updated version of the myblog class that accepts the required parameters.

Example 5-12. MyBlog Puppet manifest with parameters

```
class myblog ( $db_endpoint, $db_user, $db_password ) {

    $app_path = "/srv/mezzanine"

    class {"supervisor": }

    require myblog::requirements

}
```

Update *puppet/modules/myblog/manifests/init.pp* with the contents of this example. The first line is changed to include a list of parameters that must be set when declaring an instance of the myblog class.

The next step is to modify *site.pp* so that it retrieves the new parameters from user data and passes them to the myblog class, as shown in Example 5-13. The file reads these parameters from the $userdata variable, which is a JSON object created by reading the $ec2_userdata string variable. parsejson is a function provided by Puppet's stdlib.

Example 5-13. Puppet site.pp file for MyBlog

```
require stdlib

node default {

    $userdata = parsejson($ec2_userdata)

    # Set variables from userdata
    $role = $userdata['role']

    $db_endpoint = $userdata['db_endpoint']
    $db_user = $userdata['db_user']
    $db_password = $userdata['db_password']


    case $role {
        "web": { $role_class = "myblog::web" }
        default: { fail("Unrecognized role: $role") }
    }
```

```
# Main myblog class, takes all params
class { "myblog":

    db_endpoint => $db_endpoint,
    db_user => $db_user,
    db_password => $db_password

}
# Role-specific class, e.g. myblog::web
class { $role_class: }

}
```

Update *puppet/manifests/site.pp* with the contents of this example.

Next, we need to update the myblog::create_project class so that it creates the *local_settings.py* file. This is shown in Example 5-14.

Example 5-14. Updated MyBlog initialization Puppet manifest

```
class myblog::create_project {
    # Create the Mezzanine project
    exec { "init-mezzanine-project":
        command => "/usr/local/bin/mezzanine-project $myblog::app_path",
        user => "mezzanine",
        creates => "$myblog::app_path/__init__.py"
    }


    # Create the local_settings.py file
    file { "$myblog::app_path/myblog/local_settings.py":
        ensure => present,
        content => template("myblog/local_settings.py.erb"),
        owner => "mezzanine",
        group => "mezzanine",
        require => Exec["init-mezzanine-project"],
        notify => Exec["init-mezzanine-db"]
    }


    # Create the database
    exec { "init-mezzanine-db":
        command => "/usr/bin/python manage.py createdb --noinput",
        user => "mezzanine",
        cwd => "$myblog::app_path",
        refreshonly => true
    }
```

This file should replace *puppet/modules/myblog/manifests/create_project.pp*. The main change is to add the `File` resource that creates *local_settings.py*. Its contents will be based on the template file named *local_settings.py.erb*.

Although we specify the template name as *myblog/local_settings.py.erb*, Puppet will look for the file in *puppet/modules/myblog/templates/local_settings.py.erb*.

As before, the `require` and `notify` parameters control the ordering of Puppet resources—note the repositioning of the `notify` line in the updated file. The *local_settings.py* file must be created before `createdb` is executed.

Finally, we need to create the template file that will be used to populate the *local_settings.py* file. This is shown in Example 5-15.

Example 5-15. Updated MyBlog database manifest

```
ALLOWED_HOSTS = "*"

DEBUG = True

DATABASES = {
    "default": {
        "ENGINE": "django.db.backends.mysql",
        "NAME": "mydb",
        "USER": "<%= @db_user %>",
        "PASSWORD": "<%= @db_password %>",
        "HOST": "<%= @db_endpoint %>",
        "PORT": "3306"
    }
}
```

Save this file to *puppet/modules/myblog/templates/local_settings.py.erb*. The content is almost exactly the same as the *local_settings.py* file we created manually, except that Puppet will replace the variables with information taken from user data.

> For more information on Puppet templates, see the documentation on Using Puppet Templates (*https://docs.puppet.com/puppet/latest/reference/lang_template.html*).

Example 5-16 contains the updated `myblog::requirements` class, now including the MySQL support packages.

Example 5-16. Updated MyBlog requirements Puppet manifest

```
class myblog::requirements {
```

```
$packages = ["python-dev", "python-pip", "libtiff5-dev", "libjpeg8-dev",
"zlib1g-dev", "libfreetype6-dev", "python-mysqldb", "mysql-client-5.6",
"libmysqlclient-dev"]

package { $packages:
    ensure  => installed
}
```

Commit the updated files to the Git repository:

```
git add -A
git commit -am 'added RDS database to stack'
```

With that step complete, we can move on to the caching server.

Mezzanine's built-in web server has the capability to selectively deliver only dynamically generated content, while delegating the application's static content delivery to a more efficient external web server. The DEBUG flag controls this behavior: once it is set to false, Django will no longer answer requests for any static content and the images, CSS, and JavaScript components of the application templates need to be delivered through another mechanism.

Running the manage.py collectstatic command will copy all files from the static directory of each Django application to the location defined in STATIC_ROOT. We leave as an exercise for the reader to map the URL defined by STATIC_URL to serve files from that directory. There is something to be learned by correctly sequencing the dependencies required to set up this configuration automatically. The authors chose to focus here on scale-out caching for the application as a whole as illustrated in the next section, making this detail less important as the caching layer can be relied on to serve static files even more effectively.

Creating an ElastiCache Node

Caching is a required part of any high-traffic web application, so it makes sense to include some caching in the example stack. We will use Amazon's ElastiCache service instead of running our own Memcache cluster. ElastiCache is a drop-in replacement for Memcache, which means minimal work is required on the client side.

If a cache server is specified in Mezzanine's settings file, unauthenticated page views will be automatically cached—i.e., anonymous users will see cached copies of the Mezzanine home page. To enable caching—and start using it—we simply need to let Mezzanine know there is a caching server available, which means modifying the *local_settings.py* file again.

Just as we did earlier in the chapter, we begin by manually setting up an ElastiCache node and then automating this configuration with Puppet and CloudFormation files.

First, visit the EC2 Security Groups page and create a new security group named cache. Grant access to members of the web EC2 security group, as shown in Figure 5-4.

Figure 5-4. Setting Cache Security Group permissions

After creating the cache security group and setting its permissions, go to the ElastiCache page (*https://console.aws.amazon.com/elasticache/home*) and click Create to open the Launch Cluster Wizard, which will first prompt you to choose between Memcached and Redis—select Memcached and scroll down the page. The second section of the wizard is shown in Figure 5-5.

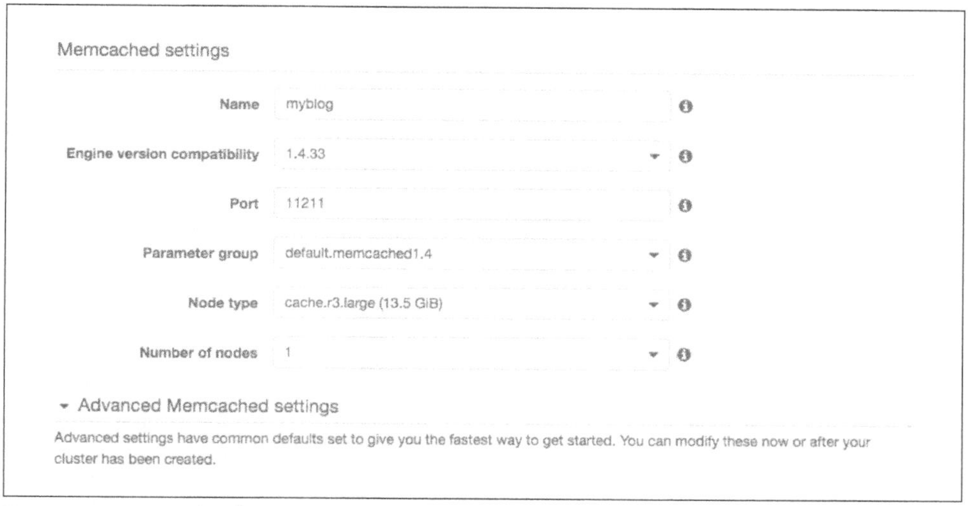

Memcached settings

Name: myblog

Engine version compatibility: 1.4.33

Port: 11211

Parameter group: default.memcached1.4

Node type: cache.r3.large (13.5 GiB)

Number of nodes: 1

▾ Advanced Memcached settings

Advanced settings have common defaults set to give you the fastest way to get started. You can modify these now or after your cluster has been created.

Figure 5-5. Launch Cluster Wizard

The key settings here are the name of the cluster and the number of nodes. We are choosing to launch a cache cluster containing a single node, which is not ideal for reliability or resilience, but is perfect to minimize costs for testing.

After selecting the options shown in the screenshot, open the Advanced Memcached setting to access the next group of settings. This is shown in Figure 5-6.

This screen has only one setting that is important for our purposes: the Security Group. Select the security group you created (cache) in addition to your preselected default subnet, and click Create.

Once the ElastiCache cluster has launched, you will see it in the Cache Clusters list. Click the name of the cache cluster to go to the description page. Here you will see a list of information describing the cache cluster, including its configuration endpoint.

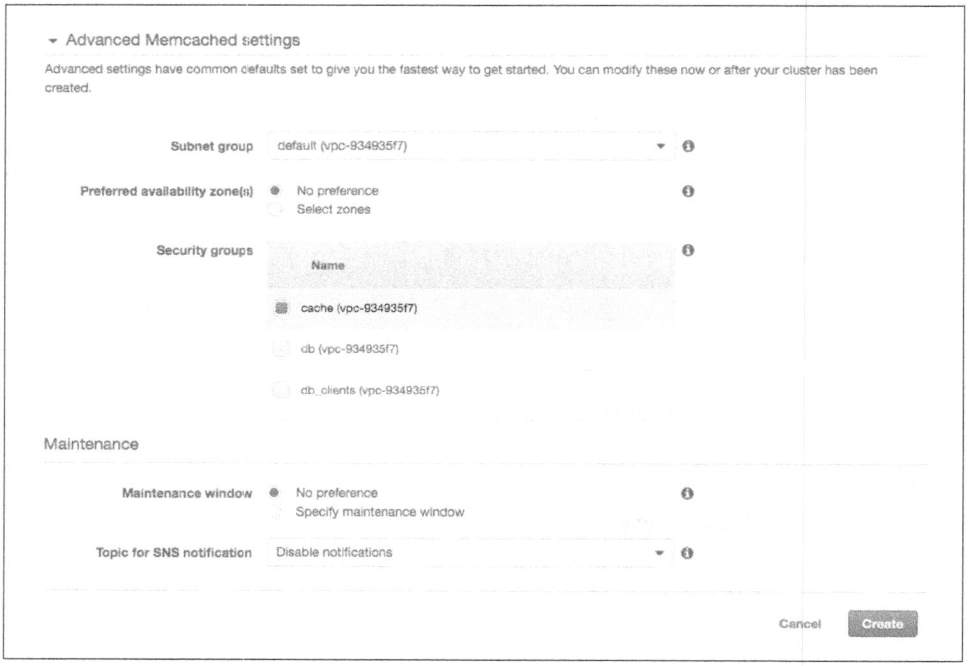

Figure 5-6. Setting the security group

ElastiCache Auto Discovery

The number of nodes in an ElastiCache cluster can change at any time, due to either planned events such as launching new nodes to increase the size of the cluster, or unplanned events such as a reduction in capacity caused by a crashed node. This can lead to problems when client applications try to connect to nodes that no longer exist, or never connect to new nodes because the client is not aware of the node's existence.

To help users build more resilient applications, Amazon has extended ElastiCache with a feature known as *Auto Discovery*. This allows clients to connect to a single address—the configuration endpoint—and retrieve information about all nodes in the cluster.

Using Auto Discovery requires a compatible client, because this feature is not part of the vanilla Memcache specification. Amazon has released compatible clients for PHP and Java, and plans to add clients for other languages in the future.

At a technical level, a configuration endpoint address is simply a CNAME DNS record. Resolving this address will return the hostname for one of the nodes in the ElastiCache cluster.

Amazon ensures that all nodes in the cluster contain up-to-date information about their sibling nodes. Auto Discovery–compatible clients use the endpoint address to

---

connect to one of the target nodes, from which they can retrieve a list of other nodes in the cluster.

If you are not using Java or PHP, you can still use Auto Discovery, albeit with a bit more effort. You will need to periodically connect to the configuration endpoint to retrieve information about members of the cluster and update your local Memcache client configuration.

In some cases, the configuration endpoint is all you need. If you maintain an ElastiCache cluster containing a single node, you can add the configuration endpoint directly to your client configuration. Because you have only one node, the configuration endpoint CNAME will always resolve to the same node address.

When running clusters with two or more nodes, using the configuration endpoint directly from an incompatible client has two drawbacks. Depending on how your client caches DNS records, traffic might become unevenly distributed between your nodes, leading to underutilized cache nodes. You will also have no control over which node your data resides on, leading to an unnecessarily high cache miss rate.

Because our cache cluster contains only a single node, we can use the configuration endpoint to configure our Memcache client.

Configuring Mezzanine to use caching is simple: if a cache host is defined in the settings file, Mezzanine will use it to cache unauthenticated page views. We first need to install the appropriate Python library so Mezzanine can communicate with ElastiCache—we will use the python-memcached library. Install it as follows:

```
sudo pip install python-memcached
```

The next step is to add the cache configuration information to Mezzanine's settings. Append the following code to */srv/mezzanine/myblog/local_settings.py*, replacing the hostname with your ElastiCache cluster's configuration endpoint:

```
CACHES = {
    "default": {
        "BACKEND": "django.core.cache.backends.memcached.MemcachedCache",
        "LOCATION": "myblog.gdkr4r.cfg.use1.cache.amazonaws.com:11211"
    }
}
```

With the configuration file updated, restart the Mezzanine process:

```
sudo supervisorctl restart myblog_app
```

Visit the Mezzanine page in your web browser. Everything should look exactly the same. However, if you refresh the page, you may notice it feels faster on subsequent requests. Of course, *it feels faster* is not the most scientific of tests, so we should verify that data is, in fact, being written to the Memcache node. We can do this by connecting to the node with Telnet and checking that it contains a record of the cached page content.

Open a connection to the node:

```
telnet myblog.gdkr4r.cfg.use1.cache.amazonaws.com 11211
```

Memcache does not contain a built-in command to list all stored keys, so we must take a slightly roundabout approach here. Within Memcache, data is stored in a series of *slabs*. We can list the slabs with the `stats slabs` command:

```
$ stats slabs
STAT 20:chunk_size 7104
STAT 20:chunks_per_page 147
STAT 20:total_pages 1
STAT 20:total_chunks 147
STAT 20:used_chunks 1
STAT 20:free_chunks 146
STAT 20:free_chunks_end 0
[output truncated]
```

The number in the first column after STAT is the slab ID; in this example, it's 20. We can then dump the keys that belong to that slab with the `stats cachedump` command. This accepts two arguments: the slab ID and the maximum number of keys to dump. Execute this command within your Telnet session:

```
$ stats cachedump 20 100
ITEM :1:e67b2514a4f5d0b3253baa637db8ba01 [6811 b; 1475464297 s]
END
```

A single key is dumped, verifying that our visit to the web page cached its data. You can delete this key:

```
$ delete :1:e67b2514a4f5d0b3253baa637db8ba01
```

After deleting the key, refresh the Mezzanine page and use the `cachedump` command to verify that a new key has been written.

 You can exit this telnet session by entering `Ctrl-]` and using the telnet client's `quit` command, like so:

```
$ ^]
telnet> quit
Connection closed.
```

Now that ElastiCache has been tested, we can make the relevant changes to the Puppet and CloudFormation files.

ElastiCache: Updating Puppet and CloudFormation

Because we laid much of the groundwork when setting up RDS, updating Puppet and CloudFormation to use Puppet will be a lot simpler than the previous section.

We will begin by ensuring that the `python-memcached` library is installed when the instance is provisioned. The *puppet/modules/myblog/manifests/requirements.pp* file contains the following line:

```
$pip_packages = ["Mezzanine"]
```

Replace it with the following:

```
$pip_packages = ["Mezzanine", "python-memcached"]
```

Next, we need to add a new parameter to the `myblog` Puppet module, which will be used to store the configuration endpoint of the cache cluster. Update *puppet/modules/myblog/manifests/init.pp*, changing the class signature to this:

```
class myblog ( $db_endpoint, $db_user, $db_password, $cache_endpoint ) {
```

The *puppet/manifests/site.pp* file must also be updated so that this parameter is passed when the `myblog` class is declared. Update this file with the following content:

```
require stdlib

node default {

    $userdata = parsejson($ec2_userdata)

    # Set variables from userdata
    $role = $userdata['role']
    $db_endpoint = $userdata['db_endpoint']
    $db_user = $userdata['db_user']
    $db_password = $userdata['db_password']
    $cache_endpoint = $userdata['cache_endpoint']

    case $role {
        "web": { $role_class = "myblog::web" }
        default: { fail("Unrecognized role: $role") }
    }

    class { "myblog":
        db_endpoint => $db_endpoint,
        db_user => $db_user,
        db_password => $db_password,
        cache_endpoint => $cache_endpoint
    }
    # Role-specific class, e.g. myblog::web
    class { $role_class: }

}
```

Finally, update *puppet/modules/myblog/templates/local_settings.py.erb* and append the cache configuration:

```
CACHES = {
    "default": {
        "BACKEND": "django.core.cache.backends.memcached.MemcachedCache",
        "LOCATION": "<%= @cache_endpoint %>:11211"
    }
}
```

Those are the changes required for the Puppet side of the equation. Updating the CloudFormation stack is equally straightforward. Rather than replicating the entire stack template again, we will just include those sections that need to be updated.

Example 5-17 shows the CloudFormation stack template section that declares the resources we need to use ElastiCache: the cache cluster itself, an ElastiCache security group, and a security group ingress rule that grants our web server instance access to the cache cluster nodes as a member of the WebSecurityGroup security group. Insert the code into the stack template, located at *cloudformation/myblog.json*, before the existing BlogDB resource.

Example 5-17. ElastiCache CloudFormation stack

```
"Resources" : {

    "CacheCluster": {
      "Type" : "AWS::ElastiCache::CacheCluster",
      "Properties" : {
        "CacheNodeType" : "cache.r3.large",
        "CacheSecurityGroupNames" : [ "CacheSecurityGroup" ],
        "Engine" : "memcached",
        "NumCacheNodes" : "1"
    }
  },
  "CacheSecurityGroup": {
    "Type": "AWS::ElastiCache::SecurityGroup",
    "Properties": {
      "Description"  : "Allow access from Web instances"
    }
  },
  "CacheSecurityGroupIngress": {
    "Type": "AWS::ElastiCache::SecurityGroupIngress",
    "Properties": {
      "CacheSecurityGroupName"  : { "Ref" : "CacheSecurityGroup" },
      "EC2SecurityGroupName"    : { "Ref" : "WebSecurityGroup" }
    }
  },

"BlogDB" : {
```

Because the cache cluster configuration endpoint address is passed to the web server instances as user data, we also need to modify the EC2 instance resource. We will again use the `Fn::GetAtt` function, this time to retrieve the configuration endpoint address.

Example 5-18 shows the updated user data—note the addition of the cache_endpoint attribute. Replace the `UserData` attribute of the `WebInstance` resource with the code shown in this example.

Example 5-18. User data with ElastiCache and database parameters

```
"UserData" : {
  "Fn::Base64" : {
    "Fn::Join" : [ "", [
      "{\"db_endpoint\": \"", { "Fn::GetAtt": [ "BlogDB", "Endpoint.Address" ] },
"\",",
      " \"db_user\": \"", { "Ref": "DBUser" }, "\",",
      " \"db_password\": \"", { "Ref": "DBPassword" }, "\",",

      " \"cache_endpoint\": \"",
      { "Fn::GetAtt": [ "CacheCluster", "ConfigurationEndpoint.Address" ] }, "\"}"

    ] ]
  }
}
```

Now, when the stack is created, the configuration endpoint will be passed to the instance as user data and used to populate the *local_settings.py* file.

As always, finish by committing the changes to the Git repository:

```
git add -A
git commit -am 'added ElastiCache cluster'
```

Installing Celery with Simple Queuing Service

The final component in the example application stack is the background task-processing service, which will be implemented using Celery. Celery (*http://www.celery project.org*) is an asynchronous task queue based on distributed message passing. The execution units, called tasks, can be executed concurrently by one or more worker servers.

Mezzanine does not, by default, use Celery, so we will briefly digress into the realm of Python programming and build a simple task that will give Celery something useful to do as part of the demonstration. In this case, *something useful* means checking user-submitted comments for spam content.

Whenever a new comment is posted on the site, Mezzanine will send a signal to notify other components in the application, letting them take action on the new comment. Signals (*https://docs.djangoproject.com/en/dev/topics/signals/*) are a feature of Django, and are an implementation of the Observer software design pattern.

We will write some code that listens for this signal. When a new comment is posted, it will be checked by our extremely simple spam filter function.

When we launch the final stack containing this infrastructure, Celery and Mezzanine will be running on separate EC2 instances. However, it is a waste of time (and money) to launch another development machine to configure Celery when we could instead use the web application instance we have used in the previous steps. So, for testing purposes, perform the steps in this section on the web application instance.

Celery works by passing messages between your application processes and the background worker processes. These messages describe the task that should be executed, along with any parameters required by the task. Celery needs somewhere to store these messages, so it uses a message broker for this purpose. In keeping with the strategy of using Amazon services for as many tasks as possible in this example stack, we will use SQS, Amazon's own message queuing service, as the message broker. Because Celery has built-in support for SQS, it is really simple to use.

We will start by creating an SQS queue to learn how the service works. In the Management Console, go to the SQS page (*https://console.aws.amazon.com/sqs/home*) and click Create New Queue. Enter **test_queue** as the queue name, select the standard queue type, and click Configure Queue. This will expose another part of the page. Scroll downward and click Create Queue—the remaining settings are default values at the time of writing.

Figure 5-7 shows the Create Queue screen.

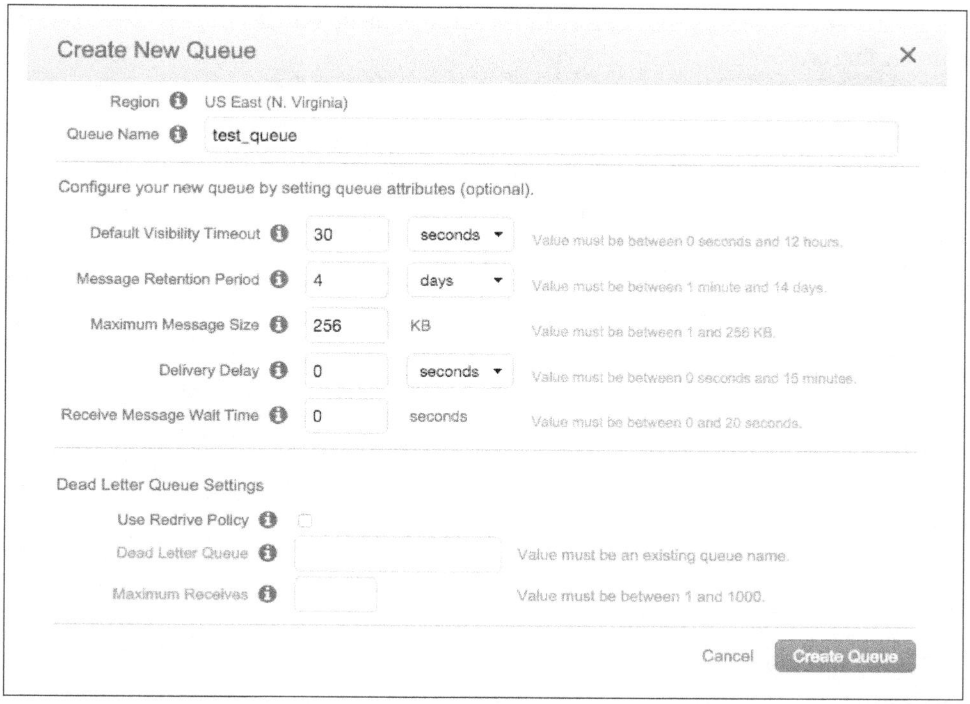

Figure 5-7. Creating a new SQS queue

Once the queue has been created, you will be returned to the Queues page, where you can see the details of the new queue. Now we need to configure the queue's access permissions so we can read from and write to it.

Select the Permissions tab and click Add a Permission, as shown in Figure 5-8 (alternatively you may use the Queue Actions pull-down menu).

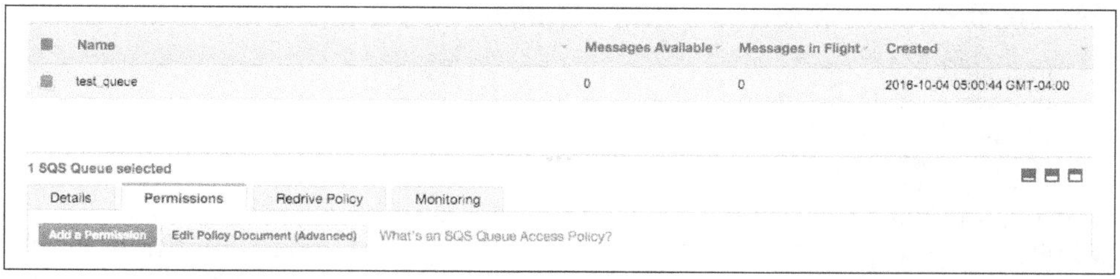

Figure 5-8. Queue permissions

On the next screen, select the options shown in Figure 5-9, replacing 740376006796 with your 12-digit AWS account ID, and click Add Permission. Now anyone in your AWS account has full permissions on this SQS queue. As we have demonstrated in

Chapter 3, it is necessary for a production setup to define a more restrictive security policy using IAM.

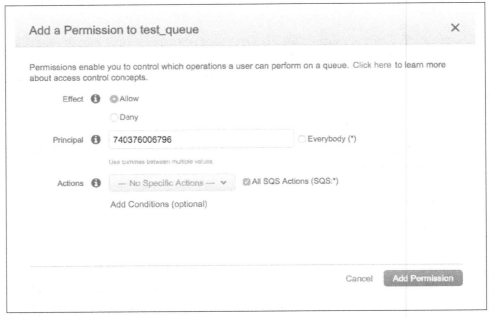

Figure 5-9. Adding a queue permission

You will not need to perform these steps for the production queue. Celery initializes an SQS queue for its own use automatically, named *celery* by default, as long as AWS credentials with adequate permissions are supplied in its configuration.

Now that we are a little more comfortable with SQS, let's build some familiarity with Celery itself to understand how all the parts fit together. Install the `celery` package by executing the following on a fresh Ubuntu instance:

```
sudo apt update
sudo apt install python-pip
sudo pip install celery
sudo pip install boto3
```

Boto version 3 is a dependency of Celery's SQS transport, which is not installed by default, as users can choose between a variety of different message broker options.

 The `django-celery` convenience package has been deprecated with Celery version 4 and above, and its use is no longer recommended.

Celery tasks are simply Python functions. By convention, these are stored in a file named *tasks.py*.

In this kind of queuing implementation, tasks are asynchronously distributed via message-passing to worker threads that idle until any such tasks become available. The system is scaled by adding more workers, while the message queue can buffer any work exceeding the capacity of the current workers. Because the system operates asynchronously, no process needs to wait for another process to complete—in our case, a comment can be submitted and the next web page can render without waiting for the spam check to complete.

The canonical example of a Celery task is asynchronously adding two numbers. Pairs of numbers are stored in the queue and retrieved by a worker thread for processing. In our version of this classic, we store tasks on Amazon SQS; see Example 5-19.

Example 5-19. The simplest Celery task

```python
from celery import Celery

import os
import urllib

AWS_KEY = os.getenv('AWS_ACCESS_KEY_ID')
AWS_SECRET = os.getenv('AWS_SECRET_ACCESS_KEY')

if not (AWS_KEY and AWS_SECRET):
        print "AWS environment variables are not set\n"
        exit(1)

app = Celery('tasks', broker = 'sqs://{0}:{1}@'.format(urllib.quote(AWS_KEY, \
            safe=''), urllib.quote(AWS_SECRET, safe='')))

@app.task
def add(x, y):
    return x + y
```

Launch a Celery worker from the scratch working directory containing your copy of *tasks.py* with this command:

```
$ celery -A tasks worker -E --loglevel=info

 -------------- celery@ip-172-31-8-239 v4.0.2 (latentcall)
---- **** -----
--- * ***  * -- Linux-4.4.0-1052-aws-x86_64-with-Ubuntu-16.04-xenial 2018-06-19
09:44:15
-- * - **** ---
- ** ---------- [config]
- ** ---------- .> app:         tasks:0x7f95ebf6aed0
- ** ---------- .> transport:   sqs://AKIAIKVKZ3IG6VXNRSIA:**@localhost//
- ** ---------- .> results:     disabled://
```

```
- *** --- * --- .> concurrency: 1 (prefork)
-- ******* ---- .> task events: ON
--- ***** -----
 ------------- [queues]
              .> celery              exchange=celery(direct) key=celery


[tasks]
  . tasks.add

[2017-12-17 03:42:17,966: INFO/MainProcess] Connected to sqs://
AKIAIKVKZ3IG6VXNRSIA:**@localhost//
[2017-12-17 03:42:18,013: INFO/MainProcess] celery@ip-172-31-8-239 ready.
```

Individual tasks are stored in an SQS queue, waiting for asynchronous retrieval and processing by a worker. You can manually inject tasks directly from Python to test our example code—try the following in another terminal session:

```
$ python
Python 2.7.6 (default, Jun 22 2015, 17:58:13)
[GCC 4.8.2] on linux2
Type "help", "copyright", "credits" or "license" for more information.
>>> from tasks import add
>>> add.delay(4, 4)
<AsyncResult: 31a46a63-576a-4fef-a299-40831cd53c8b>
>>>
```

If you now turn your attention back to the terminal running the Celery worker, you will spot the results of the worker task's processing of the input we just provided:

```
[2017-12-17 03:44:56,805: INFO/MainProcess] Received task:
tasks.add[31a46a63-576a-4fef-a299-40831cd53c8b]
[2017-12-17 03:44:56,807: INFO/ForkPoolWorker-1] Task
tasks.add[31a46a63-576a-4fef-a299-40831cd53c8b] succeeded in
0.000394316390157s: 8
```

Adding two numbers is clearly not a very impressive feat, but the queuing and asynchronous processing we just demonstrated allows an application to decouple the scaling of its components. This is an essential pattern found in microservice architectures.

We have already shown in "IAM Roles" on page 98 how the need to make credentials available in a running instance can be eliminated using IAM roles. A custom role could grant the instance access to SQS without the need for credentials, thus limiting the footprint of a breach where the instance itself is compromised—here, we tried to keep our example as simple as possible.

Now that we are familiar with Celery's design and operation, we can resume integrating the last component of our example application. We do not need to initialize an

SQS queue ourselves, as Celery will create a queue named `celery` automatically if given adequate permissions. Begin by installing the Celery package—as we did for Mezzanine, we are going to select a version that is known to work well with the rest of the stack:

```
sudo pip install celery==4.1.1
sudo pip install boto3
sudo apt install python-pycurl
```

Example 5-20 shows the code that is the backbone of our Celery application. Save it in a file named */srv/mezzanine/myblog/celery.py*, making sure it is owned by user *mezzanine*.

Example 5-20. Integrating Celery with Mezzanine

```
from __future__ import absolute_import, unicode_literals
import os
import urllib
from celery import Celery

AWS_KEY = os.getenv('AWS_ACCESS_KEY_ID')
AWS_SECRET = os.getenv('AWS_SECRET_ACCESS_KEY')
if not (AWS_KEY and AWS_SECRET):
        print "AWS environment variables are not set\n"
        exit(1)

os.environ.setdefault('DJANGO_SETTINGS_MODULE', 'myblog.settings')

app = Celery('myblog', broker = 'sqs://{0}:{1}@'.format(urllib.quote(AWS_KEY, \
safe=''), urllib.quote(AWS_SECRET, safe='')))

app.config_from_object('django.conf:settings', namespace='CELERY')

app.autodiscover_tasks()
```

This code initializes the `myblog>` Celery app itself, setting the default Django settings for the Celery app `myblog`. We then initialize a namespace for all Celery-related configuration keys. As our *tasks.py* file lives in the web application directory, we do not need to import it explicitly. Celery can autodiscover task modules that are stored within Django applications—we use this capability to load task modules from all registered Django apps.

Example 5-21 shows the configuration required to have our Celery app loaded early in the Mezzanine startup process. The `import` statement makes sure that the app is imported when Django starts up, so that `shared_task` can use it. Save it to */srv/ mezzanine/myblog/__init__.py* taking care not to alter file ownership.

Example 5-21. Loading the Celery app into Mezzanine

```
from __future__ import absolute_import, unicode_literals

default_app_config = 'myblog.apps.MyBlogConfig'

# This will make sure the app is always imported when
# Django starts so that shared_task will use this app.
from .celery import app as celery_app

__all__ = ('celery_app',)
```

Example 5-22 shows the Python code that handles the signal received when a new comment is posted.

Example 5-22. The simple asynchronous spam check

```
from celery import Celery
import os
import urllib
from django.dispatch import receiver
from django.db.models.signals import post_save
from mezzanine.generic.models import ThreadedComment

AWS_KEY = os.getenv('AWS_ACCESS_KEY_ID')
AWS_SECRET = os.getenv('AWS_SECRET_ACCESS_KEY')
if not (AWS_KEY and AWS_SECRET):
        print "AWS environment variables are not set\n"
        exit(1)

app = Celery('tasks', broker = 'sqs://{0}:{1}@'.format(urllib.quote(AWS_KEY, \
safe=''), urllib.quote(AWS_SECRET, safe='')))

def is_comment_spam(comment):
    # This check is just an example!
    if "spam" in comment.comment:
        return True

@app.task
def process_comment_async(comment_id):
    print "Processing comment"
    comment = ThreadedComment.objects.get(pk=comment_id)
    if is_comment_spam(comment):
        # The comment is spam, so hide it
        ThreadedComment.objects.filter(id=comment_id).update(is_public=False)

@receiver(post_save, sender=ThreadedComment)
def process_comment(sender, instance, **kwargs):
    process_comment_async.delay(instance.id)
```

By convention, Celery tasks are contained within a Python module named `tasks`. Django applications can contain their own tasks module that implements tasks relevant to the application's purpose. For example, a Django application that integrates with Twitter might provide tasks to asynchronously post new tweets or scrape profile information. In this case the code initializes our `tasks` module instructing it to use an SQS queue with appropriate credentials.

Save this code to */srv/mezzanine/myblog/tasks.py*, making sure it is owned by the user *mezzanine* like all others in this directory. Before moving on with the configuration, let's look at what this code is doing. This requires a brief description of a useful Django feature: signals.

Signals can be thought of as hooks for your custom code to connect to. For example, every time a database object is saved, a `post_save` signal is sent out by Django. The `@receiver` function decorator informs Django that whenever a `ThreadedComment` object sends the `post_save` signal (i.e., a new comment is posted to the blog), the `process_comment` function is called.

The `process_comment` function calls `process_Comment_async.delay`. This does not execute the code immediately—instead, it posts a message to the Celery queue. This message is picked up by a Celery worker, and the code in `process_comment_async` is executed by the worker.

This means that whenever a comment is posted to the blog, it will be initially displayed (Figure 5-10). After a worker picks up the job from the queue, the message will be hidden if it contains spammy content, as defined by the `is_comment_spam` function. In this trivial case, we simply check whether the string `spam` exists in the comment text. Alas, real spammers are not so easy to catch. You might want to update this function to perform a more reliable spam check, such as submitting the comment to Akismet's spam-checking service (*http://akismet.com*).

Figure 5-10. Comment spam hidden by our Celery task

Login credentials can be provided using the environment variables AWS_ACCESS_KEY_ID and AWS_SECRET_ACCESS_KEY, in which case the broker's URL may be simply set to sqs://. This is really convenient during development, while leaving account credentials in the shell environment would be quite ill advised in production.

 Note the @ at the end of the broker parameter URL (this is required), and that the AWS access secret may contain unsafe characters that require URL-encoding. We take care of this step in our code, but should you ever need to hardcode credentials for testing, this can be easily accomplished with the ever-handy jq:

```
$ echo -n 'hCJ/Fn3nE378Hb7WjGpSYHa9TRCsia/4UcAd+MG7' |
jq -R -r @uri
hCJ%2fFn3nE378Hb7WjGpSYHa9TRCsia%2f4UcAd%2bMG7
```

Because we created our queue in the default us-east-1 region, we do not need to add the BROKER_TRANSPORT_OPTIONS setting. If you choose to create your queue in another region, you will need to use this setting as detailed in the Django project's documentation.

With that done, you can launch the Celery worker process, which will wait for new tasks to be written to the SQS queue. Launch the process:

```
sudo -u mezzanine python manage.py runserver 0.0.0.0:8000
sudo -u mezzanine celery -A myblog worker -l info
```

If everything is configured correctly, you will see output similar to the following:

```
$ sudo -u mezzanine celery -A myblog worker -l info
 -------------- celery@ip-172-31-49-100 v4.1.1 (latentcall)
---- **** -----
--- * ***  * -- Linux-4.4.0-1052-aws-x86_64-with-Ubuntu-16.04-xenial 2018-06-20
16:38:36
-- * - **** ---
- ** ---------- [config]
- ** ---------- .> app:         myblog:0x7f7dd6a30310
- ** ---------- .> transport:   sqs://AKIAIKVKZ3IG6VXNRSIA:**@localhost//
- ** ---------- .> results:     disabled://
- *** --- * --- .> concurrency: 1 (prefork)
-- ******* ---- .> task events: OFF (enable -E to monitor tasks in this worker)
--- ***** -----
 -------------- [queues]
                .> celery           exchange=celery(direct) key=celery


[tasks]
  . myblog.tasks.process_comment_async
```

```
[2018-06-24 14:11:33,206: INFO/MainProcess] Starting new HTTPS connection (1):
queue.amazonaws.com
[2018-06-24 14:11:33,243: INFO/MainProcess] Connected to sqs://
AKIAIKVKZ6IG3VXNRSDA:**@localhost//
[2018-06-24 14:11:33,280: INFO/MainProcess] Starting new HTTPS connection (1):
queue.amazonaws.com
[2018-06-24 14:11:33,328: INFO/MainProcess] celery@ip-172-31-9-164 ready.
```

The final line of this output shows that your *tasks.py* module has been loaded successfully.

With Celery running, create a new blog post in your Mezzanine site by visiting a URL
of the form *http://example.com/admin/blog/blogpost/add/* (substitute the URL of your
instance here). After creating the blog post, browse to the post's page on the main site.
If your blog post title was *test*, for example, this will be *http://example.com/blog/test/*.

Post a comment on the blog page by filling in the comment form. After clicking the
Comment button, you will see some activity in the Celery console, as the task is
received and executed:

```
[2018-06-24 15:04:31,424: INFO/MainProcess] celery@ip-172-31-9-164 ready.
[2018-06-24 15:07:59,531: INFO/MainProcess] Received task:
myblog.tasks.process_comment_async[a4f18b4a-ecc5-42d9-8f91-4dcee35f0456]
[2018-06-24 15:07:59,533: WARNING/ForkPoolWorker-1] Processing comment
[2018-06-24 15:07:59,551: INFO/ForkPoolWorker-1] Task
myblog.tasks.process_comment_async[a4f18b4a-ecc5-42d9-8f91-4dcee35f0456] succee-
ded in 0.0183701957576s: None
```

Assuming your example comment was not particularly spammy and did not contain
the string spam, it will remain on the site after the Celery task has completed. Otherwise, it will be hidden shortly after being posted. The Mezzanine console will just
read:

```
[24/Jun/2018 15:07:59] "POST /comment/ HTTP/1.1" 302 0
```

In this example application, we are choosing to display comments by default and hide
them if they prove to be spam. Another option would be to hide comments by default
and display them only if they are not spam.

Celery: Updating Puppet and CloudFormation

With Celery working, we can update the Puppet and CloudFormation configurations.
This will differ slightly from the changes required to add ElastiCache and RDS,
because Celery and the web application will be running on separate instances. Therefore, we need to define a new role in our Puppet manifests so that the correct processes will be started on each instance.

Begin by updating the *puppet/manifests/site.pp* file, adding celery as one of the available role types:

```
case $role {
    "web": { $role_class = "myblog::web" }
    "celery": { $role_class = "myblog::celery" }
    default: { fail("Unrecognised role: $role") }
}
```

The CloudFormation stack itself will need adjustment to include a new `CeleryAMI` parameter:

```
"WebAMI": {
  "Type": "String"
},
"CeleryAMI": {
  "Type": "String"
},
"KeyPair": {
  "Type": "String"
},
```

Remember to update the `$role_class` to dynamically include Puppet modules based on the instance's user data, so instances with a `$role` of `celery` will use the `myblog::celery` module. Example 5-23 shows the `myblog::celery` module.

Example 5-23. Celery Puppet module

```
class myblog::celery {
    Class["myblog::celery"] -> Class["myblog"]

    supervisor::service { "myblog_celery":
        ensure  => present,
        enable  => true,
        command => "/usr/bin/python ${myblog::app_path}/manage.py celery -A myblog
worker",
        user    => "mezzanine",
        group   => "mezzanine"
    }

}
```

Save this module to *puppet/modules/myblog/manifests/celery.py*. This simple module ensures that Supervisor starts the Celery process. All of the heavy lifting is done in other parts of the `myblog` module—one of the many reasons for separating Puppet modules into separate manifest files.

When installing Celery, we introduced code in three files. These changes must also be made in the templates used for these files, with one modification. Append the code from Example 5-20 to *puppet/modules/myblog/templates/celery.py.erb*, the code from Example 5-21 to *puppet/modules/myblog/templates/__init__.py.erb*, and the code from

Example 5-22 to *puppet/modules/myblog/templates/tasks.py.erb*, respectively. Then replace the broker parameter with the following setting:

```
broker = 'sqs://@'
```

This removes the AWS credentials from the broker URL, telling Celery to use the keys provided by the IAM role assigned to the EC2 instance.

Now we can add Celery to the CloudFormation stack. We want to make the following changes to the stack:

1. Create an SQS queue to store Celery messages.
2. Create an IAM policy that allows web and Celery instances to write to the SQS queue.
3. Create an EC2 instance to run Celery.
4. Update the ElastiCache and RDS security groups to permit Celery access.
5. Update the Web EC2 instance so it can use the SQS queue name as a dynamic setting.

This requires changes to *cloudformation/myblog.json*. For the sake of clarity, we will gradually update this file in a series of small steps.

Begin by adding the SQS queue:

```
"CeleryQueue": {
    "Type": "AWS::SQS::Queue"
},
```

Add this snippet to the Resources section of *myblog.json*, at the same level as WebInstance.

Next, we will create the IAM policy and role that will set up the AWS access credentials that Celery and web instances use to access the SQS queue:

```
"MyBlogRole": {
  "Type": "AWS::IAM::Role",
  "Properties": {
    "AssumeRolePolicyDocument": {
      "Statement": [ {
        "Effect": "Allow",
        "Principal": {
          "Service": [ "ec2.amazonaws.com" ]
        },
        "Action": [ "sts:AssumeRole" ]
      } ]
    },
    "Path": "/"
  }
},
```

```json
"MyBlogRolePolicies": {
    "Type": "AWS::IAM::Policy",
    "Properties": {
        "PolicyName": "MyBlogRole",
        "PolicyDocument": {
            "Statement" : [ {
                "Effect" : "Allow",
                "Action" : [ "sqs:*" ],
                "Resource" : "{ "Ref" : "CeleryQueue" }"
            } ]
        },
        "Roles": [ { "Ref": "MyBlogRole" } ]
    }
},
"MyBlogInstanceProfile": {
    "Type": "AWS::IAM::InstanceProfile",
    "Properties": {
        "Path": "/",
        "Roles": [ { "Ref": "MyBlogRole" } ]
    }
},
```

Again, insert this code into *myblog.json* at the same level as `WebInstance`.

The final new resources are the Celery EC2 instance and associated security group:

```json
"CeleryInstance" : {
    "Type" : "AWS::EC2::Instance",
    "Properties" : {
        "SecurityGroups" : [ { "Ref" : "CelerySecurityGroup" } ],
        "KeyName" : "my-ssh-keypair",
        "ImageId" : { "Ref" : "CeleryAMI" },
        "IamInstanceProfile": {
            "Ref": "MyBlogInstanceProfile"
        },
        "UserData" : {
            "Fn::Base64" : {
                "Fn::Join" : [ "", [
                    "{\"role\": \"celery\",",
                    " \"db_endpoint\": \"\", { "Fn::GetAtt": [ "BlogDB", "End-
point.Address" ] }, "\",",
                    " \"db_user\": \"\", { "Ref": "DBUser" }, "\",",
                    " \"db_password\": \"\", { "Ref": "DBPassword" }, "\",",
                    " \"cache_endpoint\": \"\", { "Fn::GetAtt": [ "CacheCluster", "Configu-
rationEndpoint.Address" ] }, "\"}"
                ] ]
            }
        }
    }
},
"CelerySecurityGroup" : {
    "Type" : "AWS::EC2::SecurityGroup",
    "Properties" : {
```

```
       "GroupDescription" : "Allow SSH from anywhere",
       "SecurityGroupIngress" : [
          {
            "IpProtocol" : "tcp",
            "FromPort" : "22",
            "ToPort" : "22",
            "CidrIp" : "0.0.0.0/0"
          }
       ]
    }
  },
  "CelerySecurityGroupIngress": {
    "Type": "AWS::ElastiCache::SecurityGroupIngress",
    "Properties": {
      "CacheSecurityGroupName"  : { "Ref" : "CacheSecurityGroup" },
      "EC2SecurityGroupName"    : { "Ref" : "CelerySecurityGroup" }
    }
  },
```

Insert this code into the `Resources` section of *myblog.json*, at the same level as the
`WebInstance` resource. The `CeleryInstance` resource also uses a reference to the
AMI input, meaning it will use the same AMI as the `WebInstance`.

That's it for the new resources. We need to make a few other changes to this file
before it is complete.

The `CelerySecurityGroupIngress` resource gives the `CeleryInstance` access to the
ElastiCache cluster. We also need to allow Celery to access the RDS database instance,
which requires another modification to *myblog.json*:

```
     "DBSecurityGroup" : {
       "Type" : "AWS::EC2::SecurityGroup",
       "Properties" : {
         "GroupDescription" : "Allow inbound MySQL access from web instances",
         "SecurityGroupIngress" : [
            {
              "IpProtocol" : "tcp",
              "FromPort" : "3306",
              "ToPort" : "3306",
              "SourceSecurityGroupName" : { "Ref" : "WebSecurityGroup" }
            },
            {
              "IpProtocol" : "tcp",
              "FromPort" : "3306",
              "ToPort" : "3306",
              "SourceSecurityGroupName" : { "Ref" : "CelerySecurityGroup" }
            }
         ]
       },
```

Update the `DBSecurityGroup` resource definition as shown here, so that the
`CelerySecurityGroup` is listed in the `DBSecurityGroupIngress` attribute.

The `WebInstance` resource also requires some changes:

```json
"WebInstance" : {
  "Type" : "AWS::EC2::Instance",
  "Properties" : {
    "SecurityGroups" : [ { "Ref" : "WebSecurityGroup" } ],
    "KeyName" : "my-ssh-keypair",
    "ImageId" : { "Ref" : "WebAMI" },
    "IamInstanceProfile": {
        "Ref": "MyBlogInstanceProfile"
    },
    "UserData" : {
      "Fn::Base64" : {
        "Fn::Join" : [ "", [
          "{\"role\": \"web\",",
          " \"db_endpoint\": \"", { "Fn::GetAtt": [ "BlogDB", "End-
point.Address" ] }, "\",",
          " \"db_user\": \"", { "Ref": "DBUser" }, "\",",
          " \"db_password\": \"", { "Ref": "DBPassword" }, "\",",
          " \"cache_endpoint\": \"", { "Fn::GetAtt": [ "CacheCluster", "Configu-
rationEndpoint.Address" ] }, "\"}"
        ] ]
      }
    }
  }
},
```

This code shows the updated version of the `WebInstance` resource. Note the addition of the `IamInstanceProfile` property, which makes the EC2 instance inherit the permissions described in the IAM policy.

With that change complete, *myblog.json* now contains a full description of our stack resources.

Avoid committing security keys to a code repository as any data entering a version control system will reside there forever. This is clearly dangerous working with public code repositories like GitHub, which are routinely targeted by hackers scanning for AWS keys accidentally leaked. Perhaps less obviously, it is equally inappropriate to store security credentials in a corporate code repository with more than a single user.

Michael Dowling of the Amazon AWS team has released the git-secrets (*https://github.com/awslabs/git-secrets*) utility to validate that your code commits do not contain anything they shouldn't. `git-secrets` works equally well on macOS and Ubuntu hosts, and setup is straightforward:

```
make install
```

Macintosh users should instead use `brew install git-secrets`.

The most basic `git-secrets` configuration requires setting up `git` hooks in each monitored repository, as well as defining the forbidden patterns. To prevent accidental committing of AWS credentials, run the following in your repository's working copy:

```
git secrets --install
git secrets --register-aws
```

This will stop any commit containing strings found in *~/.aws/credentials*. This simple bit of automation can help ensure the passwords found on your development machine are not accidentally recorded for posterity along with your code.

Building the AMIs

With the Puppet configuration complete, the next step is to create the AMI we will use for the EC2 instances. We will do this using the method described in "Building AMIs with Packer" on page 166, in the previous chapter.

For demonstration purposes, we will use Packer to build two AMIs: a web AMI and a Celery AMI. Because these images are similar, you could reduce the AMI management overhead by using a single AMI for each role.

Begin by creating a directory to store the Packer configuration files. This should be at the same level as the Puppet directory:

```
mkdir ~myblog/packer
```

Copy Example 4-4 to *packer/install_puppet.sh*, as described in "Building AMIs with Packer" on page 166.

First, we will create the configuration for the web AMI, which is shown in Example 5-24. Save this file to *packer/web.json*.

Example 5-24. Packer configuration: Web

```
{
  "variables": {
    "aws_access_key": "",
    "aws_secret_key": ""
  },
  "provisioners": [
    {
      "type": "shell",
      "script": "install_puppet.sh"
    },
    { "type": "puppet-masterless",
      "manifest_file": "puppet/manifests/site.pp",
      "module_paths": ["puppet/modules"]
    }
  ],
  "builders": [{
    "type": "amazon-ebs",
    "access_key": "",
    "secret_key": "",
    "region": "us-east-1",
    "source_ami": "ami-43a15f3e",
    "instance_type": "t1.micro",
    "ssh_username": "ubuntu",
    "associate_public_ip_address": true,
    "ami_name": "myblog-web-",
    "user_data": "{\"role\": \"web\"}"
  }]
}
```

This `amazon-ebs` object contains a `user_data` parameter. This is passed to the instance that Packer uses to create the AMI. Puppet will use this user data to control which configuration classes are applied to the instance during the provisioning step. In this case, we want to build an image for the web role, so we provide a JSON string setting the `role` to `web`.

 User data can also be stored in a separate file, rather than cluttering up your Packer configuration file. This is especially useful when your user data contains large JSON strings. To do this, set `user_data_file` to the path of the file containing your user data.

Now we can create the Packer configuration file for the Celery role. The only difference is the `role` value specified as part of the `user_data`. Copy *packer/web.json* to *packer/celery.json*, changing the `user_data` and `ami_name` to read as follows:

```
    "ami_name": "myblog-celery-",
    "user_data": "{\"role\": \"celery\"}"
```

With the configuration files for each role created, we can now build the AMIs, starting with the web role:

```
packer build web.json
```

Once Packer finishes creating the AMI, it will output the AMI ID. Make note of this, as we will need it for the next section.

Now we can create an AMI for the Celery instance:

```
packer build celery.json
```

Again, make a note of the AMI ID output by Packer.

With the AMIs created, we can proceed with bringing up the CloudFormation stack.

Creating the Stack with CloudFormation

Now that we have created the AMIs containing our application, we can launch the CloudFormation stack. We will do this using the *aws* command-line tool.

The stack accepts parameters that we can specify on the command line. Execute the following command to begin creating the stack, replacing the parameter values where necessary:

```
aws cloudformation create-stack --region us-east-1 --stack-name myblog-stack \
    --template-body file://myblog.json \
    --parameters ParameterKey=CeleryAMI,ParameterValue=ami-43a15f3e \
    ParameterKey=WebAMI,ParameterValue=ami-43a15f3e \
    ParameterKey=DBUser,ParameterValue=myblog_user \
    ParameterKey=DBPassword,ParameterValue=s3cr4t \
    ParameterKey=KeyName,ParameterValue=federico
```

If there are any syntax errors in the stack template, they will be highlighted here. Common errors include unbalanced parentheses and brackets, and misplaced commas.

Use the `describe-stack-status` command to check on the status of the stack:

```
aws cloudformation describe-stacks --stack-name myblog-stack | jq
'.Stacks[0].StackStatus'
```

While the resources are being created, the stack's status will be CREATE_IN_PROGRESS. Once the resources have been successfully created, this will change to CREATED. Any other status means an error has occurred, and more information will be available in the Events tab of the Management Console, or by running the describe-stack-events command:

```
aws cloudformation describe-stack-events --stack-name myblog-stack
```

Once the stack has been created, find the public DNS name of the web instance by querying the outputs of the stack with the `describe-stacks` command:

```
aws cloudformation describe-stacks --stack-name myblog-stack | jq
  '.Stacks[0].Outputs[]'
```

Open this address in your web browser, and you should be greeted with the Mezzanine welcome page.

Adding a more friendly DNS name with Route 53 is left as an exercise for the reader.

 It is easy to get confused and mix up what AWS instance is connected to a particular terminal session—especially if you have many running concurrently. One solution for this problem that Federico is particularly fond of is Byobu (*http://byobu.org/*). Created by Google's Dustin Kirkland during his time with the Ubuntu team, this versatile terminal multiplexer introduces a status bar at the bottom of the session providing customizable system status information, including—most critically in the EC2 case—the hostname and IP address.

Application Factory

There is a lesson to be found in the prominence of integration over component-building in modern application development. It is easy to find blocks to build with (indeed, one could say there is an embarrassment of choices to be made); the hard work is in integrating them with one another, and particularly in maintaining this integration over time as the original components continue to rapidly evolve. Moving from components supplied by the Linux distribution to the freshest version available in `pip`, the burden of integration shifts from the distribution maintainers to the application developer. The distribution components may be more dated but are usually validated to inter-operate at least in some degree, while the "latest and greatest" new release carries with its shine some validation task for you to perform.

Although Mezzanine was used an example, the core concepts in this chapter are pertinent to nearly any application. Imagine you are a web design agency using Mezzanine as your CMS. Using the information in this chapter, you could set up a test environment for new clients in a few minutes, just by creating a new stack for each client.

If you follow the process shown in this chapter, incrementally building an application by first making manual changes before committing those to Puppet and CloudFormation, you may save lots of debugging time.

Auto Scaling and Elastic Load Balancing

Most applications have peaks and troughs of user activity. Consumer web applications are a good example. A website that is popular only in the United Kingdom is likely to experience very low levels of user activity at three o'clock in the morning, London time. Business applications also exhibit the same behavior: a company's internal HR system will see high usage during business hours, and often very little traffic outside these times.

Capacity planning is the process of calculating which resources will be required to ensure that application performance remains at acceptable levels. A traditional datacenter environment needs enough capacity to satisfy peak demand, leading to wasted resources during lulls in activity. If your application requires ten servers to satisfy peak demand and only one server during quiet times, up to nine of those servers are regularly going to waste.

Because of the amount of time it takes to bring physical hardware online, traditional capacity planning must take future growth into consideration; otherwise, services would be subject to outages just as they become popular, and system administrators would spend more time ordering new hardware than configuring it. Getting these growth predictions wrong presents two risks: first, if your application fails to grow as much as expected, you have wasted a lot of money on hardware. Conversely, if you fail to anticipate explosive growth, you may find the continuation of that growth restrained by the speed in which you can bring new servers online.

In a public cloud environment, Auto Scaling allows the number of provisioned instances to more closely match the demands of your application, reducing wasted resources and therefore better managing costs. Auto Scaling also eliminates the procurement aspect of capacity planning, as the lead time required to commission a new server shrinks from multiple weeks to merely a few seconds.

An Auto Scaling group is a collection of one or more EC2 instances. As the level of activity increases, the system will scale up by launching new instances into this group. A subsequent decline in activity will cause the Auto Scaling system to scale down and terminate instances.

The way in which the level of activity is measured centers on the application. In combination with the CloudWatch monitoring service, Auto Scaling can use metrics such as CPU utilization to control scaling activities.

It is possible to submit custom metrics to CloudWatch and use these to trigger Auto Scaling events (i.e., scaling up or down). In the case of a batch processing system, you might wish to launch instances based on the number of items in the queue to be processed. Once the queue is empty, the number of running instances can be reduced to zero.

This is the *elastic* in Elastic Compute Cloud.

EC2 was not always so elastic. At the time it was launched, Amazon did not yet provide the Auto Scaling service as it exists today. Although EC2 instances could be launched and terminated on demand, performing these tasks was the responsibility of the user. As such, the pioneers who made heavy use of AWS in the early days built their own systems for managing the automatic creation and deletion of instances by interacting with the EC2 APIs.

As AWS continued to grow, Amazon built this logic into the EC2 service under the name of Auto Scaling. Initially requiring the use of command-line tools, the Auto Scaling API, or CloudFormation, Auto Scaling can now be managed entirely from the AWS Management Console.

If you do not use Auto Scaling, you will need to manually recover any failed instances on AWS. Even if you have only a single instance in the group, using Auto Scaling can save a lot of headaches. When an important instance crashes, would you rather scramble to launch a new one manually, or simply read the email from Amazon letting you know that a new instance is being launched?

The benefits of Auto Scaling are not limited to changes in capacity—using Auto Scaling enhances the resilience of your application, and is a required component of any production-grade AWS infrastructure. Remember that availability zones are physically separate datacenters in which EC2 instances can be launched. Auto Scaling will distribute your instances equally between AZs. In the event of a failure in one AZ, Auto Scaling will increase capacity in the remaining AZs, ensuring that your application suffers minimal disruption.

The ability to automatically scale your instances comes with its own set of potential drawbacks. For example, consider how your application will handle distributed denial-of-service (DDoS) attacks. With a limited number of physical servers, a concentrated attack would eventually cause your site to crash. With Auto Scaling, your instances might scale up to meet the demand of the DDoS, which can become expensive very quickly. For this reason, you should always impose an upper limit on the number of instances that an Auto Scaling group can spawn, unless you are very sure that a DDoS cannot break the bank, as well as your application.

This chapter introduces the core Auto Scaling concepts (Figure 6-1) and puts them into practice by updating the example application from the previous chapter, adding resilience and scaling capabilities to the infrastructure.

Figure 6-1. The AWS console was enhanced to support Auto Scaling in December 2013

Static Auto Scaling Groups

Although Auto Scaling at its core revolves around the idea of dynamically increasing or reducing the number of running instances, you can also create a group with a specific number of instances that does not change dynamically. We refer to this as a *static* Auto Scaling group.

EC2 instances can be terminated without warning for various reasons outside of your control; this is one of the accepted downsides of operating in a public cloud. A manually launched instance—that is, an instance launched outside of an Auto Scaling group—would need to be replaced manually once its failure is noticed. Even if you are using CloudFormation to manage the instance, some manual interaction may still be required to bring the application back up. We already examined in Chapter 3 the use of Auto Scaling groups to maintain the number of instances required by an application while under security attack.

With Auto Scaling, a failed instance is automatically replaced as soon as the failure is detected by AWS. For this reason, we always use Auto Scaling for every production instance—even if there will always be only a single instance in the group. The small amount of extra work involved in configuring Auto Scaling is well worth the knowledge that if an entire AZ fails, the instance will be replaced immediately and without any effort on our part.

We will begin by modifying the CloudFormation stack from the previous example so that the web and Celery instances are contained within their own static Auto Scaling group. Example 6-1 shows a CloudFormation stack template fragment describing the resources required to launch a working Auto Scaling group.

Example 6-1. Auto Scaling groups in CloudFormation

```
"MyLaunchConfig" : {
    "Type" : "AWS::AutoScaling::LaunchConfiguration",
    "Properties" : {
        "ImageId" : "ami-XXXXXXXX",
        "SecurityGroups" : [ { "Ref" : "MySecurityGroup" } ],
        "InstanceType" : "t2.micro"
    }
},
"MyASGroup" : {
    "Type" : "AWS::AutoScaling::AutoScalingGroup",
    "Properties" : {
        "AvailabilityZones" : ["us-east-1a", "us-east-1b", "us-east-1c", "us-
east-1d", "us-east-1e"],
        "LaunchConfigurationName" : { "Ref" : "MyLaunchConfig" },
        "MinSize" : "1",
        "MaxSize" : "1",
        "DesiredCapacity" : "1"
    }
}
```

There are two components to Auto Scaling: the Auto Scaling group and a launch configuration. A launch configuration controls which parameters are used when an instance is launched, including the instance type and user data.

 A full description of valid properties for an Auto Scaling group (*https://aws.amazon.com/cloudformation/details/*) resource can be found in the CloudFormation section of the AWS documentation.

The size of an Auto Scaling group is controlled by MinSize and MaxSize, which set lower and upper bounds on the size of the group. The DesiredCapacity parameter specifies the ideal number of instances in the group. CloudFormation will consider the Auto Scaling group to have been created successfully only when this number of instances is running.

An Auto Scaling group must use at least one availability zone. The Availability Zones parameter lets you control which AZs are used for the group—ideally, as many as possible if availability is a concern. Entire availability zones can—and have—become unavailable for extended periods of time. While Amazon AWS has been enjoying the highest availability (*https://www.enterprisetech.com/2015/01/06/aws-rates-highest-cloud-reliability/*) among public cloud vendors, it has fallen short of achieving *five nines* of availability across all its regions. Any application that fails to make use of multiple availability zones in its architecture faces a high likelihood of a number of hours of outage every year. If this is not acceptable to your users, you need to design accordingly. Amazon gives you the tools to build highly available systems, but it is up to you to use them.

The parameters given to the launch configuration are similar to the ones used with an EC2 instance resource. Group-level attributes—such as the number of instances in the group—are assigned to the Auto Scaling group resource.

To update our example stack to use Auto Scaling groups, we need to perform two steps, repeated for both instance types:

1. Create a launch configuration to replace the EC2 resource, using the same user data and instance type.
2. Create an Auto Scaling group resource using this launch configuration.

Example 6-2 shows the Auto Scaling groups and launch configurations for the web and Celery instances. Update the stack template (located at *cloudformation/myblog.json*) by removing the WebInstance and CeleryInstance resources, and adding the code shown here to the Resources section.

Example 6-2. Auto Scaling web and Celery instances

```
"CeleryLaunchConfig" : {
    "Type" : "AWS::AutoScaling::LaunchConfiguration",
    "Properties" : {
        "ImageId" : { "Ref" : "CeleryAMI" },
        "SecurityGroups" : [ { "Ref" : "CelerySecurityGroup" } ]
    }
},
"CeleryGroup" : {
    "Type" : "AWS::AutoScaling::AutoScalingGroup",
    "Properties" : {
```

```
            "AvailabilityZones" : { "Fn::GetAZs" : ""},
            "LaunchConfigurationName" : { "Ref" : "CeleryLaunchConfig" },
            "MinSize" : "1",
            "MaxSize" : "2",
            "DesiredCapacity" : "1"
        }
},

"WebLaunchConfig" : {
    "Type" : "AWS::AutoScaling::LaunchConfiguration",
    "Properties" : {
        "ImageId" : { "Ref" : "WebAMI" },
        "SecurityGroups" : [ { "Ref" : "WebSecurityGroup" } ]
    }
},
"WebGroup" : {
    "Type" : "AWS::AutoScaling::AutoScalingGroup",
    "Properties" : {
        "AvailabilityZones" : { "Fn::GetAZs" : ""},
        "LaunchConfigurationName" : { "Ref" : "WebLaunchConfig" },
        "MinSize" : "1",
        "MaxSize" : "2",
        "DesiredCapacity" : "1"
    }
},
```

The instance-specific parameters have been moved from the WebInstance resource to the WebLaunchConfig resource. The new Auto Scaling group resource will launch one of each instance type, as set by the DesiredCapacity parameter.

The next step is to update the running CloudFormation stack with the new template. Do this using the Management Console or command-line tools, and wait for the stack to reach the UPDATE_COMPLETE state.

Because the WebInstance and CeleryInstance resources are no longer in the stack template, these two instances will be terminated by CloudFormation. Once the launch config and Auto Scaling group resources have been created, two new instances will be launched to replace them.

It is worth noting that instances launched as part of an Auto Scaling group are not included in the Resources panel in the Management Console. Instead, you will need to use the AWS CLI tool or the Management Console to list the members of an Auto Scaling group. Instances will also be automatically tagged with the name and ID of the CloudFormation stack to which their parent Auto Scaling group belongs, as well as any optional user-defined tags.

The fact that EC2 instances are not, technically speaking, part of the CloudFormation stack has some interesting implications when updating running stacks.

Say you want to change the parameters of a launch configuration that is in use by some running instances. When you update the running stack, CloudFormation will create a new launch configuration, update the Auto Scaling group to reference the new launch configuration, and finally delete the old launch configuration.

By default, it will make no changes to the instances that are running at the time the stack is updated. The new launch configuration will apply only to newly launched instances, meaning that currently running instances will still be using the old launch configuration. In some cases, it is acceptable to let the new launch configuration gradually propagate as new instances are launched. In others, it is necessary to immediately replace the instances so they pick up the new configuration.

An update policy can be used to automatically replace instances when their underlying launch configuration is changed. Instances will be terminated in batches and replaced with new instances by the Auto Scaling service.

Now that the web and Celery instances are part of Auto Scaling groups, we can test the resilience of our application by terminating the Celery instance via the Management Console. If you browse the Mezzanine site while the Celery instance is terminated, everything will continue to function as usual; the web application does not rely on a functioning Celery instance in order to work because of the decoupled nature of the application. As tasks are received, they are placed in the SQS queue, where they will wait until there is a working Celery instance to process them.

When Amazon's periodic instance health checks notice that the Celery Auto Scaling group no longer contains a working instance, a replacement will be launched. After a few minutes, the instance will become functional and process any tasks that are waiting in the SQS queue.

With any application, it is important to understand the failure characteristics of each component. How will your application cope when one or more of its components fail is perhaps the most important question to ask when designing an application for hosting in a public cloud environment.

In the case of Celery, the failure characteristics are very good: the application continues working almost entirely without hiccups from the user's perspective. Comments posted on the blog will be delayed for a while, which many users may not even notice.

A failed `WebInstance`, on the other hand, would cause the application to become entirely unavailable, because there is only one web instance in the group. Later in this chapter we will look at using load balancers to distribute traffic between instances.

 The authors feel strongly that CloudFormation will be a defining skill for system administrators in the coming decade. We accordingly expose the reader to copious amounts of its syntax as one of the most complex and valuable aspects of AWS worth mastering—yet there is a simpler way to draft CloudFormation templates.

In the fall of 2015, Amazon introduced CloudFormation Designer (*https://console.aws.amazon.com/cloudformation/designer*), a UI offering drag-and-drop manipulation of resources in templates. Federico likes to use it as a convenient, always up-to-date CloudFormation editor with built-in syntax validation: even when hand-crafting your templates, reducing trivial errors helps to save time (Figure 6-2).

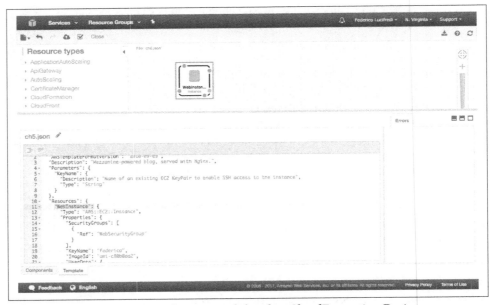

Figure 6-2. A template from Chapter 5 validated in CloudFormation Designer

Notifications of Scaling Activities

Another element of AWS is the Simple Notification Service (SNS). This is a push-based notification system through which an application can publish messages to topics. Other applications can subscribe to these topics and receive real-time notifications when new messages are available. This can be used to implement the publish/subscribe design pattern in your application.

In addition to notifying other applications when messages are published, SNS can also send notifications to email and SMS recipients, or post the message to an external HTTP web server. Auto Scaling groups can be optionally configured to publish SNS notifications when scaling activities take place, letting you receive an email each time new instances are launched or terminated.

Example 6-3 shows an updated version of our Celery scaling group with SNS notifications enabled. The example shows the four possible types of notifications that Auto Scaling will send. You can choose to subscribe to any combination of these types, but electing to choose all four can result in a lot of email traffic if your application regularly performs scaling activities.

Example 6-3. Auto Scaling with notifications

```
"ScalingSNSTopic" : {
    "Type" : "AWS::SNS::Topic",
    "Properties" : {
        "Subscription" : [ {
            "Endpoint" : "notifications@example.com",
            "Protocol" : "email"
        } ]
    }
}

"CeleryGroup" : {
    "Type" : "AWS::AutoScaling::AutoScalingGroup",
    "Properties" : {
        "AvailabilityZones" : { "Fn::GetAZs" : ""},
        "LaunchConfigurationName" : { "Ref" : "CeleryLaunchConfig" },
        "MinSize" : "1",
        "MaxSize" : "2",
        "DesiredCapacity" : "1",
        "NotificationConfiguration" : {
            "TopicARN" : { "Ref" : "ScalingSNSTopic" },
            "NotificationTypes" : [
                "autoscaling:EC2_INSTANCE_LAUNCH",
                "autoscaling:EC2_INSTANCE_LAUNCH_ERROR",
                "autoscaling:EC2_INSTANCE_TERMINATE",
                "autoscaling:EC2_INSTANCE_TERMINATE_ERROR"
            ]
        }
    }
},
```

The Importance of Error Notifications

We strongly recommend subscribing to the `INSTANCE_LAUNCH_ERROR` notification type for any important Auto Scaling groups. This will alert you to issues with Auto Scaling groups before they turn into real emergencies.

Mike once accidentally deleted an AMI that was still referenced in a production launch configuration, resulting in an Auto Scaling group no longer able to launch new instances.

This particular application—a social media website—had external monitoring that measured the performance of page-load times. Performance started to decrease as the running instances became increasingly overloaded. At the same time, Mike's inbox began filling up with emails from AWS, letting him know that there was a problem with the scaling group. He quickly realized this was due to deleting the wrong AMI and set about building a new AMI to replace it. Subscribing to these notifications saved valuable time that would otherwise have been spent investigating the problem.

Operator error is not the only time in which these messages can prove useful. For example, if AWS is experiencing problems and cannot provide an instance to satisfy an Auto Scaling request, you will be informed.

Update *cloudformation/myblog.json*, replacing the `CeleryScalingGroup` resource with the new one. Remember to replace the example email address with your own. You could also add the `NotificationConfiguration` section to the `WebScalingGroup` resource if you would like to enable notifications for both scaling groups. After saving the file, update the running stack with the new template.

If you would like to see the notifications in action, terminate the Celery instance and wait for Auto Scaling to replace it. You should start receiving emails for both the termination and launch events, each letting you know which instance is being terminated and the reason for the change.

Scaling Policies

Static Auto Scaling groups have their uses, but a primary reason to use AWS is its ability to scale compute capacity up and down on demand, shortcutting the need to purchase servers in advance.

There are two ways to configure Auto Scaling to automatically change the number of instances in a group: either at fixed time intervals, or on-demand based on measurements gathered by a monitoring system.

Scaling based on time is useful only when your usage patterns are highly predictable. The implementation process for this is described in detail on Amazon's Scaling Based on a Schedule page (*http://docs.aws.amazon.com/AutoScaling/latest/DeveloperGuide/schedule_time.html*).

Dynamic scaling is the more interesting and widely used approach. It relies on gathering metrics—such as CPU utilization or requests per second—and using this information to decide when your application needs more or less capacity. This is done by creating scaling policies that describe the conditions under which instances should be launched or terminated. Scaling policies must be triggered in order to perform any action.

A policy that controls when new instances are launched is known as a *scale-up policy*, and one that controls when instances are terminated is a *scale-down policy*. Scaling policies can adjust the size of the Auto Scaling group in three ways:

- As an exact capacity. When the policy is triggered, the number of instances will be set to a specific number defined in the policy.
- As a percentage of current capacity.
- As an absolute value. When triggered, *n* new instances will be launched, where *n* is defined by the policy.

Scaling policies are triggered as a result of changes in measured metrics, which we will look at in the next section.

Scaling on CloudWatch Metrics

CloudWatch is a monitoring system provided by Amazon, tightly integrated with most AWS services. It can be used to quickly set up a custom Auto Scaling configuration specific to your application's needs. Basic metrics gathered at five-minute intervals are available free of charge for services including compute (EC2), block storage (EBS), RDS database, and ELB load balancing. The same metrics can be gathered at one-minute intervals but in most cases you will incur an additional cost at this higher sampling rate.

Custom metrics from third-party or self-hosted monitoring systems can be published to CloudWatch, allowing you to see this data alongside AWS-provided metrics.

CloudWatch's Alarms feature can be used to send alerts when these metrics fall outside the levels that you configure. For example, you could receive an email notification when the average CPU load of an instance has been above 80% for at least 10 minutes.

By connecting alarms to scaling policies, CloudFormation metrics can be used to control the size of an Auto Scaling group. Instead of informing you by email that your CPU load is too high, Amazon can launch a new instance automatically.

CloudWatch can aggregate metrics for all instances in an Auto Scaling group and use the aggregated metrics to control scaling actions. If you have an Auto Scaling group consisting of a cluster of instances that are all processing an equal amount of work, the average CPU utilization across the entire group will probably be a good indicator as to how busy the cluster is.

Because there are so many metrics available in CloudWatch, it is worth taking some time to evaluate different scaling strategies to see which is best for your application's workload. The right choice will depend on which resources are most heavily used by your application. Sometimes, it is not possible to identify a single metric that best identifies when capacity changes are required.

Take our Celery instance as an example. The task that checks a comment for spam merely contacts an external API and returns the result to the Celery broker. This is not a particularly intensive strain on the instance's CPU because most of the task execution time will be spent waiting for responses to network requests. We could increase the parallelization of Celery by running more processes and making more efficient use of the CPU, but the instance likely will run out of RAM before saturating the CPU.

Unfortunately, it is not possible to measure RAM usage in CloudWatch directly; writing a client-side script to submit this data to the CloudWatch API is required.

Monitoring RAM Utilization in EC2 Instances

Monitoring memory use requires the instance itself to publish the relevant data to CloudWatch. Amazon Web Services maintains (but does not support) a set of sample Perl scripts reporting memory and disk usage (*http://docs.aws.amazon.com/AWSEC2/ latest/UserGuide/mon-scripts.html*) to CloudWatch. The scripts were recently updated to work out of the box on Ubuntu 14.04 and 16.04, as well as a number of older RPM-based distributions.

Standard CloudWatch pricing (*https://aws.amazon.com/cloudwatch/pricing*) for custom metrics applies to this approach. Unfortunately, the design of these scripts requires storing a set of AWS credentials on the instance itself, hardly what we would consider a security best practice.

Fortunately, Shahar Evron has devised an alternative approach (*http://arr.gr/blog/ 2013/08/monitoring-ec2-instance-memory-usage-with-cloudwatch/*) that makes use of IAM roles. You will remember that roles can be used to assign capabilities to AWS instances, in this case granting monitored instances the ability to report metrics to CloudWatch. Shahar's solution uses a small boto script (*https://gist.github.com/shev*

ron/6204349#file-cw-monitor-memusage-py) to accomplish just this, and can equally support the use of roles or AWS credentials stored in the *~/.boto* and *~/.aws/credentials* configuration files. No modules are required; boto is the sole dependency.

Following the process we outlined in Chapter 3, you will need to create a role that EC2 instances can assume, and embed a policy granting access to the *cloudwatch:PutMetricData* action on the CloudWatch resource. Once this is done, create an IAM instance profile as we have shown and use it to launch a new instance. Log in, and execute the following configuration steps:

```
sudo apt install python-pip
sudo pip install boto
curl https://gist.githubusercontent.com/shevron/6204349/raw/cw-monitor-
memusage.py | sudo tee /usr/local/bin/cw-monitor-memusage.py
sudo chmod +x /usr/local/bin/cw-monitor-memusage.py
echo "* * * * * nobody /usr/local/bin/cw-monitor-memusage.py" | sudo
tee /etc/cron.d/cw-monitor-memusage
```

This will set up Cron to report the memory usage of this instance to CloudWatch every minute—you will see an EC2/memory namespace populated by the MemUsage metric appear in your CloudWatch dashboard. This configuration can easily be automated as part of your default instance setup, and you can see how this all comes together in Figure 6-3.

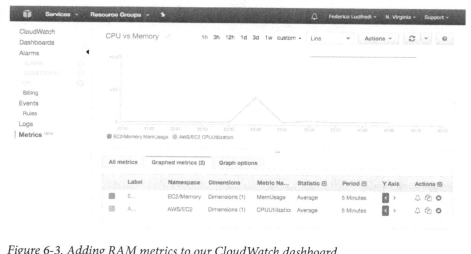

Figure 6-3. Adding RAM metrics to our CloudWatch dashboard

Because we are using the SQS service as a Celery broker, we have another option: scaling based on the number of messages in the queue, rather than on instance metrics. This is interesting because we can use one AWS service (SQS) to control another (Auto Scaling groups), even though they are not directly connected to one another.

We will use the number of messages waiting in the SQS queue to control the size of the Celery Auto Scaling group, ensuring there are enough instances in the group to process tasks in a timely manner at all times.

We know that our tasks are usually processed very quickly and the SQS queue is usually empty, so an increase in the queue length indicates either a legitimate increase in tasks or a problem with the Celery instances. Regardless, launching new instances will solve any problems caused by load and force the size of the queue to decrease.

The same metric can be used to terminate instances after the queue has been reduced to an acceptable length. Running too many instances is a waste of money, so we want to keep the Auto Scaling group as small as possible.

Starting Services on an As-Needed Basis

Scaling policies respect the minimum and maximum size of your Auto Scaling groups. Because the minimum size of our Celery group is 1, CloudFormation will never terminate the last remaining instance.

By setting the minimum size of the group to 0, you could build a system where instances are launched only when messages are published to the queue. To understand the value of such a policy, imagine using Celery to send out batches of emails at regular intervals. Most of the time the queue will be empty. When you begin publishing messages to the queue, instances will be launched to process the tasks. Once the queue is empty, all instances will be terminated. This is an incredibly cost-effective way to run a task-processing infrastructure.

To implement these changes, we need to make further additions to the stack template, as shown in Example 6-4.

Example 6-4. Auto Scaling with CloudWatch alarms

```
"CeleryScaleUpPolicy" : {
    "Type" : "AWS::AutoScaling::ScalingPolicy",
    "Properties" : {
        "AdjustmentType" : "ChangeInCapacity",
        "AutoScalingGroupName" : { "Ref" : "CeleryGroup" },
        "Cooldown" : "1",
        "ScalingAdjustment" : "1"
    }
},

"CeleryScaleDownPolicy" : {
    "Type" : "AWS::AutoScaling::ScalingPolicy",
    "Properties" : {
        "AdjustmentType" : "ChangeInCapacity",
```

```
         "AutoScalingGroupName" : { "Ref" : "CeleryGroup" },
         "Cooldown" : "1",
         "ScalingAdjustment" : "-1"
      }
   },

   "CelerySQSAlarmHigh": {
      "Type": "AWS::CloudWatch::Alarm",
      "Properties": {
         "EvaluationPeriods": "1",
         "Statistic": "Sum",
         "Threshold": "100",
         "AlarmDescription": "Triggered when SQS queue length >100",
         "Period": "60",
         "AlarmActions": [ { "Ref": "CeleryScaleUpPolicy" } ],
         "Namespace": "AWS/SQS",
         "Dimensions": [ {
            "Name": "QueueName",
            "Value": { "GetAtt": ["CeleryQueue", "QueueName"] }
         } ],
         "ComparisonOperator": "GreaterThanThreshold",
         "MetricName": "ApproximateNumberOfMessagesVisible"
      }
   },

   "CelerySQSAlarmLow": {
      "Type": "AWS::CloudWatch::Alarm",
      "Properties": {
         "EvaluationPeriods": "1",
         "Statistic": "Sum",
         "Threshold": "20",
         "AlarmDescription": "Triggered when SQS queue length <20",
         "Period": "60",
         "AlarmActions": [ { "Ref": "CeleryScaleDownPolicy" } ],
         "Namespace": "AWS/SQS",
         "Dimensions": [ {
            "Name": "QueueName",
            "Value": { "GetAtt": ["CeleryQueue", "QueueName"] }
         } ],
         "ComparisonOperator": "LessThanThreshold",
         "MetricName": "ApproximateNumberOfMessagesVisible"
      }
   },
```

Insert this template excerpt into the Resources section of the *cloudformation/myblog.json* file.

Notice that we do not need to change any aspect of the Celery Auto Scaling group resource in order to enable dynamic scaling. Our scaling policy configuration is entirely separate from the Auto Scaling group to which it applies. The scaling policy could even be in a separate CloudFormation stack.

We have separate policies for scaling up and down, and both of these policies use the ChangeInCapacity adjustment type to launch or terminate a set number of instances.

The CeleryScaleUpPolicy, when triggered, will launch two new Celery instances. The CeleryScaleDownPolicy will terminate one instance at a time. Why the difference? Launching two new instances at a time lets us quickly respond to changes in demand, springing into action as the work requirements increase. As the queue drops, we want to gradually reduce the number of instances to avoid a yo-yo effect. If we reduce the capacity of the task-processing infrastructure too quickly, it can cause the queue to begin rising again, which might trigger the scale-up policy. At times, the Elastic Compute Cloud can be a little too elastic and introducing some hysteresis through our scale planning is necessary.

The Cooldown property gives us a further means of controlling the elasticity of our Auto Scaling policy. This value, specified in seconds, imposes a delay between scaling activities to make sure the size of the group is not adjusted too frequently.

CelerySQSAlarmHigh is a CloudWatch Alarm resource that monitors the length of the SQS queue used for Celery tasks. When there are more than 100 messages in the queue, this alarm is activated, triggering the CeleryScaleUpPolicy. Conversely, CelerySQSAlarmLow triggers the CeleryScaleDownPolicy when the queue length drops below 20. In practice, it is unlikely that the queue length thresholds will be so low. However, these values make it much easier to test and demonstrate that Auto Scaling is working as planned.

After saving the updated file, update the running stack with the new template. Because the DesiredCapacity of the group is still set to 1 and none of the relevant CloudWatch alarms have been triggered, nothing will actually happen yet.

To demonstrate that Auto Scaling is working, stop the Celery process on the running instance and post some test comments, causing the number of queued messages to increase until Celery is scaled up.

Using the Management Console or command-line tools, find the public DNS name of the instance in the Celery group. Remember that it will be tagged with the name of the CloudFormation stack and role=celery. Log in to the instance and stop Celery with the following command:

```
supervisorctl celery stop
```

Visit the Mezzanine page in your web browser and post example comments. In another tab, open the CloudWatch Alarms page and watch the status of the CelerySQSHighAlarm. Once enough messages have been published to the queue, it will enter the ALARM state and trigger the CeleryScaleUpPolicy, launching two new Celery instances.

Because we configured notifications for this scaling group, you will receive a few email messages as the Auto Scaling activities are performed. After a brief period, you should see there are now three running Celery instances.

Notice that they are probably all running in different availability zones within your region. Amazon will attempt to evenly distribute an Auto Scaling group across an EC2 region to enhance resilience.

The two new instances will quickly process the tasks in the queue and take the queue length below the scale-down threshold. Once the `CelerySQSLowAlarm` is triggered, two of the instances will be terminated.

When terminating instances, the default behavior is to terminate the instance that has the oldest launch configuration. If more than one instance is running the old configuration, or all instances are running the same configuration, AWS will terminate the instance that is closest to the next instance hour. This is the most cost-effective strategy, as it maximizes the useful lifetime of instances.

If instances were launched together—as is likely in an Auto Scaling group—more than one instance will be "closest" to a full instance hour. In this case, a random instance from this subset is terminated.

This logic can be further controlled by assigning a termination policy to the Auto Scaling group, as is described in Amazon's Auto Scaling documentation (*http://docs.aws.amazon.com/autoscaling/ latest/userguide/as-instance-termination.html*).

Now that you know Auto Scaling is working, you can resume the Celery process on the original instance, assuming it was not terminated when scaling down. Do this with the following:

```
supervisorctl celery start
```

The Celery part of the infrastructure will now grow and shrink dynamically, according to the number of tasks to be processed. Tasks will be processed as quickly as possible, while ensuring that we are not wasting money by running too many instances.

Elastic Load Balancing

Whether in the cloud or on your own hardware, system failures are an inevitable part of a system administrator's life. If your application is hosted on a single server, the eventual system failure will render your application unavailable until a replacement server or virtual instance can be provisioned.

One way to improve the reliability of your application is to host it on multiple instances and distribute the traffic between them. When individual instances fail, your application will continue to run smoothly as long as the remaining instances have enough capacity to shoulder the burden of the additional requests they must now serve. This is known as *load balancing*, and the server that distributes traffic is a *load balancer*.

We have seen how Auto Scaling can be used to help solve this problem in AWS by automatically launching new instances to replace failed ones, or dynamically increasing capacity to respond to demand. So far, we have added dynamic Auto Scaling only to the Celery part of the infrastructure.

Converting the web application instance into an Auto Scaling group requires solving a problem not present with Celery: how do we distribute HTTP requests between multiple instances? For testing purposes, we have been using the public DNS name of each individual instance so far, and newly launched instances would launch with different names. Once the infrastructure is in production, users will visit it at *http://blog.example.com*. So how can we connect a single, public DNS name to a group of instances?

Elastic Load Balancing is Amazon's solution to this problem. An *Elastic Load Balancer (ELB)* is a virtual device built specifically to provide dynamic load-balancing capabilities to applications hosted on AWS. An ELB effectively sits in front of a group of EC2 instances and distributes traffic between them. A *round-robin* approach is commonly used, but alternative, application-aware strategies such as *least outstanding requests* are also popular.

Instead of pointing the *blog.example.com* DNS record toward a specific EC2 instance, we will point it at the ELB using a CNAME DNS record. All requests will be sent by the ELB to the instances behind the ELB. You can use the Management Console and API to manually add and remove instances from the ELB. The ELB will regularly perform health checks on these instances, and any instances that are deemed unhealthy will be automatically removed from the ELB.

 Mastery of ELB service requires a solid understanding of the DNS system. DNS itself is the broadest of subjects, covered by books much heftier than ours. We recommend *DNS and BIND* by Cricket Liu and Paul Albitz (O'Reilly) as the ultimate source on this topic. Federico's now dog-eared copy saw an impressive amount of use during his graduate student years!

Elastic Load Balancer and Auto Scaling Groups

ELBs are designed to work in conjunction with Auto Scaling groups. When you create a scaling group, you can specify the name of the associated ELB. New instances launched in this scaling group will be automatically placed behind the ELB, at which point they will begin receiving traffic and serving requests.

We will use this feature to convert the web application component of the example stack into an Auto Scaling group behind an ELB. Once finished, we will be able to access our example blog via the public DNS name of the ELB.

Example 6-5 shows the updated section of the application stack.

Example 6-5. Auto Scaling group with Elastic Load Balancer

```
"WebELB" : {
    "Type" : "AWS::ElasticLoadBalancing::LoadBalancer",
    "Properties" : {
      "AvailabilityZones" : { "Fn::GetAZs" : "" },
      "Listeners" : [ {
        "LoadBalancerPort" : "80",
        "InstancePort" : "80",
        "Protocol" : "HTTP"
      } ],
      "HealthCheck" : {
        "Target" : { "Fn::Join" : [ "", ["HTTP:80/"]]},
        "HealthyThreshold" : "3",
        "UnhealthyThreshold" : "5",
        "Interval" : "30",
        "Timeout" : "5"
      }
    }
},
"WebGroup" : {
    "Type" : "AWS::AutoScaling::AutoScalingGroup",
    "Properties" : {
      "AvailabilityZones" : { "Fn::GetAZs" : ""},
      "LaunchConfigurationName" : { "Ref" : "WebLaunchConfig" },
      "MinSize" : "1",
      "MaxSize" : "2",
      "DesiredCapacity" : "2",
      "LoadBalancerNames" : [ { "Ref" : "WebELB" } ]
    }
},
```

Update *cloudformation/myblog.json* to replace the `WebInstance` resource with the new code. These are almost exactly the same changes required to convert Celery into a scaling group, with two main exceptions: an Elastic Load Balancer resource has been added, and the Auto Scaling group has been updated to include the `LoadBalancerNames` parameter.

The `DesiredCapacity` for the `WebGroup` has been changed to 2, which means an additional instance will be launched when the CloudFormation stack is updated.

The ELB performs a health check that verifies that the application is responding to HTTP requests.

ELB Health Checks

An ELB can be configured with a custom health check that is performed on any instance in the group. This is done by making an HTTP request to the specified target at regular intervals. If the target server does not respond to this request with a 200 status code within the given time-out, the check fails. Once the number of failed checks reaches the UnhealthyThreshold value, the instance is considered unhealthy and removed from the ELB. As a result, an instance could be replaced if it becomes very slow or unreliable, even if it doesn't completely fail.

The health check will still be performed on unhealthy instances. Should they recover and resume operating normally, they will be automatically returned to the ELB after enough successful checks have occurred, as specified in HealthyThreshold.

Another option for the custom health check is to initiate a TCP connection. If the TCP handshake can be completed, the check is considered successful.

HTTP-based health checks are useful for more than web applications. A really useful practice is to build a custom HTTP server that represents the health of your application. This can consist of a number of tests specific to your environment, which verify that every component of the instance is working as expected. If any of these tests fail, have the server return an HTTP error code in response to the health check, which results in the instance being removed from the ELB. Anything except HTTP 200 is treated as failure and will result in the instance being considered unhealthy by the ELB.

In addition to the custom health check just described, Amazon performs an instance-level health check automatically. This checks for problems at the virtualization layer that might not be recognized by an application-level health check.

While health checks are useful, it is important to understand the implications of allowing health checks to terminate and launch new instances. A misconfigured health check will cause ELB to believe all of your instances are unhealthy, and unceremoniously remove them from the group. It is imperative that your health check return a 500 error only if the problem can be solved by removing the instance from the ELB. That is the only remedial action the ELB can take, so there is no point in alerting it about problems that require another solution, and doing so may be actually counter-productive.

Consider the example of a web application that requires a database to function properly. If the database fails, each web instance will begin returning 500 error codes for every request. Removing an individual instance of the web server from the ELB will do nothing to bring the database back to life.

If the health check page also returns 500 error codes because the database is not working, all of the instances will be removed from the ELB. At this point, visitors to your website would see the standard ELB error page, rather than the beautifully designed error page of your application.

Carefully monitor the number of unhealthy instances in each ELB by setting up a CloudWatch alarm to alert you if it remains above zero for a significant length of time.

Update the running CloudFormation stack with the modified template. The old web instance, which no longer exists in the template, will be deleted and replaced with an Auto Scaling group with a single member.

Once the stack has finished updating, use the CloudFormation Management Console or command-line tools to list the stack's resources and find out the public DNS name of the ELB. Alternatively, you could look in the Elastic Load Balancers section of the Management Console.

Visit the ELB's address in your web browser, and you should once more see the Mezzanine welcome page. This page has been served by one of the instances in the scaling group. Because they are identical, it does not matter which one actually served the request.

 The number of requests received per second is one of the Elastic Load Balancing metrics in CloudWatch. As such, it can be used to scale the number of web instances in a manner directly related to current levels of traffic.

Terminate one of the running web application instances with the Management Console. You can find it by searching for one of the values contained in the instance's tags, such as the scaling group name (WebInstanceScalingGroup).

After this instance terminates, refresh the Mezzanine page in your browser. The site will continue to function as usual even though one of the instances is no longer running.

Within a few minutes, AWS will notice the terminated instance and launch a replacement for it. Once this instance has finished the startup process, it will be marked as healthy by the ELB, and traffic will once again be split between the two instances.

With this step complete, the example application is now ready to scale at both the Celery and web levels. It is resilient to failures of individual instances and entire availability zones, and will run at the optimal capacity to ensure happy users and a low AWS bill for your organization.

Managing Outages

Amazon Web Services has come a long way from its early days, when it was routine for any medium-scale deployment to lose a few EC2 instances at least once every week. Instances no longer "disappear" as often, thanks to the dedication of the AWS team to increasing reliability for their customers, but this remains a distinctive feature of *spot priced* instances, purchased by users bidding for spare excess capacity. Any application running on EC2 must be designed to account for the possibility of an instance being terminated without any prior warning. Production datacenters present similar risks, including the loss of a hypervisor node or a network failure, but in the AWS model that opaque risk cannot be managed by the administrator in even the smallest degree, as she is unaware of Amazon's daily operational plans and needs—or the presence of any backhoes near their fiber-optic lines.

The spot instance market (*https://aws.amazon.com/ec2/spot/pricing/*) allows AWS customers to bid for spare excess capacity by specifying what maximum instance-hour price they are willing to pay. EC2 launches (or terminates) instances as the spot price fluctuates based on the supply and demand of unused EC2 capacity. Operating in this model can result in massive savings over on-demand instance pricing and is very suitable to applications that can be safely interrupted.

The spot market is becoming increasingly sophisticated over time, introducing new choices for the user. Spot priced instances now receive a two-minute notification of impending termination once the price exceeds the user-specified limit, and partially used hours are not charged. It is now also possible to define a minimum duration requirement, in which case a running instance will not be terminated even if the spot price exceeds the specified constraint.

Spot instance termination notices are provided through the *termination-time* item in the instance's metadata. If a spot instance is marked for termination, the item will be defined, its value specifying at which time the instance will receive the ACPI shutdown event. Amazon recommends polling this field at five-second intervals, which is easily accomplished as follows:

```
if curl -s http://169.254.169.254/latest/meta-data/spot/
termination-time | grep -q .*T.*Z
then
    echo terminated;
fi
```

A properly executed *Mode 2 IT* transition requires architectural design effort: we should not fall prey to the classic mistake of trying to make a new technology perform exactly like the old did. We should instead use the valuable opportunity created by the infrastructure renewal cycle to modernize applications and reduce technical debt as part of the transition. Doing so comfortably uses existing legacy systems to continue to take care of what they do best: running our applications as originally intended, while we design their next implementation making the best use of new AWS infrastructure. There is no reason to migrate everything to new infrastructure once: we can deliberately choose our timeline and application migration strategy to accomplish these goals, while remining mindful of our budget constraints. Start by migrating those applications best suited to run in the cloud, while you make your way through the redesign of ill-fitting workloads.

Netflix's Chaos Monkey (*https://github.com/Netflix/SimianArmy/wiki/Chaos-Monkey*) is the tool of choice for validating an application's response to EC2 instance outages. Chaos Monkey is a service that may be configured to randomly select and terminate instances in your AWS deployment, thereby testing the resiliency of your design and the automated responses set up to handle such contingencies. Failures happen, and unleashing Chaos Monkey on your infrastructure ensures that the flaws in its design are found during business hours and at the best time to investigate their cause, instead of being discovered at the worst possible moment in production.

AWS infrastructure outages remain rare, but are by no means unheard of. We live through the experience of a significant AWS outage every other year, and can observe its impact ripple through the most disparate services of the global internet. Failures cascade as increasingly more websites are built around core infrastructure supplied by Amazon Web Services—an AWS outage can disrupt Twitter, which uses S3 to host files, which in turn can disrupt another service relying on Twitter to deliver its user notifications. And so on.

Some of AWS's most notorious *service events* to date have included a storage component. On October 22, 2012 (*https://aws.amazon.com/message/680342/*), an unlikely combination of minor bugs in a monitoring system for the Elastic Block Storage service initiated a massive concurrent failover of volumes hosted in the `us-east-1` region. Operations in the region ground to a halt for many users, who also encountered difficulty in controlling their resources through the management API. Similarly, on February 28, 2017 (*https://aws.amazon.com/message/41926/*), an operator on the AWS team fat-fingered a routine command intended to remove a small number of servers supporting the S3 billing process. The additional servers removed supported the metadata and placement subsystems for a whole S3 region. While these systems were being restarted, S3 was unable to service requests. Services that rely on its API, like EC2 and EBS, were severely affected. Both of these events were less than a day in duration yet they were front-page news in the technical press because of the scale of their impact—the 2017 outage severely affected major sites like Twitter, Slack, and Git-Hub and was reported on CNN.

We discuss these incidents here to illustrate the complexity of an AWS outage—they typically arise from a low-probability event that becomes possible (or even eventually inevitable) with AWS's massive scale. It can be difficult for any administrator to determine if the unlikely circumstance of an AWS outage is underway at a given moment, which is why Amazon provides users with the AWS Service Health Dashboard (*http://status.aws.amazon.com/*) (Figure 6-4), publishing the most up-to-date status information available for every AWS service. A status history covering all services for the last 365 days is also provided, as well as an RSS feed to subscribe to the health status of each service.

Current Status - Apr 7, 2017 PDT

Amazon Web Services publishes our most up-to-the-minute information on service availability in the table below. Check back here any time to get current status information, or subscribe to an RSS feed to be notified of interruptions to each individual service. If you are experiencing a real-time, operational issue with one of our services that is not described below, please inform us by clicking on the "Contact Us" link to submit a service issue report. All dates and times are Pacific Time (PST/PDT).

North America	South America	Europe	Asia Pacific		Contact Us
Recent Events			Details		RSS
No recent events.					
Remaining Services			Details		RSS
Amazon API Gateway (N. California)			Service is operating normally		
Amazon API Gateway (N. Virginia)			Service is operating normally		
Amazon API Gateway (Ohio)			Service is operating normally		
Amazon API Gateway (Oregon)			Service is operating normally		
Amazon AppStream (N. Virginia)			Service is operating normally		
Amazon AppStream 2.0 (N. Virginia)			Service is operating normally		
Amazon AppStream 2.0 (Oregon)			Service is operating normally		
Amazon Athena (N. Virginia)			Service is operating normally		
Amazon Athena (Ohio)			Service is operating normally		
Amazon Athena (Oregon)			Service is operating normally		

Figure 6-4. A small section of the many pages of the AWS Service Health Dashboard

While it is standard practice to rely on multiple availability zones to guarantee services are highly availabile, some of the worst outages have affected multiple AZs within the same region. Even in the direst of circumstances, no AWS outage has ever brought down an AWS service across multiple regions concurrently. If your organization cannot afford a few hours of downtime annually as the worst-case scenario, you should analyze the cost and complexity required to operate your service from multiple AWS regions concurrently, as opposed to merely multiple availability zones.

Mastering Scale

Auto Scaling policies are tricky to get right the first time, and it is likely that you will need to tweak these as your application workload changes. Err on the side of caution —in most cases, it is best to run with a little extra capacity, rather than having too little capacity and offering users a poor experience.

Auto Scaling enables some creative thinking. Do you have an internal HR system that is used only during office hours? Use scheduled Auto Scaling to automatically launch and terminate the instance so it is running only when needed.

What about building stacks that automatically launch when needed and self-destruct once their work is complete? The minimum size of an Auto Scaling group is zero. The Celery stack could be configured to launch instances when there are more than 50 messages in the queue.

Now you're thinking with Auto Scaling groups.

## CHAPTER 7

Deployment Strategies

This chapter covers methods that should be used to deploy changes safely and reliably in a live environment, and demonstrates two of the common approaches to updating EC2 instances:

Instance-based deployment
   Each instance is updated individually at deployment time.

AMI-based deployment
   A new AMI is created every time a production version is released.

The remainder of this chapter investigates the pros and cons of each approach.

In the context of this chapter, *deploying* does not just refer to updating your application's code or executable files. It's a complete, end-to-end process that makes sure your running production environment is consistent and correct. It covers various other changes you need to manage, such as updating versions of software installed on EC2 instances and making changes to CloudFormation stack templates.

The focus here is on how to orchestrate a fleet of EC2 instances and reliably manage them. We won't cover the actions taken by the deployment script (such as restarting services), because each application has its own unique requirements.

Instance-Based Deployments

Before we look at the AWS-specific requirements of a deployment system, let's first examine the components common to nearly all such systems. Consider the deployment workflow of a typical user application. We will look at this from the perspective of a developer making a change to some application code, but the same rules apply to a designer changing a CSS file or a sysadmin changing a parameter in a configuration file:

1. A developer writes code to implement a new feature.

2. The changed files are incorporated into a version control system such as Git or Subversion.

3. Depending on the programming language being used, it might be necessary to build or compile the source files to produce an executable binary.

4. The changed source files (or compiled executables) are made available to the running instances. Instances might pull the files directly from the version control system, or perhaps use a locally hosted repository system such as Apt or Yum.

5. Once the changed files are on the instances, running services are restarted to pick up the new code or configuration files.

This is, of course, a high-level overview, and some applications might require additional steps.

Some parts of the process are not affected by the choice of hosting environment. Whether you are hosting your application on your own hardware in a shared datacenter or on AWS, you will need to perform these steps.

The elasticity of the cloud does force some changes onto the traditional datacenter deployment flow. With Auto Scaling, you can never be sure how many instances will be running when you initiate the deployment process.

Consider this example: you have 10 instances running version 1.0 of your application, and you wish to deploy an update (let's call it 1.1). You run your deployment script and update these 10 instances to v1.1. As word spreads about the amazing new features contained in this release, users flock to the site to join. The increased traffic is noticed by CloudWatch, which responds by launching two new instances to handle the load. Because these instances had not yet been launched when the deployment was originally executed, they will now be launched with whichever version of the application was baked into the AMI—in this case, v1.0. As a result, you end up running two versions of your application simultaneously.

To solve this problem, each instance must be able to update itself to the latest released version at launch time, and finish updating itself before it is added to the pool of instances behind an Elastic Load Balancer.

This approach is referred to as an *instance-based deployment*, and is very similar to the release management processes found in traditional, noncloud environments. Two additional features are required to make it AWS-compatible: finding out the hostnames of instances that should be updated, and making sure instances can update themselves on boot.

Executing Code on Running Instances with Fabric

The first problem when deploying code to running instances is a simple one: how can we reliably execute code on running EC2 instances when we don't know their hostnames in advance? Part of the answer to that question is *Fabric*, which is a Python tool used to automate system administration tasks. It provides a basic set of operations (such as executing commands and transferring files) that can be combined with custom logic to build powerful and flexible deployment systems, or simply make it easier to perform routine tasks on groups of servers or EC2 instances. Think of Fabric as an agentless system that lets you execute arbitrary Python functions via the command line, with a library of support subroutines meant to make executing shell commands over SSH easy and *pythonic*.

Because Fabric is Python-based, we can use Boto to quickly integrate it with AWS services. Tasks are defined by writing Python functions, which are usually stored in a file named *fabfile.py*. These functions use Fabric's interface to perform actions on remote hosts. Here is a simple example mirroring what we learned about Fabric in Chapter 4:

```
from fabric.api import run

def get_uptime():
    run('uptime')
```

When executed, this task will run the `uptime` command on each host and display the resulting output. It can be executed in various ways; for example:

```
fab -H localhost,www.example.com get_uptime
```

With this invocation, Fabric would execute the `get_uptime` task—and therefore the `uptime` command—on both *localhost* and *www.example.com*. The -H flag defines the list of hosts on which the task will be executed. You may need to specify which SSH key to use (-i flag) or what user ID to log in as (-u flag) when you try this example:

```
$ fab -H localhost get_uptime
[localhost] Executing task 'get_uptime'
[localhost] run: uptime
[localhost] out:  23:04:26 up 260 days, 14:29,  3 users,  load average: 0.00,
0.01, 0.05
[localhost] out:


Done.
Disconnecting from localhost... done.
```

Grouping instances through roles

Fabric includes a feature known as *roles*, which are user-defined groups of hosts. The Roles Documentation (*http://docs.fabfile.org/en/1.13/usage/execution.html#roles*) shows a simple example:

```
from fabric.api import env

env.roledefs = {
    'web': ['www1', 'www2', 'www3'],
    'dns': ['ns1', 'ns2']
}
```

A role is simply a list of hostnames (or, technically speaking, a list of *host strings*, that may or may not be fully qualified domain names). As the previous code shows, the role definition list—env.roledefs—is implemented as a Python dictionary, where a key such as 'web' is associated to an array of host strings (www1, www2, and www3). We make it available to other parts of the Python script through the global env variable.

When you combine the code just shown with the previous example, our own get_uptime task could be executed on the three web servers by executing this command:

```
fab -R web get_uptime
```

This command would execute get_uptime on the three web servers listed under env.roledefs as 'web' and display the output, making it functionally equivalent to specifying the three web server hostnames with the -H or --hosts flag.

The previous example relies on a statically defined group of hostnames, which is obviously not suitable for the dynamic nature of EC2. Having to manually create a list of web instances in the production environment before each deployment would quickly become tiresome. Fortunately, role definitions can be set dynamically: before each task is executed, it checks the role definitions to get a list of hostnames. This means one task can update the role definitions, and the updated definitions will be used for all subsequent tasks.

We can use this feature to create different role definitions for staging and production environments. Suppose we are running an infrastructure using hostnames that reference the server's role and environment. For example, a web server in the production environment is named www1-prod. Example 7-1 shows how dynamic role definitions can be used to control which hosts the tasks are executed on.

Example 7-1. Dynamic Fabric role definitions

```
from fabric.api import env

def production():
```

```
    env.roledefs = {
        'web': ['www1-prod', 'www2-prod', 'www3-prod'],
        'db': ['db1-prod', 'db2-prod']
    }

def staging():
    env.roledefs = {
        'web': ['www1-staging', 'www2-staging'],
        'db': ['db1-staging']
    }

def deploy():
    run('deploy.py')
```

Remember that Fabric tasks are simply Python functions; they do not necessarily need to execute any code on remote servers. We could then update the staging servers with the following command:

```
fab staging deploy
```

This command makes Fabric execute the `staging` task to set the role definitions and then run the *deploy.py* script on the remote instances. This example runs a nonexistent *deploy.py* script, which acts as a placeholder for your own deploy script.

That works well when we know all of our hostnames in advance, but how about dynamic fleets of EC2 instances, where we don't even know how many instances there are, let alone their hostnames?

In combination with the EC2 API, we can take advantage of this feature to selectively execute tasks on our EC2 instances without needing to know the hostnames in advance. This relies on the tagging strategy introduced in the preceding chapters, in which each instance is tagged with a role and an environment. Instead of setting `env.roledefs` to a list of predefined hostnames, we will query the EC2 API to find a list of instances that matches our target role and environment.

Dynamically finding instances

Mike has released an open source package (*https://github.com/mikery/fabric-ec2*) encapsulating the logic required to query the EC2 API and use tags to build up a list of EC2 instance hostnames. This Python module can be used to quickly convert the previous example—which showed how to deploy software to different environments —into a script that can be used to deploy code to all running instances known to EC2.

Example 7-2 uses the EC2 tags feature. It assumes that each instance was created with a web or db tag and puts the hostnames into the associated key of an associative array called roles. For each environment we need (production, staging, and deploy), we read the associative array according to our environment.

Example 7-2. Fabric role definitions and EC2 tags

```
from fabric.api import run, roles, sudo, env
from fabric_ec2 import EC2TagManager

def configure_roles(environment, region):
    """ Set up the Fabric env.roledefs, using the correct roles for the given envi-
ronment
    """
    tags = EC2TagManager(common_tags={'environment': environment},
regions=[region])

    roles = {}
    for role in ['web', 'db']:
        roles[role] = tags.get_instances(role=role)

    return roles

# select staging or production environment to filter roles accordingly,
env.roledefs = configure_roles(env.environment, env.region)

@roles('web')
def restart_web():
        sudo('/etc/init.d/nginx restart')

@roles('db')
def restart_db():
        sudo('/etc/init.d/postgresql restart')

def hostname():
        run('hostname')
```

This can be executed in our us-east-1 staging environment with the following:

```
$ fab -u ubuntu restart_web --set region='us-east-1',environment='staging'
[ec2-54-157-1-63.compute-1.amazonaws.com] Executing task 'restart_web'
[ec2-54-157-1-63.compute-1.amazonaws.com] sudo: /etc/init.d/nginx restart
[ec2-54-157-1-63.compute-1.amazonaws.com] out:  * Restarting nginx nginx
[ec2-54-157-1-63.compute-1.amazonaws.com] out:     ...done.
[ec2-54-157-1-63.compute-1.amazonaws.com] out:

[ec2-54-145-97-18.compute-1.amazonaws.com] Executing task 'restart_web'
[ec2-54-145-97-18.compute-1.amazonaws.com] sudo: /etc/init.d/nginx restart
[ec2-54-145-97-18.compute-1.amazonaws.com] out:  * Restarting nginx nginx
[ec2-54-145-97-18.compute-1.amazonaws.com] out:     ...done.
[ec2-54-145-97-18.compute-1.amazonaws.com] out:


Done.
Disconnecting from ec2-54-157-1-63.compute-1.amazonaws.com... done.
Disconnecting from ec2-54-145-97-18.compute-1.amazonaws.com... done.
```

Assuming you have some running instances bearing the relevant tags—a `role` tag with a value of `web` or `db`, and an environment tag with the value `production`—the deployment task will be executed on each of the matching EC2 hosts.

If you wanted to run a generic task only on the db instances you could execute the following example to list their instance hostnames:

```
fab -u ubuntu hostname -R db --set region='us-east-1',environment='staging'
```

The tags given are just examples. Any key/value pairs can be used with EC2 tags and queried from Fabric, making this a flexible method of orchestrating your EC2 fleet with both generic (the `hostname` example) and service-specific (like `restart_db`) tasks.

Dynamically keying on instance attributes

Omri Bahumi brought the dynamic binding concept to new heights, with a project (*https://github.com/EverythingMe/fabric-aws*) taking AWS metadata integration with Fabric even further. Omri's extension allows task decorators to key on any AWS EC2 instance attribute, including not only tags but also instance type, instance ID, and even Auto Scaling groups.

Begin by installing `fabric-aws` as follows. A configured instance of Boto is also required:

```
pip install fabric-aws
```

After setup is complete, it becomes trivial to select instances based on any metadata attribute exposed by the describe-instances (*https://docs.aws.amazon.com/cli/latest/ reference/ec2/describe-instances.html*) CLI command and corresponding API—more than 83 distinct properties are accessible as of the time of writing. Example 7-3 shows two minimalistic Fabric tasks targeting instances based on their instance ID and instance types, respectively.

Example 7-3. Fabric decorators selecting by instance ID or type

```
from fabric.api import *
from fabric_aws import *

@ec2('us-east-1',
instance_ids=['i-02f7acf3eafb0b4af','i-06eab5b7e64f5af4c','i-06eab5b7e64f5af4c'])
@task
def uptime_instance_ids():
    run('uptime')

@ec2('us-east-1', filters={'instance_type':'t2.micro'})
@task
```

```
def hostname_instance_type():
    run('hostname')
```

Service Discovery

In a highly dynamic cloud environment, the list of endpoints available to service a request may vary rather frequently. Configuration management can keep track of which servers are available and rewrite configuration files accordingly, but a Puppet run is a heavyweight process that is usually executed with hourly granularity at best. DNS can be similarly used to direct clients to the correct instance, but there is no intelligence in DNS records, so a static pool is served up for a predefined period of time, even after endpoints may have been terminated.

A service discovery tool is essentially a registry where endpoints can check in, advertising that they are available to service requests. Clients then rely on the list of servers marked as available by the service discovery tool to adjust their own configuration. The service discovery software typically monitors the health of its pool of endpoints, but endpoints are also generally expected to deregister themselves when shutting down or otherwise discontinuing service. Popular choices in this category include HashiCorp Consul (*https://www.consul.io/*) and Apache Zookeeper (*https:// zookeeper.apache.org/*), but there are many other alternatives.

Updating Instances at Launch Time

The second part of the problem is to update newly launched instances. If an AMI has a particular version of an application baked into it, that is the version that will be running when the instance is launched. If a new version has been released since the AMI was created, the instances will be running an outdated version.

Our instances therefore need to be able to check for the latest version as part of the boot process and perform an update themselves if necessary. All operating systems provide some mechanism for running user-defined scripts at boot time. On Linux systems, the update can be triggered by placing the following in the */etc/rc.local* file:

```
#!/bin/bash
```

```
/usr/local/bin/deploy.py
```

In this example, the deploy script would check a central location to find the latest version of the application and compare it with the currently installed version. The script could then update the instance to the correct version if a change is required. It is essential that a distinction between the tip of development and production releases be in place for such a process to produce consistent results.

Package Management

Many programming languages and operating systems offer their own solutions for distributing code and configuration files, such as PyPI for Python, Yum for RPM-based systems, and Apt for Debian-based systems. Using these systems wherever possible can make for a very easy upgrade path, because you can rely on the distribution's ecosystem to reduce the amount of work you need to do yourself.

For example, Python's packaging system provides a requirements text file that lists all the Python modules required by your application. The requirements file—commonly named *requirements.txt*—also tracks the installed version of the package. Moving from Boto version 1.1 to 1.5 requires a single change in *requirements.txt* (from `boto==1.1` to `boto==1.5`).

If you package your Python code as a module and publish it to an internal PyPI repository, you can then deploy your application by changing the requirements file used by your running instances. While we encourage you to make code public and participate in the global Open Source community whenever possible, we suggest you at least consider an Inner Source (*https://www.oreilly.com/ideas/getting-started-with-innersource*) approach to common resources in your organization when setting up private repositories.

Another option is to build operating system packages (e.g., RPM packages for Red Hat systems) for your custom application so that they can be installed with the OS's own package management system, and host these on your own private repository. EC2 instances can simply check this repository for any updated packages when they are launched, ensuring that they are always running the correct version of each software package.

Building such systems is not within the scope of this book, but they can be useful for managing AWS-hosted applications, and may be well worth the time required to implement. Do not underestimate the learning curve and exacting sophistication required by Linux packaging: making custom packages for Ubuntu or AWS Linux is simple enough, but making packages that upgrade correctly and work well with their host OS requires quite some mastery. If you decide to take this path, our advice is to recruit talent with published work from the appropriate Open Source community.

AMI-Based Deployments

AMIs are the building blocks of EC2. Deploying AMIs instead of individual code or configuration changes means you can offload the work of replacing instances to Amazon with varying degrees of automation.

Deploying AMIs with CloudFormation

The most automatic method involves using CloudFormation to replace running instances by changing the AMI ID referenced in the stack template. When CloudFormation receives an update request with a new AMI, it will launch some instances running the new AMI and then terminate the old instances. The number of instances launched will match the number of currently running instances to avoid a sudden reduction in capacity.

Using this method requires a high degree of confidence in the new AMI. You should first test it thoroughly in a staging environment, ideally using an automated suite of test cases. Once CloudFormation starts processing an update, there is no alternative to waiting for it to finish. If you discover early on in the update process that the application is not working as expected, you will need to wait for CloudFormation to finish applying the broken update before issuing a command to perform another update to revert to the previous AMI.

The Netflix OSS team has released Spinnaker (*https://www.spin naker.io*) as their new take on a web-based cloud management and deployment tool building on their initial experience with Asgard (*http://bit.ly/2nhytw9*).

Spinnaker can be used to automate deployments and changes to your infrastructure and control the process from a web interface, and provides a CI workflow alongside rollback capability. It acts as a supplement to the AWS Management Console and enforces local site conventions as required by Netflix's deployment process, integrating with their cloud toolset.

Deploying AMIs with the EC2 API

An alternative approach is to automate the replacement process yourself using the EC2 API. Instead of allowing CloudFormation to update the running instances, you use the API (via Boto) or script the AWS CLI to perform the same process. This gives you the opportunity to insert checkpoints and handle the rollback or reversion process with more granularity.

Using the EC2 API opens up some opportunities that were not available in traditional environments. Consider an application that has two web server instances running behind an Elastic Load Balancer, running version 1 of the AMI. The update process could then perform these steps:

1. Launch two instances running version 2 of the AMI.
2. Wait for these instances to be ready.
3. Query the health check page until the instance is serving requests correctly.

---

4. Add the new instances to the ELB and wait for them to begin receiving traffic.

5. Remove the old instances from the ELB.

At this point, the old instances are still running but not actually serving any traffic. If version 2 of the AMI turns out to be broken, you will see an increase in failed requests as measured by the ELB. You can quickly revert to version 1 of the AMI by reversing the update process—adding the old instances to the ELB and removing the newer ones.

Once you are sure the new version of the AMI is working properly, the old instances can be terminated.

With more control comes greater responsibility, as you will need to develop and maintain the custom lifecycle automation required to manage version transitions via the EC2 API. Examine what third-party tooling is available when you implement this process to avoid re-inventing the wheel—you may choose to join an existing open source project and share the maintenance burden with others instead of starting your own codebase. Nonetheless, you will need to put plans in place able to meet the recovery time you are targeting for a broken deployment of this particular application.

Webscale Thinking

Webscale computing defines a fundamentally different architecture when compared to smaller, traditional datacenter practices. The thinking that variety generates complexity is sharply reflected in the *Pets versus Cattle* metaphor we discussed in Chapter 2. The idea that hardware resources can be treated like a bag of nails, with any potentially taking the place of any other, is a central tenet of a recent paper now among Federico's favorites. In "Too Big NOT to Fail" (*https://cacm.acm.org/maga zines/2017/6/217752-too-big-not-to-fail/fulltext*), the authors base on the law of large numbers their conclusion that while individual failures cannot be predicted, the aggregated expected failure rate is entirely predictable—particularly in a large system. The reliability of individual components is not important, as long as their failure rate can be predicted and a ready supply of replacements made available.

The mandate to steer clear of bespoke hardware espoused in the webscale mindset extends to its software architecture philosophy. When remedying an anomaly, one does not repair a server's configuration, but instead replaces it with a new, identical instance configured entirely anew through automation. Troubleshooting is accomplished through *re-paving* rather than recovery. In this light, it is important to understand and embrace the *Immutable Server* pattern.

Application Immutability

The reality of configuration drift over the lifetime of a server highlights the consistency that frequent server tear-down and rebuild brings to any deployment: all of a server's configuration is set to a known state when a new instance is launched. The logical corollary is that once a server is deployed, it is never to be modified or maintained, but only replaced. This is known as the Immutable Server design pattern (*https://martinfowler.com/bliki/ImmutableServer.html*).

Application immutability is achieved by automating the operations performed on instances, and by limiting their variety to provisioning, replacement, and de-provisioning exclusively. If this design can be fully achieved, the application can then be predictably deployed, it can be just as easily rolled back, and its full state, including its security posture, is clearly understood and can be easily and exactly reproduced at any point of an instance's lifecycle.

Takeaways

The best choice for your environment will depend on how frequently you deploy code changes, and how much work is required to create an AMI. Updating running instances is tempting when you are frequently deploying small changes, and you need new code to be live as soon as possible.

Building new AMIs provides a cleaner way of deploying updates. The new AMI can be thoroughly tested in a staging environment before it is deployed, and the approach is more consistent with the Immutable Server pattern.

Updating running instances will showcase the very drawbacks illustrated by the "Pets versus Cattle" on page 67 described in metaphors of traditional datacenter environments, while maintaining AMIs more closely resembles a "golden image" process in its trade-offs, although ameliorated by the consistency of the image management process built into the EC2 APIs and its inherent versioning. If you choose to update instances, you should limit such activity to an instance's first (and only) boot time. If you choose to operate with AMIs, you should instead invest time in making the creation of a new AMI a seamless and low-effort process.

The process of deploying an update can be reduced to simply changing the AMI ID used in a CloudFormation stack, and the task of replacing running instances is handled by Amazon's internal systems. This approach opens up some interesting methods that really take advantage of the cloud and the temporary nature of EC2 instances. The following are some basic principles to take away from this chapter:

- Automate the process of building new AMIs as early as possible in your infrastructure design, to minimize *deployment friction*. The easier it is to deploy changes, the faster you will be able to iterate.

- Do not wait until you have deployed a broken application update to start thinking about how to revert.

- EC2 has many advantages over physical hardware, key among them the ability to launch new instances instead of updating code on running instances.

- The system provides support for deployment, load-balanced server swapping, and rollback. In the cloud, we replace malfunctioning servers instead of fixing them. Design your workflow accordingly.

Using the EC2 APIs creatively can save both time and headaches when maintaining custom tooling is required to deliver your application's deployment workflow—and, ultimately, its uptime objective.

## CHAPTER 8

Building Reusable Components

It is the goal of any time-pressed system administrator to avoid duplication of work where possible. There is no need to spend time building ten servers when you can build one and clone it, or implement a configuration management system that can configure ten servers as easily as one.

Within the context of AWS, there are many ways to work smarter instead of harder. Remember that AWS gives you the building blocks you need to build your infrastructure. Some of these blocks can be reused in interesting ways to remove tedious steps from your workflow.

As an example, consider an application that runs in three environments: development, staging, and production. Although the environments differ in some important ways, there will definitely be a lot of overlap in terms of the AWS resources required and the application's configuration. Considering the reuse of resources will save a lot of time as your infrastructure grows, and will let you take advantage of the flexibility that makes cloud hosting so useful.

This chapter looks at some of the ways in which AWS components can be designed for optimal reusability in order to reduce development time and minimize time spent on operations and maintenance.

The Importance of Being Reusable

Kief Morris highlights the importance of the reusability of configuration definitions in his recent *Infrastructure as Code* (O'Reilly). Kief's work defines and catalogs the patterns of server management automation in a modern computing environment. In the process, he illustrates how the reuse of configuration is essential to consistent infrastructure and repeatable processes. A key pattern of configuration reusability is parameterization.

Imagine maintaining three separate configuration definitions for testing, staging, and production environments. Most changes to one configuration would have to be manually reflected in the others—this runs counter to the aim of consistently automating infrastructure processes, and would eventually result in a human operator accidentally failing to maintain alignment between the replicated copies of the same logic. Any reasonably designed infrastructure configuration must therefore avail itself of parameters to avoid unnecessary replication.

Role-Based AMIs

It's common in both AWS infrastructures and traditional datacenters to assign each instance or server a role that describes the functions it will perform. A web application can be divided into serveral servers, each handling a separate role such as serving web requests, processing asynchronous tasks, providing a database, and so on.

The most popular configuration management tools provide some method of implementing a role-based architecture. In fact, it might be said that the *raison d'être* of configuration management tools is to provide a way to assign a role to a server or virtual instance. Applying a set of Puppet modules (or Chef recipes, or Ansible playbooks) to an instance prepares it to perform its role.

The speed with which cloud computing allows you to bring new instances online makes it even more feasible to adopt this approach fully and design your infrastructure so that each instance performs one role, and one role only. When it took days or weeks to bring a new server online, it was much more tempting to add "just one more" role to an already overburdened server.

This raises the question of how AMIs can be used to facilitate this approach. If an instance performs only a single role, do you need one AMI per role? Not necessarily. It is possible to create an AMI that can perform multiple roles, as we saw in Chapter 5.

When the instance is launched, the configuration management tool will be run. This launch-time configuration transitions the instance from the launch state to the configured state, at which point it should be ready to begin performing its role.

Using a single AMI for all roles means that each instance launched from this AMI will need to perform a lot of role-specific configuration at launch time. An AMI should always contain just the bare minimum number of installed software packages that are required by its instances. In this architecture, the AMI would need the packages required by each and every role. This leads to a lengthy launch-time configuration process, which will increase the amount of time it takes for an instance to be ready to perform its regular duties.

At the other end of the spectrum, creating an individual AMI for each role results in a much shorter launch-time configuration process, although at the cost of an increase in time spent creating and managing AMIs.

Making and testing AMIs is not difficult, but it is time-consuming. If you are using an automated AMI creation process, this cost becomes a lot easier to bear.

A third option uses a different approach to building a base AMI that can be reused for all roles. With this method, the base AMI contains all software packages required to perform any of the roles in your infrastructure. For example, it might include packages for a database server, web server, and in-memory caching server. However, none of the services are configured to start when the AMI is launched. Instead, the configuration management tool takes responsibility for starting services. This reduces the amount of time taken to perform the launch-time configuration, because software packages do not need to be downloaded and installed, only configured and started.

One downside of this third approach is that the base AMI might need to be rebuilt more frequently than role-specific AMIs. If your base AMI includes both PostgreSQL and Nginx, the release of an urgent update to either package will necessitate rebuilding the AMI and replacing any instances that are running the old version. Failing to do so would result in running insecure versions of core software, or result in running two versions of the base AMI, which will quickly become inconvenient to manage.

Package Upgrades and Service Restarts

A minor difference between the Debian APT package manager and the Red Hat RPM package manager renders RPM-based Linux distributions a better choice for the third option, where you include multiple roles in an instance but start only one role.

In Debian-inspired Linux systems like Ubuntu, policy requires that packages operate correctly once the postinit script has executed successfully. As a consequence of this design, a package update typically results in automatic service restarts, even for services that were not previously running. This is a sensible design as it eliminates the possibility of a stale process accidentally surviving the update of on-disk binaries, but it also precludes straightforward use of a single AMI for all roles.

Choosing to employ one AMI to fulfill all roles is not the most popular choice, but you should take note that the use of an RPM-based distribution like Amazon Linux is preferable in such a design. RPM distributions in the mold of Red Hat Enterprise Linux and CentOS do not automatically restart services after a package update, leaving that task to the administrator instead. This design will not result in idle services being inadvertently started by an update.

No matter which method you choose, you will need some way of mapping a running instance to a particular role, which is the topic of the next section.

Mapping Instances to Roles

Once you know that each instance will perform a given role, how do you apply that role to the instance? The answer to this question comes in two parts: assigning roles in AWS, and making this information available to your configuration management system. The second task is covered in the next section.

EC2 offers two ways to assign roles to instances or, looking at the problem from a higher level, to pass arbitrary information to your instances: user data and tags. Of course, it is also possible to store such information in a database such as RDS, SimpleDB, or your own database instance.

User data is usually the easiest method for a number of reasons. Instances can access user data without needing any IAM access credentials. User data can be retrieved from a static URL, which makes it usable from almost any programming language.

The most direct approach to using user data to control role assignation would be to use the entire user data field to specify the role. This value would then be available to scripts running on the instance from the magic address reserved by AWS to deliver metadata to instances:

```
#!/bin/bash

ROLE=$(curl -s http://169.254.169.254/latest/user-data)
echo My role is $ROLE
```

In practice, you might already be using user data for other applications and not want to reserve the entire field to define an instance's role. In this case, you should move to a more suitable data structure, such as JSON or key/value pairs. In the user data world, flexible use of metadata is enabled by the Cloud-init component of the operating system.

Cloud-init and User Data

Cloud-init is the most widespread mechanism to parse user data and configure a system at boot time. Originally designed by hacker extraordinaire Scott Moser (*https://github.com/smoser*) of the Ubuntu Server team in 2010 (*https://www.youtube.com/watch?v=-zL3BdbKyGY*), over the past decade Cloud-init has been adopted by as diverse a group of implementers as Red Hat's RHEL team and the OpenStack community as the way to deliver an instance's bootstrapping configuration. Puppet, Chef, Salt, Landscape, Rightscale, and Marionette Collective all support initialization of their management agents with short user data messages and the corresponding Cloud-init module.

The key to understanding the user data mechanism is that the cloud fabric does not enforce a format on what is delivered to the instance—it could literally be anything, and it is up to the operating system (or further up the stack in user space) to interpret the payload. Because of its large collection of modules (*http://bit.ly/2nfuPTh*), serving varied purposes for a multitude of vendors, the default inclusion of Cloud-init by the OS is as close as we get to a standard. When used in combination with the Immutable Server pattern (see "Application Immutability" on page 266), Cloud-init can be a most powerful yet lightweight mechanism to configure instances, side-stepping the need for a configuration management system in most basic cases.

Visiting the homepage of the Cloud-init project (*http://cloudinit.readthedocs.io/en/latest/*) remains perhaps the best way to learn about what is possible in the much under-documented space of user data.

Amazon Linux uses the less-featureful *CloudFormation Initialization* script `cfn-init` to fulfill the same goals. When using Amazon Linux, refer to our earlier discussion of cfn-init in Chapter 4.

Using tags is slightly more complicated because they can be retrieved only from the AWS command-line tools or APIs, the latter requiring the use of a programming language with a suitable AWS client library. An IAM account must be used to access the APIs, which means that any use of tags requires access to a set of IAM access credentials.

The simplest way to provide these credentials is to use IAM roles so that credentials do not need to be hardcoded into scripts or retrieved from user data. Instead they can be automatically detected by the underlying client library used by your scripts (such as Boto, introduced in "Launching from Your Own Programs and Scripts" on page 41).

Tags have four advantages over user data. First, they are key/value pairs by design. This fits in neatly with the idea of mapping a role to an instance: we simply need to create a tag named `role` and give it a value such as `web` or `db`.

The second advantage of tags is that they can be queried from outside the instance far more easily than user data. Tags make it possible to perform an API query to retrieve a list of instances tagged with a role like `web`. Performing the same query through user data would involve listing all your instances, parsing their user data, and compiling a list of matching instances. Let's just say it would not be fun.

Another difference between passing data with tags or through user data is that while tags can be updated at any time, an instance's user data is only initialized at first boot. While you aren't likely to change the role an instance plays once it has been deployed, this could affect your environment if you decide to change the name of a role while refactoring your code.

The final advantage of tags is more of a business reason than a technical one. Tags can be used by Amazon's billing system to produce an itemized list of instances divided into groups based on the arbitrary tags you have defined in your Cost Allocation

Report. The same source of data can then inform both technical and business decisions.

Example 8-1 shows an example of retrieving tags from a Python script.

Example 8-1. Using EC2 tags

```
from boto.utils import get_instance_metadata
from boto.ec2 import connect_to_region

metadata = get_instance_metadata()
my_instance_id = metadata['instance-id']

conn = connect_to_region('us-east-1')
for reservations in conn.get_all_instances(filters={'instance-id': my_instance_id}):
# There will be only one instance in the results
 for instance in reservations.instances:
   for tag in instance.tags:
     # Iterate through the tags, printing the keys and values
     print "Key \'%s\' has value \'%s\'" % (tag, instance.tags[tag])
```

This script does not embed any IAM credentials. It assumes that the instance it is running on has been assigned an IAM role. Boto will automatically transition to use IAM role credentials if they are available, just as it would use environment or file credentials in your development environment.

Executing the Boto script on an EC2 instance produces the following output:

```
$ python tags.py
Key 'role' has value 'web'
Key 'environment' has value 'dev'
```

This script of course requires Python and Pip (sudo `apt install python python-pip`) as well as Boto (`pip install boto`) to operate correctly, as we have seen in previous chapters.

Patterns for Configuration Management Tools

As mentioned earlier, reusability is a core goal for many configuration management tools, the entire purpose of which is to reduce duplication of effort by automating common tasks such as creating files or installing software packages. This section shows how this role-based design pattern can be used within Puppet, building on the information in the previous section. Note that, apart from the syntax used, there is nothing specific to Puppet about this pattern. It can be implemented in all the configuration management tools of which we are aware.

The usual modus operandi of Puppet is to use the hostname of an instance to control which configurations are applied to that instance. This is practically useless within

AWS, because hostnames are automatically generated based on the IP address of the instance. It is possible to work around this by setting the hostname to a "useful" value before running Puppet—a valid tactic that is used by companies such as Pinterest, and something that can be easily achieved with a Cloud-init user data setting. In our case, however, we want to bypass hostnames completely and use the role attribute that we assigned by way of user data or EC2 tags.

To find out information about the environment in which it is running, Puppet depends on a tool named *Facter*. Facter is responsible for providing Puppet with "facts" about the system it is running on. These facts can then be used within your Puppet modules. For example, the instance's hostname is a fact that Puppet modules make available via the $HOSTNAME variable.

Facter has built-in support for EC2, which means that it will automatically provide certain EC2-specific data to Puppet. Facter will query all the available meta and user data variables and provide them as facts to Puppet. For example, the AMI ID is available at a URL with a structure like *http://169.254.169.254/latest/meta-data/ami-id*. Facter will automatically set the $ec2_ami_id fact to this value. Note that the variable name is prefixed with ec2_, and any dashes are replaced with underscores.

Let's assume that we are using JSON-formatted user data to pass role information to the configuration management tool. We want to pass the following configuration over the user data channel, without precluding ourselves the possibility to later use the user data mechanism to deliver configuration data for other puposes:

```
{ "role": "web",
  "environment": "dev" }
```

Our JSON object declares two attributes: a role and an environment. To maintain compatibility with other uses of metadata, we wrap the definition of the role as a Cloud-init write_files stanza:

```
#cloud-config
# vim: syntax=yaml
write_files:
-   content: |
        { "role": "web",
          "environment": "dev" }

    path: /tmp/role.json
```

Encapsulating our configuration in Cloud-init's syntax ensures that this single purpose does not exclusively take ownership of the user data channel. The functionality supplied by the write_files module (*http://bit.ly/2LTAmOl*) supports the creation of files with text, binary or compressed payloads expanded upon delivery, as well as the setting of user ownership and permission attributes.

Including user data in an instance's configuration is one of the Advanced Details options exposed in the AWS console's Launch Instance Wizard, as shown in Figure 8-1.

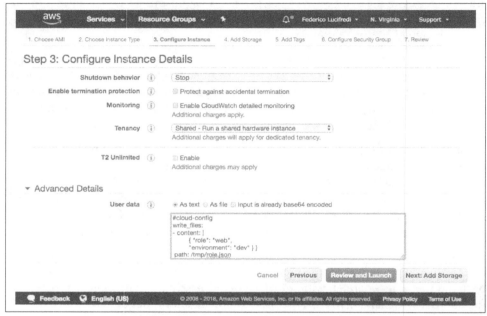

Figure 8-1. Defining an instance's user data in the AWS console

Facter populates the $ec2\_user\_data$ variable to make user data information available to Puppet. However, we choose instead to selectively place the role configuration in a *role.json* file to simplify the parsing task by limiting it to the JSON blob carrying role data and excluding any other user data that $ec2\_user\_data$ may include.

Puppet's stdlib module provides the loadjson function required to extract the keys and values you need from a JSON input source. The function converts a given file into a JSON object and returns the result as a hash. Once the data is in the hash, you can access the role and environment attributes and use them in conditional statements within Puppet modules, as shown in Example 8-2.

Facter can parse structured data fact files (*http://bit.ly/2M0f29O*) in YAML, JSON, or INI format stored in the one of the external facts directories and set facts according to their contents. For example, instructing Cloud-init to place a JSON file like the one found earlier in our example directly in */etc/facter/facts.d/* (the default external facts directory of a Linux system) would result in Facter automagically generating the role and environment facts for us. This is a powerful shortcut for occasions when writing an executable plug-in to create facts is overkill.

Example 8-2. User data roles and Puppet

```
node default {

    require stdlib

    $userdata = loadjson('/tmp/role.json')
    $role = $userdata['role']

    case $role {
        'web': {
            include role::www::dev

        }
        'db': {
            include role::db::dev
        }
        default: { fail("Unrecognized role: ${role}") }
    }

}
```

For the sake of brevity, we have not included the www and db Puppet modules. These are simply Puppet modules that perform tasks such as installing Nginx or PostgreSQL.

This example shows how the $role attribute can be used to control which modules are applied to each instance. The $userdata['environment'] variable could be used to provide a further level of abstraction, with the live environment using the role::www::live module, and the development environment using role::www::dev instead.

The module layout—in this case, `role::www::dev` and `role::db::dev`—is based on Craig Dunn's blog post "Design Puppet → Roles and Profiles" (*http://www.craigdunn.org/2012/05/239/*). This is a great way to separate business logic ("What should this instance be doing?") from technical details ("How should this instance be configured?"), and is particularly useful when adopting this pattern in AWS.

User data is only one way of providing information to AWS instances so that it can be made available to Puppet. The other option is to create tags on the instance and make these available to Puppet.

Unfortunately, tags support is not built into Facter as easily as user data. This is a minor hurdle to bypass, though—Facter makes it easy to add facts by way of a plug-in architecture. Plug-ins are simply Ruby scripts placed in a particular directory, where the name of the script is also the name of the fact that will be returned. Facter executes all the plug-ins while gathering facts about the system.

Example 8-3 shows an example Facter plug-in that retrieves all the tags for the instance and makes them available to Puppet.

Example 8-3. EC2 tag facts

```ruby
require 'facter'
require 'json'

if Facter.value("ec2_instance_id") != nil
  instance_id = Facter.value("ec2_instance_id")
  region = Facter.value("ec2_placement_availability_zone")[0..-2]

  cmd = <<eos
    aws ec2 describe-tags
      --filters \"name=resource-id,values=#{instance_id}\"
      --region #{region}
      | jq '[.Tags[] | {key: .Key, value: .Value}]'
eos
  tags = Facter::Util::Resolution.exec(cmd)

  parsed_tags = JSON.parse(tags)
  parsed_tags.each do |tag|
    fact = "ec2_tag_#{tag["key"]}"
    Facter.add(fact) { setcode { tag["value"] } }
  end
end
```

For more information about adding custom facts to Facter, and to find out where on your system this plug-in should be located, see the Custom Facts documentation page (*https://puppet.com/docs/facter/latest/custom_facts.html*).

With this plug-in in place, we can launch an instance and assign role and environment tags to it, instead of passing this information as user data. The code shown earlier in Example 8-2 has to be modified so that, instead of parsing JSON from the Cloud-init-generated */tmp/role.json* file, it obtains the same information by using the $ec2_tag_role and $ec2_tag_environment variables, as we show in the following snippet:

```
node default {

    case $ec2_tag_role {
        'web': {
            require role::www::dev
...
```

Although this section has focused on Puppet, the same result can be achieved with most other configuration management tools. The general principle of providing information to the instance at launch time, and then using this information later to control the instance configuration, can be used from configuration management tools or your own scripts.

Modular CloudFormation Stacks

CloudFormation stacks can also be designed to make them more suitable for reuse in different parts of your application. This section presents one of the most popular methods of reaching this goal.

This method uses the AWS::CloudFormation::Stack resource, which lets you embed one CloudFormation template within another. That is, a *parent* CloudFormation stack can create a number of *child* stacks. The parent stack can provide input values to the child stack and access its output values. This means that the parent stack can create multiple child stacks and use the outputs of one stack as the parameters of another stack. In this design pattern, each child stack can be self-contained and highly focused on a particular task, such as creating EC2 instances or an RDS database.

> To use embedded templates, you need to provide a TemplateURL parameter, which tells CloudFormation where to download the stack template file. This file must be in an S3 bucket configured to serve its contents over HTTP. For more information, see the AWS Stack Properties (*https://amzn.to/2M1xUFG*) documentation.

The parent stack is responsible for tying all these components together and providing the foundation your application needs to run. This is illustrated in Figure 8-2.

The architecture in the figure consists of three CloudFormation stacks: the parent stack, the DB stack, and the web stack. The DB stack is responsible for creating an RDS instance and placing it in a security group. The web stack creates an EC2 instance, also in a security group.

When the RDS instance is created, it is assigned a unique hostname generated by Amazon, which cannot be predicted in advance. How then can you let the instance know the hostname of the database instance so that it knows where to send data requests? The answer comes in the form of parameters and outputs. These can be used to provide data when launching a stack and to retrieve dynamic stack attributes after it has been created.

In this case, the DB stack outputs the hostname of the RDS instance. The parent stack uses this value as an input when creating the web stack. In turn, the web stack passes this value to the instance as user data or a tag, so it can be used in your configuration management software. More information on using parameters and outputs with embedded stacks can be found on Amazon's Stack Resource Snippets page (*https://amzn.to/2LWwfBc*).

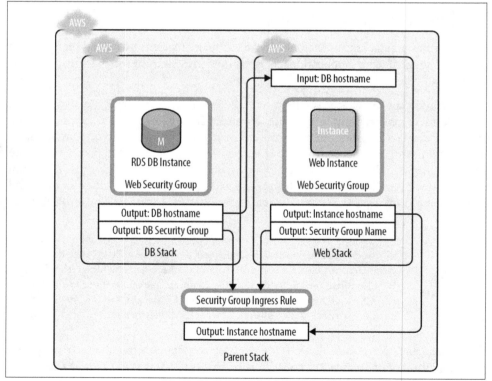

Figure 8-2. Embedded CloudFormation stacks

CloudFormation attempts to automatically determine the order in which the resources should be created, so that parameters and outputs can be passed around successfully. In this example, CloudFormation would detect that the output from the DB stack is used as an input to the web stack, and would therefore create the DB stack first.

 If you need more control over the order in which CloudFormation resources are created, you can use the DependsOn attribute (*https://amzn.to/2LZopGT*) to override CloudFormation's automatic ordering.

Note that neither the web nor DB stacks create any security group rules. Instead, these are created in the parent stack through the use of the resource type `AWS::EC2::SecurityGroupIngress`.

This resource allows you to create security group ingress rules and assign them to existing security groups. Why are these created in the parent stack? This is a personal preference more than a technical requirement. It would be possible, for example, to pass the DB security group ID as an input to the web stack and allow the web stack to create the necessary ingress rules, permitting the instance to access the database.

But the opposite is not possible: to pass the web security group as an input to the DB stack, you would need to create the web stack before the DB stack. That would make it impossible to provide the DB hostname as an input to the web stack, meaning the instance would not know the address of the database server.

By creating the ingress rules in the parent container, you are simplifying the DB and web stacks. They should not be concerned with creating security group rules, as it can be argued that ingress rules are not specifically tied to the function of the stack.

Moving some of the resource creation—such as ingress rules—to the parent stack increases the reusability of the child stacks. Consider the familiar example of development and production environments. Both will need web and DB stacks, but the development instance should be accessible only from a specific list of IP addresses, whereas the production environment will be accessible from the public internet.

To enforce this distinction, you could create a separate CloudFormation stack for each environment, each of which embeds the web and DB stacks as children. The development and production stacks would be almost identical, except when it comes to creating the security group ingress rules. When you want to make changes to the DB stack, you have only a single template to update.

This provides a clean way of breaking your infrastructure into logical components that can be reused to create flexible environments without duplication of effort.

CloudFormation will automatically tag your resources with some information about the stack itself. If you configure Cost Allocation Reports to track these tags, you can get a high-level overview of where your money is going.

Other tricks can be used in CloudFormation templates to allow easy recycling of stacks. Let's suppose that we need each developer on the team to have his own development environment, which should be accessible via SSH at a given hostname such as *mryan.dev.example.com*.

The development stack template could accept an `EnvironmentName` input parameter, which is used to create a Route 53 resource record mapping the desired hostname to the instance's public DNS name. Each developer can create his own copy of the stack, using the same template, entering his username when the stack is launched.

Although the CloudFormation template language is not as flexible as a full programming or scripting language, it can be useful to think of your CloudFormation stacks in the same way that you think of your scripts, programs, or even Puppet modules. Each of these presents various methods that can be used to dramatically reduce the time it takes to add new features or deploy new resources.

## CHAPTER 9

Log Management

Despite the best efforts of system administrators everywhere, logging in the cloud can quickly become more complicated (and more expensive) than logging in a physical hardware environment. Because EC2 instances come and go dynamically, the number of instances producing log files can grow and shrink at any time. Your logging system must therefore be designed with this in mind, to ensure that it keeps up with peaks in demand when processing log files.

Another area that requires some advance planning is log storage. Running a large number of instances will produce large log files, which need to be stored somewhere. Without some advance planning, the storage requirements can grow rapidly, leading to an increase in costs.

This chapter presents some popular logging tools that can be useful in AWS environments and introduces some strategies for managing log files without breaking the bank. Logstash is used to demonstrate the concepts in this chapter, but the principles also apply to most other logging software.

Central Logging

A common solution to the problem of viewing logs from multiple machines is to set up a central logging server to which all servers in your infrastructure send their logs. The central logging server is responsible for parsing and processing log files and managing the policies for log retention.

This pattern works well within AWS, with a few caveats. It is critical to ensure that your logging system does not struggle to keep up when many instances are sending their log files back to the central server and become a bottleneck in the process.

Another potential issue is related to hostnames within EC2. Remember that, by default, most instances will set their hostname to match their internal IP address. This is not particularly useful when it comes to viewing log files. For this reason, many log-viewing tools provide a method of adding key/value pairs to log data. These can be used in conjunction with EC2 tags to make it easier to keep track of the source of a particular log entry.

Overriding Default Hostnames

The default address-derived hostname of AWS EC2 instances can be easily overridden using the Cloud-init mechanism. To name an instance after our cover animal, use the following user data when booting a new instance:

```
#cloud-config
hostname: peccary
```

Note that configuring the Linux hostname will not set the name attribute in the AWS console instance listing. To assign a name to an instance in that user interface, one needs to define a tag with the case sensitive key Name as in this example:

```
aws ec2 create-tags --resources i-0c53dee6aa8708287 --tags
Key=Name,Value=peccary
```

Another option is to click the name field in the AWS console itself, and then fill-in the desired name interactively, which is convenient when remedying an inconsistency in a pinch or during development.

Building a central logging system requires three main components. *Log shippers* and *log receivers* such as syslog, rsyslog, and syslog-ng are responsible for sending and receiving log files. The third component is *log viewers*, such as Kibana and Graylog2, which handle the task of displaying this gathered data through a web interface. To further complicate things, most log shippers can also act as log receivers, and some packages provide all three components.

A comparison of the many tools that can be used to build such a system is beyond the scope of this book, because the issues surrounding them are not really specific to AWS. However, one tool deserves special mention, because it has several AWS-specific features.

Logstash is an open source log management tool that provides a framework for receiving, processing, and storing logs. It also includes a web interface for browsing logged data.

Like many log-receiving tools, it can accept data in the standard syslog format (RFC 3164). It also has a plug-in architecture that allows it to consume log data from a variety of additional sources. Most interestingly, it can read and write logs stored in S3

---

buckets, read logs from SQS queues, and write output messages to SNS topics. This integration with AWS services makes Logstash an ideal candidate for building a logging system within AWS.

Logstash itself consists of multiple components, collectively known as the *ELK Stack*. It includes the core functionality for consuming and producing log files, as well as a web interface, known as Kibana. It also uses an instance of Elasticsearch, which is a powerful distributed search server based on Apache Lucene. Elasticsearch provides search capabilities, allowing you to quickly and easily find the log entries you are searching for.

All of these components can be run on a single machine for development and testing purposes. Once Logstash is dealing with a large amount of log data, these components can be moved to separate instances, so they can be scaled independently.

Many third-party logging services can entirely obviate the need to build your own logging system. Some of these services provide convenient features, such as automatically retrieving EC2 tags and assigning them to log data, so that EC2 tags can be used to quickly drill down through log files. As you define your logging strategy, make sure to examine the hosted log management offerings currently leading the market, and weigh the functionality and cost of maintaining your own infrastructure against what third-party vendors can offer to do for you in exchange for a monthly service fee.

Logstash Configuration

To demonstrate Logstash in action, we will set up a simple centralized logging infrastructure suitable for use in EC2 (see Figure 9-1). Before going ahead and setting up the instances, we need to first prepare the security groups that will be used in the demonstration.

To keep this demonstration simple, we will manually install and configure Logstash on the client and server instances. Of course, when it comes to moving this into production, the configuration should be handled by a DevOps automation tool like Puppet. The Logstash documentation site contains links to Logstash Puppet modules (*https://github.com/elastic/puppet-logstash*) that can be used to automate installing and configuring the Logstash components.

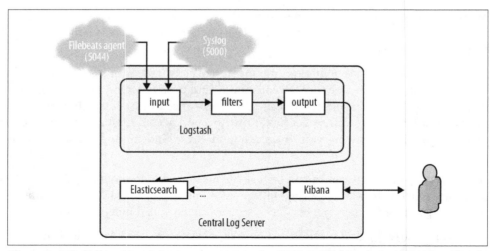

Figure 9-1. Relationship of the components in the ELK stack as integrated in our central-ized logging infrastructure

Using the AWS Management Console or command-line tools, create two security groups, named log_client and log_receiver. The rules for log_client could be left empty, but we include SSH access for convenience.

The log_receiver security group will be used for the Logstash server. It must be able to accept syslog traffic from logging clients and allow administrators to access the Kibana web interface and Elasticsearch API.

Create five rules in the log_receiver group:

Rule	Description
Inbound TCP 5601 from your network	Kibana web interface
Inbound TCP 9300 from your network	Elasticsearch API
Inbound TCP 5000 from log_client security group	Logstash (Syslog)
Inbound TCP 5044 from log_client security group	Logstash (Filebeats)
Inbound TCP 22 from your network	SSH

Create a single rule in the log_client group:

Rule	Description
Inbound TCP 22 from your network	SSH

Once you save these changes, the security group configuration is complete.

Creating and configuring a Logstash server

After creating the security groups, you can launch and configure the Logstash server instance. Launch a new EC2 i3.large instance using the most recent Ubuntu 16.04 AMI, assigning it to the log_receiver security group. Optionally, you could use Route 53 to set up a DNS record for this instance, so that a URL like *logging.example.com* points to the public DNS name of the new instance, as described in Chapter 10.

When the instance is ready, connect to it via SSH and configure Elastic's private repository:

```
$ wget -qO - https://artifacts.elastic.co/GPG-KEY-elasticsearch | \
sudo apt-key add -
OK
$ echo "deb https://artifacts.elastic.co/packages/6.x/apt stable main" | \
sudo tee -a /etc/apt/sources.list.d/elastic-6.x.list
```

This slightly unusual process is required to install Logstash due to its absence from the Ubuntu Archive—none of Elastic's projects have been packaged for the Archive as of the time of writing, so it is either using the custom repository or performing a direct download and execution.

Ensure that you have a recent version of Java—Java is the key dependency and Logstash install will fail in post-install if it is not available. Currently Logstash requires Java 8 and does not support Java 9:

```
sudo apt install openjdk-8-jre-headless
```

Finally, after retrieving metadata for the new repository, download and install Logstash and the rest of the ELK stack:

```
sudo apt update
sudo apt install -y logstash elasticsearch kibana
```

Logstash, Elasticsearch, and Kibana are not automatically started upon installing their respective packages. Let's start with Elasticsearch, which will serve as the storage and search backend for all of our logging data. Configure the system and start the Elasticsearch service first with the following commands:

```
sudo systemctl enable elasticsearch logstash kibana
sudo systemctl start elasticsearch
```

Verify that the service has started correctly by checking if there are new servers listening. Elasticsearch runs by default on ports 9200 and 9300—we will be using port 9200 to enter and query data via the API interface, while the port range starting at 9300 is used for cluster communication, which does not take place in our single-node setup:

```
$ netstat -ntl
Active Internet connections (only servers)
Proto Recv-Q Send-Q Local Address          Foreign Address         State
```

```
tcp        0    0 0.0.0.0:22          0.0.0.0:*          LISTEN
tcp6       0    0 127.0.0.1:9200      :::*               LISTEN
tcp6       0    0 ::1:9200            :::*               LISTEN
tcp6       0    0 127.0.0.1:9300      :::*               LISTEN
tcp6       0    0 ::1:9300            :::*               LISTEN
tcp6       0    0 :::22               :::*               LISTEN
```

Logstash is configured by way of files located by default in */etc/logstash/conf.d/*. Create a file named *logstash.conf* with the following contents:

```
input {
  tcp {
    port => 5000
    type => syslog
  }
  udp {
    port => 5000
    type => syslog
  }
  beats {
    port => "5044"
  }
}

output {
  elasticsearch { hosts => ["localhost:9200"] }
  stdout { codec => rubydebug }
}
```

Logstash pipeline configuration files consist of three sections, two of which are shown here. The input section specifies the sources of logging data that Logstash will consume. We default to Logstash's lightweight Filebeat client as a convenient option for all cases where we can run an agent in the monitored instance (or device), while also offering an endpoint for syslog traffic to provide the broadest compatibility. The output section controls what Logstash does with this data after it has been filtered. The final section (filter) is not used in this simple setup. Filters are used to control the flow of messages and to add supplementary data to log entries. An extensive library of filters (*http://bit.ly/2LTNumq*) is available to manipulate log data.

Our pipeline configuration instructs Logstash to listen on port 5000 on all available interfaces, including localhost, the instance's local IP address, as well as any public IP address. This seems like a reasonable approach, as it may be difficult to predict upfront on what networks all the devices forwarding logs may happen to be located. We configure Logstash in the most generic configuration, and limit access to it at the network level through the log_client security group. Changing the inbound rules of a security group can be done in a single CLI call, without reconfiguring (and potentially, redeploying) the server. This approach presents us with an advantage when operating under the *Immutable Server* pattern (see "Application Immutability" on page 266), but is not always the right choice, as we will see later in this chapter.

Tracking Temporary Configuration

You may have noticed that twice already in this chapter we told you to take actions that will need to be undone at some point in the future (the other occasion was when we added SSH to a security group as a convenience in the previous page).

The authors do not have perfect recall, and so we similarly presume you may fail to go back and correct all of your temporary decisions. This is one of the most common sources of security breaches occurring in AWS infrastructure; see, for example, published reports of S3 bucket configurations left unintentionally open by the Department of Defense's Central Command,[1] by an independent agency processing security clearance applications,[2] by Federal Express,[3] and security researcher Kevin Beaumont's very recent report of the ubiquity of JavaScript website logic found in world-writable S3 buckets.[4] These incidents have one thing in common: they are not originated by lax AWS defaults (bucket permissions default to private at creation); they were most likely originated by settings that were convenient during development, then forgotten in place and persisted into production.

Temporary implementation choices are a necessity during development, but our recommendation is to put in place good hygiene and track these future work items as technical debt that needs to be cleared before production. A lightweight process can be easily put in place by adding notes to a file dedicated exclusively for this purpose in your version control system. If your version control system itself is for any reason unavailable, start with a private instance of Etherpad (*http://etherpad.org*) instead.

Do not rely on your memory: not only it is not perfect, it is also not a shared medium accessible by your teammates.

For more information on using filters to parse and modify syslog data, see the Logstash documentation (*http://bit.ly/2nfKYbu*).

---

1 Terabytes of scraped social media data leaked by CENTCOM (*http://bit.ly/2ngl737*).

2 Thousands of files containing the personal information of US citizens with classified security clearance have been exposed by an unsecured Amazon server (*http://bit.ly/2nfH5n1*).

3 Fedex stored customer passports, driver licenses, and more in public Amazon bucket (*http://bit.ly/2nglFWJ*).

4 Lots of websites sites found to have world-writable JavaScript files embedded (*http://bit.ly/2M0xqQ9*).

In this case, all data is output to an instance of Elasticsearch, as well as stdout. We output to stdout so we can easily see logged messages on the console. The use of the console is for development purposes only and should be removed when moving into production.

With the configuration file saved, restart Logstash to force loading of the new pipeline configuration:

```
sudo systemctl restart logstash
```

Launching Logstash might take a few seconds, as is the case with any other large Java executable. Once Logstash has launched, you should see something similar to the following:

```
$ sudo systemctl status logstash
● logstash.service - logstash
   Loaded: loaded (/etc/systemd/system/logstash.service; enabled; vendor pre-
set: enabled)
   Active: active (running) since Wed 2018-04-25 02:11:19 UTC; 13s ago
 Main PID: 29378 (java)
    Tasks: 15
   Memory: 363.0M
      CPU: 25.533s
   CGroup: /system.slice/logstash.service
           └─29378 /usr/bin/java -Xms256m -Xmx1g -XX:+UseParNewGC -XX:+UseConc-
MarkSweepGC -XX:CMSInitiatingOccupancyFraction=75 -XX:+UseCMSInitiatingOccupancy

Apr 25 02:11:19 ip-172-31-11-202 systemd[1]: Started logstash.
lines 1-11/11 (END)
```

In another SSH session, verify that Logstash is listening for incoming syslog data on TCP port 5000 by using the lsof command:

```
$ sudo lsof -i :5000,5044
COMMAND   PID       USER   FD   TYPE DEVICE SIZE/OFF NODE NAME
java    29378 logstash  106u  IPv6 109277      0t0  TCP *:5000 (LISTEN)
java    29378 logstash  119u  IPv4 109288      0t0  UDP *:5000
java    29480 logstash  123u  IPv6 110120      0t0  TCP *:5044 (LISTEN)
```

Finally, use the netcat command to send a test message to Logstash. This message will be echoed to Logstash's stdout by the pipeline we previously defined, and as such will also be conveniently displayed in the systemd status view:

```
echo "testing logging" | nc localhost 5000
```

Once this command is executed, you should see some output printed to the Logstash console. This is a JSON representation of the logged message:

```
$ sudo systemctl status logstash
[...] Started logstash.
[...]Sending Logstash's logs to /var/log/logstash which is now configured via
log4j2.properties
```

```
[...]{
[...]              "port" => 54780,
[...]        "@timestamp" => 2018-04-25T02:24:53.034Z,
[...]              "host" => "localhost",
[...]              "type" => "syslog",
[...]           "message" => "testing logging",
[...]          "@version" => "1"
[...] }
```

Setting up a minimal Kibana configuration is slightly more complex, but it affords us
the opportunity to showcase an important automation technique which will come in
handy regardless of your choice of Puppet, Ansible, or Chef as your automation
framework. Our design calls for Kibana's web interface to be available exclusively on
the local network, not on the internet at large. This requires the Kibana configuration
file (found in */etc/kibana/kibana.yml*) to incorporate information available to the
instance only after boot if dynamic IP addressing is in use. This gives us the perfect
reason to pull off a little bit of shell scripting magic:

```
$ ec2metadata | grep local-ipv4 | cut -f 2 -d' '
172.31.11.202
```

As we previously discussed (see "Querying information about the instance" on page
32), the `ec2metadata` command provides any instance with convenient access to
some key configuration values, including its network interfaces. A little bit of standard shell string manipulation does the rest. To bind with the local interface, we need
to set Kibana's `server.host` configuration variable to the address of the desired interface. Splitting on two lines to improve readability, we have the following:

```
ADDRESS=$(ec2metadata | grep local-ipv4 | cut -f 2 -d' ')
sudo sed -i "s/\#server.host: \"localhost\"/server.host: \"$ADDRESS\"/" /etc/
kibana/kibana.yml
```

The first expression extracts the IP address from the output of `ec2metadata`—something that you can easily reuse for every value it makes available—while the second
uses `sed` to match and edit in-place the configuration line we needed to change.
Using the same approach, we also uncomment two lines that are required for proper
operation:

```
sudo sed -i 's_\#elasticsearch.url: "http://localhost:9200"_elasticsearch.url:
"http://localhost:9200"_' /etc/kibana/kibana.yml
sudo sed -i 's/\#kibana.index: ".kibana"/\kibana.index: ".kibana"/' /etc/kibana/
kibana.yml
```

With the configuration file updated, start Kibana:

```
sudo systemctl start kibana
```

Navigate to the Kibana web interface with your web browser. If you set up a Route 53
record pointing to *logging.example.com* to your instance, you can visit the interface at
http://logging.example.com:5601/. Otherwise, use the public DNS name of your

instance, making sure to specify port 5601 such as in the following: *ec2-35-172-226-10.compute-1.amazonaws.com:5601/*.

The first time you start Kibana, you will have to navigate to the Management tab, and create an index pattern. The system will guide you through the steps required.

Using Kibana's search function, search for the string *testing logging*. Do this by entering the Lucene query syntax `message:"testing logging"` in the search box of the Discover tab. The results window will show the test message you logged with `netcat`, as shown in Figure 9-2.

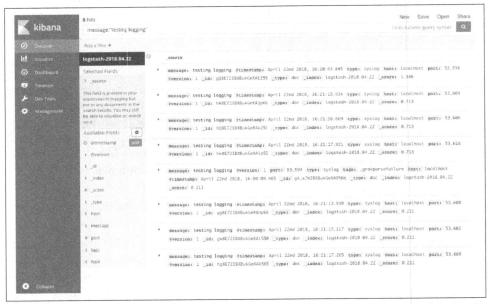

Figure 9-2. Test messages received by Logstash and archived in Elasticsearch, visualized in a Kibana search query

Kibana and Elasticsearch are extremely powerful tools, and we haven't even begun scratching the surface of their functionality. One could easily pen an entire book just on this subject. We shall focus on completing the design of a working logging infrastructure, and leave the pleasure of completing the exploration of these tools to our readers.

Configuring the Logstash clients

With the logging server listening, we can move on to configuring the logging client that will represent the other servers in your infrastructure.

Launch a second EC2 instance (a t2.micro will suffice) and make it a member of the log_client security group. Once the instance is ready to accept SSH connections, you can log in to set up Elastic's private repository:

```
$ wget -qO - https://artifacts.elastic.co/GPG-KEY-elasticsearch | \
sudo apt-key add -
OK
$ echo "deb https://artifacts.elastic.co/packages/6.x/apt stable main" | \
sudo tee -a /etc/apt/sources.list.d/elastic-6.x.list
```

Now install and enable the Filebeat log forwarding agent:

```
sudo apt install filebeat
sudo apt systemctl enable filebeat
```

While a local Logstash instance is sometimes used to forward logs to our central server, Logstash is a hefty Java executable including code that supports sophisticated format conversion functionality. The ELK stack also provides a lightweight solution for the log forwarding of individual nodes that is easier to configure and more nimble in its resource consumption: Filebeat. Instead of sending the log files directly to Elasticsearch, we instead send them to the central Logstash instance using the beats protocol.

Create a client configuration file named *filebeat.yml* in */etc/filebeat/* with the following contents:

```
filebeat.prospectors:
- type: log
  paths:
    - /var/log/*.log
    - /var/log/syslog
output.logstash:
  hosts: ["logging.example.com"]
```

This configuration file defines what inputs (known as *prospectors*) the filebeat agent will forward to the Logstash server. The input source in this example is a list of file paths, assigned to the log prospector, but alternative prospectors exist for as varied sources as Docker, Redis, stdin, and others. The path attribute can accept a list of paths, which can either be glob paths (including an asterisk or other wildcard) or paths to single files, as in the case of */var/log/syslog*.

If you did not set up a Route 53 DNS record for your central log server, you will need to replace the instance's public DNS name in the client configuration file, instead of *logging.example.com*.

This configuration file will cause `filebeat` to monitor the specified files and send their input via TCP to the *logging.example.com* host, where Logstash is listening on port 5044. We are not yet using any filters to modify or parse the logged data.

You can check the validity of your configuration by running the self-tests conveniently built into `filebeat` itself. The first test validates the syntax of the configuration file, while the second helpfully attempts to connect to the designated Logstash output and checks the health of the connection:

```
$ sudo filebeat test config
Config OK
$ sudo filebeat test output
logstash: logging.example.com:5044...
  connection...
    parse host... OK
    dns lookup... OK
    addresses: 172.31.11.202
    dial up... OK
  TLS... WARN secure connection disabled
  talk to server... OK
```

We are now ready to start the `filebeat` agent on the client instance:

```
sudo apt systemctl start filebeat
```

Use the `logger` command to write some example text to the local syslog system:

```
logger "testing client logging"
```

If everything is configured correctly, you should see the test message repeated in `syslog`. In addition, this message will be passed to Elasticsearch, so it can also be viewed by searching for `message:"testing client logging"` in the Kibana web interface.

With these steps complete, your central logging system is up and running. Any log messages produced on the client system and written to one of the monitored files will be passed to the central Logstash server.

 In the interest of brevity and readability, we made a determined effort to keep the setup steps of our example configuration to a minimum. In doing so, we did not configure password security for any of the ELK services. While we have limited the network access to `localhost` in several cases, you will need to evaluate Kibana and Elasticsearch access controls in the context of your own architectural layout.

Logging to S3

Like any critical component, the logging system should be loosely coupled to the other core services in your infrastructure. That is, a failure in the logging system should not propagate and cause other services to fail.

In the previous section, we set up a central Logstash server that will accept log messages from clients via TCP. What happens if the central Logstash instance crashes or otherwise becomes unavailable? In that case, clients will be unable to send log messages. Any attempt to do so would result in *broken pipe* error messages, because the client is unable to open a TCP connection to the central server. Fortunately, the Filebeat client will recognize this type of failure and track the log messages locally. Once the central Logstash server is back in action, these messages will be resent once again.

> If we were using the UDP transport, transmission would fail silently, and messages would be lost instead of being stored at the senders. The same may apply to instances that are forwarding Syslog instead of running a local Filebeat or Logstash client. This may or may not be acceptable, depending on your log retention policies.

The process of storing the messages locally until they can be sent to a server is known as *store and forward*, and is conceptually similar to the way in which systems like email work. If the Logstash server is only temporarily unavailable, briefly retaining the messages on the client will not cause any problems. However, prolonged outages might cause an excessive amount of spooled data to pile up on the client instance. This can cause problems if the temporary files grow so large that they interfere with the proper running of the client instance. This is not an unlikely situation in cases where Logstash is used as a logging client instead of `filebeat`, perhaps providing intermediate aggregation for multiple services.

In this case, it can be helpful to have an intermediary storage location for your log files, to further decouple the client/master Logstash instances. One method of doing this is to use S3 as temporary storage for your log files: instead of sending its log files directly to the Logstash server, the client writes all log files to an agreed-upon S3 bucket. A central Logstash agent is then responsible for regularly downloading these log files from S3 and processing them as usual.

The use of S3 as an intermediary has several benefits, the primary one being decoupling. Even if the Logstash server is unavailable for an extended period of time, you can be safe in the knowledge that your log files will be queued up on S3 and processed after the log server is back in action.

A secondary benefit relates to scaling your logging system. Consider what would happen if the number of instances sending their log files to a central Logstash instance were to grow rapidly. Because log messages are sent to Logstash as soon as they are generated, logs are effectively processed in real time. Sending too many logs could cause the central instance to become overloaded.

By temporarily storing the files in S3, you can remove the instantaneous nature of the processing. Instead, the central server has more control over when log files are pulled from S3 for processing. While the amount of work remains the same, the peaks and troughs are evened out by storing the data on S3 and allowing the central server to pull it at a steady rate.

Because Logstash has built-in support for some Amazon services, including S3, modifying our existing system to support the new setup is very straightforward. We need to make two changes to the system. First, instead of clients sending files directly to the Logstash server, they should be written to an S3 bucket. On the server side of things, we need to tell Logstash to read incoming log files from the S3 bucket, in addition to listening for TCP connections.

To start with, we need to create a new S3 bucket to store our log files. Using the Management Console or command-line tools, create a new bucket with a name like `logs-example-com`. Remember that S3 bucket names must be unique, so you will not be able to use this exact example.

Once the bucket is set up, create a new IAM user named `logging`. This will be used on both the client and central Logstash instances to read and write to the bucket.

Assign an IAM policy to the new user, granting it permissions to read from and write to the logging bucket with the following IAM policy:

```
{
  "Statement": [
    {
      "Action": "s3:*",
      "Effect": "Allow",
      "Resource": [
        "arn:aws:s3:::my-s3-bucket",
        "arn:aws:s3:::my-s3-bucket/*"
      ]
    }
  ]
}
```

Note that this policy explicitly references the S3 bucket. You will need to change the example to match the name of your S3 bucket.

Once the policy has been assigned to the IAM user, the AWS side of the configuration is complete, and you can return to the EC2 instances running your Logstash client and server.

Begin by configuring a Logstash client so that it writes log entries to the S3 bucket. Begin by installing Java and Logstash as previously detailed in this chapter. Create a configuration file named *logstash-client-s3.conf* in */etc/logstash/conf.d/* with the following content:

```
input {
  file {
    type => "syslog"
    path => [ "/var/log/*.log", "/var/log/syslog" ]
  }
}

output {
  s3 {
    access_key_id => "my-aws-access-key-id"
    secret_access_key => "my-aws-secret-access-key"
    region => "us-east-1"
    bucket => "logging-example-com"
  }
}
```

You will, of course, need to update this example to reflect the name of your S3 bucket and the AWS access credentials we created for the new logging user. It is also necessary to grant the logstash user permission to read the local log files:

```
sudo usermod -G adm logstash
```

On the Logstash server instance, create a configuration file named *logstash-central-s3.conf* with the following contents:

```
input {
  s3 {
    access_key_id => "my-aws-access-key-id"
    secret_access_key => "my-aws-secret-access-key"
    bucket => "logging-example-com"
    region => "us-east-1"
    delete => true
  }
}

output {
  stdout { codec => rubydebug }
  elasticsearch { hosts => ["localhost:9200"] }
}
```

The Logstash S3 plug-in downloads data from the bucket using the credentials you configure here. So the server's input section is totally new in this example, but the output section remains the same as the one in our original example. Again, you will need to replace the S3 bucket name and IAM access credentials with your own data. Note the delete attribute, instructing Logstash to remove files from the S3 bucket once they have been transferred to our central log archive.

Note the different configuration file options required for the S3 input and S3 output. Logstash has not yet settled on conventions for naming attributes in plug-ins, so each plug-in author chooses his own variable naming scheme. The documentation for plug-ins also varies dramatically in terms of detail and finish. Hopefully, both of these will improve as Logstash continues to grow in popularity.

With these changes in place, you will need to stop and restart the Logstash agents on both the client and central servers. Start the Logstash process on the client first:

```
sudo systemctl enable logstash
sudo systemctl start logstash
```

The central Logstash instance should be restarted as follows:

```
sudo systemctl restart logstash
```

Once both processes are running, create some log file entries on the client Logstash instance with a `logger` command:

```
echo "testing s3 logger" | logger
```

After a few minutes, this log message should be printed in the central Logstash agent log. This will take a little longer than the preceding examples, because you will need to wait for the Logstash client to write this message to the S3 bucket, and then wait again for the central Logstash agent to retrieve the updated file and process its contents.

This method of using S3 as a temporary storage location greatly increases the reliability of your logging infrastructure, as it is no longer dependent on having a central server running. Of course, without the Logstash instance running, log files will still not be processed or visible in the Kibana web interface. However, a failure in the central agent will have no ill effect on logging client instances, which will happily continue shipping their log files to the temporary S3 bucket for later processing.

AWS Service Logs

So far, we have been looking at application and operating system logs, but another class of logs must also be considered. Many of the AWS services produce log files that might need to be stored and reviewed. For example, a CloudFront distribution will produce log files providing details about requests it receives, such as the URL that was requested or the resulting HTTP response code.

All of Amazon's services use the same basic logging methodology: logs are written to a specified S3 bucket at regular intervals. This makes retrieving and processing the log files very simple. You just need to regularly download and process the files. The kind of decoupling described in the previous section is already built into this system:

if you do not process the log files, they will pile up in the S3 bucket, but CloudFront will continue to function as usual.

Given that we already have a system for processing log files that have been written to an S3 bucket, we can reuse the example from the previous section to read CloudFront logs, as well as our application and operating system logs. Logstash is already configured to process logs from an S3 bucket, so we can easily add another section to our central Logstash agent's configuration file to make it process CloudFront log files.

The first step is to create a CloudFront distribution to serve some static or dynamic files and configure that distribution to store its access logs in an S3 bucket. This is described in Amazon's CloudFront documentation (*https://amzn.to/2M0xZcJ*). During this process, you will have the option to create a new S3 bucket in which to store the logs, or enter the name of an existing bucket. Either way, keep track of the bucket name you choose, because this will be required in the following steps. For this example, we have used a bucket named `cloudfront-logs-example-com`.

Once these steps in the Amazon documentation have been completed, you will have a CloudFront distribution that writes its access logs to an S3 bucket periodically. Next, you can configure Logstash to consume these logs, feeding them into the same system that processes your application and operating system logs.

On the Logstash instance, stop the `logstash` process if it is still running from the previous example. Update the *logstash-central-s3.conf* file so that it matches the following:

```
input {
  s3 {
    bucket => "logging-example-com"
    credentials => [ "my-aws-access-key-id", "my-aws-secret-access-key"]
    region => "us-east-1"
  }
  s3 {
    bucket => "cloudfront-logs-example-com"
    credentials => [ "my-aws-access-key-id", "my-aws-secret-access-key"]
    region => "us-east-1"
    type => "cloudfront"
  }
}

output {
  stdout { codec => rubydebug }
  elasticsearch { hosts => ["localhost:9200"] }
}
```

The newly inserted `s3` section configures Logstash so that it will read log files from the CloudFront log bucket, as well as the original `logging-example-com` bucket.

All logs retrieved from the `cloudfront-logs-example-com` bucket will have their `type` attribute set to `cloudfront`. You can refer to this to keep track of the source of log data, and the type will be visible when these logs are viewed in the Kibana web interface.

After saving the file, start Logstash again:

```
sudo systemctl restart logstash
```

To see this in action, you will need to wait for CloudFront to write the first log file, which it will do after receiving a certain number of HTTP requests. For testing, it can be helpful to use `curl` or `wget` to quickly make a large number of requests to your CloudFront distribution, which will cause the access log to be written to. Once this file reaches a certain size, it will be written to S3, at which point Logstash will notice the new file and process the logs contained therein.

Other Amazon services, such as Elastic Beanstalk and S3 itself, use the same mechanism for storing access logs, so this technique can also be easily reused for those services.

S3 Lifecycle Management

Managing ever-growing log files is an old problem for system administrators. Working in the AWS cloud introduces some additional challenges, but the same principles can be used to solve the problem. On an individual system, `logrotate` is used to ensure that log files are regularly rotated and deleted. Without `logrotate`, log files might grow to the point where they exhaust all available space on the system, causing problems for running applications.

Storing logs on S3 creates a different problem: instead of worrying about shrinking available capacity, you need to worry about an increasing AWS bill. Constantly throwing log files into S3 buckets and ignoring them indefinitely will lead to an unnecessarily high bill at the end of the month.

S3 lifecycles can be used to manage this problem, by allowing you to create rules that control when your data is automatically archived to AWS Glacier or permanently deleted. Glacier is an offline storage service that optimizes storage costs for data that your users do not require regular or rapid access to. If you are logging to S3, you should ensure that your lifecycle rules are configured to automatically delete objects when they are no longer needed. We show how to accomplish this in Chapter 12.

Lifecycle rules can also be used to potentially increase the security of your log files after they have been moved to storage. In most use cases, log files should be considered read-only after they have been written. In the strictest cases, this is enforced by using WORM (write once, read many) devices, which provide hardware-level protection to prevent modification of files after they have been written. This type of requirement is usually driven by an industry or government regulator.

While lifecycle rules cannot provide this level of protection, they can be used to separate the credentials used for reading operations from those used for writing operations. As an example, envision writing your log files to an S3 bucket for storage in */backups/logs/*. Your logging application uses a set of IAM credentials that give it permission to write to this location in the bucket.

To ensure that once log files have been written it would be difficult for a malicious user or application to overwrite them, we put in place a regularly executing process to relocate the log files. A really simple way to accomplish this is configuring lifecycle rules that archive the objects after a certain time has elapsed. After this interval, the log files would be moved to the Glacier S3 storage class, where they would become inaccessible to the IAM credentials that were used to create the files originally. You will learn how to manipulate S3 buckets via lifecycle rules in Chapter 12.

## CHAPTER 10

DNS with Route 53

The venerable Domain Name System remains a critical component in the knowledge toolbox of a system administrator. Amazon's Route 53 service can provide a tighter integration between DNS and other AWS systems such as Elastic Load Balancers and the Elastic Compute Cloud. Although DNS is incredibly simple at its core, a broken or misconfigured DNS server can result in some very interesting problems. Kris Buytaert, one of the original proponents of the DevOps movement, highlights this with the title of his blog: Everything Is a Freaking DNS Problem (*http://www.krisbuytaert.be/blog/*).

This book assumes that our readers are already familiar with the general concepts surrounding DNS. This chapter therefore focuses on the AWS-specific implementation provided by Route 53, and demonstrates a few techniques that can be used to configure a cloud-aware DNS service.

Creating DNS records to identify the server entry points of an application enables a smoother user experience for your internal users or developers, even when it is not downright required by external public access. It also enables you as the operator to easily replace published entry points with more powerful resources, without having to explicitly inform users of a change taking place. By redirecting a service-specific domain name record to a more powerful instance (or even a load-balancer), an administrator can perform but with a sleight of hand the magic trick of having all users march in a different direction from the one they used a few seconds ago. That is the operational value delivered by identifying key points in your application such as images.example.com or db.example.com with their own distinct name records.

Why Use Route 53?

Many AWS services are similar to their noncloud counterparts, and Route 53 is no exception. It is possible to use Route 53 as a replacement for a traditional web-based DNS service, and indeed many people are using Route 53 in exactly this way. However, some features specific to Route 53 make it the ideal method of managing DNS when operating or managing an AWS infrastructure.

The main reason for this is its tight integration with services like the Elastic Load Balancer (ELB). Using an external DNS service in combination with AWS can require a significant custom development effort to glue these two otherwise independent services together, including writing and maintaining scripts to query the status and hostname of an Elastic Load Balancer and continuously updating your DNS records to reflect changes to the ELB.

Route 53 provides this feature through the *ALIAS* resource record type. This is an Amazon-specific record type and should not be confused with the CNAME record type, which can also be used to alias one hostname to another. In Amazon AWS terms, an ALIAS resource record type allows a hostname to be linked to a specific AWS service endpoint, such as the hostname of an ELB or a website hosted in an S3 bucket (see Chapter 12).

Other Amazon-specific features include Latency-Based Routing, whereby the result of a DNS query can change depending on the location of the end user and other factors such as network link speed. The idea is to route a user's request to the service that can provide the best experience. For example, one might be serving a web application from two AWS regions, such as Sydney and London. Using Latency-Based Routing, you can ensure that requests from London-based users are routed to the web application servers in Ireland, which will deliver much faster service than Sydney-based servers in this particular case. However good Amazon's service is, the speed of light remains a hard limit to the rate at which one can serve up web applications to a geographically diverse user base.

From an operational perspective, Route 53 is *just another AWS service*, meaning it can be managed from the Management Console, command-line tools, or even Cloud-Formation. One common complaint about DNS services that provide only a web interface is that they allow no way to back up and restore your resource records. Many sysadmins prefer a command-line option for managing their DNS records, or at least an API. Route 53 can provide all of these options, making it a good choice for DNS management even if you are not yet using many other AWS systems.

Failure Is an Option: Service Failover with Route 53

The first scenario we will look at is using DNS to manage service failure. As much as we might wish otherwise, services will break from time to time, and we need to ensure that the interruption is as brief as possible from the user's perspective.

Consider a PostgreSQL database cluster that consists of a master (which can handle both read and write traffic) and a slave (which can handle only read traffic). In this common scenario, either a high level of uptime is required or the single master is not capable of handling all of the application load on its own. Using tools such as repmgr (*http://www.repmgr.org*), you can easily configure a PostgreSQL cluster consisting of a single master and multiple slaves. Furthermore, repmgr can be used to periodically check the health of the master server and automatically promote one of the slaves in the event of a failure.

Many applications can be configured to send read traffic to one address, while read/write traffic is sent to another address. This makes scaling up the application traffic much easier, because you can offload read-only traffic from the master to the slave. For example, all read-only traffic would be sent to *slave.example.com*, while read/write traffic is sent to *master.example.com*.

The *slave.example.com* DNS record can be configured to return multiple addresses in response to client queries, in an arrangement known as *round-robin DNS*. In this configuration, your application can send all traffic to a single hostname without being actually aware of how many PostgreSQL slaves are currently in service.

Consider how the dynamic nature of Route 53 can be used in combination with PostgreSQL, or indeed the failover of many other services.

In the initial state where everything is working correctly, the *master.example.com* record points to the working master. Repmgr exposes hooks allowing users to run custom scripts when a failover or promotion event occurs. Using these hooks, it is possible to automatically update the *master.example.com* DNS record to point to the newly promoted master server, which was previously in operation as a slave. It is also necessary to remove the corresponding entry from the *slave.example.com* record pool.

It is important to consider DNS caching and how it will affect failover time when using this method. The DNS record's time-to-live (TTL) setting indicates how long the result should be cached by clients, but not all DNS clients honor this setting. Some (arguably broken) applications may cache the results of a DNS query permanently, and will recognize updated DNS records only after being restarted.

Depending on your infrastructure and the services you are running, this method can be implemented in various ways. To make this example more concrete, we will implement the features just described using a PostgreSQL cluster with streaming replication and failover.

Configuring a PostgreSQL cluster is beyond the scope of this book, and is superbly documented in the official PostgreSQL documentation. Using this in combination with repmgr failover documentation (*http://bit.ly/2nfZKPq*), begin by configuring a PostgreSQL cluster with a master and at least one slave. The master and slave(s) should of course be running on separate EC2 instances.

For the sake of this demonstration, it is suitable to launch individual instances for each role. In production, the instances likely would be running in an Auto Scaling group so that instances are automatically replaced by additional slaves if they fail.

Prepare the runtime environment with the following steps:

```
sudo apt install python python-pip
pip install boto
```

Head to the Route 53 section of the AWS console (*https://console.aws.amazon.com/route53/home?region=us-east-1*) and create a new zone, as shown in Figure 10-1. AWS Route53 will create for you the initial NS (namespace) and SOA (Statement of Authority) records in what those readers conversant with DNS will recognize to be a zone file. You will need to use a valid domain name instead of the customary exam ple.com placeholder.

Figure 10-1. Initialize the DNS zone to be used in our round-robin failover design

If the root nameservers are not pointing to AWS Route 53 for the domain you select, even entering a domain under your control will not result in the internet at large (which includes your browser) becoming aware of these changes. This should not stop you from experimenting, but if you are new to the subject of DNS, you may want to ask a colleague to give you a quick primer to help you ramp up faster.

As each PostgreSQL instance is launched, it must register itself with Route 53 by creating a CNAME record pointing to its hostname. This is done by running a script at launch time that creates the relevant DNS record. An example of such a script is shown in Example 10-1.

Example 10-1. PostgreSQL launch script

```python
#!/usr/bin/python

import argparse
import boto.route53
from boto.utils import get_instance_metadata

def do_startup():
    """ This function is executed when the instance launches. The instance's
            IP address will be added to the master or slave DNS record. If the
            record does not exist it will be created.
    """
    # Check if the master resource record exists
    if zone.get_cname(master_hostname) is None:
        print 'Creating master record: %s' % master_hostname
        status = zone.add_cname(master_hostname, instance_ip, ttl)
        return
    print "Master record exists. Assuming slave role"
# Check if the slave resource record exists - if more than one result is
# found by get_cname, an exception is raised. This means that more than
# one record exists so we can ignore it.
    try:
        slave_rr_exists = (zone.get_cname(slave_hostname) != None)
    except boto.exception.TooManyRecordsException:
        slave_rr_exists = True

    if slave_rr_exists:
        print 'Slave record exists. Adding instance to pool: %s' \
            % slave_hostname
    else:
        print 'Creating slave record: %s' % slave_hostname
    # Create or update the slave Weighted Resource Record Set
    status = zone.add_cname(slave_hostname, instance_ip, ttl, slave_identifier)
```

```
def do_promote():
        master_rr = zone.get_cname(master_hostname)
        print 'Updating master record: %s %s' % (master_hostname, instance_ip)
        zone.update_cname(master_hostname, instance_ip)
        # Remove this instance from the slave CNAME pool by deleting its WRRS
        print 'Removing slave CNAME: %s %s' % (slave_hostname, slave_identifier)
        zone.delete_cname(slave_hostname, slave_identifier)



parser = argparse.ArgumentParser(description='Update Route 53 master/slave DNS
records')
parser.add_argument('action', choices=['startup', 'promote'])
#parser.add_argument('--hosted-zone-id', required=True)
parser.add_argument('--domain', required=True)
parser.add_argument('--cluster-name', required=True)
parser.add_argument('--test')


args = parser.parse_args()

metadata = get_instance_metadata()

instance_ip = metadata['local-ipv4']
instance_id = metadata['instance-id']

ttl = 60 # seconds

master_hostname = 'master-%s.%s' % (args.cluster_name, args.domain)
slave_hostname = 'slave-%s.%s' % (args.cluster_name, args.domain)
# Identifier used for slave Weighted Resource Record Set
slave_identifier = ('slave-%s' % instance_id, 10)



conn = boto.route53.connect_to_region('us-east-1')
zone = conn.get_zone(args.domain)

if args.action == 'startup':
        do_startup()
elif args.action == 'promote':
        do_promote()
```

Execute this script manually on each of the instances, making sure to run it on the master first. You will also need to provide the hosted zone ID of your Route 53 zone and set AWS credentials in either the environment, the *~/.aws/credentials* file, or better yet by using an IAM role for the instance:

```
python update_route53.py --domain example.com --cluster-name db startup
```

After executing the script on both instances, you should see two new records in the Route 53 web console. Figure 10-2 shows the updated record set for the `example.com` zone after the master's mapping has been created.

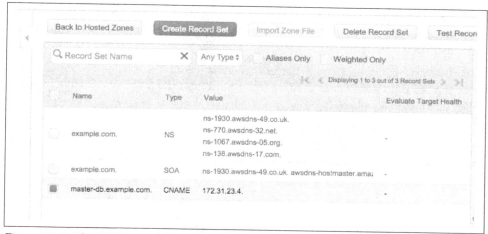

Name	Type	Value	Evaluate Target Health
example.com.	NS	ns-1930.awsdns-49.co.uk. ns-770.awsdns-32.net. ns-1067.awsdns-05.org. ns-138.awsdns-17.com.	-
example.com.	SOA	ns-1930.awsdns-49.co.uk. awsdns-hostmaster.ama;	-
master-db.example.com.	CNAME	172.31.23.4.	-

Figure 10-2. The DNS record for the DB master instance has successfully been created

This script is very simple and will require a few tweaks to make it robust enough for production. For example, what happens if the master DNS record already exists, but the PostgreSQL service has failed? Should the script forcefully "take" the hostname and point it to the instance on which it is running? Automatic database failover requires plenty of careful thought before implementation.

Each node in the cluster will have its own *repmgr.conf* file, usually located at */etc/repmgr/repmgr.conf*. This contains a PROMOTE_COMMAND parameter that specifies the path to a script that will be executed when a failover event occurs. This is the hook we will use to update the DNS records when a slave is promoted to the master role.

The script in Example 10-2 will be executed on the slave that is being promoted. Note that this script is also responsible for initiating the repmgr failover process.

Example 10-2. repmgr promote script

```
#/bin/bash

# Use repmgr to initiate the failover process
repmgr promote

# Run the script to update the DNS records
python update_route53.py --domain example.com --cluster-name db promote
```

Save the script on both the master and slave instances, perhaps in */etc/repmgr/promote_script.py*, and make it executable. Update the *repmgr.conf* file so that the PROMOTE_COMMAND parameter points to the path of the script.

With the DNS records created and the promote script in place, you can test the failover process. You might want to refer to the repmgr documentation again at this point for additional detail.

Stop the PostgreSQL service on the master instance and watch the repmgr log file. Once the repmgr daemon notices that the master has failed, the slave will be promoted by calling the script.

Once the process has completed, check the Route 53 Management Console. You will see that the *master.example.com* record now points to the instance that was previously a slave, and the corresponding *slave.example.com* record has been deleted.

When the PostgreSQL service was stopped on the master, any client attempting to connect to it would have begun generating error messages. As the DNS change propagates to the clients, they will begin connecting to the new master and begin functioning correctly.

Ramping Up Traffic

In the process described in the preceding section, traffic was abruptly shunted from one instance to another by changing the hostname. The new instance is thrown in at the deep end and must immediately handle all traffic destined for its hostname, which could overload some instances, as they have not had time to warm up their caches. Sometimes, it is desirable to send traffic to an instance in a more controlled and gradual fashion. This is often true in the case of database services.

Let's continue with our PostgreSQL example. A highly efficient PostgreSQL server relies on data being stored in memory and not read from spinning disks. Immediately sending a large number of queries to a recently started PostgreSQL instance will result in much of the data being read from disks, resulting in poor performance until PostgreSQL has had a chance to warm up the cache by storing recently used data and indices in memory.

To work around this, we can begin by sending a small amount of traffic to a new PostgreSQL instance and gradually increasing this amount over time. For example, we could start by sending 10% of traffic to the instance and increasing this by 5% every five minutes. This can be done using weighted resource record sets (WRRS) (*https://amzn.to/2LXFfWG*), which are used to return multiple records in response to a query for a single DNS hostname.

 Remember that DNS caching affects how quickly your application responds to changes in the resource record set. You can control this with an individual record's and zone-wide TTL default values.

When creating an entry (a member of the pool) in a WRRS, a weight value must be provided. This is used to calculate how frequently this record will be returned in response to client queries. For example, the *slave.example.com* hostname used for our slave database in the previous example could be configured to return multiple records, allowing traffic to be distributed across multiple slaves. If the records all have the same weight, traffic will be distributed in a round-robin fashion.

This method can also be used to perform a phased rollout of software updates. For example, a small percentage of web application traffic can be sent to instances running a new version of the software, while the majority of traffic is sent to instances running the existing stable version.

Once the new version is confirmed to be working as expected, the rest of the traffic can be shifted over to the new instances in the proper cloud-native approach, or alternatively the already existing instances could be updated in place using a traditional datacenter strategy.

Surviving ELB and Application Outages with Route 53

Elastic Load Balancers are reliable, but just as is the case for any other component, accounting for the possibility of their failure must be part of your design. A robust infrastructure will take this into consideration and include a way to work around temporarily unavailable ELBs. The default failure condition of a nonresponsive ELB does not make for a good user experience: users will see a blank, unstyled error page.

Outside AWS, one common method of working around failures is to have a separate web server that is responsible for serving your error page, or a message informing the user that the site is currently down for maintenance (scheduled or otherwise).

Within AWS, this process can be automated so that Route 53 will begin returning the IP address of your maintenance server instead of the IP address of your ELB. Furthermore, AWS can be used to serve your error pages from S3 buckets, removing the requirement of running an additional server solely for the purpose of serving error pages.

This is achieved using failover record sets. These work in the same way as weighted resource record sets with one important change: Route 53 will periodically perform health checks against your ELB (or other specified health check endpoint). Route 53 will respond to queries based on the results of this health check. For example, when your ELB is working normally, Route 53 will provide the ELB's IP addresses in response to DNS queries. If the ELB (or the application behind it) fails these health checks, Route 53 will provide a different result to DNS queries.

In this example, we will use this feature to set up an S3 bucket capable of serving error pages, which will be used as a failover in case the ELB or application fails.

Without any action on our part, Route 53 will automatically route users to this error page in the event of an ELB or application failure.

The first step is to create a bucket that will serve our error page. Using the S3 panel of the AWS Management Console, create a new bucket and assign it a name like my-error-page. Follow the instructions in Amazon's Configure a Bucket for Website Hosting documentation (*https://amzn.to/2LXFDEC*) to configure this bucket to serve web pages. When configuring the bucket to serve web pages, you will need to provide the name of the index document and error document. Set both of these to *index.html* to ensure that any requests that reach this bucket will result in your error page being served.

Next, create a file named *index.html* containing the error message you wish to display to your users when the main application is down for maintenance or otherwise not available. This page should reference only media that is guaranteed to be available, no matter the state of your application. For example, if you reference a CSS file that is served by your application, your error page will not work correctly, and your users will see an unstyled error page.

 Amazon AWS itself made the mistake of relying on a service to provide its own outage page in 2017, when a large-scale AWS S3 outage (*https://aws.amazon.com/message/41926/*) concurrently made the AWS operations team unable to update the AWS Service Health Dashboard to update users.

With those steps complete, we can move on to the ELB-related steps. The various methods of setting up an ELB are described in earlier chapters and will not be duplicated here. Refer to Chapter 6 for more information on setting up an Elastic Load Balancer.

For the sake of this example, we will assume you have created an ELB named my-elb, which has a single EC2 instance behind it running your custom application.

The next step is creating a failover resource record set that includes a health check. This will periodically check the status of your ELB and application.

First, we must create the primary record set that will be used when the ELB is working as expected. Open the Route 53 Management Console, navigate to your Hosted Zones, click Go To Record Sets, and then click Create Record Set. The corresponding setup is shown in Figure 10-3.

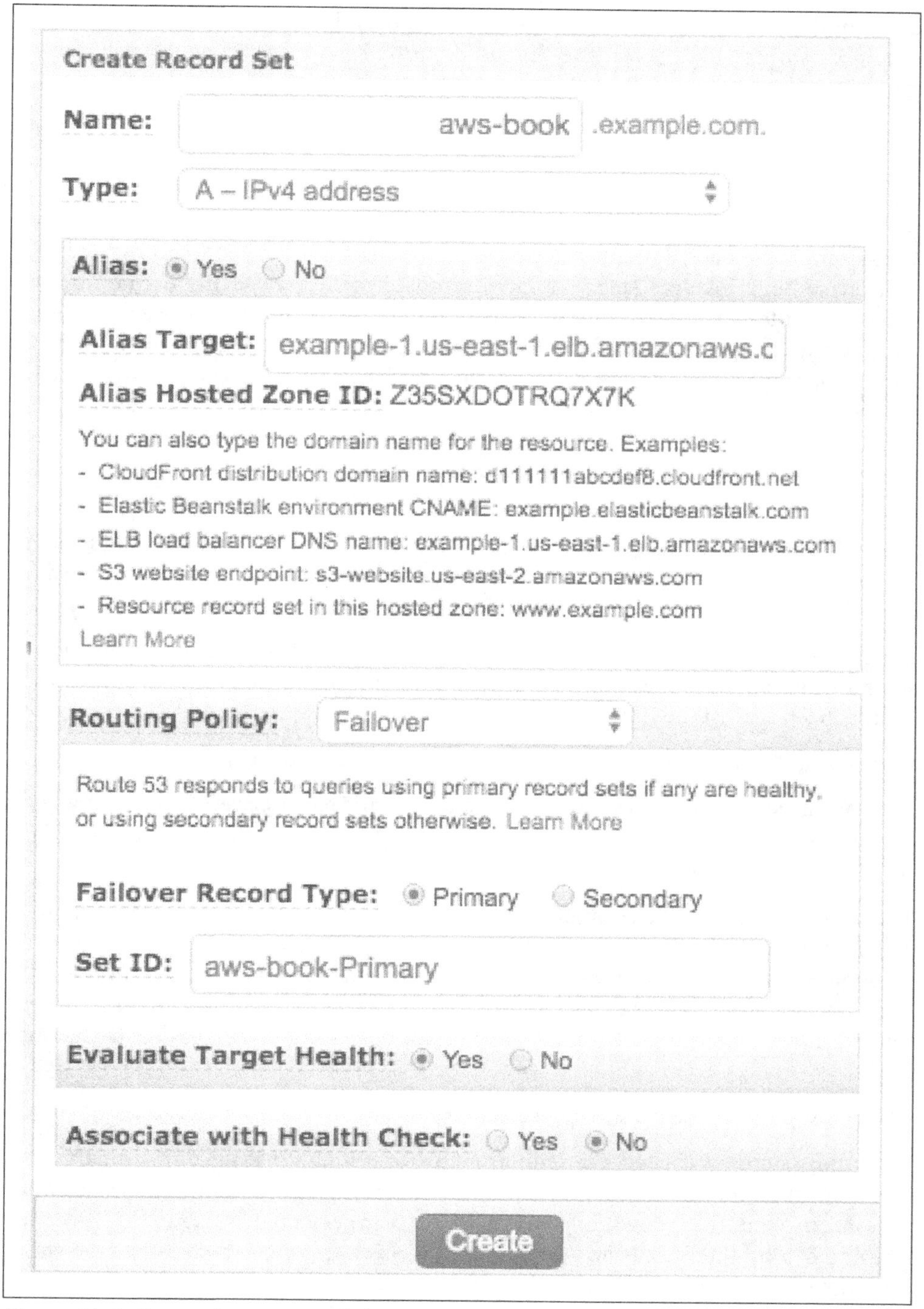

Create Record Set

Name: [aws-book] .example.com.

Type: [A – IPv4 address   ⬍]

Alias: ⦿ Yes ○ No

> **Alias Target:** [example-1.us-east-1.elb.amazonaws.c]
> **Alias Hosted Zone ID:** Z35SXDOTRQ7X7K
>
> You can also type the domain name for the resource. Examples:
> - CloudFront distribution domain name: d111111abcdef8.cloudfront.net
> - Elastic Beanstalk environment CNAME: example.elasticbeanstalk.com
> - ELB load balancer DNS name: example-1.us-east-1.elb.amazonaws.com
> - S3 website endpoint: s3-website.us-east-2.amazonaws.com
> - Resource record set in this hosted zone: www.example.com
> Learn More

Routing Policy: [Failover   ⬍]

Route 53 responds to queries using primary record sets if any are healthy, or using secondary record sets otherwise. Learn More

Failover Record Type: ⦿ Primary ○ Secondary

Set ID: [aws-book-Primary   ]

Evaluate Target Health: ⦿ Yes ○ No

Associate with Health Check: ○ Yes ⦿ No

[Create]

Figure 10-3. Create the primary failover record set

Some of the values you enter in this screen—such as the Name—will differ from the example configuration. Select the Yes radio button next to Alias, which will cause a new input box to appear. Type the name of your ELB in this new Alias Target input box.

In this particular case, records of the special class *ALIAS* were created in the hosted DNS zone. Route 53 uses these records to define what it serves as resource mappings to client DNS resolvers, and under what conditions. Details are hidden from us, and the system is pleasantly simple to operate despite its sophisticated logic. Whenever a failover strategy involves standard DNS resource records explicitly defined by our zone, the underlying TTL values will affect the client's ability to fail over independently of any changes made to the server's configuration. This is the case with the hostname mapping and aliasing provided by the standard *A* and *CNAME* records. If your failover strategy involves traditional DNS records, it is important to choose a low TTL so that failover can occur quickly. If this value is set too high, clients will cache the old value for a longer period of time, resulting in more requests hitting your failed ELB or application.

In the Routing Policy drop-down, select Failover and select Primary as the Failover Record Type. Enter a Set ID, such as `Primary`, to help you remember which record set is which.

Finally, select the Yes radio button next to Evaluate Target Health. Because this record set is an alias to an ELB, Route 53 already has the information it needs to perform the health check against the ELB.

Click Create Record Set to save this information and close the window.

Next, we need to repeat these steps for the secondary resource record set that will be used when the ELB fails its health check. Repeat the previous steps for the secondary resource record set, as shown in Figure 10-4.

This record set should be configured like the primary record set, with a few changes. The name should be the same as in the primary. This record set should also be an alias, but instead of pointing to an ELB, type the name of your S3 bucket in the Alias Target input. Select Failover as the Routing Policy and Secondary as the Failover Record Type. The Set ID should be Secondary, or some other easy-to-remember name.

Click Create Record Set to save the secondary record set.

With those steps completed, the setup is ready for testing. Visit the domain name you chose for the record sets, replacing our unadventurous placeholder *www.example.com*, in your web browser. You should see a page served by your EC2 instance running behind the ELB. If not, go back and recheck the steps to confirm everything is set up as described in the instructions.

If you see your application's web page, you are ready to test the failover scenario. Terminate the EC2 instance or stop the application process running on it so that the ELB's health check fails. It can take a few minutes for the failure to be recognized, depending on how you configured the ELB. Remember that you can also examine the current status of the health check in CloudWatch.

Once the health check eventually fails, visit the web page again. You should now see the error page you uploaded to your S3 bucket. Retrace your steps to ensure that everything is configured as described in this section if this does not occur.

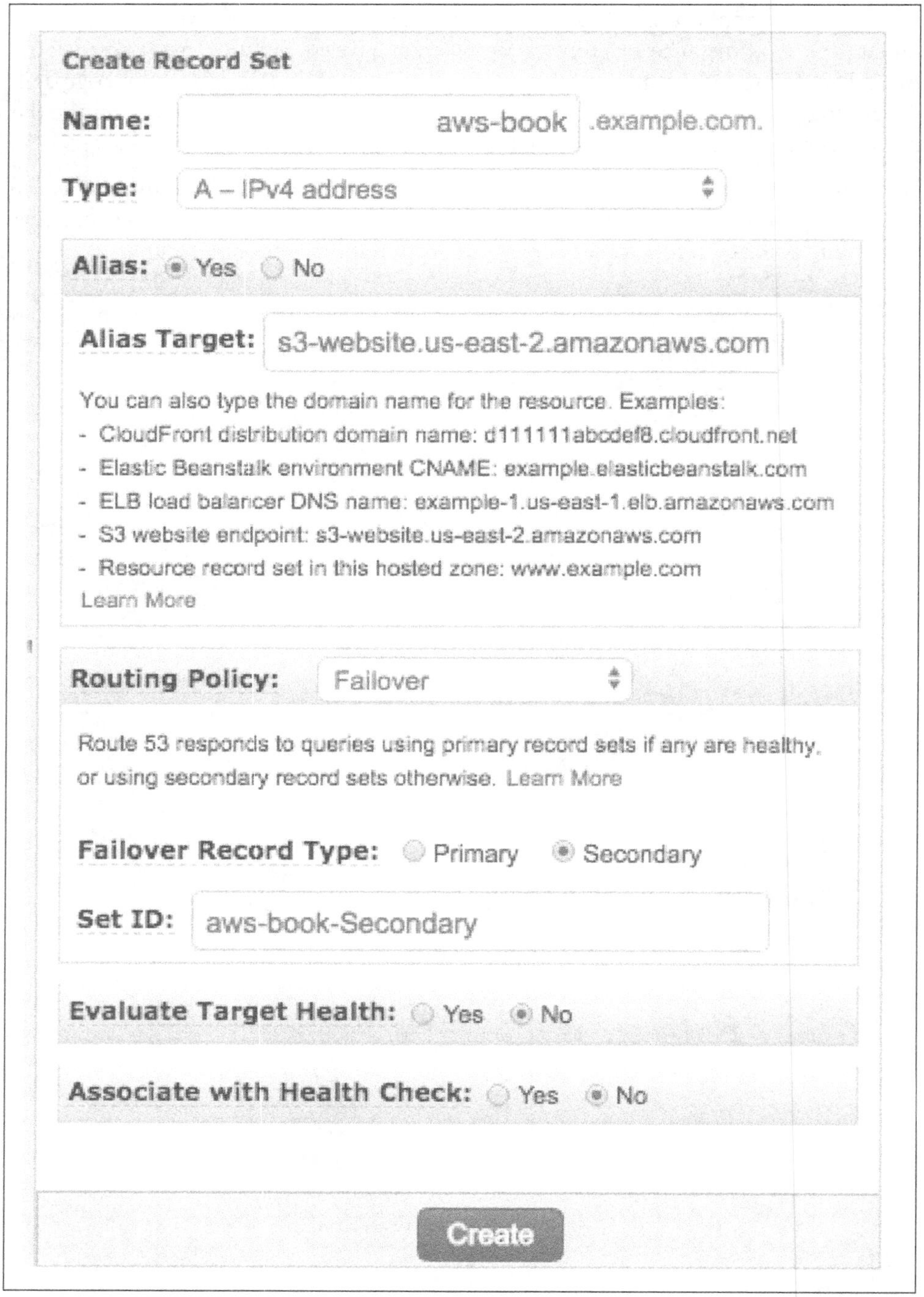

Create Record Set

Name: aws-book .example.com.

Type: A – IPv4 address ⬍

Alias: ● Yes ○ No

Alias Target: s3-website.us-east-2.amazonaws.com

You can also type the domain name for the resource. Examples:
- CloudFront distribution domain name: d111111abcdef8.cloudfront.net
- Elastic Beanstalk environment CNAME: example.elasticbeanstalk.com
- ELB load balancer DNS name: example-1.us-east-1.elb.amazonaws.com
- S3 website endpoint: s3-website.us-east-2.amazonaws.com
- Resource record set in this hosted zone: www.example.com

Learn More

Routing Policy: Failover ⬍

Route 53 responds to queries using primary record sets if any are healthy, or using secondary record sets otherwise. Learn More

Failover Record Type: ○ Primary ● Secondary

Set ID: aws-book-Secondary

Evaluate Target Health: ○ Yes ● No

Associate with Health Check: ○ Yes ● No

Create

Figure 10-4. Create secondary resource record set

Finally, we need to make sure that failover takes place correctly in reverse when your application returns to a healthy state. If you terminated the instance behind the ELB, launch a new one and place this new instance behind the ELB. If you stopped the application process instead, restart it.

After a few minutes, the health check should recognize that the application has returned to a healthy status. When you refresh the web page, you should once again see a page served by your application.

One potential downside of this approach is that DNS records might be cached by your user's DNS client or by a caching DNS server that exists on the path between your users and Route 53. Some DNS caching servers do not honor the TTL either you or Route 53 chose when serving your record set. Unfortunately, there is no way to work around these misconfigured DNS servers. This can result in the failover appearing to take longer to succeed than it really does, which means that some users might see your error page for longer than they should.

Regardless of this, DNS failover provides a useful way of automatically displaying an error or maintenance page when circumstances beyond your immediate control take down your web application. Furthermore, the complete automation of the process means you do not need to worry about putting your error page in place when your application is experiencing problems—instead, you can get on with the more useful task of diagnosing and fixing the problem.

In the likely event that your DNS records are not all hosted by Route 53, a tool capable of managing domain configuration across multiple providers like GitHub's octoDNS (*https://github.com/github/octodns*) is a handy way to coordinate automatic zone updates across multiple providers. octoDNS currently supports Cloudflare, Dyn, and AWS Route 53 among several others.

Takeaways

Summing up what we learned in this chapter:

- Route 53 is not just a web interface for a BIND-like service. It is a configurable and programmable service, just like the other components of AWS.
- Use Route 53 DNS names as the public face of your application and to route traffic to your internal services.
- Be careful when updating DNS records for high-traffic services. A sudden massive increase in traffic could overload your servers. Instead, gradually ramp up traffic by using weighted resource record sets.

- Remember to keep your TTLs low when using Route 53 for high availability between servers. Higher TTL values will result in clients using old cached DNS records longer than necessary, and not failing over as quickly.

## CHAPTER 11

Monitoring

Monitoring dynamic instances can be a challenge. The classic monitoring tools expect your systems to be around for a long time, and can have difficulty recognizing the difference between an instance that has failed and an instance that has been terminated as part of an Auto Scaling event or other planned termination in response to changes in capacity requirements.

AWS provides its own CloudWatch monitoring service, designed from the ground up to work in such an environment. Additionally, with some planning and custom scripting, most traditional monitoring tools can be used to monitor dynamic instances without spamming operators with false alarms when instances are terminated. This chapter showcases some of these methods as well as how to best use Amazon's CloudWatch service, and how the two can be integrated.

A cottage industry of cloud-based monitoring tools has sprung up around AWS and other cloud providers. There are far too many tools to mention in this book, and each has its own strengths and weaknesses.

The tighter these tools integrate with AWS, the more useful they are. Most advanced tools automatically query the EC2 tags associated with instances and use them to aggregate metrics. This allows the same tool to generate a high-level overview of your application across all EC2 regions, or drill down to view the performances of instances in a particular availability zone.

Why Are You Monitoring?

There are many reasons for setting up a monitoring system for your application and infrastructure. The most obvious reason is that when things break, operators should be alerted by automated systems, rather than phone calls from upset customers or C-level executives.

Another good reason is to allow system administrators to identify trends in application usage so they can make informed decisions about capacity requirements. Knowing how your application performed last month is critical when it comes to planning your requirements for the next month.

Yet another reason is to allow administrators and developers to accurately measure the effects of infrastructure changes and new application features. It is difficult to improve what you do not measure. If your application is running slowly, a well-planned monitoring system will allow you to quickly identify and remove bottlenecks. You need metrics demonstrating that your changes are having a positive effect in order to make continual, incremental improvements, to keep the aforementioned C-level executives happy. The opposite is also true—it is easy to accidentally reduce the performance of your application when deploying new code on a frequent basis. In this case, it is imperative to recognize which changes are negatively affecting performance so that they can be reverted or fixed.

CloudWatch

Amazon's own CloudWatch service is the starting point for many administrators when it comes to monitoring AWS services. In fact, many AWS services, such as Auto Scaling, rely on CloudWatch to perform scaling operations, making it an essential part of the infrastructure. CloudWatch is responsible for monitoring metrics such as the CPU load of EC2 instances. When these metrics cross certain thresholds, the Auto Scaling system is alerted so that it can take the relevant action of spawning or terminating instances according to an Auto Scaling policy.

CloudWatch is also an integral part of Amazon's Health Check feature, used by Elastic Load Balancers to identify instances that have failed or are otherwise "unhealthy."

In addition to tracking built-in metrics, such as disk usage and CPU load, Cloud-Watch can monitor custom metrics (*https://amzn.to/2LV3aWC*) provided by external sources. If the built-in metrics do not provide the detail required to inform your Auto Scaling requirements, these custom metrics can provide more granular control when scaling Auto Scaling groups up or down. The sky's the limit when using custom metrics. Typically, administrators monitor values such as requests per second, although more outlandish metrics, ranging from solar flare activity to the phase of the moon, could be used if it makes sense in your application. CloudWatch retains data for a fifteen-month period, allowing you to track the latest values as well as comparing them against the historical baseline.

Although powerful, CloudWatch is not perfect and has some drawbacks. The largest is its web-based interface. When monitoring a large number of metrics, the interface can become slow and cumbersome, taking some time to display the results you are looking for. This is because the graphs are generated on demand each time they are viewed. If you have many metrics, or are viewing data across a large time range, generating these graphs can take time and become quite frustrating. Fortunately, Cloud-Watch supports the creation of as many dashboards as your monitoring needs require, which also makes it rather easy to avoid overloading the web interface with too much data—you could say that there is an actual time saving to neatly categorizing your data in this case.

Another consideration is the cost associated with submitting custom metrics to CloudWatch. The cost is based on the number of metrics submitted, and the number of API requests required to submit these requests. At the time of writing, in the us-east-1 region the cost is $0.30 per metric per month for the first 10,000 samples, plus $0.01 per 1,000 API requests. In most cases, each metric submission will require one API PUT request. Assuming you are submitting your custom metric every minute, this will result in a cost of around $0.83 per month. While not overly expensive, these costs can quickly add up given the high usefulness of custom metrics, and must be taken into consideration when designing your monitoring system. The cost factor is particularly evident when tracking metrics with a per-minute granularity. Of course, building any custom monitoring system will also have many other capital costs: the time taken to implement it, licensing costs for a third-party monitoring service, and so on.

CloudWatch Basics

Native monitoring in AWS is a multifaceted system revolving around CloudWatch (Figure 11-1) but extending beyond a single service's limits and integrating with a fast increasing set of other AWS services. Collectively, AWS monitoring facilities enable administrators to track data, generate notifications, visualize the status of services or resources, and even respond automatically to changes in the conditions of your environment.

Four key abstractions define the core mechanisms provided by CloudWatch. *Events* are the asynchronous notification system provided by CloudWatch (and other services supporting CloudWatch) to alert the administrator that something has occurred. Events have a very wide-ranging scope, including as diverse circumstances as the reboot of an instance due to cloud maintenance (one of a number of possible triggers for an AWS Health Event) to the account's root user logging into the AWS Management Console (causing a CloudTrail event to be published, as we have previously shown in "CloudTrail" on page 91).

Events are optionally filtered and fed by simple rules through Amazon's Simple Notification Service (SNS). In circumstances where the operator chooses to be alerted, SNS can be used to deliver updates to mobile devices in the form of text messages or even generate platform-specific push notifications to iOS and macOS (Apple Push Notification Service), Android (Google Cloud Messaging for Android), and even Windows and Baidu Cloud. An alternative approach is to filter the appropriate events into an SQS queue or a dedicated AWS Lambda function for automated processing, without requiring administrator intervention by generating an immediate notification event. A real-world deployment will make use of both strategies to address different circumstances as represented by event types or sample values.

Figure 11-1. CloudWatch basic monitoring dashboard, found in the Monitoring tab of an EC2's instance details in the AWS console

Metrics are the bread and butter of CloudWatch monitoring, measuring both the operational status and present utilization condition of your AWS resources. As previously discussed, metrics are at the core of the CloudWatch pricing model, with the sampling frequency of the metrics and the total number of samples constituting the key cost dimensions. In what every datacenter administrator should immediately recognize as a remarkable demonstration of the power of integrated public cloud architecture, AWS had been providing monitoring of EC2 instances out of the box to all its users at five-minute sampling frequency, as early as 2010. Up to 10 metrics are automatically defined at boot time as the "basic monitoring" *dashboard* CloudWatch populates at no additional cost for each EC2 instance. Such metrics can be viewed in the Monitoring tab preloaded on each EC2 instance in the AWS console (see Figure 11-1 for an example), and include inbound and outbound network traffic (measured in either packets or bytes), disk reads and writes (measured in both IOPS and bytes), as well as CPU load. Note that additional metrics are often presented here: for example,

EC2 will automatically include graphs of CPU credit use and balance for burstable instance types like t2. Finally, *alarms* can be defined on metrics to cause an automated system or a human administrator to respond to circumstances predefined as requiring a response.

Auto Scaling and Custom Metrics

One of the most useful features of CloudWatch is its integration with Auto Scaling. This is commonly used to increase or decrease capacity in an Auto Scaling group according to metrics such as CPU utilization. When your instances are becoming too busy to cope with demand, more instances are launched. As demand decreases, the surplus instances are gradually terminated.

Auto Scaling is not limited to metrics that are built into CloudWatch: it is also possible to scale up or down based on the values of custom metrics that you provide to CloudWatch. As an example, consider a task-processing application in which tasks are queued in a messaging system and processed by EC2 instances. When running such an application, you might want the number of EC2 instances to scale dynamically according to the number of tasks waiting in the queue. If your message processing system is based on Amazon's Simple Queue Service, you are able to use CloudWatch's built-in metrics (such as the ApproximateNumberOfMessagesVisible SQS metric, which shows the number of messages available for retrieval in the queue) to control the size of your Auto Scaling group.

If you are using something other than SQS to store your queued messages for your task-processing application, you will need to provide CloudWatch with the data yourself so that Auto Scaling can make decisions based on these metrics.

Custom metrics do not need to be predefined: simply send the metric to CloudWatch, and it will begin storing and graphing it for you. This can be done in a number of ways. The Amazon API can be used from language-specific libraries (such as Boto for Python or Fog for Ruby), or by sending requests using the AWS REST API. The most straightforward method is to use the AWS CLI.

In the following example, we create a WaitingTasks custom metric, which performs the same function as the ApproximateNumberOfMessagesVisible metric for SQS-based systems. Once CloudFormation has some data on your custom metric, it can be used in the same way as built-in metrics to control Auto Scaling processes.

Begin sending your new custom metric to CloudWatch with the following command:

```
aws cloudwatch put-metric-data --namespace "MyAppMetrics" --metric-name Waiting-
Tasks --value 20 --unit Count
```

This example creates a WaitingTasks metric and provides an initial value of 20. We introduce a dedicated namespace to prevent the accidental aggregation of similarly named metrics that belong to different applications. The CLI command itself runs silently and generates no output, but after a few moments the new metric will become visible in the CloudWatch Management Console, as shown in Figure 11-2.

Figure 11-2. The first WaitingTasks value appears in our CloudWatch dashboard

Instead of providing sample values on the command line, you can achieve the same result by sending a JSON file containing the metric data. For example, you could create a file named *metric_data.json* with the following contents to define the same metric—and load the same initial value:

```
[
  {
    "MetricName": "WaitingTasks",
    "Value": 20,
    "Unit": "Count"
  }
]
```

Upload the file with this command:

```
aws cloudwatch put-metric-data --namespace "MyAppMetrics" \
--metric-data file://metric_data.json
```

This command is equivalent to the first example in this section and is most useful when providing more complex or detailed metrics, or to perform bulk upload of multiple samples. It similarly runs silently with no default terminal output.

Chapter 6 explained how to create and manage Auto Scaling groups. In this section, we create a CloudFormation stack that describes an Auto Scaling group that dynamically shrinks and grows based on the value of our WaitingTasks metric. An example of such a stack is shown in Example 11-1.

Example 11-1. Auto Scaling group driven by a custom CloudWatch metric

```
{
    "AWSTemplateFormatVersion" : "2010-09-09",
    "Description" : "Auto Scaling on Custom Metrics",
    "Resources" : {
        "CustomMetricLaunchConfig" : {
            "Type" : "AWS::AutoScaling::LaunchConfiguration",
            "Properties" : {
              "ImageId" : "ami-43a15f3e",
              "InstanceType" : "m3.medium"
            }
        },
        "CustomMetricScalingGroup" : {
            "Type" : "AWS::AutoScaling::AutoScalingGroup",
            "Properties" : {
                "AvailabilityZones" : [ "us-east-1a" ],
                "Cooldown" : "300",
                "DesiredCapacity" : "1",
                "LaunchConfigurationName" : { "Ref" : "CustomMetricLaunchConfig" },
                "MaxSize" : "10",
                "MinSize" : "1"
            }
        },
        "ScaleUpPolicy" : {
            "Type" : "AWS::AutoScaling::ScalingPolicy",
            "Properties" : {
                "AdjustmentType" : "ChangeInCapacity",
                "AutoScalingGroupName" : { "Ref" : "CustomMetricScalingGroup" },
                "ScalingAdjustment" : "1"
            }
        },
        "ScaleDownPolicy" : {
            "Type" : "AWS::AutoScaling::ScalingPolicy",
            "Properties" : {
                "AdjustmentType" : "ChangeInCapacity",
                "AutoScalingGroupName" : { "Ref" : "CustomMetricScalingGroup" },
                "ScalingAdjustment" : "-1"
            }
        },
        "WaitingTasksAlarm" : {
            "Type" : "AWS::CloudWatch::Alarm",
            "Properties" : {
                "AlarmActions" : [ { "Ref" : "ScaleUpPolicy" } ],
                "ComparisonOperator" : "GreaterThanThreshold",
                "EvaluationPeriods" : "1",
                "MetricName" : "WaitingTasks",
                "Namespace" : "MyAppMetrics",
                "OKActions" : [ { "Ref" : "ScaleDownPolicy" } ],
                "Period": "60",
                "Statistic" : "Maximum",
                "Threshold" : "10",
```

```
            "Unit" : "Count"
        }
    }
  }
}
```

This stack consists of several components that are all required to make everything work correctly.

`CustomMetricLaunchConfig` and `CustomMetricScalingGroup` should be a familiar sight from Chapter 6. These are a required part of any Auto Scaling group.

Next, we define `ScaleUpPolicy` and `ScaleDownPolicy`. These scaling policy resources control *how* the capacity of an Auto Scaling group should be changed. The scale-up policy has a `ScalingAdjustment` parameter of 1, which means a single additional EC2 instance should be launched into the Auto Scaling group every time this policy is triggered. Similarly, the scale-down policy's `ScalingAdjustment` parameter is –1, meaning that a single instance will be removed from the group if this is triggered.

The `ScalingAdjustment` parameter controls what changes will be made to the size of the Auto Scaling group when this policy is triggered. The `AutoScalingGroupName` parameter associates the scaling policy with a particular Auto Scaling group.

The final component is `WaitingTasksAlarm`, which ties everything together and controls *when* the capacity should be changed. The important parts of this resource are the `AlarmActions` and `OKActions` parameters, which state what should happen when the stack enters and leaves the `Alarm` state. The stack enters the `Alarm` state when the specified metric—in this case, the `WaitingTasks` metric in the `MyAppMetrics` namespace—is over the threshold of 10 for a single evaluation period. That is, as soon as CloudWatch notices this value is above 10, it will enter into the `Alarm` state, triggering the `ScaleUpPolicy`.

This will cause an additional instance to be launched into the Auto Scaling group. Once this instance begins processing tasks, the `WaitingTasks` value will drop below 10, which puts the `WaitingTasksAlarm` in the `OK` state. This causes `ScaleDownPolicy` to be triggered, resulting in a single instance in the scaling group being terminated.

The `CustomMetricScalingGroup` has its `Cooldown` parameter set to `300`. This value, measured in seconds, controls how frequently Auto Scaling events occur for this group. By setting it to five minutes (300 seconds), we ensure that there is a gap between instances being created and deleted. Setting `Period` to 60 seconds similarly defines what time interval CloudFormation should use to evaluate samples of our custom metric. This value is required to match multiples of a minute.

To see all this in action, create the CloudFormation stack using the template just shown:

```
$ aws cloudformation create-stack --template-body file://scaling_metric.json \
  --stack-name autoscaled-metric
{
    "StackId": "arn:aws:cloudformation:us-east-1:740376006796:stack/autoscaled-
metric/ba4f1030-ff36-11e7-8395-5044334e0ab3"
}
```

You can follow along in the AWS console as the resources defined in the template are being created (see Figure 11-3 for an example).

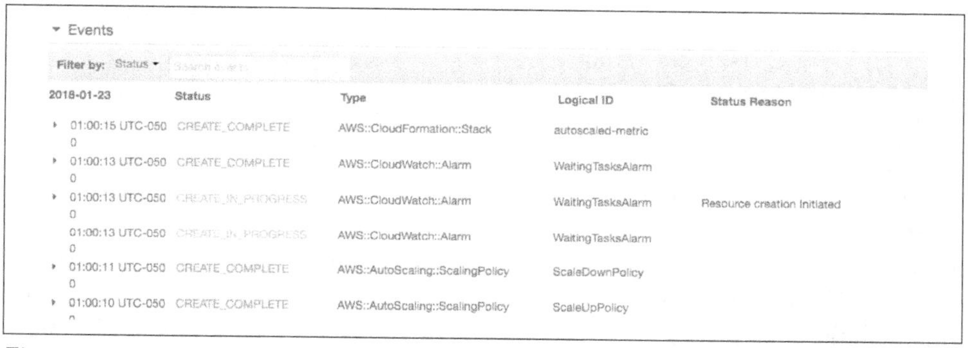

Figure 11-3. Progress creating the resources of our stack as shown in the AWS console (https://console.aws.amazon.com/cloudformation/home?region=us-east-1#/stacks?filter=active)

After a minute, verify that the stack was successfully created with the following command:

```
$ aws cloudformation list-stacks --stack-status-filter CREATE_COMPLETE
{
    "StackSummaries": [
        {
            "StackId": "arn:aws:cloudformation:us-east-1:740376006796:stack/
autoscaled-metric/ba4f1030-ff36-11e7-8395-5044334e0ab3",
            "StackName": "autoscaled-metric",
            "CreationTime": "2018-01-22T05:40:17.723Z",
            "StackStatus": "CREATE_COMPLETE",
            "TemplateDescription": "Auto Scaling on Custom Metrics"
        }
    ]
}
```

Listing a stack's resources is accomplished through the describe-stack-resources CLI command. With a little magic and the --query option we can generate a format that will fit on the printed page:

```
$ aws cloudformation describe-stack-resources --stack-name autoscaled-metric \
--query 'StackResources[*].[StackName,ResourceType,LogicalResourceId]'\
--output text
```

```
autoscaled-metric  AWS::AutoScaling::LaunchConfiguration  CustomMetricLaunchConfig
autoscaled-metric  AWS::AutoScaling::AutoScalingGroup     CustomMetricScalingGroup
autoscaled-metric  AWS::AutoScaling::ScalingPolicy        ScaleDownPolicy
autoscaled-metric  AWS::AutoScaling::ScalingPolicy        ScaleUpPolicy
autoscaled-metric  AWS::CloudWatch::Alarm                 WaitingTasksAlarm
```

The resources listed do not include the EC2 instances created by the stack's auto scaling actions. To find the relevant instances we exploit the fact that any instances associated with the stack are automatically tagged with several metadata attributes, including its name, which is found in the `aws:cloudformation:stack-name` tag:

```
$ aws ec2 describe-tags  --output text \
--filters Name=tag-key,Values="aws:cloudformation:stack-name" \
Name=tag-value,Values="autoscaled-metric"
TAGS    aws:cloudformation:stack-name   i-01d1f65898f90977b    instance
autoscaled-metric
TAGS    aws:cloudformation:stack-name   i-03cc8125c8e3c7c02    instance
autoscaled-metric
```

Because we previously set the value of the `WaitingTasks` metric to 20, a new instance will be launched if the data point arrived in the interval specified by `Period`—the last minute in the case of our metric (re-issue the `put-metric-data` command if a longer time has elapsed). The `WaitingTasksAlarm` alarm in the scaled metric will switch to the alarm state within a minute, with results similar to those shown in Figure 11-4.

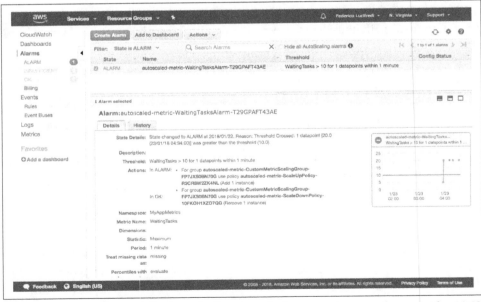

Figure 11-4. Triggering of the Auto Scaling group's alarm resource, as shown in the AWS console (https://console.aws.amazon.com/cloudwatch/home?region=us-east-1#alarm:alarmFilter=ANY)

Wait for the two instances to finish launching and then issue the following command:

```
aws cloudwatch put-metric-data --namespace "MyAppMetrics" --metric-name Waiting-
Tasks --value 5 --unit Count
```

This makes CloudWatch think there are only five messages remaining in the queue, putting the WaitingTasksAlarm in OK status, which in turn will trigger the ScaleDown Policy action. After a few moments, one of the instances in the scaling group will be terminated. The system will continue to adjust between the minimum and maximum sizes defined by the scaling group according to the custom metric's sampling in the specified period and cooldown intervals.

If no data is available for the requested metric, Auto Scaling will, by default, take no action. This defines a third possible state for CloudWatch alarms alongside alarm and ok, called insufficient. This behavior can be controlled by adding an Insufficient DataActions parameter to the WaitingTasksAlarm resource. For more information on how to control this behavior, see the documentation for the AWS::Cloud Watch::Alarm resource type (*https://amzn.to/2LYWMxK*).

In the real world, we would be periodically executing a command that checks the size of the waiting tasks queue and submits the value to CloudWatch, making this an entirely automated process. If you have experimented with the example we provided, you should now have a good understanding of what is involved in designing a custom metric and using it to control an Auto Scaling group. Attention is required to tune the availability of data, as well as what behavior is expected in those situations when the data source fails: the system needs to maintain its availability while avoiding failure modes that allocate a lot of costly resources when they are not actually required by the service.

Old Tools, New Tricks

Many common monitoring tools predate AWS significantly. Nagios, a popular open source monitoring tool, has been around since 1999, seven years before the introduction of EC2. One of the advantages of mature monitoring tools like Nagios is the ecosystem surrounding them, providing features such as graphing, reporting, and integration with third-party services. Using such tools, one can build a replacement for CloudWatch that leverages existing datacenter monitoring infrastructure, helping to consolidate the number of technology choices that are in use at any one time as your operations migrate to the public cloud.

The Nagios Exchange (*http://exchange.nagios.org*) contains plug-ins that can be used to integrate Nagios and AWS. In addition to plug-ins that directly monitor the status of your EC2 instances, there are plug-ins that query CloudWatch and other AWS components, allowing you to monitor your AWS infrastructure in a variety of ways. Remember that any tools that pull data from CloudWatch will do so by querying the CloudWatch API. Pulling these metrics too frequently will result in a higher AWS bill.

As Robert Heinlein pointed out in *The Moon Is a Harsh Mistress* (G.P. Putnam's Sons, 1966), there's no such thing as a free lunch. The time taken to implement a custom monitoring solution is time taken away from building your core application infrastructure, so this undertaking should be carefully considered against off-the-shelf tools, or indeed simply using CloudWatch and learning to love its limitations.

At a high level, there are two main ways of dynamically configuring tools like Nagios within an AWS infrastructure.

The first is to use a configuration management tool such as Puppet. Puppet provides a feature known as exported resources (*http://bit.ly/2LVCpRT*), which allows the configuration of one node to influence the configuration of another node. For example, when Puppet runs on one of your web application instances, it can use the data collected on this node to dynamically configure your monitoring instances. If Puppet recognizes that Nginx is running on the web application node, the Nagios instance can be automatically configured to run Nginx-specific checks against the web application node, such as making sure HTTP requests to port 80 respond with an HTTP 200 status code.

This feature relies on PuppetDB (*http://bit.ly/2ni2WdC*), which means it will work only when Puppet is running in the traditional master/client mode.

Implementing this system requires two entries in your Puppet manifest files. The first is the declaration stage, where you declare the virtual resource type. This stanza is placed in the Puppet manifest for the host to be monitored. For example, to monitor Nginx as just described, the following virtual resource declaration can be used:

```
@@nagios_service { "check_http${hostname}":
    use                 => 'http-service',
    host_name           => "$fqdn",
    check_command       => 'check_http',
    service_description => "check_http${hostname}",
    target              => '/etc/nagios/conf.d/dynamic_${fqdn}.cfg',
    notify              => Service[$nagios::params::nagios_service],
}
```

Notice that the resource type (in this case, `nagios_service`) is prefixed with `@@`. This lets Puppet know that this is a virtual resource that will be realized on another node.

Declaring this virtual resource will not cause any changes to be made on the monitored instance itself. Rather, it causes the relevant data to be stored in PuppetDB for later use by another node.

This declaration configures Nagios to perform a simple HTTP service check, using the check_http command. The target parameter writes this configuration to a file whose name contains the fully qualified domain name (FQDN) of the monitored instance. If your monitored instance has an FQDN of *web01.example.com*, this configuration segment would be written to a file named */etc/nagios/conf.d/ dynamic_web01.example.com.cfg* on the Nagios host. By default, Nagios will include all *.cfg* files contained within the */etc/nagios/conf.d* directory when the configuration is read. The notify parameter causes Nagios to be restarted whenever this file changes, so that the new monitoring configuration is picked up automatically.

The second component is the collection stage, which affects the Nagios instance. The following line should be added to the node definition for the Nagios instance in your Puppet manifest file:

```
Nagios_service <<|  |>>
```

When Puppet is run on the Nagios instance, any previously declared virtual resources describing Nagios resources will be realized on the Nagios instance. This is the point at which the */etc/nagios/conf.d/dynamic_web01.example.com.cfg* file is created, and the Nagios service restarted.

Although support for Nagios is explicitly built into Puppet's exported resources feature, there is nothing to stop Puppet from being used for other packages. In fact, it can be used to configure any service that relies on text-based configuration files, making it a flexible tool for dynamic configuration.

The alternative approach to achieving this goal is to use a custom script to query the AWS API and write Nagios configuration files based on the retrieved data. This is a good option if you do not have an existing Puppet master/client infrastructure in place. Implementing Puppet merely to take advantage of exported resources could be considered overkill, making the custom script route a more attractive option.

One potential downside of this system relates to instances that get terminated as part of expected Auto Scaling operations. Nagios must be informed that the instance no longer exists and shouldn't be monitored. We recommend addressing this by using a separate configuration file in the Nagios configuration directory for each instance, hence the use of *dynamic_${fqdn).cfg* in the example.

Auto Scaling can be configured to send a notification to Amazon's Simple Notification Service when instances are launched or terminated. Subscribing to these notifications makes it simple to delete all the Nagios configuration files for a particular host after it is terminated. After Nagios is restarted, the host will no longer be monitored, and will not cause any false alarms after Nagios notices that the instance is no longer accessible to its checks.

Cleverly scripted integration enables us to adapt a monitoring system designed for the immutability of the datacenter to the public cloud, but this exercise can stretch any traditional tool only so far. There is a minimum time granularity to Puppet runs, and Nagios restarts at any reasonable scale are not rapid events. There are inherent limitations to what a static monitoring tool like Nagios can accomplish when paired to a highly dynamic system like AWS. Looking at our example again, the practical limits of this system are defined by how often Puppet runs, combined with the time interval between Auto Scaling events. This kind of approach is most suitable as a temporary stopgap, extending existing infrastructure monitoring while a more permanent cloud native solution is investigated.

Other Custom Monitoring Options

The preceding section described how to use Nagios to monitor EC2 instances. Of course, Nagios is only one of the wide range of tools that can be used for system monitoring, and we chose it because it enjoys a surprisingly high level of popularity among system administrators. This is due to the number of plug-ins available for Nagios, allowing almost any service or application to be monitored.

Many other highly regarded monitoring tools can be used to monitor your services. One example is Icinga (*https://www.icinga.org*), which is a fork of the open source version of Nagios. Icinga aims to provide compatibility with all existing Nagios plug-ins while making enhancements to the web interface and core software.

Another package in this space is Sensu (*https://sensuapp.org*). Sensu has features that make it an excellent choice for monitoring cloud-based infrastructure. Chief among these is the architecture of Sensu itself. Rather than operating in a client/server mode (as do Nagios and Icinga), it uses RabbitMQ, an AMQP-based messaging system. This makes it inherently more scalable than software that relies on a single central master server.

When a service is checked, the Sensu client writes the check result to a RabbitMQ queue, where it is read by the Sensu server process. Decoupling the submission of a check from the reading process in this way enables a much higher throughput than an architecture in which clients submit their check results directly to the master. Because RabbitMQ can operate in a highly available cluster, it is also more resilient to failure. As long as both the master and client processes know the address of the RabbitMQ server, check results can be submitted. If the master server is briefly unavailable, messages will wait in the queue until the master is available again.

When combined with Auto Scaling groups, this configuration of Sensu makes the entire monitoring system more reliable. Should the EC2 instance running the master server be terminated due to failure, a new one can be brought into service, and it will begin processing all of the waiting check results automatically.

 The rise of Software-as-a-Service solutions did not turn a blind eye to the monitoring field. Vendors like Datadog (*https://www.data doghq.com*) and Loggly (*https://www.loggly.com*) provide system monitoring and log management as a service for a monthly fee. SaaS creates a middle ground between using Amazon AWS services and the "build your own" approach. Whenever the services provided by AWS do not meet your needs, we advise that you research third-party service-based options before going all out and rolling your own: at the very least, you will learn how others have approached the problem—or possibly why they chose not to.

## CHAPTER 12

Backups

If one relies solely on marketing materials provided by cloud hosts and resellers, one might be forgiven for thinking that the cloud is a magical place where nothing breaks and everything Just Works. Unfortunately, this is not the case. Cloud-based infrastructure requires just as much backup planning as a traditional self-hosted architecture—sometimes more, because of the dynamic nature of the cloud. Fortunately there is a silver lining: along with new challenges, the cloud provides new features to make backups simpler and reduce implementation time. For example, ticking a checkbox is figuratively all that it takes to set up scheduled backups for the RDS service, as shown in Figure 12-1.

Figure 12-1. Built-in cloud backup facility in the AWS Relational Database Service

Although business types can think of the *cloud* as a single logical entity, we must look beyond that high-level presentation to view our cloud as a series of datacenters spread across multiple regions, and plan our backups accordingly. To run a highly available service, you would not put all of your servers in a single datacenter. You should plan backups with the same consideration in mind.

Furthermore, it is also important to think about off-site backups. When working with AWS, this can mean one of two things: storing backups outside your primary region, or going a step further and storing them entirely outside AWS.

You are trying to protect yourself against two separate risks. If a single AWS region goes down, it would be relatively simple to deploy your operations to another region. For example, if you host your application in us-east-1 and store your backups in eu-west-1, you can redeploy your application to us-east-2, and restore servers from the backups in eu-west-1 to get your application up and running again.

However, if the AWS API is unavailable, it can become impossible to retrieve these backups, no matter which region they are hosted in, rendering them useless in protecting against this particular failure mode.

Backups are a means to an end, not an end in themselves. What we are trying to achieve is a way to restore operations in the event of failure, no matter the cause or severity of this failure. Unless your backups put you in a position where you can restore after failures, they are of no use whatsoever.

An untested backup procedure is useless. In fact, an untested backup procedure can be worse than no backups at all, as it provides a false sense of security. Perform regularly scheduled restore tests to make sure that your documented backup procedure works as planned.

This chapter presents some of the ways traditional tools and AWS-specific features can be used to implement reliable backup procedures.

RDS Database Snapshot

If you are using Amazon's RDS service to host your database, you can use the RDS Database Snapshot feature. This process can be automated so that Amazon automatically backs up your database according to your specified schedule, or you can manually create backup snapshots before performing potentially destructive operations.

When you use RDS, automated snapshots are automatically enabled and will be carried out during the maintenance window specified when creating the database instance. The process of enabling and disabling automated backups is described in Amazon's Working with Automated Backups documentation (*https://amzn.to/2uZquHs*). You can find a more general explanation of how automated backups work in DB Instance Backups (*https://amzn.to/2uZq7g2*). The Related Topics section of the latter page provides more detail on working with automated backups.

If you rely on RDS snapshots, it is important to keep track of the most recent snapshot ID when backing up the other files required for your application to ensure that the database schema referenced in your code matches the data contained in the snapshot. This can be done by regularly querying the ID of the most recent snapshot and storing it in a text file alongside the other application files and making sure it is included in the backup. When restoring from backups, this file will let you know which corresponding DB snapshot should be restored.

Finally, even if you are using RDS, you might wish to follow the other steps in this chapter to regularly take a full dump of the database. This will ensure that you can restore the backup to a non-RDS database. RDS snapshots can be used only to restore to RDS databases, and do not provide any facility to make off-site backups.

At the time of writing, RDS supports MySQL, MariaDB, Oracle, Microsoft's SQL Server, and PostgreSQL in addition to Amazon's own Aurora—all of which can be generate cloud-automated backups. Later in this chapter, we will look at ways to manually back up databases that are not part of RDS.

Backing Up Static Files from EC2 Instances to S3

One of the earliest and most popular uses for EC2 has been to host web applications, such as WordPress blogs. This section describes how an EC2-hosted WordPress blog can be backed up, with the backup archive being stored on S3 (Figure 12-2). Although the steps taken will differ if you are using a different application—or indeed, your own custom application—the general steps will be the same.

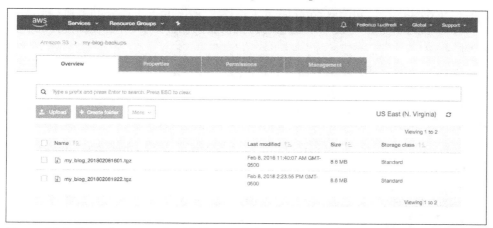

Figure 12-2. Over the years, the AWS console has developed into a full graphical user interface to manipulate S3 storage

Dynamic websites usually consist of two major components that need to be backed up: the database in which content and configuration options are stored, and static files such as images and HTML files. Furthermore, these websites might allow users to upload their own files, such as profile images for blog authors. All of these components need to be backed up to ensure that the entire site can be restored in the event of an EC2 instance failing.

If you are backing up a custom application, we will assume that the code that powers your application is stored in an external version control system such as GitHub. Therefore, backing up these files is outside the scope of this section. If, for whatever reason, you are not using version control for your application, you could back up the code files as part of the file-based backup archive—we also strongly encourage you to revisit your decision not to use version control: choosing to operate in an anti-pattern is OK, but you ought to justify to your satisfaction why you are doing so.

The first step in the backup process is to create a snapshot of your database contents.

For the sake of simplicity, we will assume the WordPress blog is configured to use a MySQL instance running on the same host as WordPress. If your database is hosted on a separate instance, you will need to modify some of the example commands to connect to the correct host in order to dump the contents of the database.

We will begin by creating a database dump file containing the SQL statements required to re-create your database. MySQL helps you do this with the conveniently named mysqldump command. For example, if your WordPress database is named my_blog, the following command can be used to dump its contents to a file located at */var/backups/my_blog/database.sql*:

```
mysqldump my_blog > /var/backups/my_blog/database.sql
```

After the database dump has completed, you can move on to backing up the application files. Let's assume they are stored in */srv/vhosts/my_blog*. First, copy all the files into the backups directory with the following command:

```
rsync -av /srv/vhosts/my_blog/ /var/backups/my_blog/
```

This command will copy all files. The -a option indicates that rsync should run in archive mode, which, among other things, ensures that file permissions and ownerships are copied.

To reduce the amount of data stored in S3, you can create a compressed tar archive before transferring it to S3. This is done with the following:

```
DATE=`date -u +"%Y%m%d%H%M"`
BACKUP_FILE="/var/backups/my_blog_${DATE}.tgz"
tar zcvf ${BACKUP_FILE} /var/backups/my_blog/
```

The first time, you will need to set up transfer tooling and an S3 bucket as the remote endpoint:

```
sudo apt install s3cmd python-magic
s3cmd --configure
s3cmd mb s3://my-blog-backups --acl-private
```

Finally, you can transfer the resulting file to S3 with the s3cmd command:

```
$ s3cmd put "${BACKUP_FILE}" s3://my-blog-backups/ --acl-private
/var/backups/my_blog_201802081922.tgz -> s3://my-blog-backups/
my_blog_201802081922.tgz  [1 of 1]
 8986351 of 8986351   100% in    0s    14.40 MB/s  done
```

To keep the WordPress instance clean, delete the temporary files used during the backup:

```
rm -rf /var/backups/my_blog/*
```

This last step is optional. Leaving these files in place would not negatively affect the speed of subsequent backups, because rsync would need to transfer only the files that have changed since the last backup. When choosing to leave backup files in place in a temporary location the key factor to consider is security, as backup archives often straddle permission schemes and may contain passwords or other sensitive information. Theft of backup files is a common vector for data confidentiality loss; take care to secure both any temporary locations as well as the final S3 endpoint.

Put these commands together to make a script that can be easily used to automatically back up the database and files required to recover your blog in the event of a disaster.

Restoring the resulting archive is simply a case of extracting the files to the correct location and importing the SQL statements file into the database. For example:

```
cd /srv/vhosts/myblog
tar xcvf my_blog_201206011200.tar.gz
mysql my_blog < myblog/database.sql
rm myblog/database.sql
```

Later in this section, we will look at ways to move this data out of S3 and into off-site storage for additional reliability.

Rolling Backups with S3 and Glacier

When keeping backups on S3, it is important to keep track of how much data you are storing. Each additional byte will gradually increase your monthly Amazon bill, so there is no point in storing data that you will never need to use. Your backup strategy should reflect this. In many ways, the traditional approaches used with tape backups are still applicable: one tape per day of the week, one tape for each of the last four weeks, and finally one tape for each month. A total of 23 tapes would allow you to restore from any day of the previous week, any week of the previous month, and any month of the previous year.

A similar approach can also be used in S3 to keep your data storage requirements to a minimum. In this section, we will look at how this can be implemented using S3's Object LifeCycle Management and Object Archival features. This method relies on S3 for the last month's worth of backups, and older daily backups are automatically transitioned to the Glacier archival service on the assumption that they will be required less frequently than daily or monthly backups.

Launched in 2012, Glacier (*https://aws.amazon.com/glacier/*) is AWS's storage service for data backup and archival. Targeted at unfrequently accessed data, Glacier is best thought of as the least available AWS storage class (*https://amzn.to/2LZEpbN*). In the S3 service, storage classes enable operators to balance cost with the resiliency and availability of data. Data stored in Glacier needs to be asynchronously retrieved from the archive before it is made available, and is stored at the lowest prices offered by AWS (a rock-bottom $0.004 per GB/month at the time of writing).

Let's assume that you are using one of the methods described in this chapter to store your backups in S3. We will configure S3 to automatically transition backup objects to Glacier after they reach a certain age and remove them from S3. This will keep your S3 backups bucket clean and ensure that you do not gradually build up a huge Amazon bill for storing unnecessary files.

For this example, we will assume that your daily backup archives are prefixed with *backups/daily/* in your S3 bucket—for example, *backups/daily/201802081601.tar.gz*.

The rules that govern when S3 objects are transitioned to Glacier are stored as a lifecycle subresource on your S3 bucket. A lifecycle configuration can contain up to 1,000 rules controlling when your files—or subsets thereof—are transitioned to Glacier. Lifecycle configurations can be created and modified using the AWS API, or via the AWS Management Console. In this example, we will use the Management Console to create our lifecycle configuration.

Begin by finding your S3 bucket (*https://s3.console.aws.amazon.com/s3/buckets/my-blog-backups/*) in the AWS Management Console. Select the Management tab; then navigate to the lifecycle wizard shown in Figure 12-3 by clicking the button to add a lifecycle rule.

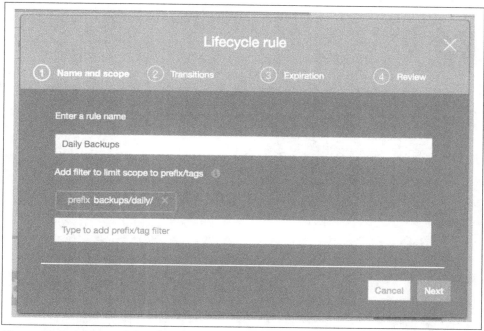

Figure 12-3. Adding a lifecycle rule in the Console

The first screen lets us name the rule and choose which objects the action that we are about to define will be applied to. In the Prefix box, enter *backups/daily/*, as we want this particular rule to apply only to the daily backup archives. Name the rule "Daily Backups" and click Next to proceed to the next screen shown in Figure 12-4. This screen lets us choose what action will be performed on the objects. A great feature of the Simple Storage Service is the ability to maintain a versioned history of all objects that were ever stored in a bucket—as our backup bucket is not versioned, the Current Version checkbox is all that we need to select for this rule definition. Click the "+ Add transition" link to see the options available to the rule we are creating.

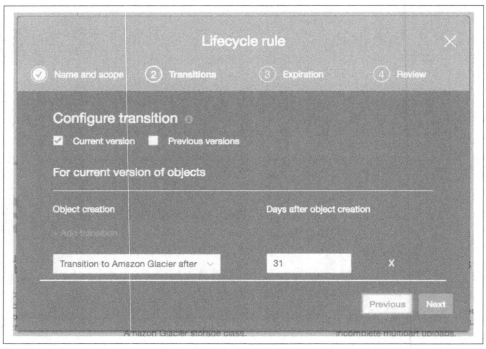

Figure 12-4. Configuring the transition rule

Our desired rule consists of two actions: transitioning our backups to Glacier once a month has elapsed, and removing those objects altogether two months after their creation. Because this is such a common pattern, Amazon allows us to configure both of these actions at once, as you will see on the next screen.

Enter 31 in the Archive to the Glacier Storage Class input box, then click Next once again. Enter 62 in the expiration input box as shown in Figure 12-5. It is generally considered a best practice to allow AWS to perform the available cleanup options on the bucket, so that we avoid having to eventually carry this task out manually. In this case, the *incomplete multipart uploads* cleanup is certainly applicable.

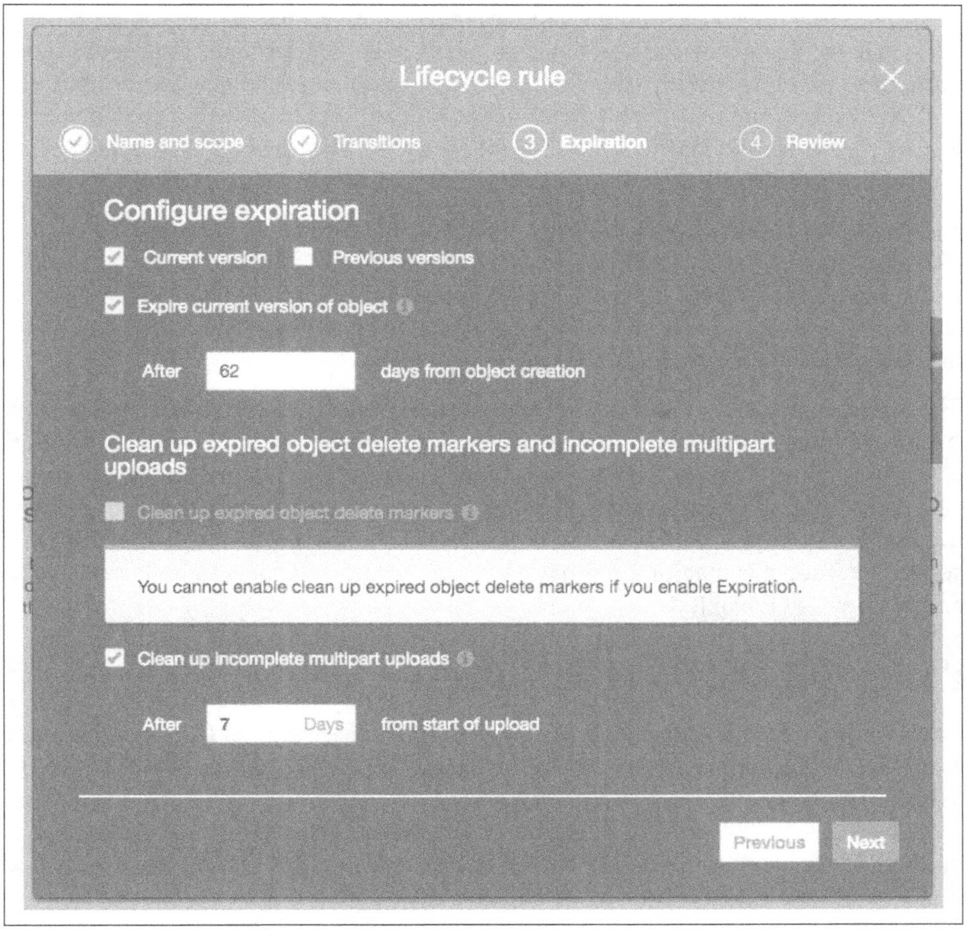

Figure 12-5. Configure Rule

Lifecycle rules can be set only in daily increments, so we set archiving to 31 to ensure that we do not transition objects too early in months with fewer than 31 days. The reader should define a similar policy for the monthly backup path—the authors recommend keeping monthly backups as long as possible if cost is the only concern: unlike the dailies, a decade will need to pass for their number to significantly accumulate. Publicly traded companies may be subject to a number of data-retention policies limiting not only the minimum but also, and somewhat unexpectedly from a pure IT perspective, the maximum time data should be retained. If such policies apply to you, they should guide your definition of the expiration rule for the monthly backup path.

Click Next to confirm the options you have selected on a final review screen. Finally, click Save to create and activate the rules. Your AWS Glacier vault also needs to be initialized, which is trivially easy to do and only requires selecting a few notification preferences as of the time of this writing. You will be prompted with a guided wizard during your first visit and only need to follow the steps presented by Glacier's management console (*https://console.aws.amazon.com/glacier/*).

You can now store your daily backups in S3, and all objects will be moved to Glacier after they are older than 31 days. We do recommend you make liberal use of the Glacier storage class to limit the cost of storing rarely used objects like backups. When choosing the time window for moving data to Glacier, consider that objects archived in Glacier must be restored to S3 before they can be accessed.

The speed (and cost) of Glacier retrieval operations depends on the service class specified by the restore request: expedited requests will make the data available in under 5 minutes, whereas bulk requests could take up to 12 hours. Restore requests generate a temporary copy of the object that is automatically expunged from S3 after the number of days specified in the request itself. A side effect of this operationally convenient model is that for a few days, storage charges will apply to both the Glacier and S3 copies of the object.

PostgreSQL and Other Databases

Amazon offers hosted and managed PostgreSQL databases via its RDS service. For a long time, RDS supported only MySQL databases, so it was common for PostgreSQL users to run their own PostgreSQL instances on EC2 instances. This also meant that users were responsible for providing their own backup procedures instead of relying on the backup features provided by RDS. For this reason, this section goes into some detail about the manual process of backing up databases that are hosted on EC2 instances, as opposed to running on RDS. While this section uses PostgreSQL-specific commands, the general principles are applicable to most database engines including those, like MongoDB, that AWS RDS does not yet support.

Backing up dynamic databases is not as simple as copying the database files to a remote location. First, PostgreSQL must be informed that a database backup is about to execute. If you forget this step, the database files could be copied while they are effectively in an unusable state, making restoration procedures either very time-consuming or in some cases impossible. PostgreSQL must be informed that a database backup is about to be executed so that it can flush any in-memory data to disk and ensure that the files on disk are in a state that will allow them to be used to restore data.

There are two main methods of backing up a PostgreSQL database running on EC2: pg_dump and snapshots. The latter is more complicated, but better for large databases.

pg_dump

pg_dump and its companion commands are distributed with PostgreSQL. pg_dump dumps all the data from the specified database, without interfering with reads and writes. Any changes made to the database after you start pg_dump will not appear in the dump, but the dump will be consistent. Data can be dumped in a variety of formats, which can be restored with the pg_restore command. The default option is to create a file containing SQL statements, but it is also possible to dump data in a PostgreSQL-specific format or create a tar archive of the data.

This method is especially suited for smaller databases (less than 5 GB) because the resulting dump file can be transferred directly to S3. For example, to dump the my_db database and store it in an S3 bucket named my-db-backups, you could use the following script:

```
#!/bin/bash -e

DB_NAME="my_db"
BUCKET_NAME="my-db-backups"
DATE=`date -u +"%Y%m%d%H%M"`
BACKUP_DIR="/var/backups"
BACKUP_FILE="${BACKUP_DIR}/${DB_NAME}_${DATE}.tar"
mkdir -p $BACKUP_DIR

# Dump the database as a tar archive
pg_dump ${DB_NAME} --file="${BACKUP_FILE}" --format=tar

# Copy the tar file to S3
s3cmd put "${BACKUP_FILE}" s3://${BUCKET_NAME}

# Delete the local tar file
rm ${BACKUP_FILE}
```

This script first dumps the data from PostgreSQL using the pg_dump command. Once the backup file has been created, it is copied to an S3 bucket. Finally, the local copy of the tar file is deleted to ensure that you do not gradually use up all the space available on the device on which /var is mounted or inadvertently leak data meant to be secured in a known location. Bash's -e option is used to ensure that the script fails immediately if any of the commands in the script fail.

To restore a database backed up using this script, simply copy the backup file from the S3 bucket onto the new PostgreSQL instance and use the pg_restore command to load the data into the new database. For example:

```
pg_restore --dbname=my_db /path/to/backup/file.tar
```

As your database grows, the time taken to run the pg_dump and pg_restore commands will increase, making this option less attractive. If you want to make backups once per hour, this process will become useless as soon as it takes longer than 60 minutes to complete, as you will never be able to complete a backup before a new one is started.

Snapshots and Continuous Archiving

Another option for backing up EC2-hosted PostgreSQL databases is to use the snapshotting capabilities of EBS volumes. This is slightly more complex, but provides a much quicker way of backing up larger databases. This method does not produce a single file that can be used with the `pg_restore` command. Instead, it uses PostgreSQL's base backup feature (*http://bit.ly/2M1Aqf6*) to produce one or more EBS snapshots that can be used to provision new EBS volumes containing your backed-up data.

This method relies on PostgreSQL's continuous archiving features. Configuring this is beyond the scope of this book. Refer to the PostgreSQL documentation on Continuous Archiving (*http://bit.ly/2LZHDvQ*) for information on how to configure and test this feature.

In a nutshell, continuous archiving will periodically store your data in an external location so that it can be used for a restore later. This is done by archiving the *write-ahead log* (WAL) files, which essentially play back all operations performed on your database. This allows you to restore the database to a time of your choosing (point-in-time recovery). However, playing back all the WAL files can take some time. To reduce restoration time, create a *base backup* that is used as a starting point for recovery. This allows you to restore a smaller number of WAL files in external storage and play back only WAL files that were created after a particular base backup was taken.

WAL-E (*https://github.com/wal-e/wal-e*) is a program designed to help create and manage PostgreSQL WAL files and create base backups. Although it is still worth learning and understanding how the underlying concepts of WAL and base backups work, WAL-E can make the day-to-day usage of continuous archiving a lot simpler and more reliable.

For performance reasons, it is recommended that you put PostgreSQL's data directory on its own EBS volume. The data directory location will vary depending on the version of PostgreSQL and the operating system in use. For example, a PostgreSQL 9.4 instance on Ubuntu will be stored in */var/lib/postgresql/9.3/main*. Attaching an additional EBS volume to your instance and mounting the data directory on this volume will improve performance, because PostgreSQL will not be contending with the operating system for disk I/O operations.

A bit of generally applicable advice: EBS is AWS's recommended storage option to run a database on Amazon EC2, with provisioned IOPS volumes offering a performant storage option to even the largest databases. It often makes sense to provision even a smaller database instance with a dedicated EBS volume for DBMS storage to guard against load growth over time.

PostgreSQL's tablespace feature allows you to store each table in a separate on-disk location. This feature makes it possible to store each table on a different EBS volume, further improving performance. In conjunction with EBS Provisioned IOPS, which provide a higher level of performance than vanilla EBS volumes, this can dramatically improve the performance of disk-bound workloads.

Backing up

This section, and the following, assume that you have at least two EBS volumes attached to your PostgreSQL EC2 instance. The first volume is used to mount the root of the filesystem (the / directory). The second volume is used solely for PostgreSQL's data directory and is mounted at */var/lib/postgresql/9.3/main*. For example purposes, the data EBS volume will be created with the device name */dev/sda2*, a typical name for a local Linux storage device defined by the SCSI interface. We will further assume that you have installed PostgreSQL and created a database for testing purposes according to PostgreSQL's documentation.

Begin by connecting to the PostgreSQL instance as the superuser by running the psql command. Depending on how you configured your database, you might need to provide the superuser password at this point. Once connected to the database, issue the pg_start_backup command:

```
SELECT pg_start_backup('test_backup');
```

This command will create a *backup label* file in the data directory containing information about the backup, such as the start time and label string. It is important to retain this file with the backed-up files, because it is used during the restore process. It will also inform PostgreSQL that a backup is about to be performed so that a new checkpoint can be created and any pending data can be written to disk. This can take some time, depending on the configuration of the database.

Once the command completes, take a snapshot of the EBS volume on which the PostgreSQL database is stored.

The filesystem type you are using might require a slightly different approach at this stage. This example assumes you are using XFS, which requires that the filesystem be frozen before a snapshot is made. This ensures that any attempts to modify files on this filesystem will be blocked until the snapshot is completed, ensuring the integrity of the files.

First, freeze the filesystem with the `xfs_freeze` command:

```
xfs_freeze -f /var/lib/postgresql/9.3/main
```

Once the filesystem has been frozen, it is safe to take a snapshot using the EBS snap-shotting tools. This can be done from the AWS Management Console or from the command-line tools. Because the final goal is to use this process as part of an auto-mated backup script on the database host itself, we will use the command-line approach.

There are a multitude of ways to find the ID of the instance running our database, including of course the AWS console and CLI, as well as our favorite approach of using tags to identify an instance's logical function. One more way to accomplish this is to interrogate the EC2 metadata from the instance itself, something very suitable for scripting in that it requires no EC2 management privileges to access:

```
# Find out the ID of the instance on which this command is executed
EC2_INSTANCE_ID=$(ec2metadata --instance-id)
# The device name is used to filter the list of volumes attached to the instance
DEVICE="/dev/sda2"
```

Finding out the ID of the EBS volume on which the data is stored requires EC2 API access. This is another use case for IAM roles as described in "IAM Roles" on page 98: to maintain the highest security, you should not need to place AWS credentials on the instance. The following IAM policy grants the required access level:

```
{
    "Version": "2012-10-17",
    "Statement": [
        {
            "Sid": "1",
            "Effect": "Allow",
            "Action": [
                "ec2:CreateSnapshot",
                "ec2:DescribeVolumes",
                "ec2:DescribeInstances"
            ],
            "Resource": [
                "*"
            ]
        }
    ]
}

# Find the ID of the EBS volume on which PostgreSQL data is stored
VOLUME_ID=$(aws ec2 describe-instance-attribute \
--instance-id i-0e369cdca165b562a --attribute blockDeviceMapping \
--query "BlockDeviceMappings[?DeviceName==\`$DEVICE\`].{Id:Ebs.VolumeId}" --
output text)
```

Now we have everything we need to trigger the snapshot:

```
$ aws ec2 create-snapshot --volume-id ${VOLUME_ID}
{
    "Description": "",
    "Encrypted": false,
    "VolumeId": "vol-037501dc81d584227",
    "State": "pending",
    "VolumeSize": 8,
    "Progress": "",
    "StartTime": "2018-02-11T19:59:44.000Z",
    "SnapshotId": "snap-0daafbeb9409cb652",
    "OwnerId": "740376006796"
}
```

These commands will query the EC2 API to find out the ID of the EBS volume containing the PostgreSQL data before using the `aws ec2 create-snapshot` command to create a snapshot of this volume. Note the ID of the new snapshot printed as part of the output from `ec2-create-snapshot`.

Although the snapshot has not yet been fully created, it is safe to begin using the volume again. AWS will create a snapshot of the volume in the state it was in when the `ec2-create-snapshot` command was executed, even if data is subsequently changed.

As soon as the snapshotting command finishes, the XFS volume should be unfrozen:

```
xfs_freeze -u /var/lib/postgresql/9.3/main
```

Finally, you can inform PostgreSQL that the backup has been completed and that it should resume normal operations:

```
SELECT pg_stop_backup();
```

Note that the backup is not entirely complete until the WAL archives identified by the `pg_stop_backup` command have been archived (by way of the `archive_command` configuration directive in *postgresql.conf*).

 Eric Hammond of Alestic (*https://alestic.com*) fame has authored a tool to create consistent snapshots of databases, with dedicated support for MongoDB and MySQL in particular. Even when not using a database instance outside of RDS, Eric's work on `ec2-consistent-snapshot` (*https://github.com/alestic/ec2-consistent-snapshot*) is valuable for its support of drives spanning multiple volumes.

Restoring

Restoring from a backup created with this method is much simpler, but more time-consuming. Whether your original PostgreSQL instance has suffered from some kind of catastrophic failure or you are restoring the data to a new machine (perhaps for development or testing purposes), the procedure is essentially the same.

First, you will need to launch a new instance using the same EBS configuration. That is, the new instance should use the same EBS volume layout as the original instance. There is one difference, however: the data volume (*/dev/sda2*) should use the most recent snapshot created using the method described in the previous section. When the instance is launched, the snapshot will be used to create the sda2 device, ensuring that the PostgreSQL data is already in place when the instance is launched.

The preferred approach when manually attaching a volume to a new instance is to create a volume from the appropriate backup snapshot, making sure it is located in the same availability zone you launched the new database instance in:

```
$ aws ec2 create-volume --availability-zone us-east-1b --snapshot-id
snap-0daafbeb9409cb652 --output text
us-east-1b       2018-02-11T22:51:32.830Z       False   8
snap-0daafbeb9409cb652  creating        vol-06394e3cae23070b9   standard
$ aws ec2 attach-volume --volume-id vol-06394e3cae23070b9 --instance-id
i-0e369cdca165b562a --device "/dev/sda2" --output text
2018-02-11T23:36:20.018Z       /dev/sda2       i-0e369cdca165b562a     attach-
ing     vol-06394e3cae23070b9
```

A more direct approach can be taken when launching the new instance by using a block device mapping to add the volume at boot time. The following *mappings.json* file creates a new volume from the previous snapshot, and presents it to the system as /dev/sda2:

```
[
    {
        "DeviceName": "/dev/sda2",
        "Ebs": {
            "DeleteOnTermination": false,
            "SnapshotId": "snap-0daafbeb9409cb652"
        }
    }
]
```

In this approach, building a new server from our block device mapping only requires the system AMI and the data volume snapshot:

```
$ aws ec2 run-instances --image-id ami-43a15f3e --region us-east-1 --key feder
ico --security-groups ssh --instance-type t2.micro --block-device-mappings
file://mappings.json --output text
740376006796      r-0741b6189faec54c5
INSTANCES       0       x86_64          False   xen     ami-43a15f3e
i-06a4d321e51347397     t2.micro        federico        2018-02-11T23:52:45.000Z
ip-172-31-51-195.ec2.internal   172.31.51.195           /dev/sda1       ebs
True            subnet-2a45b400 hvm     vpc-934935f7
MONITORING      disabled
NETWORKINTERFACES               12:81:c8:7e:b0:4e       eni-2a546ae7
740376006796    ip-172-31-51-195.ec2.internal   172.31.51.195   True    in-use
subnet-2a45b400 vpc-934935f7
ATTACHMENT      2018-02-11T23:52:45.000Z        eni-attach-9d232850     True
```

```
0          attaching
GROUPS    sg-4ebd8b36      ssh
PRIVATEIPADDRESSES         True      ip-172-31-51-195.ec2.internal    172.31.51.195
PLACEMENT      us-east-1a                default
SECURITYGROUPS    sg-4ebd8b36      ssh
STATE     0       pending
STATEREASON       pending pending
```

Once the instance is ready, you can log in and start PostgreSQL with this command:

```
/etc/init.d/postgresql-9.3 start
```

PostgreSQL must be configured using the same configuration files used for the original instance. The continuous archiving configuration directives will let PostgreSQL know how to restore the archived WAL files. This is controlled through the restore_command configuration directive.

During the startup process, PostgreSQL will recognize that the files in the data directory were created as part of a base backup and will automatically restore the required WAL files by executing the restore command. This can take some time depending on how much data was changed since the base backup was taken, and how quickly the archived WAL files can be restored from remote storage.

PostgreSQL will begin accepting connections as soon as it has finished restoring the WAL files and the database is up-to-date. At this point, the state of the data should match the state it was in just before the original database was terminated. If the original database was uncleanly terminated (for example, the actual EC2 instance was terminated), some data might be missing if PostgreSQL did not have time to archive the final WAL file(s).

As mentioned, this approach is a tad more complex than simply dumping a file full of SQL statements representing your data. However, it does provide a lot more flexibility in restoring your data, and is the only valid option after your database grows to the point where dumping SQL statements is no longer viable.

Off-Site Backups

As we explained earlier, you may want to move some backups outside of the AWS ecosystem altogether for those rare times when AWS goes down (*https:// aws.amazon.com/message/41926/*) and even the region's AWS API endpoint becomes unavailable. You can use another cloud storage provider to host your off-site backups, or provision a new server entirely outside AWS to act as a backup host. Planning should be explicitly mindful of the difference between disaster recovery, defined here as possession of your business-critical data in a total datacenter loss, and service restoration. If your business requires services to be restored in a matter of hours, a strategy to provision alternative compute services and modify DNS records needs to be put in place along with off-site data backup—the most common approach in this case is to set up operations in multiple AWS regions independently.

Assuming that your data has been backed up to S3 using one of the other methods described in this chapter, you can use tools such as s3cmd or s3funnel to regularly pull this data from S3 and store it on another server.

 Backups without a reliable and regularly tested restore procedure can be worse than useless, providing nothing but a false sense of security. End-to-end testing of your restore procedures needs to be a regularly scheduled occurrence. As the saying goes, if you haven't tested restore, you do not have a backup.

A final consideration we want to offer is a reminder to focus on protecting configuration, in the form of automation that can be used to rapidly rebuild lost infrastructure, and to avoid diluting the cloud-native approach by protecting the servers themselves with backups. Backups are properly reserved to protecting the stateful data set of your application, which should be structured to permit data-only backups and rapid re-attach of that data to infrastructure rebuilt *from scratch* through automation.

Index

Symbols
@@ prefix, 330

A
A DNS record, 314
access credentials
    about, 5, 35
    auditing, 87-90, 97
    generating, 76
    passing as arguments, 42
    tracking usage, 74
access key IDs
    about, 4, 35
    generating, 76
    passing as arguments, 42
access management (see IAM)
accounts
    activating, 3
    auditing usage, 88-90, 97
    CloudTrail service, 71, 73, 91-94
    creating, 2-3, 84
    on-demand instance limits for, 47
    OwnerID attribute, 63
    resetting to original state, 14
    security strategy for, 71, 83
    service limits for, 94
actions
    defined, 75
    Simple Storage Service, 79
activate script (Python), 8
administration tasks, automating, 55-56
Advanced Message Queuing Protocol (AMQP),
    173
Advanced Vector Extensions instruction set, 21

AES encryption, 21
AKIDs (key IDs), 89
Akismet spam-checking service, 217
Alarms feature (CloudWatch), 35, 239-245, 249,
    323
Albitz, Paul, 246
Alestic blog, 11-13, 31
ALIAS resource record type, 304
Allow permission, 79
ALLOWED_HOSTS setting (Django), 193
Amazon Machine Images (see AMIs)
Amazon Resource Names (see ARNs)
Amazon Web Services (see AWS)
AMI Locator tool, 37, 38
AMI-based deployments
    about, 255, 263
    CloudFormation and, 264
    EC2 and, 264
AMIs (Amazon Machine Images)
    about, 16, 26, 56-58
    building, 59-62, 225-227
    building with Packer, 166-170
    default user, 30-31
    deployments based on, 255, 263-265
    deregistering, 63-67
    finding using command-line tools, 37
    HVM virtualization, 19, 38
    launching instances of, 25-29, 43
    role-based, 270-279
    tagging strategy, 63, 74
AMQP (Advanced Message Queuing Protocol),
    173
Ansible, 132
Apache Zookeeper, 262

HashiCorp Consul, 262
head command, 53
Health Check feature (ELB), 246-250, 314, 320
Heinlein, Robert, 330
$HOSTNAME variable, 275
hostnames, overriding default, 284
HVM virtualization, 19, 38

I

I2 instance type, 19, 22
IAM (Identity and Access Management)
    about, 4, 72
    Amazon Resource Names, 73, 78-80, 99-100
    CloudFormation stacks and, 107-112
    IAM policies, 74-83, 98, 107-112
    IAM roles, 28, 98-107
    IAM users and groups, 4, 71-73, 84-97,
        231-236, 246
IAM policies
    about, 74-77
    CloudFormation stacks and, 107-112
    creating, 79
    dynamic, 81-82
    IAM roles and, 98
    limitations of, 83
    referencing resources, 78-80
    validating, 76
    wildcards in, 87
IAM Policy Simulator, 78
IAM roles
    about, 98-107
    IAM policies and, 98
    instances and, 28
    privilege escalation, 99
    security best practices, 71
    using from other AWS accounts, 106
IAM users and groups
    about, 84
    auditing and rotating access keys, 87-90
    authentication and, 4, 73
    Auto Scaling and, 231-236, 246
    CloudTrail service, 71, 73, 91-94
    creating separate accounts for, 84
    organizing with paths, 85-87
    password policy, 71, 90
    security best practices, 71
    Trusted Advisor support, 95-97
iam:PassRole permission, 99
Icinga package, 332

id CPU metric, 20
Identity and Access Management (see IAM)
identity validation (accounts), 2
Immutable Server design pattern, 266
Immutable Server pattern, 273, 289
init-mezzanine-db command, 185
init-mezzanine-project command, 184
instance storage, 21-23
instance store–backed AMI, 57
instance types, 18-21, 26
instance-based deployments
    about, 255-256
    executing code with Fabric, 257-261
    updating instances at launch time, 262
instances
    about, 15-17
    backing up static files to S3, 337-339
    deployments based on, 255-262
    displaying metadata for, 103
    downloading metadata, 33
    dynamically keying on attributes, 261
    finding dynamically, 259
    grouping through roles, 258-259
    IAM roles and, 28
    images of, 17
    instance types, 18-21
    IP addresses and, 23
    key pairs and, 30-32
    launching from Management Console,
        25-33
    launching from programs and scripts, 41-45
    launching with command-line tools, 34-40
    mapping to roles, 272-274
    networking and, 23-25
    processing power, 18-21
    protecting with SSH whitelists, 116-118
    purchase options, 21
    querying information about, 32
    storage options, 21-23
    terminating, 22, 33, 40, 62, 245, 249
    upgrading hardware, 58
    user data, 27
    waiting for, 32
INSTANCE_LAUNCH_ERROR notification
    type, 238
ip addr show command, 23
IP addresses, instances and, 23

J

JavaScript Object Notation (see JSON)
JAVA_HOME environment variable, 12
jitter, EBS and, 21
jq tool, 9-10, 88, 123
JSON (JavaScript Object Notation)
   CloudFormation and, 45
   creating stacks, 47-50
   jq tool and, 9-10
   JSONview Chrome extension, 93
   metric data and, 324
   user data and, 197
JSONview Chrome extension, 93

K

Kanies, Luke, 133
key IDs (AKIDs), 89
key pairs
   about, 4, 35
   instances and, 30-32
   SSH, 30-32, 35, 43, 103
   tags as, 273
key rotation, 87-90, 99
Kibana log viewer, 284, 291
Kirkland, Dustin, 228

L

latency, EBS and, 21
Latency-Based Routing feature, 304
Launch Cluster Wizard, 202
launch configuration, 232
Launch Instance Wizard, 25-33, 103, 120, 276
launch-wizard-1 security group, 29, 113
LDAP (Lightweight Directory Access Protocol), 85
life cycle management (S3), 300, 340
Lifecycle Rules Wizard, 340
Lightweight Directory Access Protocol (LDAP), 85
Limoncelli, Thomas A., 56
Liu, Cricket, 246
load balancers, 246-248
load balancing, 246
loadjson() function, 276
log management
   about, 283
   AWS service logs, 298-300
   central logging, 283-298

   logging to S3, 295-298
   Logstash configuration, 285-294
   S3 life cycle management, 300
log receivers, 284
log shippers, 284
log viewers, 284
logger command, 294
Logstash tool
   about, 284
   configuring, 285
   configuring clients, 293
   creating and configuring servers, 287-292

M

M3 instance type, 19
M4 instance type, 19, 23
magnetic disks, EBS and, 21
Management Console
   about, 3, 16
   adding lifecycle rule, 340
   administration tasks, 55
   Chef and, 130
   creating policies, 80
   creating RDS database, 189
   inspecting access credentials, 36
   launching instances from, 25-33
   managing ELBs from, 246
   mobile app interface, 34
   permissions and, 75
   stack template and, 48
   termination protection, 28
manifests (Puppet), 133-135, 330
mapping instances to roles, 272-274
masters (Puppet), 133-141
Memcache software, 172, 203-206
memory management
   monitoring RAM utilization in EC2 instances, 240
   processing power and, 20
MemUsage metric, 241
message brokers, 173
metadata
   accessing attributes, 33
   configuration data, 141
   displaying for instances, 103
   downloading for instances, 33
Metadata attribute, 142
metrics

CloudWatch-supported, 239-245, 320, 322-329
CPU shares, 20
Mezzanine CMS, 172, 174, 192, 201
MFA (multi-factor authentication), 72
Micro instance class, 27
mobile app interface, 34
Mode 1 IT, 67
Mode 2 IT, 67, 251
modular CloudFormation stacks, 279-282
modules (Puppet), 132, 134
monitoring
    about, 319-320
    CloudWatch support, 239-245, 320-329
    Nagios support, 329-332
    RAM utilization in EC2 instances, 240
Morris, Kief, 269
Moser, Scott, 272
mounts module (Cloud-init), 22
multi-factor authentication (MFA), 72
Munroe, Randall, 56, 91, 132
mysqldump command, 338

N

Nagios tool, 329-332
native at-rest encryption, 23
Nayak, Anay, 115
netcat command, 290
netstat command, 287
networking
    about, 23-25
    security groups and, 112
Nginx service, 59-61, 176
node definitions (Puppet), 133-139
noisy neighbor effect, 20
notifications of scaling activities, 236-238
NotResource keyword, 80
Nunnikhoven, Mark, 114

O

Object Archival feature (S3), 340
off-site backups, 336, 351
OpenVPN, 119-126
OpsWorks service, 130
outages, managing, 250-252
--output option, aws command, 7
OwnerID (accounts), 63

P

package management
    about, 263
    package upgrades and service restarts, 271
Packer tool, 166-170, 225-227
parameterization, reusability and, 269
paravirtualized virtualization, 19, 38
parent stack (CloudFormation), 280
parsejson() function, 158, 198
password policy, 71, 90
PATH environment variable, 8, 12
paths
    organizing users and groups with, 85-87
    validating path location, 6
patterns for configuration management tools, 266, 274-279
.pem file extension, 31
pending state (AMI), 61
pending state (instance), 32, 39, 43
permissions
    about, 75
    ARN syntax, 100
    conflicting, 79
    EC2 syntax, 75
    evaluating, 81
    Management Console and, 75
    resources and, 75, 83
    Simple Storage Service and, 78-80
Pets versus Cattle metaphor, 67, 265
pg_dump command, 345
pg_restore command, 345
pg_start_backup command, 347
pg_stop_backup command, 349
phone verification (accounts), 2
ping command, 41
pip tool, 5, 42, 174
playbooks (Ansible), 132
PostgreSQL
    AMIs and, 271
    backups and, 344-351
    master/slave scenario, 305-310
    ramping up traffic and, 310
    security and, 113
private hostnames, 24
private IP addresses, 23
private keys, 30
privilege escalation, IAM roles and, 99
programs, launching instances from, 41-45
prospectors, 293

provisioners (Packer), 168
psql command, 347
public hostnames, 24
public IP addresses, 23
Puppet
    $HOSTNAME variable and, 275
    about, 133-141
    Celery updating, 219-224
    CloudFormation and, 135-141, 141-155
    ElastiCache updating, 207-209
    executing tasks with Fabric, 158-161
    exported resources feature, 330
    installing, 157
    Logstash support, 285
    master-less, 161-165
    preparing for web applications, 179-186
    provisioning runtime and modules, 182
    RDS updating, 194-201
    tags and, 155-158
    user data and, 155-158
puppet command, 139, 180
Puppet Forge site, 132, 180
puppet-lint tool, 135
puppet-server package, 141
PuTTY terminal program, 32
PyPl package management system, 174
Python environments, creating isolated, 8
python-memcached library, 205

Q

--query option, aws command, 10, 65, 327
querying
    information about instances, 32
    snapshot ID, 337
    tags, 273
queuing (see SQS)

R

R3 instance type, 19, 22
RabbitMQ message broker, 173, 332
RDS (Relational Database Service), 54, 172,
    188-201, 335
RDS Database Snapshot feature, 336
recipes (Chef), 132
Ref function, 108-109
--region option, aws command, 12
regions (AWS), 17
regular expressions, 134

Relational Database Service (RDS), 54, 172,
    188-201, 335
Repmgr tool, 305
requirements file, 263
Resource attribute, 78-80
resources
    permissions and, 75, 83
    service limits, 94
    Trusted Advisor support, 95-97
    virtual, 330
restoring from backups, 349-351
Retain deletion policy, 54
reusability
    mapping instances to roles, 272-274
    modular CloudFormation stacks, 279-282
    parameterization and, 269
    patterns for configuration management
        tools, 274-279
    role-based AMIs and, 270-279
revision control systems, 225
RFC 3164, 284
RFC 6238, 72
Rhett, Jo, 141
role tag, 29
role-based AMIs
    about, 270-271
    mapping instances to roles, 272-274
    patterns for configuration management
        tools, 274-279
roles (IAM) (see IAM roles)
roles feature (Fabric), 159, 258-259
rolling backups, 339-344
root credentials, security best practices, 5, 71,
    84
rootkey.csv credentials file, 5
Route 53 service
    about, 303-304
    application outages and, 311-317
    ELB outages and, 311-317
    handling failover, 305-311
    ramping up traffic, 310
    setting up DNS records, 287
rsync command, 338
RunInstances method (EC2 API), 42
running state (instance), 32, 39, 44
run_instances() function, 43

S

S3 (Simple Storage Service)

ssh-agent program, 31
ssh-import-id command, 39
SSL (Secure Sockets Layer), 82
st CPU metric, 20
stack templates
    controlling changes to, 53
    creating, 46
    embedding configuration data into, 141
    Management Console and, 48
    SSH whitelists and, 117
stacks
    creating, 46-50, 227, 324
    deleting, 54
    IAM policies and, 107-112
    initial version displayed, 186-187
    modular, 279-282
    Puppet example, 143-155, 162-165
    security groups and, 117
    updating, 50-53
state tag, 63
state-changed tag, 63
Statement attribute, 77
static Auto Scaling groups, 231-236
STATIC_ROOT setting (Django), 201
STATIC_URL setting (Django), 201
stats cachedump command, 206
stats slab command, 206
stdlib module (Puppet), 182, 198, 276
stolen CPU time, 20
stopped state (instance), 50
storage options for instances, 21-23
store and forward process, 295
Supervisor process-control system, 178, 194, 244
support plans (accounts), 3
SUSE Studio, 62
sy CPU metric, 20

T

T2 instance type, 19
tags
    about, 28
    AMI strategy, 63, 74
    applying to resources, 53
    CloudFormation and, 155
    passing information to instances via, 273
    Puppet and, 155-158
tasks module (Python), 217
terminate() function, 44

terminated state (instance), 45
"Too Big NOT to Fail" paper, 265
TOTP algorithm, 72
Trusted Advisor, 95-97
TTL value, failover and, 305, 314
The Twelve-Factor App, 192

U

Ubuntu images, 36, 37
update policy, 235
update() function, 43
update-stack command, 156
UPDATE_COMPLETE state, 234
us CPU metric, 20
user data
    about, 27
    Cloud-init and, 272
    JSON and, 197
    passing information to instances via, 272
    Puppet and, 155-158
    running instances and, 50
users and groups (see IAM users and groups)

V

validating
    IAM policies, 76
    path location, 6
    puppet-lint tool, 135
    stack templates, 48
version control systems, 180-181
--version option, aws command, 6
virtual appliances, 26, 56
Virtual Private Cloud (VPC), 23-24, 119
virtual private networks (VPNs), 118-126
virtual resources, 330
virtual servers (see instances)
Virtualenv tool, 8
virtualization types, 19, 38
VPC (Virtual Private Cloud), 23-24, 119
VPNs (virtual private networks), 118-126

W

wa CPU metric, 20
WAL (write-ahead log) files, 346
WAL-E program, 346
web applications
    background task processing, 172
    building AMIs, 225-227

About the Authors

Mike Ryan runs a DevOps and blockchain consultancy based in Amsterdam, and is obsessed with automation and cloud services. He can be reached on Twitter, GitHub, and LinkedIn as @mikery.

Federico Lucifredi was the lead product manager for Ubuntu Server, Amazon Web Services' most popular operating system. While at Canonical, Federico led the Certified Public Cloud program, ensuring the seamless integration of Ubuntu into AWS and other public clouds. He is currently the Ceph product management director at Red Hat, and can be reached on Twitter as @0xF2.

Colophon

The animal on the cover of *AWS System Administration* is a peccary (*Tayassuidae*). Sometimes called javelina, peccaries are medium-sized, hoofed mammals that live throughout Central and South America as well as the southwestern portion of North America. Peccaries grow to about 3–4.3 feet in length and adults weigh from 44–88 pounds.

Peccary bear a strong resemblance to pigs, with small eyes and a snout that ends in a disc made up of cartilage. However, its three-chambered, nonruminating stomach is more complex than that of pigs.

The peccary's short, straight tusk is also markedly different from the long, curved tusk found on European pigs. The tusks serve a dual purpose: peccaries rub their tusks together to create a chattering noise as a warning against potential predators, but also utilize them for crushing hard seeds and slicing into plant roots. Peccaries are omnivores and prefer to feed on roots, grass, seeds, fruit, and cacti such as the prickly pear. They will also eat small animals.

Peccaries often travel in herds and are considered social animals. Using scent glands below each eye, peccaries mark their territory and other members of their herds with a pungent odor that can be detected by humans, hence the nickname "skunk pig."

Many of the animals on O'Reilly covers are endangered; all of them are important to the world. To learn more about how you can help, go to *animals.oreilly.com*.

The cover image is from loose plates, source unknown. The cover fonts are URW Typewriter and Guardian Sans. The text font is Adobe Minion Pro; the heading font is Adobe Myriad Condensed; and the code font is Dalton Maag's Ubuntu Mono.

Learn from experts.
Find the answers you need.

Sign up for a **10-day free trial** to get **unlimited access** to all of the content on Safari, including Learning Paths, interactive tutorials, and curated playlists that draw from thousands of ebooks and training videos on a wide range of topics, including data, design, DevOps, management, business—and much more.

Start your free trial at:
oreilly.com/safari

(No credit card required)

CPSIA information can be obtained
at www.ICGtesting.com
Printed in the USA
BVHW05s0124110818
524089BV00010B/52/P